ANTI-INFLAMMATORY DIET COOKBOOK FOR BEGINNERS

800 Quick, Easy & Delicious Recipes with 1000-Day Diet Meal Plan(10 Tips for Success)

Betty K. Billings

Meat **251**

Description

It might look a daunting task trying to cut some food types from your menu for others but don't look at it that way. The anti-inflammatory diet is for your benefit both in the short and long run, and you should commit to it. The temptation might be there for you to slip up, most especially when you are out with friends, or you are in an event, but if you value your health, you can weather the storm and don't allow for any slip-up. Before you start to tell yourself the following;

It is not difficult: Sure, it looks challenging, after all, you are cutting out some of your favorite food types, but the truth is it is not hard. Don't ever tell yourself it is hard because you've done much harder things in life than not eating your favorite sloppy joes.

Do not slip: Don't even consider slipping. You have no excuse or reason to slip. Commit to the process wholeheartedly. Don't attempt this haphazardly; you will only give yourself an excuse to fail. The effort, commitment, and discipline: There is no lying about this; it is going to require effort, dedication, and discipline. You would have to plan your meals, shop for ingredients, let your family and friends know your plan, and follow the rules. But the effort is worth it, and the rewards are too numerous both in the short-run and long-run.

Learn to say no and stick with the plan: there will be gatherings, events, hangouts with friends that might give you an excuse to compromise on your plans, but learn to be though and say "No" in a polite way though. You have a choice, and that choice is to follow your plan to the letter. Don't fall for peer pressure.

Getting Yourself Back On

The premise behind the anti-inflammatory diet is simple: focus on foods that reduce inflammation while avoiding those that contribute to it. While simple in concept, it can be more challenging in practice.

Yes, we know we live in a society where convenience is essential when it comes to the foods we select. Unfortunately, many of the more convenient foods are highly processed and full of inflammatory ingredients such as refined sugars and grains, chemical additives, and unhealthy fats. Still, the foods are readily available and, in some cases, taste delicious, which makes the thought of giving them up difficult.

But the good news is that your convenience will not be compromised when you adopt anti-inflammatory diets. This is not to flatter you or pull your legs; there are still some fantastic anti-inflammatory dishes that taste just as good as your junk meals. What's more, you don't need to spend hours preparing them. You can have your breakfast, lunch and dinner ready in a matter of minutes when it comes to anti-inflammatory meals.

Introduction

Inflammation refers to your body's process of fighting against things that damages it, like infections, accidents, and toxins, in an attempt to heal itself. When something damages your cells, your body releases chemicals that activate a reaction from your immune system.

This reaction includes the release of proteins and antibodies, along with increased blood flow into the damaged area. The entire process generally lasts for a few hours or days in the case of acute inflammation.

Chronic inflammation occurs when this reaction lingers, leaving your body at a continuous state. Over time, chronic inflammation might have a negative impact on your tissues and organs. Some research indicates that chronic inflammation may play a role in a range of conditions, anything from cancer to asthma.

What are the symptoms of chronic inflammation?
Acute inflammation frequently causes noticeable symptoms, such as redness, pain, or swelling. But chronic inflammation symptoms are usually subtler. This makes them simple to overlook. Common symptoms of chronic inflammation include:

- Fatigue
- Fever
- Mouth problems
- Rashes
- Stomach pain
- Chest pain

These symptoms may range from mild to severe and last for several months or years.

What causes chronic inflammation?
A number of things can cause chronic inflammation, for example:

- Untreated causes of acute inflammation, like an infection or harm
- An autoimmune disorder, which involves the immune system mistakenly attacking healthy tissue
- Long-term exposure to irritants, such as industrial chemicals or polluted atmosphere

Keep in mind that these do not cause chronic inflammation in everyone. In addition, some cases of chronic inflammation don't have a definite underlying cause.
Experts also believe that a range of variables may also lead to chronic inflammation, for example:

- Smoking supply
- Obesity source
- Alcohol supply
- Chronic stress

Breakfast

1. Chili Tomato Salad

Preparation Time: 10 minutes
Cooking Time: 0 minutes
Servings: 4
Ingredients:
1 tablespoon avocado oil
3 scallions, chopped
1-pound cherry tomatoes, halved
2 chili peppers, minced
Salt and black pepper to the taste
1 tablespoon chives, chopped
Directions:
In a salad bowl, combine the tomatoes with the chili peppers and the other ingredients, toss and serve for breakfast.
Nutrition: calories 30, fat 5.7, fiber 1.8, carbs 5.6, protein 1.3

2. Cumin Mushroom Bowls

Preparation Time: 5 minutes
Cooking Time: 20 minutes
Servings: 4
Ingredients:
2 spring onions, chopped
1 pound white mushrooms, halved
Salt and black pepper to the taste
1 teaspoon sweet paprika
1 tablespoon olive oil
½ teaspoon cumin, ground
1 zucchini, sliced
1 cucumber, sliced
Directions:
Heat up a pan with the oil over medium heat, add the spring onions and the mushrooms and sauté for 5 minutes.
Add the rest of the ingredients, toss, cook everything for 15 minutes more, divide into bowls and serve.
Nutrition: calories 78, fat 4.1, fiber 2.5, carbs 9.1 , protein 4.9

3. Bell Peppers and Tomato Salad

Preparation Time: 10 minutes
Cooking Time: 0 minutes
Servings: 4
Ingredients:

2 tablespoons olive oil
4 scallions, chopped
2 garlic cloves, minced
1 red bell pepper, cut into strips
1 yellow bell pepper, cut into strips
1 green bell pepper, cut into strips
½ cup cherry tomatoes, halved
1 teaspoon basil, dried
Salt and black pepper to the taste
1 tablespoon chives, chopped
Directions:
In a salad bowl, combine the scallions with the bell peppers and the other ingredients, toss, divide into bowls and serve for breakfast.
Nutrition: calories 100, fat 7.3, fiber 1.9, carbs 9.1, protein 1.5

4. Avocado and Spinach Salad

Preparation Time: 5 minutes
Cooking Time: 0 minutes
Servings: 4
Ingredients:
1 pound baby spinach
2 avocados, peeled, pitted and cubed
1 cucumber, sliced
1 tablespoon chives, chopped
Salt and black pepper to the taste
1 tablespoon balsamic vinegar
1 tablespoon avocado oil
Directions:
In a bowl, combine the spinach with the avocado and the other ingredients, toss and serve for breakfast.
Nutrition: calories 248, fat 20.6, fiber 9.8, carbs 15.8, protein 5.7

5. Zucchini Bowls

Preparation Time: 10 minutes
Cooking Time: 0 minutes
Servings: 4
Ingredients:
2 zucchinis, cut with a spiralizer
2 tablespoons olive oil
1 avocado, peeled, pitted and cubed
2 tomatoes, cubed
2 spring onions, chopped
1 tablespoon olive oil
Salt and black pepper to the taste
1 tablespoon lime juice

1 tablespoon chives, chopped
Directions:
In a bowl, combine the zucchinis with the avocado, tomatoes and the other ingredients, toss, divide into smaller bowls and keep in the fridge for 10 minutes before for breakfast.
Nutrition: calories 225, fat 20.6, fiber 5.5, carbs 11.5, protein 2.9

6. Lime Berries Salad

Preparation Time: 5 minutes
Cooking Time: 0 minutes
Servings: 4
Ingredients:
1 cup blackberries
1 cup blueberries
1 tablespoon stevia
1 tablespoon lime juice
1 teaspoon vanilla extract
Directions:
In a bowl, combine the berries with the stevia and the other ingredients, toss and serve for breakfast.
Nutrition: calories 42, fat 0.3, fiber 2.8, carbs 9.8, protein 0.8

7. Garlicky Green Beans and Olives Pan

Preparation Time: 10 minutes
Cooking Time: 20 minutes
Servings: 4
Ingredients:
2 shallots, chopped
2 tablespoons tomato passata
1 pound green beans, trimmed and halved
1 cup black olives, pitted and halved
1 tablespoon avocado oil
3 garlic cloves, minced
Salt and black pepper to the taste
1 tablespoon cilantro, chopped
1 teaspoon sweet paprika
Directions:
Heat up a pan with the oil over medium heat, add the shallots, garlic and the paprika and sauté for 5 minutes.
Add the green beans and the other ingredients, toss, cook everything for 15 minutes more, divide into bowls and serve.
Nutrition: calories 83, fat 4.3, fiber 5.4, carbs 11.4, protein 2.6

8. Greek Tomato and Olives Salad

Preparation Time: 5 minutes
Cooking Time: 0 minutes

Servings: 4
Ingredients:
2 cups cherry tomatoes, halved
1 cup kalamata olives, pitted and halved
½ cup baby spinach
2 scallions, chopped
1 tablespoon lime juice
A pinch of salt and black pepper
1 tablespoon avocado oil
Directions:
In a salad bowl, combine the tomatoes with the olives, spinach and the other ingredients, toss and serve for breakfast.
Nutrition: calories 66, fat 4.2, fiber 2.7, carbs 7.4, protein 1.4

9. Zucchini Spread

Preparation Time: 10 minutes
Cooking Time: 10 minutes
Servings: 4
Ingredients:
1-pound zucchinis, grated
1 tablespoon olive oil
2 garlic cloves, minced
3 scallions, chopped
1 tablespoon lime juice
2 tablespoons coconut cream
Salt and black pepper to the taste
1 tablespoon chives, chopped
Directions:
Heat up a pan with the oil over medium heat, add the garlic and the scallions and sauté for 2 minutes.
Add the zucchinis and the other ingredients except the cream, stir and cook for 8 minutes more.
Add the cream, blend the mix using an immersion blender, divide into bowls and serve as a spread.
Nutrition: calories 74, fat 5.5, fiber 1.8, carbs 6.5, protein 1.9

10. Paprika Olives Spread

Preparation Time: 10 minutes
Cooking Time: 0 minutes
Servings: 4
Ingredients:
1 cup kalamata olives, pitted and halved
1 cup black olives, pitted and halved
1 avocado, peeled, pitted and cubed
2 scallions, chopped
2 teaspoons sweet paprika
1 tablespoon olive oil

1 tablespoon lime juice
Salt and black pepper to the taste
½ cup coconut cream
Directions:
In a blender, combine the olives with the avocado, scallions and the other ingredients, pulse well, divide into bowls and serve for breakfast.
Nutrition: calories 287, fat 27.8, fiber 6.8, carbs 12.2, protein 2.5

11. Chives Avocado Mix

Preparation Time: 5 minutes
Cooking Time: 0 minutes
Servings: 4
Ingredients:
2 avocados, peeled, pitted and roughly cubed
1 tomato, cubed
1 cucumber, sliced
1 celery stalk, chopped
2 tablespoons avocado oil
1 tablespoon lime juice
Salt and black pepper to the taste
2 scallions, chopped
½ teaspoon cayenne pepper
1 tablespoon chives, chopped
Directions:
In a bowl, combine the avocados with the tomato, cucumber and the other ingredients, toss, divide between plates and serve for breakfast.
Nutrition: calories 232, fat 20.7, fiber 8, carbs 13.2, protein 2.9

12. Zucchini Pan

Preparation Time: 5 minutes
Cooking Time: 15 minutes
Servings: 4
Ingredients:
2 shallots, chopped
1 tablespoon olive oil
3 zucchinis, roughly cubed
2 garlic cloves, minced
2 sun-dried tomatoes, chopped
1 tablespoon capers, drained
Salt and black pepper to the taste
1 tablespoon dill, chopped
Directions:
Heat up a pan with the oil over medium heat, add the shallots, garlic and tomatoes and sauté for 5 minutes.

Add the zucchinis and the other ingredients, toss, cook over medium heat for 10 minutes more, divide between plates and serve.
Nutrition: calories 73, fat 4, fiber 2.6, carbs 9.2, protein 2.8

13. Chili Spinach and Zucchini Pan

Preparation Time: 5 minutes
Cooking Time: 15 minutes
Servings: 4
Ingredients:
1-pound baby spinach
1 tablespoons olive oil
2 zucchinis, sliced
1 tomato, cubed
2 shallots, chopped
1 tablespoon lime juice
2 garlic cloves, minced
2 teaspoons red chili flakes
1 teaspoon chili powder
Salt and black pepper to the taste
Directions:
Heat up a pan with the oil over medium heat, add the shallots, garlic, chili powder and chili flakes, stir and sauté for 5 minutes.
Add the spinach, zucchinis and the other ingredients, toss, cook over medium heat for 10 minutes more, divide into bowls and serve for breakfast.
Nutrition: calories 85, fat 4.3, fiber 4.1, carbs 10.6, protein 4.9

14. Basil Tomato and Cabbage Bowls

Preparation Time: 5 minutes
Cooking Time: 0 minutes
Servings: 4
Ingredients:
1 pound cherry tomatoes, halved
1 cup red cabbage, shredded
2 tablespoons balsamic vinegar
2 shallots, chopped
1 tablespoon avocado oil
Salt and black pepper to the taste
1 tablespoon basil, chopped
Directions:
In a bowl, combine the cabbage with the tomatoes and the other ingredients, toss and serve for breakfast.
Nutrition: calories 35, fat 0.7, fiber 2, carbs 6.6, protein 1.4

15. Spinach and Zucchini Hash

Preparation Time: 5 minutes
Cooking Time: 15 minutes
Servings: 4
Ingredients:
2 zucchinis, cubed
2 cups baby spinach
A pinch of salt and black pepper
1 tablespoon olive oil
1 teaspoon chili powder
1 teaspoon rosemary, dried
½ cup coconut cream
1 tablespoon chives, chopped
Directions:
Heat up a pan with the oil over medium heat, add the zucchinis and the chili powder, stir and cook for 5 minutes.
Add the rest of the ingredients, toss, cook the mix for 10 minutes more, divide between plates and serve fro breakfast.
Nutrition: calories 121, fat 11.1, fiber 2.5, carbs 6.1, protein 2.4

16. Tomato and Zucchini Fritters

Preparation Time: 5 minutes
Cooking Time: 10 minutes
Servings: 4
Ingredients:
1 pound zucchinis, grated
2 tomatoes, cubed
2 garlic cloves, minced
Salt and black pepper to the taste
1 tablespoon coconut flour
1 tablespoon flaxseed mixed with 2 tablespoons water
1 tablespoon dill, chopped
2 tablespoons olive oil
Directions:
In a bowl, mix the zucchinis with the tomatoes and the other ingredients except the oil, stir well, shape medium fritters out of this mix and flatten them
Heat up a pan with the oil over medium heat, add the fritters, cook them for 5 minutes on each side, divide between plates and serve for breakfast.
Nutrition: calories 111, fat 8.2, fiber 3.4, carbs 9, protein 2.8

17. Peppers Casserole

Preparation Time: 10 minutes
Cooking Time: 25 minutes
Servings: 4
Ingredients:
1 pound mixed bell peppers, cut into strips

Salt and black pepper to the taste
4 scallions, chopped
½ teaspoon cumin, ground
½ teaspoon oregano, dried
½ teaspoon basil, dried
2 garlic cloves, minced
1 tablespoon avocado oil
2 tomatoes, cubed
1 cup cashew cheese, grated
2 tablespoons parsley, chopped
Directions:
Heat up a pan with the oil over medium heat, add the scallions and the garlic and sauté for 5 minutes.
Add the rest of the ingredients except the cheese, stir and cook for 5 minutes more.
Sprinkle the cashew cheese on top and bake everything at 380 degrees F for 15 minutes.
Divide the mix between plates and serve for breakfast.
Nutrition: calories 85, fat 3.6, fiber 3.9, carbs 11.8, protein 3.3

18. Peanut Butter Banana Yogurt Parfait

Preparation Time: 5 Minutes
Cooking Time: 10 Minutes
Servings: 4
5 Ingredients:
3 cups vanilla yogurt
1 cup dried banana chips, crushed
1 cup granola cereal
2 large ripe bananas, sliced
1/4 cup unsalted roasted peanuts, chopped
None
Directions:
In a glass, layer the yogurt, banana chips, and cereal in alternating manner.
Top with ripe bananas and roasted peanuts.
Put in the fridge to chill for at least 10 minutes to set.
Nutrition:
Calories: 457; Fat: 17g; Carbs: 67g; Protein:14g

19. Mini Eggs in Cups

Preparation Time: 10 Minutes
Cooking Time: 20 Minutes
Servings: 6
5 Ingredients:
6 eggs, beaten
1 tablespoon Dijon mustard
¾ cup smoked salmon, finely chopped
½ cup cheddar cheese, shredded

¼ cup green onion, chopped
Cooking oil
Directions:
Preheat the oven to 4000F.
In a bowl, whisk the egg together with the mustard. Set aside.
In another bowl, mix the smoked salmon, cheese, and green onions.
Grease a mini muffin pan with cooking oil.
Place mixture and salmon mixture into the muffin pan.
Bake for 20 minutes until the eggs have set.
Allow to cool before taking out of the muffin cup.
Nutrition:
Calories: 98; Fat: 6g; Carbs: 0.5g; Protein:9g

20. Crème Brulee

Preparation Time: 15 Minutes
Cooking Time: 50 Minutes
Servings: 2
5 Ingredients:
3 tablespoons white sugar
1 cup heavy cream
3 eggs
¼ teaspoon vanilla extract
2 tablespoons white sugar
None
Directions:
Preheat the oven to 3500F.
In a bowl, whisk 3 tablespoons of sugar and cream until well-combined.
Heat the mixture in a saucepan for 2 minutes until warm and to dissolve the sugar.
Remove from the heat and stir in the egg yolks and vanilla. Whisk until smooth.
Place the cream mixture into ramekins.
Place the ramekins into a roasting pan with enough hot water to reach halfway of the sides of the ramekin.
Place in the oven and bake for 50 minutes.
Remove the ramekins from the hot water and allow to chill in the fridge for 2 hours.
Sprinkle with the remaining sugar on top and brown using a torch.
Nutrition:
Calories: 612; Fat: 51g; Carbs: 35g; Protein:7g

21. Cottage Cheese Fluff

Preparation Time: 10 Minutes
Cooking Time: 35 Minutes
Servings: 6
5 Ingredients:
3 cups low-fat cottage cheese
3 ounces sugar-free lemon-flavored Jell-O mix, mixed in warm water

8 ounces frozen whipped cream
½ cup berries of your choice
2 tablespoons toasted almond nuts, chopped
None
Directions:
Place the cottage cheese in a food processor and blend until creamy.
Whisk in the flavored gelatin and fold.
Place in molds and allow to set in the fridge.
Before, top with whipped cream, fruits, and nuts.
Nutrition:
Calories: 283; Fat: 15g; Carbs: 21g; Protein:18g

22. Strawberries and Cream Trifle

Preparation Time: 10 Minutes
Cooking Time: 45 Minutes
Servings: 12
5 Ingredients:
6 ounces packaged cream cheese, softened
1 ½ cups condensed milk
12 ounces frozen whipped cream, thawed
1 angel food cake, cubed
3 pints fresh strawberries, hulled and sliced
None
Directions:
In a bowl, mix the cream cheese, sweetened condensed milk, and whipped topping in a bowl until smooth.
In a trifle bowl, place a layer of angel food cake cubes. Add a layer of strawberries and cream on top. Repeat the layers.
Place in the fridge to cool for at least 35 minutes.
Nutrition:
Calories: 378; Fat: 17g; Carbs: 51g; Protein: 7g

23. Maple Toast and Eggs

Preparation Time: 20 Minutes
Cooking Time: 20 Minutes
Servings: 6
5 Ingredients:
12 bacon strips, diced
½ cup maple syrup
¼ cup butter
12 slices white bread
12 large eggs
Salt and pepper to taste
Directions:

Cook the bacon on a skillet over medium heat until the fat has rendered. Take the bacon out and place on paper towels to drain excess fat.

In a saucepan, heat the maple syrup and butter until melted. Set aside.

Trim the edges of the bread and flatten the slices with rolling pin. Brush one side with the syrup mixture and press the slices into greased muffin cups.

Divide the bacon into the muffin cups.

Break one egg into each cup.

Sprinkle with salt and pepper to taste

Cover with foil and bake in the oven at 4000F for 20 minutes or until the eggs have set.

Nutrition:

Calories: 671; Fat: 46g; Carbs: 44g; Protein:21g

24. Eggs Baked in Avocado

Preparation Time: 5 Minutes
Cooking Time: 30 Minutes
Servings: 2
5 Ingredients:
2 eggs
1 teaspoon olive oil
1 avocado, halved and pit removed
1/8 teaspoon salt
1 teaspoon chopped mint leaves
None
Directions:
Preheat the oven to 400oF.
Separate the egg yolks from the whites and put them in separate bowls.
Add salt into the egg whites and mix well.
In a skillet, sear the avocado halves under medium flame.
Place the egg whites into the depression made from the pit of the avocado.
Place the avocado in the oven and cook for 15 minutes.
Slide in the yolks and put in the oven to cook for another 15 minutes.
Garnish with chopped mint leaves before.
Nutrition:
Calories: 310; Fat: 27g; Carbs: 10g; Protein:11g

25. Baked Egg Stuffed Cups

Preparation Time: 10 Minutes
Cooking Time: 25 Minutes
Servings: 4
5 Ingredients:
1 cup cooking stuffing
4 eggs
¼ teaspoon salt
¼ teaspoon pepper
Chopped sage leaves for garnish

Cooking spray
Directions:
Preheat the oven to 3250F.
Press the stuffing into greased ramekins. Form wells in the center.
Break and slip the egg at the center of the stuffing.
Season with salt and pepper to taste.
Bake in the oven for 25 minutes.
Garnish with chopped sage.
Nutrition:
Calories: 200; Fat: 10g; Carbs: 20g; Protein:9g

26. Sweet Onion and Egg Pie

Preparation Time: 20 Minutes
Cooking Time: 35 Minutes
Servings: 10
5 Ingredients:
2 sweet onions, halved and sliced
1 tablespoons butter
6 eggs
1 cup evaporated milk
11 frozen deep-dish pie crust
Salt and pepper to taste
Directions:
Preheat the oven 4000F.
Melt the butter in a non-stick skillet. Sauté the onions over medium low heat until very tender.
Place the onions in a bowl. Add in eggs and evaporated milk. Season with salt and pepper to taste.
Pour the egg and onion mixture into the commercial pie crust.
Bake in the oven for 35 minutes.
Nutrition:
Calories: 169; Fat: 7g; Carbs: 21g; Protein:7g

27. Easy Sweet Potatoes and Eggs

Preparation Time: 10 Minutes
Cooking Time: 35 Minutes
Servings: 2
5 Ingredients:
2 teaspoons coconut oil
1 medium sweet potato, peeled and grated
3 large eggs
1 cup shredded cheddar cheese
Salt and pepper to taste
None
Directions:
Set your oven to broil on high.
Brush a baking dish with oil.

Spread the grated potatoes in a baking dish and create wells.
Crack one egg for each well created and sprinkle with cheddar cheese.
Season with salt and pepper to taste.
 Bake in the oven for 35 minutes.
Nutrition:
Calories: 685; Fat: 36g; Carbs: 46g; Protein:44g

28. Apple Yogurt Parfait

Preparation Time: 10 Minutes
Cooking Time: 10 Minutes
Servings: 4
5 Ingredients:
1 ½ cups vanilla yogurt
½ cup granola cereals
½ cup raisins, chopped
1 cup sweetened applesauce
A dash of ground nutmeg
None
Directions:
Layer each glass with yogurt and top with granola and raising. Repeat the layer twice.
Top with applesauce and nutmeg.
Place in the fridge to cool before.
Nutrition:
Calories: 158; Fat: 2g; Carbs: 30g; Protein:5g

29. Basic Poached Eggs

Preparation Time: 5 Minutes
Cooking Time: 3 Minutes
Servings: 4
5 Ingredients:
4 eggs, cold
3 tablespoons vinegar
Salt and pepper to taste
4 slices of bread, toasted
Chopped green onions for garnish
Water
Directions:
Put water in a saucepan.
Bring to a boil and add vinegar.
Crack eggs into separate bowls.
Give the boiling water a swirl and pour gently the eggs into the mixture.
Allow to cook for 3 minutes.
Take the eggs out and serve on toast
Season with salt and pepper to taste.
Garnish with green onions.

Nutrition:
Calories: 237; Fat: 11g; Carbs: 22g; Protein:12g

30. Mini Breakfast Pizza

Preparation Time: 5 Minutes
Cooking Time: 10 Minutes
Servings: 4
5 Ingredients:
4 eggs, beaten
1/3 cup commercial pizza sauce
2 English muffins, split and toasted
½ cup shredded Italian cheese
Dried oregano leaves
Cooking spray
Salt and pepper to taste
Directions:
Preheat the oven to 4000F.
Coat a skillet with cooking spray and heat over medium flame.
Season the eggs with salt and pepper to taste and pour into the skillet. As the eggs begin to set, pull the eggs across the pan with an inverted turner. Continue cooking and folding the egg. Set aside.
Spread pizza sauce evenly on English muffin halves and top with eggs and cheese.
Place on a baking sheet and bake for 5 minutes.
Garnish with oregano last.
Nutrition:
Calories: 282; Fat: 13g; Carbs: 25g; Protein:17g

31. Microwaved Ham and Mushroom Coffee Cup Scramble

Preparation Time: 3 Minutes
Cooking Time: 1 minute
Servings: 1
5 Ingredients:
1 egg, beaten
¼ cup chopped mushrooms
1 thin slice ham, diced
2 tablespoons Swiss cheese, shredded
Green onion for garnish
1 tablespoon water
Salt and pepper to taste
Directions:
In a mug, beat the egg and water. Season with salt and pepper to taste.
Stir in the mushrooms, ham, and cheese.
Place inside the microwave oven and cook for 1 minute.
Garnish with green onions last.
Nutrition:
Calories: 627; Fat: 40g; Carbs: 29g; Protein:36g

32. Microwaved Egg and Cheese Breakfast Burrito

Preparation Time: 2 Minutes
Cooking Time: 1 minute
Servings: 1
5 Ingredients:
1 flour tortilla, warm
1 egg, beaten
1 tablespoon Mexican cheese blend, shredded
1 red tomato, chopped
1 tablespoon coriander leaves, chopped
Salt and pepper to taste
Directions:
Press tortilla in a microwave-safe bowl and pour in the egg.
Microwave for 30 seconds.
Remove from the microwave and add in cheese blend on top.
Microwave for another 30 seconds.
Top with chopped tomato and coriander leaves.
Nutrition:
Calories: 309; Fat: 14g; Carbs: 30g; Protein:16g

33. Easy Egg Breakfast Quesadillas

Preparation Time: 5 Minutes
Cooking Time: 5 Minutes
Servings: 2
5 Ingredients:
½ cup Mexican cheese blend, shredded
2 whole wheat flour tortillas
4 slices bacon, cooked
4 eggs, beaten
Commercial salsa for garnish
Cooking spray
Salt and pepper to taste
Directions:
Sprinkle half of the cheese on one side of each tortilla and top with bacon slices. Set aside.
Coat a non-stick skillet with cooking spray and heat over medium flame.
Beat the eggs and season with salt and pepper.
Pour in the eggs and allow to set. Gently pull the eggs across the pan using a turner and continue folding until cooked.
Spoon eggs on top of bacon.
Top with cheese.
Fold the tortillas over the filling and press gently.
On a clean skillet, toast the quesadillas over low heat until the cheese is melted.
Cut into wedges and serve with salsa.
Nutrition:
Calories: 698; Fat: 51g; Carbs: 21g; Protein:35g

34. Broccoli Cheddar Omelet

Preparation Time: 5 Minutes
Cooking Time: 5 Minutes
Servings: 2
5 Ingredients:
2 eggs, beaten
2 tablespoons milk
1/3 cup cooked broccoli florets
2 tablespoons shredded cheddar cheese
Parsley for garnish
Cooking spray
Salt and pepper to taste
Directions:
Beat the eggs and milk in a bowl until well-combined. Season with salt and pepper to taste.
Coat an omelet pan with cooking spray and heat over medium flames.
Pour in the egg mixture. While the eggs are setting, push the cooked portion to the center using an inverted turner. Continue cooking the eggs.
Place the omelet and cheese on one side of the egg then fold.
Slide on to a plate.
Garnish with parsley last.
Nutrition:
Calories: 177; Fat: 14g; Carbs: 4g; Protein:13g

35. Breakfast Pudding

Preparation Time: 5 Minutes
Cooking Time: 7 Minutes
Servings: 6
5 Ingredients:
½ cup sugar
¼ cup cornstarch
3 cups milk
4 egg yolks
2 tablespoons butter
¼ teaspoon salt
2 teaspoon vanilla
Fresh fruit for garnish
Directions:
In a bowl, mix sugar, cornstarch, and salt.
Place in a saucepan and pour in milk and eggs until smooth.
Turn on the heat and allow to simmer over medium flame until the sauce thickens. Remove from the heat and stir in butter and vanilla.
Pour into custard cups and refrigerate.
Garnish with fresh fruits of your choice before.
Nutrition:
Calories: 195; Fat: 11g; Carbs: 18g; Protein:6g

36. Sausage Cheddar Breakfast Bowl

Preparation Time: 5 Minutes
Cooking Time: 5 Minutes
Servings: 1
5 Ingredients:
2 eggs, beaten
2 tablespoons milk
2 tablespoons breakfast sausage, cooked and crumbled
1 tablespoon cheddar cheese, shredded
1 red tomato, chopped
Cooking spray
Salt and pepper to taste
Directions:
Whisk the egg and milk in a bowl. Season with salt and pepper to taste.
Heat skillet sprayed with cooking oil over medium flame and cook the eggs.
Stir the eggs until fluffy.
Place in a bowl and add in breakfast sausages, cheddar cheese and tomatoes.
Serve immediately.
Nutrition:
Calories: 365; Fat: 25g; Carbs: 9g; Protein:24g

37. Broccoli Cheese Soup

Preparation Time: 5 Minutes
Cooking Time: 15 Minutes
Servings: 4
5 Ingredients:
2 cloves of garlic, minced
1 head broccoli, cut into florets
26 ounces cream of chicken soup
1 can milk
2 cups shredded cheddar cheese
Cooking oil
Directions:
Heat oil in a large saucepan over medium flame and sauté the garlic until fragrant.
Add in the broccoli and sauté for 1 minute.
Stir in the cream of chicken soup and allow to boil for 8 minutes.
Reduce the heat and simmer.
Pour in the milk and cheese and continue cooking for another 5 minutes.
Serve warm.
Nutrition:
Calories: 460; Fat: 31g; Carbs: 23g; Protein:23g

38. Bacon and Egg Breakfast Chili

Preparation Time: 25 minutes

Servings: 8
Ingredients:
1 pound of breakfast sausage, thawed and roughly chopped
½ pound of bacon, chopped
6 large organic eggs
1 medium white onion, finely chopped
2 tablespoons of olive oil
1 (28-ouncecan of diced tomatoes with green chiles
2-3 cups of homemade low-sodium chicken broth
2 teaspoons of smoked paprika or regular paprika
2 teaspoons of chili powder
2 teaspoons of garlic powder
1 teaspoon of onion powder
1 teaspoon of fine sea salt
Avocado slices (for
Directions:
Press the "Sauté" function on your Instant Pot and add the bacon. Cook until brown and crispy, stirring occasionally. Transfer the bacon to a plate lined with paper towels.
Add the breakfast sausage and onions to the bacon grease and cook until the sausage has browned.
Add the remaining ingredients except for the eggs to your Instant Pot. Lock the lid and cook at high pressure for 10 minutes.
When the cooking is done, naturally release the pressure and remove the lid.
Meanwhile, fry or scramble your eggs on a stovetop skillet the way you like. You can skip this step if you only want to use your Instant Pot.
Once everything is done, scoop the breakfast chili onto bowls and top with eggs, bacon and avocado slices. Serve and enjoy!
Nutrition:
Calories: 441
Fat: 34.9g
Net Carb: 3.4g
Protein: 26.5g

39. Lemon Blueberry Muffins

Preparation Time: 15 minutes
Servings: 6
Ingredients:
2 cups of almond flour
1 cup of heavy whipping cream
2 large organic eggs, beaten
¼ cup of coconut butter or ghee, melted
1 tablespoon of granulated erythritol or other keto-friendly sweeteners
½ cup of fresh or frozen blueberries
1 teaspoon of fresh lemon zest
1 teaspoon of lemon extract
1/8 teaspoon of fine sea salt
Directions:

In a large bowl, add all the ingredients and gently stir until well combined.
Grease 6 silicone muffin cups with nonstick cooking spray.
Divide and add the muffin batter into each muffin cup.
Add 1 cup of water and a trivet inside your Instant Pot. Place the muffin cup on top of the trivet and cover with aluminum foil.
Lock the lid and cook at high pressure for 8 minutes. When the timer beeps, naturally release the pressure for 10 minutes. Carefully remove the lid.
Check if the muffins are cooked through using a toothpick. Serve and enjoy!
Nutrition:
Calories: 220
Fat: 21g
Net Carb: 3g
Protein: 4g

40. Zucchini Muffins

Preparation Time: 15 minutes
Servings: 6
Ingredients:
1 large zucchini, finely grated
6 medium bacon slices, chopped
4 large organic eggs
½ cup of heavy whipping cream
1 cup of shredded cheddar cheese
1 cup of almond flour
4 tablespoons of flax meal
½ cup of parmesan cheese, finely grated
1 tablespoon of dried Italian herbs
2 teaspoons of onion powder
1 teaspoon of baking powder
½ teaspoon of garlic powder
½ teaspoon of fine sea salt
½ teaspoon of freshly cracked black pepper
Directions:
Grease 6 silicone muffin cups with nonstick cooking spray.
In a large bowl, add all the ingredients and gently stir until well combined.
Divide and spoon the batter into each muffin cup.
Add 2 cups of water and a trivet inside your Instant Pot. Place the muffin cups on top and cover with aluminum foil.
Lock the lid and cook at high pressure for 10 minutes. When the cooking is done, naturally release the pressure for 10 minutes. Carefully remove the lid and check if the muffins are done.
Serve and enjoy!
Nutrition:
Calories: 216
Fat: 17g
Net Carb: 2.7g
Protein: 12.9g

41. Italian Sausage Breakfast Cups

Preparation Time: 20 minutes
Servings: 4
Ingredients:
1 pound of Italian sausage links, cut into bite-sized pieces
4 large eggs, beaten
1 medium yellow or white onion, finely chopped
1 teaspoon of fine sea salt
1 teaspoon of freshly cracked black pepper
½ cup of mushrooms, finely chopped
½ cup of broccoli florets, chopped
½ cup of spinach, roughly chopped
1 tablespoon of fresh parsley, finely chopped
2 tablespoons of olive oil
Directions:
Press the "Sauté" function on your Instant Pot and add the olive oil. Once hot, add the onions, mushrooms, and broccoli. Cook until softened, stirring occasionally. Remove and set aside.
Add the Italian sausage and cook until brown, stirring occasionally. Turn off "Sauté" function on your Instant Pot.
In a large bowl, add the vegetables, cooked Italian sausage and remaining ingredients. Stir until well combined. Divide the mixture between 6 silicon muffin cups or greased ramekins.
Add 1 cup of water and a trivet inside your Instant Pot. Place the muffin cups on top and lock the lid. Cook at high pressure for 10 minutes.
When the cooking is done, naturally release the pressure and carefully remove the lid.
Serve and enjoy!
Nutrition:
Calories: 288
Fat: 23g
Net Carb: 1g
Protein: 16.5g

42. Zucchini Bread with Walnuts

Preparation Time: 1 hour and 15 minutes
Servings: 16
Ingredients:
3 large organic eggs, beaten
½ cup of extra-virgin olive oil
1 cup of zucchini, finely grated
½ cup of walnuts, chopped
1 teaspoon of pure vanilla extract
2 ½ cups of almond flour
½ cup of erythritol or other keto-friendly sweeteners
½ teaspoon of fine sea salt
1 teaspoon of baking soda or baking powder
¼ teaspoon of grated ginger

1 teaspoon of cinnamon

Directions:

In a large bowl, add all the ingredients and gently stir until well blended together.

Grease a 7-inch pan that fits inside your Instant Pot with nonstick cooking spray.

Add the bread batter to the pan and cover with aluminum foil.

Add 1 cup of water and place a trivet inside your Instant Pot. Place the pan on top of the trivet.

Lock the lid and cook at high pressure for 55 minutes. When the cooking is done, naturally release the pressure for 10 minutes. Carefully remove the lid. Unfold the aluminum foil and allow to cool. Serve and enjoy!

Nutrition:

Calories: 200

Fat: 19g

Net Carb: 3g

Protein: 6g

43. Breakfast Chicken and Egg

Preparation Time: 30 minutes

Servings: 6

Ingredients:

1 pound of boneless, skinless chicken breasts

6 large organic eggs

2 tablespoons of extra-virgin olive oil

1 large onion, finely chopped

1 cup of water

½ cup of cauliflower rice

2 tablespoons of fresh parsley, finely chopped

1 teaspoon of fine sea salt

1 teaspoon of freshly cracked black pepper

Directions:

Press the "Sauté" function on your Instant Pot and add the olive oil. Once hot, add the onions and cook until fragrant, stirring occasionally. Remove and set aside.

Add the chicken and cook for 4 minutes per side or until brown.

Pour in 1 cup of water and lock the lid. Cook at high pressure for 15 minutes.

When the cooking is done, naturally release the pressure and remove the lid. Transfer the chicken to a cutting board and shred using two forks.

In a large bowl, add the shredded chicken, eggs, onions, cauliflower rice, fresh parsley, salt and black pepper. Stir until well combined.

Grease an oven-proof dish that fits inside your Instant Pot. Add the egg mixture and cover with foil.

Place a trivet inside your Instant Pot and place the dish on top. Lock the lid and cook at high pressure for another 8 minutes.

When the cooking is done, naturally release the pressure and remove the lid. Serve and enjoy!

Nutrition:

Calories: 275

Fat: 13g

Net Carb: 2g

Protein: 35g

44. Eggs en Cocotte

Preparation Time: 20 minutes
Servings: 3
Ingredients:
3 tablespoons of unsalted butter
3 tablespoons of heavy whipping cream
3 large organic eggs
1 tablespoon of fresh chives, chopped
½ teaspoon of fine sea salt
½ teaspoon of freshly cracked black pepper
1 cup of water
Directions:
Grease 3 ramekins with unsalted butter and add 1 tablespoon of heavy whipping cream into each one.
Crack an egg into each ramekin and sprinkle with fresh chives, salt and black pepper.
Add 1 cup of water and a trivet inside your Instant Pot. Place the ramekins on top of the trivet and cover with aluminum foil. Lock the lid and cook at low pressure for 2 minutes.
When the timer beeps, naturally release the pressure and carefully remove the lid. Serve and enjoy!
Nutrition:
Calories: 420
Fat: 44.5g
Net Carbs: 0.8g
Protein: 6.2g

45. Breakfast Chocolate Zucchini Muffins

Preparation Time: 40 minutes
Servings: Around 24 muffin bites
Ingredients:
2 large organic eggs
½ cup of coconut oil, melted
2 teaspoons of pure vanilla extract
1 tablespoon of unsalted butter
3 tablespoons of unsweetened cocoa powder
1 cup of almond flour
½ teaspoon of baking soda or baking powder
1 cup of evaporated cane juice
1 cup of water
½ teaspoon of ground cinnamon
1 cup of finely grated zucchini
1/3 cup of mini chocolate chips
A small pinch of fine sea salt
Directions:
In a large bowl, add all the ingredients one by one and gently stir until well blended together.
Fill silicone muffin cups with the batter.

Add 1 cup of water and a trivet inside your Instant Pot. Layer the muffins on top of the trivet. Cover with aluminum foil.

Lock the lid and cook at high pressure for 8 minutes. When the cooking is done, naturally release the pressure and remove the lid.

Remove the muffins and check if done using toothpicks. Serve and enjoy!

Nutrition:

Calories: 71

Fat: 6.8g

Net Carbs: 1.8g

Protein: 1g

46. Cauliflower Oatmeal

Preparation Time: 15 minutes

Servings: 1

Ingredients:

1 cup of fine cauliflower rice

½ cup of coconut cream

½ teaspoon of organic ground cinnamon

¼ teaspoon of granulated erythritol

½ tablespoon of peanut butter

A small pinch of fine sea salt

Directions:

Add all the ingredients except for the peanut butter and stir until well combined.

Lock the lid and cook at high pressure for 2 minutes.

When the cooking is done, naturally release the pressure and remove the lid.

Transfer to bowls and top with peanut butter. Serve and enjoy!

Nutrition:

Calories: 140

Fat: 7g

Net Carbs: 8g

Protein: 7g

47. Chocolate Cauliflower Rice Pudding

Preparation Time: 16 minutes

Servings: 2

Ingredients:

2 cups of fine cauliflower rice

1 cup of heavy whipping cream

1/3 cup of granulated erythritol or other keto-friendly sweeteners

1 to 2 egg whites

1 teaspoon of pure vanilla extract

3 tablespoons of unsweetened cocoa powder

A small pinch of fine sea salt

Directions:

Add all the ingredients and stir until well combined.

Lock the lid and cook at high pressure for 2 minutes. When the cooking is done, naturally release the pressure and carefully remove the lid. Serve and enjoy!
Nutrition:
Calories: 313
Fat: 27.7g
Net Carbs: 5g
Protein: 10g

48. Mushroom and Cauliflower Risotto

Preparation Time: 25 minutes
Servings: 4
Ingredients:
1 medium cauliflower head, cut into florets
1 pound of shiitake mushrooms, sliced
3 medium garlic cloves, peeled and minced
2 tablespoons of coconut aminos
1 cup of homemade low-sodium chicken stock
1 cup of full-fat coconut milk
1 tablespoon of coconut oil, melted
1 small onion, finely chopped
2 tablespoons of almond flour
¼ cup of nutritional yeast
Directions:
Press the "Sauté" function on your Instant Pot and add the coconut oil.
Once hot, add the onions, mushrooms and garlic. Sauté for 5 minutes or until softened, stirring occasionally.
Add the remaining ingredients except for the almond flour. Lock the lid and cook at high pressure for 2 minutes.
When the cooking is done, naturally release the pressure and remove the lid.
Sprinkle the almond flour over the risotto and stir to thicken. Serve and enjoy!
Nutrition:
Calories: 230
Fat: 18.5g
Net Carbs: 8g
Protein: 7.5g

49. Coconut and Lime Cauliflower Rice

Preparation Time: 15 minutes
Servings: 4
Ingredients:
1 large cauliflower, chopped
2 tablespoons of extra-virgin olive oil
1 large yellow onion, finely chopped
3 medium garlic cloves, peeled and minced
1 (15-ouncecan of full-fat coconut milk

1 medium lime, zest and juice
½ teaspoon of fine sea salt
¼ teaspoon of freshly cracked black pepper
Directions:
Add the cauliflowers to a food processor and pulse until resembles rice-like consistency.
Press the "Sauté" function on your Instant Pot and add the olive oil. Once hot, add the onions and garlic. Sauté for 2 to 3 minutes or until fragrant, stirring occasionally.
Add the remaining ingredients and lock the lid. Cook at high pressure for 3 minutes.
When the cooking is done, quick release the pressure and remove the lid. Serve and enjoy!
Nutrition:
Calories: 160
Fat: 11g
Net Carbs: 6g
Protein: 5g

50. Eggs with Avocados and Feta Cheese

Preparation Time: 10 minutes
Servings: 2
Ingredients:
4 large organic eggs
1 large avocado, peeled and cut into 12 slices
2 tablespoons of crumbled feta cheese
1 tablespoon of fresh parsley, finely chopped
½ teaspoon of fine sea salt
½ teaspoon of freshly cracked black pepper
Directions:
Grease 2 gratin dishes with nonstick cooking spray..
Arrange 6 avocado slices into each gratin dish. Crack 2 eggs into each dish. Sprinkle with crumbled feta cheese, fresh parsley, salt and black pepper. Wrap with aluminum foil.
Add 1 cup of water and a trivet inside your Instant Pot. Place the gratin dish on top of the trivet.
Lock the lid and cook at high pressure for 4 minutes. When the cooking is done, quick release or naturally release the pressure. Carefully remove the lid and check if the eggs are done.
Serve and enjoy!
Nutrition:
Calories: 362
Fat: 30g
Net Carb: 4g
Protein: 16g

51. Giant Keto Pancake

Preparation Time: 50 minutes
Servings: 6
Ingredients:
2 cups of almond flour or coconut flour
2 teaspoons of baking powder

2 tablespoons of granulated erythritol or another keto-friendly sweetener
2 large organic eggs
1 ½ cup of unsweetened almond milk or coconut milk
Directions:
In a large bowl, add all the ingredients and stir until well combined.
Grease a springform pan with nonstick cooking spray and add the pancake batter.
Add 1 cup of water and a trivet inside your Instant Pot. Place the springform pan on top of the trivet.
Lock the lid and cook at low pressure for 45 minutes. When the cooking is done, remove the lid and allow the pancake to cool. Serve and enjoy!
Nutrition:
Calories: 280
Fat: 24g
Net Carbs: 1g
Protein: 9g

52. Breakfast Burrito Casserole

Preparation Time: 25 minutes
Servings: 6
Ingredients:
4 large organic eggs
1 cup of cheddar cheese, cubed
¼ cup of white or yellow onion, finely chopped
1 medium jalapeno, finely chopped
1 cup of cooked ham, cut into cubes
½ teaspoon of fine sea salt
½ teaspoon of freshly cracked black pepper
½ teaspoon of chili powder
Lettuce leaves (for
Salsa (for
Avocado slices (for
Ingredients:
In a large bowl, add all the ingredients and stir until well combined.
Grease a springform pan or a round metal bowl with nonstick cooking spray. Add the egg mixture.
Add 1 cup of water and a trivet inside your Instant Pot. Place the pan on top of the trivet and cover with aluminum foil.
Lock the lid and cook at high pressure for 12 minutes. When the cooking is done, naturally release the pressure and remove the lid. Remove the pan and spoon the egg mixture onto lettuce leaves.
Top with salsa and avocado slices. Serve and enjoy!
Nutrition:
Calories: 165
Fat: 11.5g
Net Carbs: 1.5g
Protein: 13g

53. Breakfast Ratatouille

Preparation Time: 30 minutes
Servings: 6
Ingredients:
12 large organic eggs
¼ cup of extra-virgin olive oil
1 medium yellow onion, finely chopped
6 medium garlic cloves, peeled and finely minced
1 (28-ouncecan of plum tomatoes, drained
1 medium eggplant, chopped
1 zucchini, sliced
1 medium yellow bell pepper, seeded and chopped
1 tablespoon of capers, chopped
1 tablespoon of red wine vinegar
2 teaspoons of fresh thyme, finely chopped
1 teaspoon of fresh oregano, finely chopped
3 tablespoons of fresh basil, finely chopped
3 tablespoons of fresh parsley, finely chopped
Directions:
Press the "Sauté" function on your Instant Pot and add olive oil and onions. Sauté for 4 minutes or until slightly softened, stirring occasionally.
Add the garlic and herbs. Sauté until fragrant, stirring occasionally.
Add the tomatoes, eggplant, bell peppers and zucchini. Stir until well combined.
Lock the lid and cook at high pressure for 5 minutes. When the cooking is done quick release the pressure and remove the lid.
Stir in the capers and red wine vinegar.
In a small skillet over medium-high heat, add the vegetables. Make small cavities and crack eggs into the cavity. Cover and allow the eggs to cook through.
Serve and enjoy!
Nutrition:
Calories:
Fat:
Net Carbs:
Protein:

54. Spanish Chorizo and Cauliflower Hash

Preparation Time: 20 minutes
Servings: 4
Ingredients:
1 pound of cauliflower florets, cut into florets
1 tablespoon of extra-virgin olive oil
1 medium sweet potato, cut into bite-sized pieces
1 pound of chorizo sausage, crumbled
1 large onion, finely chopped
2 medium garlic cloves, peeled and minced
3 tablespoons of fresh rosemary, finely chopped
3 tablespoons of fresh basil, finely chopped

1 teaspoon of fine sea salt
1 teaspoon of freshly cracked black pepper
½ cup of homemade low-sodium vegetable stock
Directions:
Press the "Sauté" function on your Instant Pot and add the olive oil. Once hot, add the onions and garlic. Sauté for 2 minutes or until softened, stirring occasionally.
Add the sweet potato pieces, chorizo sausage and cauliflower. Sauté for 3 minutes, stirring occasionally.
Add the remaining ingredients and stir until well combined.
Pour in the vegetable stock and lock the lid. Cook at high pressure for 10 minutes. When the cooking is done, naturally release the pressure and remove the lid. Serve and enjoy!
Nutrition:
Calories: 550
Fat: 35g
Net Carbs: 12g
Protein: 23g

55. BLT Egg Casserole

Preparation Time: 30 minutes
Servings: 4
Ingredients:
6 large organic eggs
6 medium slices of bacon, chopped
1 medium Roma tomato, sliced
½ cup of cheddar cheese, shredded
2 green onions, thinly sliced
½ cup of heavy whipping cream
½ cup of fresh spinach
1 teaspoon of fine sea salt
1 teaspoon of freshly cracked black pepper
Directions:
In a large bowl, add all the ingredients and stir until well combined.
Grease a large springform pan with nonstick cooking spray and add the egg mixture.
Add 1 cup of water and place a trivet inside your Instant Pot. Place the springform pan on top of the trivet and cover with aluminum foil.
Lock the lid and cook at high pressure for 13 minutes.
When the cooking is done, naturally release the pressure for 10 minutes, then quick release the remaining pressure. Remove the lid. Serve and enjoy!
Nutrition:
Calories: 360
Fat: 29g
Net Carbs: 2g
Protein: 23g

56. Coconut Oatmeal

Preparation Time: 20 minutes
Servings: 4
Ingredients:
2 cups almond milk
1 cup coconut; shredded
2 tsp. vanilla extract
2 tsp. stevia
Directions:
In a pan that fits your air fryer, mix all the ingredients, stir well, introduce the pan in the machine and cook at 360°F for 15 minutes
Divide into bowls and serve for breakfast.
Nutrition: Calories: 201; Fat: 13g; Fiber: 2g; Carbs: 4g; Protein: 7g

57. Cheesy Tomatoes

Preparation Time: 20 minutes
Servings: 4
Ingredients:
1 lb. cherry tomatoes; halved
1 cup mozzarella; shredded
1 tsp. basil; chopped.
Cooking spray
Salt and black pepper to taste.
Directions:
Grease the tomatoes with the cooking spray, season with salt and pepper, sprinkle the mozzarella on top, place them all in your air fryer's basket, cook at 330°F for 15 minutes
Divide into bowls, sprinkle the basil on top and serve.
Nutrition: Calories: 140; Fat: 7g; Fiber: 3g; Carbs: 4g; Protein: 5g

58. Banana Nut Cake

Preparation Time: 35 minutes
Servings: 6
Ingredients:
1 cup blanched finely ground almond flour
2 large eggs.
¼ cup unsalted butter; melted.
¼ cup full-fat sour cream.
¼ cup chopped walnuts
½ cup powdered erythritol
2 tbsp. ground golden flaxseed.
2 ½ tsp. banana extract.
1 tsp. vanilla extract.
2 tsp. baking powder.
½ tsp. ground cinnamon.
Directions:

Take a large bowl, mix almond flour, erythritol, flaxseed, baking powder and cinnamon. Stir in butter, banana extract, vanilla extract and sour cream
Add eggs to the mixture and gently stir until fully combined. Stir in the walnuts
Pour into 6-inch nonstick cake pan and place into the air fryer basket. Adjust the temperature to 300 Degrees F and set the timer for 25 minutes
Cake will be golden and a toothpick inserted in center will come out clean when fully cooked. Allow to fully cool to avoid crumbling.
Nutrition: Calories: 263; Protein: 7.6g; Fiber: 3.1g; Fat: 23.6g; Carbs: 18.4g

59. Olives and Kale

Preparation Time: 25 minutes
Servings: 4
Ingredients:
4 eggs; whisked
1 cup kale; chopped.
½ cup black olives, pitted and sliced
2 tbsp. cheddar; grated
Cooking spray
A pinch of salt and black pepper
Directions:
Take a bowl and mix the eggs with the rest of the ingredients except the cooking spray and whisk well.
Now, take a pan that fits in your air fryer and grease it with the cooking spray, pour the olives mixture inside, spread
Put the pan into the machine and cook at 360°F for 20 minutes. Serve for breakfast hot.
Nutrition: Calories: 220; Fat: 13g; Fiber: 4g; Carbs: 6g; Protein: 12g

60. Cheesy Turkey

Preparation Time: 30 minutes
Servings: 4
Ingredients:
1 turkey breast, skinless, boneless; cut into strips and browned
2 cups almond milk
2 cups cheddar cheese; shredded
2 eggs; whisked
2 tsp. olive oil
1 tbsp. chives; chopped.
Salt and black pepper to taste.
Directions:
Take a bowl and mix the eggs with milk, cheese, salt, pepper and the chives and whisk well.
Preheat the air fryer at 330°F, add the oil, heat it up, add the turkey pieces and spread them well
Add the eggs mixture, toss a bit and cook for 25 minutes. Serve right away for breakfast
Nutrition: Calories: 244; Fat: 11g; Fiber: 4g; Carbs: 5g; Protein: 7g

61. Mushrooms and Cheese Spread

Preparation Time: 25 minutes
Servings: 4
Ingredients:
¼ cup mozzarella; shredded
½ cup coconut cream
1 cup white mushrooms
A pinch of salt and black pepper
Cooking spray
Directions:
Put the mushrooms in your air fryer's basket, grease with cooking spray and cook at 370°F for 20 minutes.
Transfer to a blender, add the remaining ingredients, pulse well, divide into bowls and serve as a spread
Nutrition: Calories: 202; Fat: 12g; Fiber: 2g; Carbs: 5g; Protein: 7g

62. Cheesy Sausage Balls

Preparation Time: 22 minutes
Servings: 16 balls
Ingredients:
1 lb. pork breakfast sausage
1 large egg.
1 oz. full-fat cream cheese; softened.
½ cup shredded Cheddar cheese
Directions:
Mix all ingredients in a large bowl. Form into sixteen (1-inchballs. Place the balls into the air fryer basket.
Adjust the temperature to 400 Degrees F and set the timer for 12 minutes. Shake the basket two or three times during cooking
Sausage balls will be browned on the outside and have an internal temperature of at least 145 Degrees F when completely cooked.
Nutrition: Calories: 424; Protein: 22.8g; Fiber: 0.0g; Fat: 32.2g; Carbs: 1.6g

63. Blackberries Bowls

Preparation Time: 20 minutes
Servings: 4
Ingredients:
1 ½ cups coconut milk
½ cup coconut; shredded
½ cup blackberries
2 tsp. stevia
Directions:
In your air fryer's pan, mix all the ingredients, stir, cover and cook at 360°F for 15 minutes.
Divide into bowls and serve
Nutrition: Calories: 171; Fat: 4g; Fiber: 2g; Carbs: 3g; Protein: 5g

64. Cilantro Omelet

Preparation Time: 25 minutes
Servings: 4
Ingredients:
6 eggs; whisked
1 cup mozzarella; shredded
1 cup cilantro; chopped.
Cooking spray
Salt and black pepper to taste.
Directions:
Take a bowl and mix all the ingredients except the cooking spray and whisk well.
Grease a pan that fits your air fryer with the cooking spray, pour the eggs mix, spread, put the pan into the machine and cook at 350°F for 20 minutes
Divide the omelet between plates and serve for breakfast.
Nutrition: Calories: 270; Fat: 15g; Fiber: 3g; Carbs: 5g; Protein: 9g

65. Tomatoes and Swiss Chard Bake

Preparation Time: 20 minutes
Servings: 4
Ingredients:
4 eggs; whisked
3 oz. Swiss chard; chopped.
1 cup tomatoes; cubed
1 tsp. olive oil
Salt and black pepper to taste.
Directions:
Take a bowl and mix the eggs with the rest of the ingredients except the oil and whisk well.
Grease a pan that fits the fryer with the oil, pour the swish chard mix and cook at 359°F for 15 minutes.
Divide between plates and serve for breakfast
Nutrition: Calories: 202; Fat: 14g; Fiber: 3g; Carbs: 5g; Protein: 12g

66. Pumpkin Spice Muffins

Preparation Time: 25 minutes
Servings: 6
Ingredients:
2 large eggs.
1 cup blanched finely ground almond flour.
¼ cup unsalted butter; softened.
¼ cup pure pumpkin purée.
½ cup granular erythritol.
¼ tsp. ground nutmeg.
1 tsp. vanilla extract.
½ tsp. ground cinnamon.

½ tsp. baking powder.
Directions:
Take a large bowl, mix almond flour, erythritol, baking powder, butter, pumpkin purée, cinnamon, nutmeg and vanilla. Gently stir in eggs.
Evenly pour the batter into six silicone muffin cups. Place muffin cups into the air fryer basket, working in batches if necessary.
Adjust the temperature to 300 Degrees F and set the timer for 15 minutes. When completely cooked, a toothpick inserted in center will come out mostly clean. Serve warm.
Nutrition: Calories: 205; Protein: 6.3g; Fiber: 2.4g; Fat: 18.0g; Carbs: 17.4g

67. Strawberries Oatmeal

Preparation Time: 20 minutes
Servings: 4
Ingredients:
½ cup coconut; shredded
¼ cup strawberries
2 cups coconut milk
¼ tsp. vanilla extract
2 tsp. stevia
Cooking spray
Directions:
Grease the Air Fryer's pan with the cooking spray, add all the ingredients inside and toss
Cook at 365°F for 15 minutes, divide into bowls and serve for breakfast
Nutrition: Calories: 142; Fat: 7g; Fiber: 2g; Carbs: 3g; Protein: 5g

68. Tuna and Spring Onions Salad

Preparation Time: 20 minutes
Servings: 4
Ingredients:
14 oz. canned tuna, drained and flaked
2 spring onions; chopped.
1 cup arugula
1 tbsp. olive oil
A pinch of salt and black pepper
Directions:
In a bowl, all the ingredients except the oil and the arugula and whisk.
Preheat the Air Fryer over 360°F, add the oil and grease it. Pour the tuna mix, stir well and cook for 15 minutes
In a salad bowl, combine the arugula with the tuna mix, toss and serve.
Nutrition: Calories: 212; Fat: 8g; Fiber: 3g; Carbs: 5g; Protein: 8g

69. Scrambled Eggs

Preparation Time: 20 minutes
Servings: 2

Ingredients:

4 large eggs.

½ cup shredded sharp Cheddar cheese.

2 tbsp. unsalted butter; melted.

Directions:

Crack eggs into 2-cup round baking dish and whisk. Place dish into the air fryer basket.

Adjust the temperature to 400 Degrees F and set the timer for 10 minutes

After 5 minutes, stir the eggs and add the butter and cheese. Let cook 3 more minutes and stir again

Allow eggs to finish cooking an additional 2 minutes or remove if they are to your desired liking. Use a fork to fluff. Serve warm.

Nutrition: Calories: 359; Protein: 19.5g; Fiber: 0.0g; Fat: 27.6g; Carbs: 1.1g

70. Herbed Eggs

Preparation Time: 25 minutes

Servings: 4

Ingredients:

½ cup cheddar; shredded

10 eggs; whisked

2 tbsp. chives; chopped.

2 tbsp. basil; chopped.

2 tbsp. parsley; chopped.

Cooking spray

Salt and black pepper to taste.

Directions:

Take a bowl and mix the eggs with all the ingredients except the cheese and the cooking spray and whisk well

Preheat the air fryer at 350°F, grease it with the cooking spray and pour the eggs mixture inside

Sprinkle the cheese on top and cook for 20 minutes. Divide everything between plates and serve.

Nutrition: Calories: 232; Fat: 12g; Fiber: 4g; Carbs: 5g; Protein: 7g

71. Cherry Tomatoes Omelet

Preparation Time: 25 minutes

Servings: 4

Ingredients:

1 lb. cherry tomatoes; halved

4 eggs; whisked

1 tbsp. cheddar; grated

1 tbsp. parsley; chopped.

Salt and black pepper to taste.

Cooking spray

Directions:

Put the tomatoes in the air fryer's basket, cook at 360°F for 5 minutes and transfer them to the baking pan that fits the machine greased with cooking spray

Take a bowl and mix the eggs with the remaining ingredients, whisk, pour over the tomatoes and cook at 360°F for 15 minutes.

Nutrition: Calories: 230; Fat: 14g; Fiber: 3g; Carbs: 5g; Protein: 11g

72. Basil Eggs

Preparation Time: 25 minutes
Servings: 4
Ingredients:
1 cup mozzarella cheese; grated
6 eggs; whisked
2 tbsp. basil; chopped.
2 tbsp. butter; melted
6 tsp. basil pesto
A pinch of salt and black pepper
Directions:
Take a bowl and mix all the ingredients except the butter and whisk them well.
Preheat your Air Fryer at 360°F, drizzle the butter on the bottom, spread the eggs mix, cook for 20 minutes and serve for breakfast
Nutrition: Calories: 207; Fat: 14g; Fiber: 3g; Carbs: 4g; Protein: 8g

73. Zucchini and Artichokes Mix

Preparation Time: 25 minutes
Servings: 4
Ingredients:
8 oz. canned artichokes, drained and chopped.
2 tomatoes; cut into quarters
4 eggs; whisked
4 spring onions; chopped.
2 zucchinis; sliced
Cooking spray
Salt and black pepper to taste.
Directions:
Grease a pan with cooking spray and mix all the other ingredients inside.
Put the pan in the Air Fryer and cook at 350°F for 20 minutes. Divide between plates and serve
Nutrition: Calories: 210; Fat: 11g; Fiber: 3g; Carbs: 4g; Protein: 6g

74. Paprika Eggs and Broccoli

Preparation Time: 25 minutes
Servings: 4
Ingredients:
1 broccoli head, florets separated and roughly chopped.
4 oz. sour cream
Cooking spray
2 eggs; whisked
Salt and black pepper to taste.
1 tbsp. sweet paprika

Directions:
Grease a pan that fits your air fryer with the cooking spray and mix all the ingredients inside.
Put the pan in the Air Fryer and cook at 360°F for 20 minutes. Divide between plates and serve
Nutrition: Calories: 220; Fat: 14g; Fiber: 2g; Carbs: 3g; Protein: 2g

75. Raspberries Oatmeal

Preparation Time: 20 minutes
Servings: 4
Ingredients:
1 ½ cups coconut; shredded
½ cups raspberries
2 cups almond milk
¼ tsp. nutmeg, ground
2 tsp. stevia
½ tsp. cinnamon powder
Cooking spray
Directions:
Grease the air fryer's pan with cooking spray, mix all the ingredients inside, cover and cook at 360°F for 15 minutes. Divide into bowls and serve
Nutrition: Calories: 172; Fat: 5g; Fiber: 2g; Carbs: 4g; Protein: 6g

76. Zucchini Spread

Preparation Time: 20 minutes
Servings: 4
Ingredients:
4 zucchinis; roughly chopped.
1 tbsp. butter; melted
1 tbsp. sweet paprika
Salt and black pepper to taste.
Directions:
Grease a baking pan that fits the Air Fryer with the butter, add all the ingredients, toss and cook at 360°F for 15 minutes
Transfer to a blender, pulse well, divide into bowls and serve for breakfast.
Nutrition: Calories: 240; Fat: 14g; Fiber: 2g; Carbs: 5g; Protein: 11g

Sides

77. Spinach with Kale

Servings: 2
Preparation Time: 15 minutes
Cooking Time: 22 minutes
Ingredients:
3 tablespoons extra-virgin olive oil, divided
8 garlic cloves, minced
½ of red onion, chopped finely
1 bunch fresh kale, trimmed and chopped
Water, as required
1 bag fresh baby spinach
Salt and freshly ground black pepper, to taste
Directions:
In a big nonstick skillet, heat 2 tablespoons of oil on medium heat.
Add garlic and sauté for approximately 1 minute.
Reduce the heat to medium-low.
Add onion and a pinch of salt sauté for about 4-5 minutes.
Stir fry kale along with a few teaspoons of water and improve the heat to medium.
Cook, covered for approximately 2-3 minutes.
Stir in spinach and 1-2 teaspoons of water.
Cook, covered approximately 5-8 minutes.
Stir in remaining oil and improve the heat to medium-high.
Stir fry for about 3-4 minutes.
Stir in sat and black pepper and take away from heat.
Serve warm.
Nutrition:
Calories: 207, Fat: 4g, Carbohydrates: 21g, Fiber: 7g, Protein: 28g

78. Garlicky Bok Choy

One from the quickest recipes of a side dish. The amazing combo of fresh ginger and garlic gives Bok Choy a delicious taste.
Servings: 2
Preparation Time: 15 minutes
Cooking Time: 6 minutes
Ingredients:
1 tablespoon coconut oil
5 Bok Choy bunches, trimmed and cut into 1-inch chunks
1 teaspoon fresh ginger, grated finely
2 minced garlic cloves
Salt, to taste

Directions:

In a skillet, melt coconut oil on medium heat.

Add Bok Choy and stir fry approximately 3-4 minutes.

Add ginger, garlic and salt and stir fry for approximately 2 minutes more.

Serve warm.

Nutrition:

Calories: 156, Fat: 4g, Carbohydrates: 15.5g, Fiber: 2.4g, Protein: 27.3g

79. Turmeric Potato

Servings: 1

Preparation Time: 15 minutes

Cooking Time: 10 minutes

Ingredients:

2 tablespoons olive oil

1 medium potato, scrubbed and sliced thinly

1 garlic oil, minced

½ teaspoon ground turmeric

1 small onion, sliced thinly

Directions:

In a frying pan, heat oil on medium heat.

Add potato slices, garlic and turmeric and cook for about 10 min.

Add onion and cook, stirring occasionally for about 4 minutes.

Nutrition:

Calories: 140.3, Fat: 7.5g, Carbohydrates: 25.6g, Fiber: 5.8g, Protein: 5.2g

80. Citrus Carrot

Servings: 4

Preparation Time: 15 minutes

Cooking Time: 5 minutes

Ingredients:

2 teaspoons extra virgin olive oil
2 teaspoons fresh ginger, minced
3 cups carrots, peeled and grated
½ cup fresh orange juice
Salt and freshly ground black pepper, to taste
Directions:
In a large nonstick skillet, heat oil on medium-high heat.
Add ginger and carrot and cook, stirring occasionally for approximately 2 minutes.
Reduce heat and stir in orange juice, salt and black pepper.
Simmer for approximately 1-2 minutes or till desired doneness of carrots.
Nutrition:
Calories: 69, Fat: 3g, Carbohydrates: 6g, Fiber: 2g, Protein: 1g

81. Roasted Honey Carrot

Servings: 4
Preparation Time: 15 minutes
Cooking Time: 40 minutes
Ingredients:
1-pound carrots, peeled and halved lengthwise
1 (1-inchpiece fresh ginger, grated
¼ cup honey
¼ cup essential olive oil
3 tablespoons coconut aminos
Salt, to taste
1 tablespoon sesame seeds

Directions:

Preheat the oven to 400 degrees F.

In a baking dish, arrange the carrot halves.

In a bowl, mix together remaining ingredients except sesame seeds.

Place the honey mixture over carrots evenly.

Roast for about 30-40 minutes.

Serve with all the sprinkling of sesame seeds.

Nutrition:

Calories: 203, Fat: 6g, Carbohydrates: 26g, Fiber: 44g, Protein: 25g

82. Roasted Spicy Baby Carrot

Servings: 2-4

Preparation Time: 15 minutes

Cooking Time: 20 minutes

Ingredients:

1-pound baby carrots, trimmed

1 teaspoon fresh lime zest, grated finely

½ teaspoon ground cumin

¼ teaspoon smoked paprika

¼ teaspoon ground coriander

Salt, to taste

1 teaspoon organic honey

2 tablespoons fresh lime juice

1 tbsp. organic olive oil

2 scallions, sliced thinly

2 tablespoons fresh mint leaves, chopped

Directions:

Preheat the oven to 400 degrees F.

In a baking dish, arrange the carrots.

In a bowl, mix together remaining ingredients except scallion and mint.

Place the honey mixture over carrots evenly.

Roast for approximately 20 min.

Serve with the garnishing of scallion and mint.

Nutrition:

Calories: 191, Fat: 3g, Carbohydrates: 6g, Fiber: 4.4g, Protein: 25.3g

83. Sweet & Citrus Glazed Carrot

Servings: 4

Preparation Time: 15 minutes

Cooking Time: 8 minutes

Ingredients:

1 cup water

1-pound carrots, peeled and cut into ½-inch slices

Salt, to taste

1 tablespoon coconut oil

2 teaspoons fresh orange zest, grated finely

2 tablespoons organic honey

2 tablespoons fresh orange juice

½ teaspoon ground ginger

Freshly ground black pepper, to taste

Directions:

In a pan, add water, carrots as well as a pinch of salt and provide with a boil on high heat.

Reduce the temperature to medium and simmer approximately 5 minutes.

Drain the river well.

In the same pan, add remaining ingredients with carrot on medium heat.

Sauté for about 2-3 minutes or till glaze becomes slightly thick.

Nutrition:

Calories:163, Fat: 5g, Carbohydrates: 27g, Fiber: 10g, Protein: 29g

84. Spicy Cabbage

Servings: 2-4

Preparation Time: 15 minutes

Cooking Time: 13 minutes

Ingredients:

1 teaspoon extra-virgin extra virgin olive oil

1 onion, sliced thinly

2 teaspoons curry powder

1 teaspoon ground cumin

1 teaspoon ground turmeric

8 cups cabbage, sliced thinly

Salt and freshly ground black pepper, to taste

2 tablespoons fresh lemon juice

¼ cup water

Directions:

In a skillet, heat oil on medium heat.

Add onion and sauté for approximately 4-5 minutes.

Add curry powder and spices and sauté for about 1 minute.

Add cabbage and cook approximately 2-3 minutes.

Stir in water and cook, covered for around 4-5 minutes or till desired doneness.

Nutrition:

Calories: 187, Fat: 4.1g, Carbohydrates: 12g, Fiber: 7.3g, Protein: 29g

85. Cabbage with Apple

Servings: 2-4

Preparation Time: 15 minutes

Cooking Time: 9 minutes

Ingredients:

2 teaspoons coconut oil

1 large apple, cored and sliced thinly

1 onion, sliced thinly

1½ pound cabbage, chopped finely

1 tablespoon fresh thyme, chopped

1 red chili, chopped

1 tablespoon using apple cider vinegar

2/3 cup almonds, chopped

Directions:

In a nonstick skillet, melt 1 teaspoon of coconut oil on medium heat.

Add apple and stir fry for around 2-3 minutes.

Transfer the apple right into a bowl.

In a similar skillet, melt 1 teaspoon of coconut oil on medium heat.

Add onion and sauté for about 1-2 minutes.

Add cabbage and stir fry for about 3 minutes.

Add apple, thyme and vinegar and cook, covered for approximately 1 minute.

Serve warm with all the garnishing of almonds.

Nutrition:

Calories: 200, Fat: 2.9g, Carbohydrates: 19g, Fiber: 7g, Protein: 22g

86. Roasted Sweet Potato

Servings: 2-3
Preparation Time: 15 minutes
Cooking Time: 20 minutes
Ingredients:
1 teaspoon coconut oil
1 onion, chopped
2 medium sweet potatoes, peeled and cubed
½ tablespoon ground turmeric
1-2 fresh parsley sprigs
Salt and freshly ground black pepper, to taste
Water, as required
Directions:
In a skillet, melt coconut oil on low heat.
Add onion and sauté approximately 8-10 minutes.
Stir in sweet potato turmeric, parsley, salt and black pepper.
Add enough water that covers the sweet potato midway.
Cook for around 68 minutes or till desired doneness.
Nutrition:
Calories: 175, Fat: 3.1g, Carbohydrates: 21g, Fiber: 4g, Protein: 30g

87. Beetroot with Coconut

Servings: 2
Preparation Time: 15 minutes
Cooking Time: 20 minutes
Ingredients:
4 beetroots, peeled and cubed
1 small onion, cubed
¼ cup extra virgin olive oil
1 small cinnamon stick
2 whole cardamoms
2 whole cloves
1 teaspoon garlic paste

1 teaspoon ginger paste
Pinch of ground turmeric
1 tablespoon red chili powder
Salt, to taste
2-3 tablespoons fresh coconut powder
1 tablespoon garam masala powder
Directions:
In a mixer grinder, add beetroot and onion and grind till chopped very finely. (Mixture needs to be just a little chunky. Keep aside.
In a skillet, heat oil on medium heat.
Add cinnamon stick, cardamoms and cloves and sauté for about 1 minute.
Add garlic paste, ginger paste, turmeric, chili powder and salt and sauté approximately 1 minute.
Add beetroot mixture and stir fry for about fifteen minutes.
Add coconut powder and garam masala powder and cook for about 2-3 minutes.
Serve hot.
Nutrition:
Calories: 136, Fat: 6.4g, Carbohydrates: 19g, Fiber: 4.7g, Protein: 26g

88. Roasted Summer Squash & Fennel Bulb

Servings: 4
Preparation Time: 15 minutes
Cooking Time: 15 minutes
Ingredients:
2 small summer squash, cubed into 1-inch size
1½ cups fennel bulb, sliced
1 tablespoon fresh thyme, chopped
1 tablespoon extra-virgin organic olive oil
Salt and freshly ground black pepper, to taste
¼ cup garlic, sliced thinly
1 tablespoon fennel fronds, chopped
Directions:
Preheat the oven to 450 degrees F.
In a substantial bowl, add all ingredients except garlic and fennel fronds and toss to coat well.
Transfer a combination right into a large rimmed baking sheet.
Roast for approximately 10 min.
Remove from oven and stir in sliced garlic.
Roast for 5 minutes more.
Remove from oven and stir inside the fennel fronds.
Serve immediately.
Nutrition:
Calories: 166, Fat: 4g, Carbohydrates: 8g, Fiber: 2g, Protein: 2g

89. Roasted Brussels Sprouts & Sweet Potato

Servings: 6-8
Preparation Time: 15 minutes

Cooking Time: 45 minutes
Ingredients:
1 large sweet potato, peeled and cut into 1-2-nch pieces
1-pound Brussels sprouts, trimmed and halved
2 minced garlic cloves
1 teaspoon ground cumin
½ teaspoon garlic salt
Salt and freshly ground black pepper, to taste
1/3 cup olive oil
1 tablespoon apple cider vinegar
Chopped fresh thyme, for garnishing
Directions:
Preheat the oven to 400 degrees F. Grease a sheet pan.
In a large bowl, add all ingredients except vinegar and thyme and toss to coat well.
Transfer the mix into prepared baking pan.
Roast for 40-45 minutes more.
Transfer the vegetable mixture in a plate and drizzle with vinegar.
Garnish with thyme and serve.
Nutrition:
Calories: 133, Fat: 6g, Carbohydrates: 27g, Fiber: 11g, Protein: 36g

90. Potato Mash

Servings: 32
Preparation Time: 15 minutes
Cooking Time: 20 minutes
Ingredients:
10 large baking potatoes, peeled and cubed
3 tablespoons organic olive oil, divided
1 onion, chopped
1 tablespoon ground turmeric
½ teaspoon ground cumin
Salt and freshly ground black pepper, to taste
Directions:
In a large pan of water, add potatoes and produce with a boil on medium-high heat.
Cook approximately twenty or so minutes.
Drain well and transfer in to a large bowl.
With a potato masher, mash the potatoes.
Meanwhile in a very skillet, heat 1 tablespoon of oil on medium-high heat.
Add onion and sauté for about 6 minutes.
Add onion mixture in the bowl with mashed potatoes.
Add turmeric, cumin, salt and black pepper and mash till well combined.
Stir in remaining oil and serve.
Nutrition:
Calories: 103, Fat: 1.4g, Carbohydrates: 21.3g, Fiber: 2g, Protein: 1.8g

91. Creamy Sweet Potato Mash

Servings: 4
Preparation Time: 15 minutes
Cooking Time: 21 minutes
Ingredients:
1 tbsp. extra virgin olive oil
2 large sweet potatoes, peeled and chopped
2 teaspoons ground turmeric
1 garlic herb, minced
2 cups vegetable broth
2 tablespoons unsweetened coconut milk
Salt and freshly ground black pepper, to taste
Chopped pistachios, for garnishing
Directions:
In a big skillet, heat oil on medium-high heat.
Add sweet potato and stir fry for bout 2-3 minutes.
Add turmeric and stir fry for approximately 1 minute.
Add garlic and stir fry approximately 2 minutes.
Add broth and provide to a boil.
Reduce the heat to low and cook for approximately 10-15 minutes or till every one of the liquids is absorbed.
Transfer the sweet potato mixture in to a bowl.
Add coconut milk, salt and black pepper and mash it completely.
Garnish with pistachio and serve.
Nutrition:
Calories: 110, Fat: 5g, Carbohydrates: 16g, Protein: 1g

92. Gingered Cauliflower Rice

Servings: 3-4
Preparation Time: 15 minutes
Cooking Time: 10 minutes
Ingredients:
3 tablespoons coconut oil
4 (1/8-inch thickfresh ginger slices
1 small head cauliflower, trimmed and processed into rice consistency
3 garlic cloves, crushed
1 tablespoon chives, chopped
1 tablespoon coconut vinegar
Salt, to taste
Directions:
In a skillet, melt coconut oil on medium-high heat.
Add ginger and sauté for about 2-3 minutes.
Discard the ginger slices and stir in cauliflower and garlic.
Cook, stirring occasionally approximately 7-8 minutes.
Stir in remaining ingredients and take off from heat.
Serve immediately
Nutrition:

Calories: 67, Fat: 3.5g, Carbohydrates: 4.5g, Fiber: 2g, Protein: 7g

93. Spicy Cauliflower Rice

Servings: 4
Preparation Time: 15 minutes
Cooking Time: 10 minutes
Ingredients:
3 tablespoons coconut oil
1 small white onion, chopped
3 garlic cloves, minced
1 large head cauliflower, trimmed and processed into rice consistency
½ teaspoon ground cumin
½ teaspoon paprika
Salt and freshly ground black pepper, to taste
1large tomato, chopped
¼ cup tomato paste
¼ cup fresh cilantro, chopped
Chopped fresh cilantro, for garnishing
2 limes, quarters

Directions:

In a sizable skillet, melt coconut oil on medium-high heat.

Add onion and sauté for approximately 2 minutes.

Add garlic and sauté approximately 1 minute.

Stir in cauliflower rice.

Add cumin, paprika, salt and black pepper and cook, stirring occasionally approximately 2-3 minutes.

Stir in tomato, tomato paste and cilantro and cook approximately 2-3 minutes.

Garnish with cilantro and serve alongside lime.

Nutrition:

Calories: 246, Fat: 11g, Carbohydrates: 26g, Fiber: 4g, Protein: 21g

94. Simple Brown Rice

Servings: 4
Preparation Time: 10 minutes
Cooking Time: 50 minutes
Ingredients:
1 cup brown rice
2 cups chicken broth
1 tablespoon ground turmeric
1 tbsp. extra virgin olive oil
Directions:

In a pan, add rice, broth and turmeric and provide with a boil.

Reduce the warmth to low.

Simmer, covered for about 50 minutes.

Add the organic olive oil and fluff using a fork.

Keep aside, covered approximately 10 minutes before.

Nutrition:

Calories: 320, Fat: 6g, Carbohydrates: 285g, Fiber: 4g, Protein: 21g

95. Spicy Quinoa

Servings: 4
Preparation Time: 10 minutes
Cooking Time: 25 minutes
Ingredients:
2 tablespoons extra-virgin essential olive oil
1 teaspoon curry powder
1 teaspoon ground turmeric
12 teaspoon ground cumin
1 cup quinoa, rinsed and drained
2 cups chicken broth
¾ cup almonds, toasted
½ cup raisins
¾ cup fresh parsley, chopped
Directions:

In a medium pan, heat oil on medium-low heat.
Add curry powder, turmeric and cumin and sauté for approximately 1-2 minutes.
Add quinoa and sauté approximately 2-3 minutes.
Add broth and stir to blend.
Cover reducing the warmth to low.
Simmer for around twenty minutes.
Remove from heat whilst aside, covered approximately 5 minutes.
Just before, add almonds and raisins and toss to coat.
Drizzle with lemon juice and serve.
Nutrition:
Calories: 237, Fat: 3g, Carbohydrates: 17g, Fiber: 6g, Protein: 31g

96. Quinoa with Apricots

Servings: 4
Preparation Time: 15 minutes
Cooking Time: 12 minutes
Ingredients:

2 cups water
1 cup quinoa
½ teaspoon fresh ginger, grated finely
½ cup dried apricots, chopped roughly
Salt and freshly ground black pepper, to taste
Directions:
In a pan, add water on high heat and bring to your boil.
Add quinoa and reduce the heat to medium.
Cover and reduce the heat to low.
Simmer for about 12 minutes.
Remove from heat and immediately, stir in ginger and apricots.
Keep aside, covered for approximately fifteen minutes before.
Nutrition:
Calories: 267, Fat: 3.5g, Carbohydrates: 4g, Fiber: 5g, Protein: 17g

97. Easy Zucchini Slaw

Preparation Time: 10 minutes
Servings: 3
Nutrition: 96 Calories; 9.4g Fat; 2.8g Carbs; 0.7g Protein; 0.4g Fiber
Ingredients
2 tablespoons extra-virgin olive oil
1 zucchini, shredded
1 teaspoon Dijon mustard
1 yellow bell pepper, sliced
1 red onion, thinly sliced
Directions
Combine all ingredients in a salad bowl. Season with the salt and black pepper to taste.
Let it sit in your refrigerator for about 1 hour before. Bon appétit!

98. Broc n' Cheese

Preparation Time: 25 minutes
Servings: 5
Nutrition: 179 Calories; 10.3g Fat; 7.6g Carbs; 13.5g Protein; 3.6g Fiber
Ingredients
1 ½ pounds broccoli florets
3 tablespoons olive oil
1/2 cup cream of mushrooms soup
1 teaspoon garlic, minced
6 ounces Swiss cheese, shredded
Directions
Start by preheating your oven to 380 degrees F. Brush the sides and bottom of a baking dish with 1 tablespoon of olive oil.
In a small nonstick skillet, heat 1 tablespoon of the olive oil over a moderate heat. Sauté the garlic for 30 seconds or until just beginning to brown.

In a soup pot, parboil the broccoli until crisp-tender; place the rinsed broccoli in the prepared baking dish. Place the sautéed garlic on top. Drizzle the remaining tablespoon of olive oil over everything.

Season with the salt and black pepper. Pour in the cream of mushroom soup. Top with the Swiss cheese.

Bake for 20 minutes until the cheese is hot and bubbly. Enjoy!

99. Greek Avgolemono Soup

Preparation Time: 25 minutes
Servings: 6
Nutrition: 86 Calories; 6.1g Fat; 6g Carbs; 2.8g Protein; 2.4g Fiber
Ingredients
1 pound fennel bulbs, sliced
1 celery stalk, chopped
1 tablespoon freshly squeezed lemon juice
2 eggs
5 cups chicken stock
Directions
Heat 2 tablespoons of olive oil in a soup pot over medium-high heat. Sauté the fennel and celery until tender but not browned, approximately 7 minutes.

Add in Mediterranean seasoning mix and continue to sauté until they are fragrant.

Add in the chicken stock and bring to a rapid boil. Turn the temperature to medium-low; let it simmer for 10 to 13 minutes.

Puree your soup using a food processor or an immersion blender.

Thoroughly whisk the eggs and lemon juice until well combined; pour 2 cups of the hot soup into the egg mixture, whisking continuously.

Return the mixture to the pot; continue cooking for 2 to 3 minutes more until cooked through. Spoon into individual bowls and enjoy!

## 100.	Italian Zuppa Di Pomodoro

Preparation Time: 35 minutes
Servings: 4
Nutrition: 104 Calories; 7.2g Fat; 6.2g Carbs; 2.6g Protein; 3.1g Fiber
Ingredients
1/2 cup scallions, chopped
1 ½ pounds Roma tomatoes, diced
2 cups Brodo di Pollo (Italian broth
2 tablespoons tomato paste
2 cups mustard greens, torn into pieces
Directions
Heat 2 teaspoon of olive oil in a large pot over medium-high heat. Sauté the scallions for 2 to 3 minutes until tender.

Add in Roma tomatoes, Italian broth, and tomato paste and bring to a boil. Reduce the temperature to medium-low and continue to simmer, partially covered, for about 25 minutes.

Puree the soup with an immersion blender and return it to the pot. Add in the mustard greens and continue to cook until the greens wilt.

Taste, adjust seasonings and serve immediately.

101.   Easy Zucchini Croquets

Preparation Time: 40 minutes
Servings: 6
Nutrition: 111 Calories; 8.9g Fat; 3.2g Carbs; 5.8g Protein; 1g Fiber
Ingredients
1 egg
1/2 cup almond meal
1 pound zucchini, grated and drained
1/2 cup goat cheese, crumbled
2 tablespoons olive oil
Directions
Combine the egg, almond milk, zucchini and cheese in a mixing bowl. Refrigerate the mixture for 20 to 30 minutes.

Heat the oil in a frying pan over medium-high heat. Scoop the heaped tablespoons of the mixture into the hot oil.

Cook for about 4 minutes per side; cook in batches. Serve warm.

102.   Pork and Cheese Stuffed Peppers

Preparation Time: 30 minutes
Servings: 2
Nutrition: 313 Calories; 21.3g Fat; 5.7g Carbs; 20.2g Protein; 1.9g Fiber
Ingredients
2 sweet Italian peppers, deveined and halved
1/2 Spanish onion, finely chopped
1 cup marinara sauce
1/2 cup cheddar cheese, grated
4 ounces pork, ground
Directions
Heat 1 tablespoon of canola oil in a saucepan over a moderate heat. Then, sauté the onion for 3 to 4 minutes until tender and fragrant.

Add in the ground pork; cook for 3 to 4 minutes more. Add in Italian seasoning mix. Spoon the mixture into the pepper halves.

Spoon the marinara sauce into a lightly greased baking dish. Arrange the stuffed peppers in the baking dish.

Bake in the preheated oven at 395 degrees F for 17 to 20 minutes. Top with cheddar cheese and continue to bake for about 5 minutes or until the top is golden brown. Bon appétit!

103. Stewed Cabbage with Goan Chorizo Sausage

Preparation Time: 30 minutes
Servings: 3
Nutrition: 235 Calories; 17.7g Fat; 6.1g Carbs; 9.8g Protein; 2.4g Fiber
Ingredients
6 ounces Goan chorizo sausage, sliced
3/4 cup cream of celery soup
1 pound white cabbage, outer leaves removed and finely shredded
2 cloves garlic, finely chopped
1 teaspoon Indian spice blend
Directions
In a large frying pan, sear the sausage until no longer pink; set aside.
Then, sauté the garlic and Indian spice blend until they are aromatic. Add in the cabbage and cream of celery soup.
Turn the heat to simmer; continue to simmer, partially covered, for about 20 minutes or until cooked through.
Top with the reserved Goan chorizo sausage and serve.

104. Cauliflower and Ham Casserole

Preparation Time: 10 minutes
Servings: 6
Nutrition: 236 Calories; 13.8g Fat; 7.2g Carbs; 20.3g Protein; 2.3g Fiber
Ingredients
1 ½ pounds cauliflower, broken into small florets
6 ounces ham, diced
4 eggs, beaten
1/2 cup Greek-Style yogurt
1 cup Swiss cheese, preferably freshly grated
Directions
Parboil the cauliflower in a saucepan for about 10 minutes or until tender. Drain and puree in your food processor.
Add in the ham, eggs, and Greek-Style yogurt; stir to combine well.
Spoon the mixture into a lightly buttered baking dish. Top with the Swiss cheese and bake in the preheated oven at 385 degrees F for about 20 minutes. Enjoy!

105. Stuffed Spaghetti Squash

Preparation Time: 1 hour
Servings: 4
Nutrition: 219 Calories; 17.5g Fat; 6.9g Carbs; 9g Protein; 0.9g Fiber
Ingredients
1/2 pound spaghetti squash, halved, scoop out seeds
1 garlic clove, minced

1 cup cream cheese
2 eggs
1/2 cup Mozzarella cheese, shredded
Directions
Drizzle the insides of each squash with 1 teaspoon of olive oil. Bake in the preheated oven at 380 degrees F for 45 minutes.
Scrape out the spaghetti squash "noodles" from the skin. Fold in the remaining ingredients; stir to combine well.
Spoon the cheese mixture into squash halves. Bake at 360 degrees F for about 9 minutes, until the cheese is hot and bubbly. Enjoy!

106.   Spicy and Warm Coleslaw

Preparation Time: 45 minutes
Servings: 4
Nutrition: 118 Calories; 10.2g Fat; 6.6g Carbs; 1.1g Protein; 1.9g Fiber
Ingredients
1 medium-sized leek, chopped
1 tablespoon balsamic vinegar
1 teaspoon yellow mustard
1/2 pound green cabbage, shredded
1/2 teaspoon Sriracha sauce
Directions
Drizzle 2 tablespoons of the olive oil over the leek and cabbage; sprinkle with salt and black pepper. Bake in the preheated oven at 410 degrees F for about 40 minutes. Transfer the mixture to a salad bowl.
Toss with 1 tablespoon of olive oil, mustard, balsamic vinegar, and Sriracha sauce. Serve warm!

107.   Easy Mediterranean Croquettes

Preparation Time: 40minutes
Servings: 2
Nutrition: 463 Calories; 36g Fat; 7.6g Carbs; 27.5g Protein; 2.8g Fiber
Ingredients
1/2 pound zucchini, grated
1/2 cup Swiss cheese, shredded
3 eggs, whisked Mediterranean
1/3 cup almond meal
2 tablespoons pork rinds
Directions
Place the grated zucchini in a colander, sprinkle with 1/2 teaspoon of salt, and let it stand for 30 minutes. Drain the zucchini well and discard any excess water.
Heat 2 tablespoons of olive oil in a frying pan over medium-high heat. Mix the zucchini with the remaining ingredients until well combined.
Shape the mixture into croquettes and cook for 2 to 3 minutes per side. Enjoy!

108. Tuscan Asparagus with Cheese

Preparation Time: 20 minutes
Servings: 5
Nutrition: 140 Calories; 11.5g Fat; 5.5g Carbs; 5.6g Protein; 2.9g Fiber
Ingredients
1 ½ pounds asparagus, trimmed
1 tablespoon Sriracha sauce
1 tablespoon fresh cilantro, roughly chopped
4 tablespoons Pecorino Romano cheese, grated
4 tablespoons butter, melted
Directions
Toss the asparagus with the cheese, melted butter, and Sriracha sauce; season with Italian spice mix, if desired.
Arrange your asparagus on a baking sheet and roast in the preheated oven at 410 degrees F for 12 to 15 minutes.
Garnish with fresh cilantro and enjoy!

109. Brown Mushroom Stew

Preparation Time: 20 minutes
Servings: 6
Nutrition: 123 Calories; 9.2g Fat; 5.8g Carbs; 4.7g Protein; 1.4g Fiber
Ingredients
2 pounds brown mushrooms, sliced
1 bell pepper, sliced
2 cups chicken broth
1/2 cup leeks, finely diced
1 cup herb-infused tomato sauce
Directions
Heat 4 tablespoons of oil in a soup pot over a moderate flame. Sauté the pepper and leeks for about 4 to 5 minutes.
Stir in the mushrooms and continue to sauté for about 2 minutes. Pour in a splash of broth to deglaze the bottom of the pan.
After that, add in the tomato sauce and the remaining broth; bring to a boil. Turn the heat to simmer.
Continue to cook, partially covered, for about 10 minutes or until the mushrooms are tender and thoroughly cooked.
Ladle into soup bowls and serve. Bon appétit!

110. Wax Beans in Wine Sauce

Preparation Time: 15 minutes
Servings: 4
Nutrition: 56 Calories; 3.5g Fat; 6g Carbs; 1.5g Protein; 2.2g Fiber
Ingredients
1/2 pound wax beans, trimmed
2 tablespoons dry white wine
1 tablespoon butter
1/2 teaspoon mustard seeds
1/2 cup tomato sauce with garlic and onions
Directions
Melt the butter in a soup pot over medium-high heat. Then, fry wax beans in hot butter for 2 to 3 minutes.
Add in tomato sauce, wine, and mustard seeds; season with salt and black pepper.
Turn the temperature to medium-low and continue to simmer for about 8 longer or until wax beans are tender and the sauce has thickened slightly. Bon appétit!

111. Lebanese Mushroom Stew with Za'atar

Preparation Time: 1 hour 50 minutes
Servings: 4
Nutrition: 155 Calories; 13.9g Fat; 6g Carbs; 1.4g Protein; 2.9g Fiber
Ingredients
8 ounces Chanterelle mushroom, sliced
1 cup tomato sauce with onion and garlic
4 tablespoons olive oil
2 bell peppers, chopped
1/2 teaspoon Za'atar spice
Directions
Heat olive oil in a heavy-bottomed pot over medium-high heat. Once hot, sauté the peppers until tender or about 3 minutes.
Stir in the mushrooms and continue to sauté until they have softened.
Add in Za'atar spice and tomato sauce; bring to a rapid boil. Immediately, turn the heat to medium-low.
Continue to simmer for about 35 minutes until cooked through. Bon appétit!

112. Skinny Cucumber Noodles with Sauce

Preparation Time: 35 minutes
Servings: 2
Nutrition: 194 Calories; 17.1g Fat; 7.6g Carbs; 2.5g Protein; 4.6g Fiber
Ingredients
1 cucumber, spiralized
1/2 teaspoon sea salt
1 tablespoon olive oil
1 tablespoon fresh lime juice

1 California avocado, pitted, peeled and mashed
Directions
Sprinkle your cucumber with salt; let it stand for 30 minutes; after that, discard the excess water and pat the cucumber dry with kitchen towels.
In the meantime, combine olive oil, lime juice, and avocado. Season with salt and black pepper.
Toss the cucumber noodles with sauce and serve. Bon appétit!

113. Balkan-Style Stir-Fry

Preparation Time: 25 minutes
Servings: 5
Nutrition: 114 Calories; 7.6g Fat; 6g Carbs; 3.4g Protein; 1.5g Fiber
Ingredients
8 bell peppers, deveined and cut into strips
1 tomato, chopped
2 eggs
1 yellow onion, sliced
3 garlic cloves, halved
Directions
Heat 2 tablespoons of olive oil in a saucepan over medium-low flame. Sweat the onion for about 4 minutes or until tender and translucent.
Stir in the garlic and peppers and continue to sauté for 5 to 6 minutes. Fold in chopped tomato along with salt and black pepper.
Stir fry for a further 7 minutes. Stir in the eggs and continue to cook for 4 to 5 minutes longer. Serve immediately.

114. Italian Zoodles with Romano Cheese

Preparation Time: 15 minutes
Servings: 3
Nutrition: 160 Calories; 10.6g Fat; 7.4g Carbs; 10g Protein; 3.4g Fiber
Ingredients
1 ½ tablespoons olive oil
3 cups button mushrooms, chopped
1 cup tomato sauce with garlic and herbs
1 pound zucchini, spiralized
1/3 cup Pecorino Romano cheese, preferably freshly grated
Directions
In a saucepan, heat the olive oil over a moderate heat. Once hot, cook the mushrooms for about 4 minutes until they have softened.
Stir in the tomato sauce and zucchini, bringing to a boil.
Immediately reduce temperature to simmer. Continue to cook, partially covered, for about 7 minutes or until cooked through. Season with salt and black pepper.
Top with Pecorino Romano cheese and serve. Bon appétit!

115. Garden Vegetable Mash

Preparation Time: 15 minutes
Servings: 3
Nutrition: 162 Calories; 12.8g Fat; 7.2g Carbs; 4.7g Protein; 3.5g Fiber
Ingredients
1 ½ tablespoons butter
4 tablespoons cream cheese
1/2 pound cauliflower florets
1/2 pound broccoli florets
1/2 teaspoon garlic powder
Directions
Parboil the broccoli and cauliflower for about 10 minutes until they have softened. Mash them with a potato masher.
Add in garlic powder, cream cheese, and butter; mix to combine well.
Season with salt and black pepper to taste. Bon appétit!

116. Spicy and Cheesy Roasted Artichokes

Preparation Time: 1 hour 10 minutes
Servings: 2
Nutrition: 368 Calories; 33g Fat; 7.2g Carbs; 10.6g Protein; 3.8g Fiber
Ingredients
2 small-sized globe artichokes, cut off the stalks
2 tablespoons butter, melted
2 tablespoons fresh lime juice
1/2 cup Romano cheese, grated
2 tablespoons mayonnaise
Directions
Start by preheating your oven to 420 degrees F.
To prepare your artichokes, discard the tough outer layers; cut off about 3/4 inches from the top. Slice them in half lengthwise.
Toss your artichokes with butter and fresh lime juice; season with the salt and pepper to taste.
Top with the grated Romano cheese; wrap your artichokes in foil and roast them in the preheated oven for about 1 hour.
Serve with mayonnaise and enjoy!

117. Cheesy Stuffed Peppers with Cauliflower Rice

Preparation Time: 45 minutes
Servings: 6
Nutrition: 244 Calories; 12.9g Fat; 3.2g Carbs; 1g Fiber; 16.5g Protein;
Ingredients
6 medium-sized bell peppers, deveined and cleaned
1 cup cauliflower rice

1/2 cup tomato sauce with garlic and onion
1 pound ground turkey
1/2 cup Cheddar cheese, shredded
Directions
Heat 2 tablespoons of olive oil in a frying pan over medium-high heat. Then, cook ground turkey until nicely browned or about 5 minutes.
Add in cauliflower rice and season with salt and black pepper. Continue to cook for 3 to 4 minutes more.
Add in tomato sauce. Stuff the peppers with this filling and cover with a piece of aluminum foil.
Bake in the preheated oven at 390 degrees F for 17 to 20 minutes. Remove the foil, top with cheese, and bake for a further 10 to 13 minutes. Bon appétit!

118.   Broccoli and Bacon Soup

Preparation Time: 20 minutes
Servings: 4
Nutrition: 95 Calories; 7.6g Fat; 4.1g Carbs; 3g Protein; 1g Fiber
Ingredients
1 head broccoli, broken into small florets
1 carrot, chopped
1 celery, chopped
1/2 cup full-fat yogurt
2 slices bacon, chopped
Directions
Fry the bacon in a soup pot over a moderate flame; reserve.
Then, cook the carrots, celery and broccoli in the bacon fat. Season with salt and pepper to taste.
Pour in 4 cups of water or vegetable stock, bringing to a boil. Turn the temperature to a simmer and continue to cook, partially covered, for 10 to 15 minutes longer.
Add in yogurt and remove from heat. Puree your soup with an immersion blender until your desired consistency is reached.
Garnish with the reserved bacon and serve.

119.   Aromatic Kale with Garlic

Preparation Time: 20 minutes
Servings: 3
Nutrition: 93 Calories; 4.4g Fat; 6.1g Carbs; 7.1g Protein; 2.7g Fiber
Ingredients
1/2 tablespoon olive oil
1/2 cup cottage cheese, creamed
1/2 teaspoon sea salt
1 teaspoon fresh garlic, chopped
9 ounces kale, torn into pieces
Directions

Heat the olive oil in a pot over medium-high flame. Once hot, fry the garlic until just tender and fragrant or about 30 seconds.

Add in kale and continue to cook for 8 to 10 minutes until all liquid evaporates.

Add in cottage cheese and sea salt, remove from heat, and stir until everything is combined. Bon appétit!

120.   Spanish-Style Keto Slaw

Preparation Time: 10 minutes
Servings: 4
Nutrition: 122 Calories; 9.1g Fat; 5.9g Carbs; 4.5g Protein; 3g Fiber
Ingredients
1 teaspoon fresh garlic, minced
4 tablespoons tahini (sesame paste
1/2 pound Napa cabbage, shredded
2 cups arugula, torn into pieces
1 Spanish onion, thinly sliced into rings
Directions
Make a dressing by whisking the garlic and tahini; add in 2 teaspoons of balsamic vinegar along with salt and black pepper.

In a salad bowl, combine Napa cabbage, arugula, and Spanish onion. Toss the salad with dressing. Garnish with sesame seeds if desired and serve.

121.   Cheesy Breakfast Broccoli Casserole

Preparation Time: 40 minutes
Servings: 4
Nutrition: 188 Calories; 11.3g Fat; 5.7g Carbs; 14.9g Protein; 1.1g Fiber
Ingredients
1 (1/2-poundhead broccoli, broken into florets
1 cup cooked ham, chopped
1/2 cup Greek-style yogurt
1 cup Mexican cheese, shredded
1/2 teaspoon butter, melted
Directions
Begin by preheating an oven to 350 degrees F. Now, butter the bottom and sides of a casserole dish with melted butter.

Cook broccoli for 6 to 7 minutes until it is "mashable". Mash the broccoli with a potato masher.

Now, stir in Greek-style yogurt, Mexican cheese, and cooked ham. Season with Mexican spice blend, if desired.

Press the cheese/broccoli mixture in the buttered casserole dish. Bake in the preheated oven for 20 to 23 minutes. Serve and enjoy!

122.   Cauli Mac and Cheese

Preparation Time: 15 Minutes
Cooking Time: 15 Minutes
Servings: 6
5 Ingredients:
1 head cauliflower, blanched and cut into florets
½ cup nutritional yeast
1 cup heavy cream
5 tablespoons butter, melted
1 ½ cup cheddar cheese
Salt and pepper to taste
½ cup water or milk
Directions:
In a heat-proof dish, place the cauliflower florets. Set aside.
In a mixing bowl, combine the rest of the ingredients.
Pour over the cauliflower florets.
Bake in a 3500F preheated oven for 15 minutes.
Place in containers and put the proper label.
Store in the fridge and consume before 3 days.
Microwave or bake in the oven first before eating.
Nutrition:
Calories: 329; Fat: 30.3g; Carbs: 10.1g; Protein: 12.1g

123. Baked Vegetable Side

Preparation Time: Minutes
Cooking Time: 15 Minutes
Servings: 4
5 Ingredients:
2 large zucchinis, sliced
2 bell peppers, sliced
½ cup peeled garlic cloves, sliced
A dash of oregano
4 tablespoons olive oil
Salt and pepper to taste
Directions:
Place all ingredients in a mixing bowl. Stir to coat everything.
Place in a baking sheet.
Bake in a 3500F preheated oven for 15 minutes.
Serve and enjoy.
Nutrition:
Calories: 191; Fat: 23.0g; Carbs: 12.0g; Protein: 3.0g

124. Shrimp Fra Diavolo

Preparation Time: 15 Minutes
Cooking Time: 5 Minutes
Servings: 3

5 Ingredients:
3 tablespoons butter
1 onion, diced
5 cloves of garlic, minced
1 teaspoon red pepper flakes
¼ pound shrimps, shelled
2 tablespoons olive oil
Salt and pepper to taste
Directions:
Heat the butter and the olive oil in a skillet and sauté the onion and garlic until fragrant.
Stir in the red pepper flakes and shrimps. Season with salt and pepper to taste.
Stir for 3 minutes.
Serve and enjoy.
Nutrition:
Calories: 145; Fat: 32.1g; Carbs: 4.5g; Protein: 21.0g

125.   Zucchini and Cheese Gratin

Preparation Time: 15 Minutes
Cooking Time: 15 Minutes
Servings: 8
5 Ingredients:
5 tablespoons butter
1 onion, sliced
½ cup heavy cream
4 cups raw zucchini, sliced
1 ½ cups shredded pepper Jack cheese
Salt and pepper to taste
Directions:
Place all ingredients in a mixing bowl and give a good stir to incorporate everything.
Pour the mixture in a heat-proof baking dish.
Place in a 3500F preheated oven and bake for 15 minutes.
Serve and enjoy.
Nutrition:
Calories: 280; Fat: 20.0g; Carbs: 5.0g; Protein: 8.0g

126.   Soy Garlic Mushrooms

Preparation Time: 20 Minutes
Cooking Time: 10 Minutes
Servings: 8
5 Ingredients:
2 pounds mushrooms, sliced
3 tablespoons olive oil
2 cloves of garlic, minced
¼ cup coconut aminos
Salt and pepper to taste

Directions:

Place all ingredients in a dish and mix until well-combined.

Allow to marinate for 2 hours in the fridge.

In a large saucepan on medium fire, add mushrooms and sauté for 8 minutes. Season with pepper and salt to taste.

Serve and enjoy.

Nutrition:

Calories: 383; Fat: 10.9g; Carbs: 86.0g; Protein: 6.2g

127.   Old Bay Chicken Wings

Preparation Time: 5 Minutes
Cooking Time: 30 Minutes
Servings: 4
5 Ingredients:
3 pounds chicken wings
¾ cup almond flour
1 tablespoon old bay spices
1 teaspoon lemon juice, freshly squeezed
½ cup butter
Salt and pepper to taste
Directions:
Preheat oven to 400oF.
In a mixing bowl, combine all ingredients except for the butter.
Place in an even layer in a baking sheet.
Bake for 30 minutes. Halfway through the cooking time, shake the fryer basket for even cooking.
Once cooked, drizzle with melted butter.
Nutrition:
Calories: 640; Fat: 59.2g; Carbs: 1.6g; Protein: 52.5g

128.   Tofu Stuffed Peppers

Preparation Time: 5 Minutes
Cooking Time: 10 Minutes
Servings: 8
5 Ingredients:
1 package firm tofu, crumbled
1 onion, finely chopped
½ teaspoon turmeric powder
1 teaspoon coriander powder
8 banana peppers, top end sliced and seeded
Salt and pepper to taste
3 tablespoons oil
Directions:
Preheat oven to 400oF.
In a mixing bowl, combine the tofu, onion, coconut oil, turmeric powder, red chili powder, coriander power, and salt. Mix until well-combined.

Scoop the tofu mixture into the hollows of the banana peppers.
Place the stuffed peppers in one layer in a lightly greased baking sheet.
Cook for 10 minutes.
Serve and enjoy.
Nutrition:
Calories: 67; Fat: 5.6g; Carbs: 4.1g; Protein: 1.2g

129.   Air Fryer Garlic Chicken Wings

Preparation Time: 5 Minutes
Cooking Time: 25 Minutes
Servings: 4
5 Ingredients:
16 pieces chicken wings
¾ cup almond flour
4 tablespoons minced garlic
¼ cup butter, melted
Salt and pepper to taste
2 tablespoons stevia powder
Directions:
Preheat oven to 400oF.
In a mixing bowl, combine the chicken wings, almond flour, stevia powder, and garlic Season with salt and pepper to taste.
Place in a lightly greased cookie sheet in an even layer and cook for 25 minutes.
Halfway through the cooking time, turnover chicken.
Once cooked, place in a bowl and drizzle with melted butter. Toss to coat.
Serve and enjoy.
Nutrition:
Calories: 365; Fat: 26.9g; Carbs: 7.8g; Protein: 23.7g

130.   Sautéed Brussels Sprouts

Preparation Time: 5 Minutes
Cooking Time: 8 Minutes
Servings: 4
5 Ingredients:
2 cups Brussels sprouts, halved
1 tablespoon balsamic vinegar
Salt and pepper to taste
2 tablespoons olive oil
Directions:
Place a saucepan on medium high fire and heat oil for a minute.
Add all ingredients and sauté for 7 minutes.
Season with pepper and salt.
Serve and enjoy.
Nutrition:
Calories: 82; Fat: 6.8g; Carbs: 4.6g; Protein: 1.5g

131. Bacon Jalapeno Poppers

Preparation Time: 15 Minutes
Cooking Time: 10 Minutes
Servings: 8
5 Ingredients:
4-ounce cream cheese
¼ cup cheddar cheese, shredded
1 teaspoon paprika
16 fresh jalapenos, sliced lengthwise and seeded
16 strips of uncured bacon, cut into half
Salt and pepper to taste
Directions:
Preheat oven to 400oF.
In a mixing bowl, mix the cream cheese, cheddar cheese, salt, and paprika until well-combined.
Scoop half a teaspoon onto each half of jalapeno peppers.
Use a thin strip of bacon and wrap it around the cheese-filled jalapeno half.
Place in a single layer in a lightly greased baking sheet and roast for 10 minutes.
Serve and enjoy.
Nutrition:
Calories: 225; Fat: 18.9g; Carbs: 3.2g; Protein: 10.6g

132. Basil Keto Crackers

Preparation Time: 30 Minutes
Cooking Time: 15 Minutes
Servings: 6
5 Ingredients:
1 ¼ cups almond flour
½ teaspoon baking powder
¼ teaspoon dried basil powder
A pinch of cayenne pepper powder
1 clove of garlic, minced
Salt and pepper to taste
3 tablespoons oil
Directions:
Preheat oven to 350oF and lightly grease a cookie sheet with cooking spray.
Mix everything in a mixing bowl to create a dough.
Transfer the dough on a clean and flat working surface and spread out until 2mm thick. Cut into squares.
Place gently in an even layer on prepped cookie sheet. Cook for 10 minutes.
Cook in batches.
Serve and enjoy.
Nutrition:
Calories: 205; Fat: 19.3g; Carbs: 2.9g; Protein: 5.3g

133. Crispy Keto Pork Bites

Preparation Time: 20 Minutes
Cooking Time: 30 Minutes
Servings: 3
5 Ingredients:
½ pork belly, sliced to thin strips
1 tablespoon butter
1 onion, diced
4 tablespoons coconut cream
Salt and pepper to taste
Directions:
Place all ingredients in a mixing bowl and allow to marinate in the fridge for 2 hours.
When 2 hours is nearly up, preheat oven to 400oF and lightly grease a cookie sheet with cooking spray.
Place the pork strips in an even layer on the cookie sheet.
Roast for 30 minutes and turnover halfway through cooking.
Nutrition:
Calories: 448; Fat: 40.6g; Carbs: 1.9g; Protein: 19.1g

134.   Fat Burger Bombs

Preparation Time: 30 Minutes
Cooking Time: 20 Minutes
Servings: 6
5 Ingredients:
12 slices uncured bacon, chopped
1 cup almond flour
2 eggs, beaten
½ pound ground beef
Salt and pepper to taste
3 tablespoons olive oil
Directions:
In a mixing bowl, combine all ingredients except for the olive oil.
Use your hands to form small balls with the mixture. Place in a baking sheet and allow to set in the fridge for at least 2 hours.
Once 2 hours is nearly up, preheat oven to 400oF.
Place meatballs in a single layer in a baking sheet and brush the meat balls with olive oil on all sides.
Cook for 20 minutes.
Nutrition:
Calories: 448; Fat: 40.6g; Carbs: 1.9g; Protein: 19.1g

135.   Onion Cheese Muffins

Preparation Time: 20 Minutes
Cooking Time: 20 Minutes
Servings: 6
5 Ingredients:
¼ cup Colby jack cheese, shredded

¼ cup shallots, minced
1 cup almond flour
1 egg
3 tbsp sour cream
½ tsp salt
3 tbsp melted butter or oil
Directions:
Line 6 muffin tins with 6 muffin liners. Set aside and preheat oven to 350oF.
In a bowl, stir the dry and wet ingredients alternately. Mix well using a spatula until the consistency of the mixture becomes even.
Scoop a spoonful of the batter to the prepared muffin tins.
Bake for 20 minutes in oven until golden brown.
Serve and enjoy.
Nutrition:
Calories: 193; Fat: 17.4g; Carbs: 4.6g; Protein: 6.3g

136.   Bacon-Flavored Kale Chips

Preparation Time: 20 Minutes
Cooking Time: 25 Minutes
Servings: 6
5 Ingredients:
2 tbsp butter
¼ cup bacon grease
1-lb kale, around 1 bunch
1 to 2 tsp salt
Directions:
Remove the rib from kale leaves and tear into 2-inch pieces.
Clean the kale leaves thoroughly and dry them inside a salad spinner.
In a skillet, add the butter to the bacon grease and warm the two fats under low heat. Add salt and stir constantly.
Set aside and let it cool.
Put the dried kale in a Ziploc back and add the cool liquid bacon grease and butter mixture.
Seal the Ziploc back and gently shake the kale leaves with the butter mixture. The leaves should have this shiny consistency which means that they are coated evenly with the fat.
Pour the kale leaves on a cookie sheet and sprinkle more salt if necessary.
Bake for 25 minutes inside a preheated 350-degree oven or until the leaves start to turn brown as well as crispy.
Serve and enjoy.
Nutrition:
Calories: 148; Fat: 13.1g; Carbs: 6.6g; Protein: 3.3g

137.   Keto-Approved Trail Mix

Preparation Time: 10 Minutes
Cooking Time: 3 Minutes
Servings: 8

5 Ingredients:
½ cup salted pumpkin seeds
½ cup slivered almonds
¾ cup roasted pecan halves
¾ cup unsweetened cranberries
1 cup toasted coconut flakes
None
Directions:
In a skillet, place almonds and pecans. Heat for 2-3 minutes and let cool.
Once cooled, in a large re-sealable plastic bag, combine all ingredients.
Seal and shake vigorously to mix.
Serve and enjoy.
Nutrition:
Calories: 184; Fat: 14.4g; Carbs: 13.0g; Protein: 4.4g

138. Reese Cups

Preparation Time: 15 Minutes
Cooking Time: 1 Minutes
Servings: 12
5 Ingredients:
½ cup unsweetened shredded coconut
1 cup almond butter
1 cup dark chocolate chips
1 tablespoon Stevia
1 tablespoon coconut oil
Directions:
Line 12 muffin tins with 12 muffin liners.
Place the almond butter, honey and oil in a glass bowl and microwave for 30 seconds or until melted. Divide the mixture into 12 muffin tins. Let it cool for 30 minutes in the fridge.
Add the shredded coconuts and mix until evenly distributed.
Pour the remaining melted chocolate on top of the coconuts. Freeze for an hour.
Carefully remove the chocolates from the muffin tins to create perfect Reese cups.
Serve and enjoy.
Nutrition:
Calories: 214; Fat: 17.1g; Carbs: 13.7g; Protein: 5.0g

139. Curry ' n Poppy Devilled Eggs

Preparation Time: 20 Minutes
Cooking Time: 8 Minutes
Servings: 6
5 Ingredients:
½ cup mayonnaise
½ tbsp poppy seeds
1 tbsp red curry paste
6 eggs

¼ tsp salt
Directions:
Place eggs in a small pot and add enough water to cover it. Bring to a boil without a cover, lower fire to a simmer and simmer for 8 minutes.
Immediately dunk in ice cold water once done cooking. Peel eggshells and slice eggs in half lengthwise.
Remove yolks and place them in a medium bowl. Add the rest of the ingredients in the bowl except for the egg whites. Mix well.
Evenly return the yolk mixture into the middle of the egg whites.
Serve and enjoy.
Nutrition:
Calories: 200; Fat: 19.0g; Carbs: 1.0g; Protein: 6.0g

140.   Bacon and Cheddar Cheese Balls

Preparation Time: 10 Minutes
Cooking Time: 8 Minutes
Servings: 10
5 Ingredients:
½ tsp chili flakes (optional
5 1/3-oz bacon
5 1/3-oz cheddar cheese
5 1/3-oz cream cheese
½ tsp pepper (optional
Directions:
Pan fry bacon until crisped, around 8 minutes.
Meanwhile, in a food processor, process remaining ingredients. Then transfer to a bowl and refrigerate. When ready to handle, form into 20 equal balls.
Once bacon is cooked, crumble bacon and spread on a plate.
Roll the balls on the crumbled bacon to coat.
Nutrition:
Calories: 225.6; Fat: 21.6g; Carbs: 1.6g; Protein: 6.4g

141.   Cheese Roll-Ups the Keto Way

Preparation Time: 15 Minutes
Cooking Time: 0 Minutes
Servings: 4
5 Ingredients:
4 slices cheddar cheese
4 ham slices
None
Directions:
Place one cheese slice on a flat surface and top with one slice of ham.
Roll from one end to the other. Repeat process to remaining cheese and ham.
Serve and enjoy.
Nutrition:

Calories: 60; Fat: 2.6g; Carbs: 2.5g; Protein: 6.7g

142. Cheddar Cheese Chips

Preparation Time: Minutes
Cooking Time: 8 Minutes
Servings: 4
5 Ingredients:
8 oz. cheddar cheese or provolone cheese or edam cheese, in slices
½ tsp paprika powder
None
Directions:
Line baking sheet with foil and preheat oven to 400oF.
Place cheese slices on baking sheet and sprinkle paprika powder on top.
Pop in the oven and bake for 8 to 10 minutes.
Pay particular attention when timer reaches 6 to 7 minutes as a burnt cheese tastes bitter.
Serve and enjoy.
Nutrition:
Calories: 228; Fat: 19.0g; Carbs: 2.0g; Protein: 13.0g

143. Cardamom and Cinnamon Fat Bombs

Preparation Time: Minutes
Cooking Time: 3 Minutes
Servings: 10
5 Ingredients:
¼ tsp ground cardamom (green
¼ tsp ground cinnamon
½ cup unsweetened shredded coconut
½ tsp vanilla extract
3-oz unsalted butter, room temperature
None
Directions:
Place a nonstick pan on medium fire and toast coconut until lightly browned.
In a bowl, mix all ingredients.
Evenly roll into 10 equal balls.
Let it cool in the fridge.
Serve and enjoy.
Nutrition:
Calories: 90; Fat: 10.0g; Carbs: 0.4g; Protein: 0.4g

144. No Cook Coconut and Chocolate Bars

Preparation Time: 15 Minutes
Cooking Time: 0 Minutes
Servings: 6
5 Ingredients:

1 tbsp Stevia
¾ cup shredded coconut, unsweetened
½ cup ground nuts (almonds, pecans, or walnuts
¼ cup unsweetened cocoa powder
4 tbsp coconut oil
Done
Directions:
In a medium bowl, mix shredded coconut, nuts and cocoa powder.
Add Stevia and coconut oil.
Mix batter thoroughly.
In a 9x9 square inch pan or dish, press the batter and for 30-minutes place in the freezer.
Serve and enjoy.
Nutrition:
Calories: 148; Fat: 7.8g; Carbs: 2.3g; Protein: 1.6g

145.   Coleslaw

Preparation Time: 10 minutes
Servings: 2
Ingredients:
1 cup white cabbage
1 tablespoon mayonnaise
½ teaspoon ground black pepper
½ teaspoon salt
Directions:
Shred the white cabbage and place it in the big salad bowl.
Sprinkle it with ground black pepper and salt.
Add mayonnaise and mix up coleslaw very carefully.
Nutrition: calories 39, fat 2.5, fiber 1, carbs 4.1, protein 0.6

146.   Roasted Zucchini and Pumpkin Cubes

Preparation Time: 10 minutes
Cooking Time: 20 minutes
Servings: 3
Ingredients:
1 cup zucchini, chopped
¼ cup pumpkin, chopped
¼ teaspoon thyme
½ teaspoon ground coriander
½ teaspoon ground cloves
1 tablespoon olive oil
½ teaspoon butter
1 teaspoon dried dill
Directions:
Toss butter in the skillet and melt it.
Add olive oil, zucchini, and pumpkin.

Start to roast vegetables over the medium heat for 5 minutes.
Hen sprinkle them with thyme, ground coriander, ground cloves, and dried dill.
Mix up well and close the lid.
Cook the vegetables on the low heat for 15 minutes.
Nutrition: calories 66, fat 5.5, fiber 1.2, carbs 3.4, protein 0.8

147.   Chile Casserole

Preparation Time: 15 minutes
Cooking Time: 15 minutes
Servings: 4
Ingredients:
1 cup chili peppers, green, raw
1 teaspoon olive oil
3 oz Cheddar cheese, shredded
1 teaspoon butter
2 eggs, whisked
¼ cup heavy cream
½ teaspoon salt
Directions:
Preheat the grill well and place chili peppers on it.
Grill the chili peppers for 5 minutes. Stir them from time to time.
Then chill the peppers little and peel them. Remove the seeds.
Place the peppers in the casserole tray.
Add butter and sprinkle with salt.
In the separated bowl, mix up together heavy cream, whisked eggs, and cheese.
Pour the liquid over the chili peppers and transfer casserole in the [reheated to the 365F oven.
Cook casserole for 10 minutes.
Nutrition: calories 169, fat 14.2, fiber 0.3, carbs 2.4, protein 8.6

148.   Pickled Jalapeno

Preparation Time: 10 minutes
Cooking Time: 10 minutes
Servings: 6
Ingredients:
6 jalapeno peppers
¼ cup apple cider vinegar
1/3 cup water
¼ teaspoon peppercorns
1 garlic clove, peeled
½ teaspoon ground coriander
Directions:
Pour apple cider vinegar in the saucepan.
Add water, peppercorns, and bring the liquid to boil.
Wash the jalapeno peppers and slice them.
Put the sliced jalapenos in the glass jar.

Add ground cinnamon and garlic clove.

After this, add boiled apple cider vinegar liquid and close the lid.

Marinate the jalapenos as a minimum for 1 hour.

Nutrition: calories 9, fat 0.2, fiber 0.6, carbs 1.4, protein 0.2

149.   Naan

Preparation Time: 10 minutes
Cooking Time: 4 minutes
Servings: 2
Ingredients:
1 tablespoon butter
1 tablespoon almond flour
¾ teaspoon baking powder
¼ teaspoon lemon juice
1 teaspoon coconut oil, softened
1 teaspoon psyllium husk powder
Directions:
In the mixing bowl, mix up together almond flour, baking powder, lemon juice, coconut oil, and psyllium husk powder.

Knead the dough and cut it into 2 pieces.

Roll up the dough pieces to get naan bread shape.

Toss butter in the skillet and bring it to boil.

Place naan bread in the preheated butter and roast for 1 minute from each side.

The time of cooking depends on the naan size.

It is recommended to serve naan bread warm.

Nutrition: calories 157, fat 15.1, fiber 2.7, carbs 5.2, protein 3.1

150.   Sauteed Tomato Cabbage

Preparation Time: 10 minutes
Cooking Time: 35 minutes
Servings: 4
Ingredients:
1 tablespoon tomato paste
1 bell pepper, chopped
½ oz celery, grated
2 cups white cabbage, shredded
1 tablespoon butter
1 tablespoon dried oregano
1/3 cup water
¼ cup coconut cream
1 teaspoon salt
Directions:
Mix up together tomato paste, coconut cream, and water.

Pour the liquid in the saucepan.

Add bell pepper, grated celery, white cabbage, butter, and dried oregano.

Sprinkle the mixture with salt and mix up gently.
Close the lid and saute cabbage for 35 minutes over the medium-low heat.
Nutrition: calories 86, fat 6.7, fiber 2.3, carbs 6.7, protein 1.4

151.   Tender Radicchio

Preparation Time: 10 minutes
Cooking Time: 8 minutes
Servings: 4
Ingredients:
8 oz radicchio
1 teaspoon canola oil
½ teaspoon apple cider vinegar
¼ cup heavy cream
1 teaspoon minced garlic
1 teaspoon dried dill
Directions:
Slice the radicchio into 4 slices.
Line the baking dish with parchment and put sliced radicchio on it.
Sprinkle the vegetables with canola oil, apple cider vinegar, and dried dill.
Bake radicchio in the preheated to the 360F oven for 8 minutes.
Meanwhile, whisk together heavy cream with minced garlic.
Transfer the cooked radicchio on the plates and sprinkle with minced heavy cream mixture.
Nutrition: calories 43, fat 4, fiber 0.2, carbs 1.5, protein 0.5

152.   Green Salad with Walnuts

Preparation Time: 10 minutes
Servings: 2
Ingredients:
1 cup arugula
2 tablespoons walnuts, chopped
1 tablespoon avocado oil
½ teaspoon sesame seeds
1 teaspoon lemon juice
½ teaspoon lemon zest, grated
1 tomato, chopped
Directions:
Chop arugula roughly and put in the salad bowl.
Add walnuts, sesame seeds, and chopped tomato.
Make the dressing: mix up together avocado oil, sesame seeds, lemon juice, and grated lemon zest.
Pour the dressing over salad and shake it gently.
Nutrition: calories 71, fat 6, fiber 1.5, carbs 3.1, protein 2.7

153.   Jicama Slaw

Preparation Time: 10 minutes

Servings: 4
Ingredients:
1 cup jicama, julienned
1 bell pepper, julienned
1 onion, sliced
1 tablespoon fresh cilantro, chopped
½ carrot, julienned
2 tablespoons olive oil
1 teaspoon apple cider vinegar
½ teaspoon cayenne pepper
½ teaspoon salt
1/3 cup red cabbage, shredded
¼ teaspoon liquid stevia
Directions:
In the mixing bowl, combine together jicama, bell pepper, sliced onion, fresh cilantro, carrot, olive oil, apple cider vinegar, and liquid stevia. Mix up the salad mixture.
Then sprinkle slaw with cayenne pepper, salt, and red cabbage.
Mix up the cooked slaw one more time and transfer on the plates.
Nutrition: calories 98, fat 7.2, fiber 2.9, carbs 8.7, protein 1

154.   Peanut Slaw

Preparation Time: 10 minutes
Servings: 4
Ingredients:
1 cup white cabbage
1 teaspoon peanut butter
1 teaspoon lemon juice
1 tablespoon peanuts, chopped
½ teaspoon ground black pepper
1 tablespoon canola oil
1 oz scallions, chopped
1 teaspoon sriracha
¼ cup fresh parsley, chopped
Directions:
Shred the white cabbage and transfer in the mixing bowl.
Add peanuts, chopped fresh parsley, and scallions.
Then make the slaw dressing: whisk together peanut butter, lemon juice, ground black pepper, and canola oil.
Pour the dressing over the white cabbage mixture.
Add sriracha and chopped parsley.
Shake the slaw gently and transfer on the plates.
Nutrition: calories 62, fat 5.4, fiber 1.1, carbs 2.9, protein 1.4

155.   White Mushroom Saute

Preparation Time: 15 minutes

Cooking Time: 25 minutes
Servings: 6
Ingredients:
10 oz white mushrooms, chopped
1 carrot, chopped
1 onion, chopped
½ cup of water
3 tablespoons coconut cream
1 teaspoon salt
½ teaspoon turmeric
1 teaspoon chili flakes
1 teaspoon coconut oil
½ teaspoon Italian seasoning
Directions:
In the saucepan, combine together white mushrooms, chopped carrot, onion, and mix up gently.
Sprinkle the vegetables with coconut cream, salt, turmeric, chili flakes, and coconut oil.
Add Italian seasoning and mix up well.
Cook the mixture over the high heat for 5 minutes.
Stir the vegetables constantly.
Then add water and close the lid.
Saute the meal for 20 minutes over the medium heat.
Then let saute rest for 10 minutes before.
Nutrition: calories 47, fat 2.9, fiber 1.3, carbs 4.9, protein 1.9

156.   Caesar Salad

Preparation Time: 15 minutes
Servings: 5
Ingredients:
1 tablespoon capers
2 cups lettuce, chopped
1 teaspoon walnuts, chopped
1 teaspoon mustard
2 tablespoons canola oil
1 teaspoon lime juice
½ teaspoon white pepper
1 avocado, peeled, chopped
Directions:
Place walnuts, mustard, canola oil, lime juice, white pepper, and avocado in the blender.
Blend the mixture until smooth.
After this, transfer the avocado smooth mixture in the salad bowl.
Add chopped lettuce.
Sprinkle the salad with capers. Don't stir the salad before.
Nutrition: calories 142, fat 14, fiber 3.1, carbs 4.6, protein 1.2

157.   Cranberry Relish

Preparation Time: 5 minutes
Servings: 6
Ingredients:
1 cup cranberries
1 orange, peeled, chopped
1 tablespoon Erythritol
3 tablespoons lemon juice
Directions:
Place cranberries and chopped orange in the blender.
Add Erythritol and lemon juice.
Pulse the ingredients for 1 minute.
Transfer the relish in the plate.
The side dish tastes the best with meat meals.
Nutrition: calories 26, fat 0.1, fiber 1.4 carbs 5.4, protein 0.4

158.   Vegetable Tots

Preparation Time: 15 minutes
Cooking Time: 12 minutes
Servings: 8
Ingredients:
2 cups cauliflower
1 cup broccoli
4 eggs
1/3 cup almond flour
3 oz Parmesan, grated
1 teaspoon ground coriander
½ teaspoon ground thyme
1 teaspoon olive oil
Directions:
Grate the broccoli and cauliflower.
Transfer the grated vegetables in the cheesecloth and squeeze the liquid.
Then put vegetables in the mixing bowl.
Beat the eggs in the mixture and add grated cheese.
Then add almond flour, ground coriander, ground thyme, and mix it up.
Line the baking tray with baking paper and brush with 1 teaspoon of olive oil.
Make the medium size tots from the vegetable mixture and put them in the baking tray.
Bake the vegetable tots for 12 minutes at 365F.
Chill the meal to the room temperature before.
Nutrition: calories 88, fat 5.7, fiber 1.1, carbs 2.9, protein 7.3

159.   Hasselback Zucchini

Preparation Time: 15 minutes
Cooking Time: 20 minutes
Servings: 3
Ingredients:

3 small zucchini
4 oz Parmesan, sliced
1 tablespoon cream
½ teaspoon chili flakes
½ teaspoon butter
½ teaspoon ground black pepper
½ teaspoon olive oil
Directions:
Trim zucchini and cut them in the shape of the Hasselback.
Fill the zucchini Hasselback with sliced Parmesan.
Then whisk together cream, chili flakes, butter, ground black pepper, and olive oil.
Brush the zucchini with the cream mixture generously.
Wrap the zucchini Hasselback in the foil.
Preheat the oven to 365F.
Put the wrapped zucchini in the oven and cook for 20 minutes.
When the time is over, chill the zucchini for 5 minutes and then discard the foil.
Transfer the meal on the plates.
Nutrition: calories 156, fat 9.9, fiber 1.4, carbs 5.7, protein 13.7

160.   Lime Fennel Bulb

Preparation Time: 10 minutes
Cooking Time: 15 minutes
Servings: 4
Ingredients:
9 oz fennel bulb
½ lime
2 tablespoons butter
1 teaspoon olive oil
1 teaspoon harissa
½ teaspoon salt
Directions:
Cut every fennel bulb into 4 pieces.
Sprinkle the fennel with olive oil, harissa, and salt. Massage the fennel pieces with the help of the fingertips and transfer in the tray.
Add butter and bake fennel for 15 minutes at 360F. Stir the vegetables once during cooking.
Nutrition: calories 87, fat 7.3, fiber 2.2, carbs 6, protein 1

161.   Baked Garlic

Preparation Time: 5 minutes
Cooking Time: 20 minutes
Servings: 3
Ingredients:
3 big garlic cloves, peeled
3 teaspoons olive oil
1 teaspoon salt

½ teaspoon apple cider vinegar
Directions:
Place the garlic cloves in the parchment.
Add olive oil, salt, and apple cider vinegar.
Wrap the garlic to get the parchment pocket and place it in the oven.
Cook the garlic for 20 minutes at 355F.
When the time is over, the garlic should be very soft.
Serve the garlic with all remaining gravy.
Nutrition: calories 54, fat 4.7, fiber 0.2, carbs 3, protein 0.6

162. Roasted Okra

Preparation Time: 10 minutes
Cooking Time: 15 minutes
Servings: 4
Ingredients:
1 ½ cup okra
1 tablespoon almond flour
1 teaspoon salt
1 tablespoon coconut oil
½ teaspoon cayenne pepper
½ teaspoon dried cilantro
1 tablespoon heavy cream
Directions:
Slice the okra roughly.
Put coconut oil in the skillet.
Add sliced okra and start to cook it over the medium-high heat.
Sprinkle the vegetables with salt, cayenne pepper, and dried cilantro.
Then add heavy cream and mix up well.
Cook okra for 5 minutes more.
Sprinkle the vegetables with almond flour and close the lid.
Cook the side dish for 5 minutes over the medium heat.
Nutrition: calories 98, fat 8.4, fiber 2, carbs 4.5, protein 2.3

163. Broccoli Gratin

Preparation Time: 10 minutes
Cooking Time: 30 minutes
Servings: 6
Ingredients:
2 cups broccoli florets
1 teaspoon salt
1 teaspoon chili flakes
3 eggs, whisked
2 oz Swiss cheese, grated
1 onion, diced
1 cup heavy cream

Directions:

Whisk together chili flakes, salt, eggs, and heavy cream.

Add the diced onion in the mixture and stir gently.

After this, place broccoli florets into the non-sticky gratin mold.

Sprinkle the vegetables with Swiss cheese and heavy cream mixture.

Cover the gratin with foil and secure the edges.

Cook gratin for 30 minutes in the preheated to the 360F oven.

When the time is over, discard the foil and check if the broccoli is tender.

Chill the gratin little and transfer on the plates.

Nutrition: calories 154, fat 12.3, fiber 1.2, carbs 5, protein 6.8

Seafood

164.   Poached Halibut and Mushrooms

Preparation Time: 5 Minutes
Cooking Time: 30 Minutes
Servings: 8
Ingredients:
2 pounds halibut, cut into bite-sized pieces
1 teaspoon fresh lemon juice
½ teaspoon soy sauce
1/8 teaspoon sesame oil
4 cups mushrooms, sliced
¼ cup water
Salt and pepper to taste
¾ cup green onions
Directions:
Place a heavy bottomed pot on medium high fire.
Add all ingredients and mix well.
Cover and bring to a boil. Once boiling, lower fire to a simmer. Cook for 25 minutes.
Adjust seasoning to taste.
Serve and enjoy.
Nutrition:
Calories 217, Total Fat 15.8g, Saturated Fat 5.3g, Total Carbs 1.1g, Net Carbs 0.7g, Protein 16.5g, Sugar: 0g, Fiber 0.4g, Sodium 97mg, Potassium 234mg

165.   Halibut Stir Fry

Preparation Time: 5 Minutes
Cooking Time: 20 Minutes
Servings: 6
Ingredients:
2 pounds halibut fillets
2 tbsp olive oil
½ cup fresh parsley
1 onion, sliced
2 stalks celery, chopped
2 tablespoons capers
4 cloves of garlic minced
Salt and pepper to taste
Directions:
Place a heavy bottomed pot on high fire and heat for 2 minutes. Add oil and heat for 2 more minutes.
Stir in garlic and onions. Sauté for 5 minutes.
Add remaining ingredients, except for parsley and stir fry for 10 minutes or until fish is cooked.
Adjust seasoning to taste and serve with a sprinkle of parsley.
Nutrition:

Calories 331, Total Fat 26g, Saturated Fat 4g, Total Carbs 2g, Net Carbs 1.5g, Protein 22g, Sugar: 0.6g, Fiber 0.5g, Sodium 197mg, Potassium 485mg

166.   Steamed Garlic-Dill Halibut

Preparation Time: 5 Minutes
Cooking Time: 25 Minutes
Servings: 4
Ingredients:
1-pound halibut fillet
1 lemon, freshly squeezed
Salt and pepper to taste
1 teaspoon garlic powder
1 tablespoon dill weed, chopped
Directions:
Place a large pot on medium fire and fill up to 1.5-inches of water. Place a trivet inside pot.
In a baking dish that fits inside your large pot, add all ingredients and mix well. Cover dish with foil.
Place the dish on top of the trivet inside the pot.
Cover pot and steam fish for 15 minutes.
Let fish rest for at least 10 minutes before removing from pot.
Serve and enjoy.
Nutrition:
Calories 270, Total Fat 6.5g, Saturated Fat 0.5g, Total Carbs 3.9g, Net Carbs 1.8g, Protein 47.8g, Sugar: 0g, Fiber 2.1g, Sodium 565mg, Potassium 356mg

167.   Italian Halibut Chowder

Preparation Time: 5 Minutes
Cooking Time: 20 Minutes
Servings: 8
Ingredients:
2 tablespoons olive oil
1 onion, chopped
3 stalks of celery, chopped
3 cloves of garlic, minced
2 ½ pounds halibut steaks, cubed
1 red bell pepper, seeded and chopped
1 cup tomato juice
½ cup apple juice, organic and unsweetened
½ teaspoon dried basil
1/8 teaspoon dried thyme
Salt and pepper to taste
Directions:
Place a heavy bottomed pot on medium high fire and heat pot for 2 minutes. Add oil and heat for a minute.
Sauté the onion, celery and garlic until fragrant.
Stir in the halibut steaks and bell pepper. Sauté for 3 minutes.

Pour in the rest of the ingredients and mix well.

Cover and bring to a boil. Once boiling, lower fire to a simmer and simmer for 10 minutes.

Adjust seasoning to taste.

Serve and enjoy.

Nutrition:

Calories 318, Total Fat 23g, Saturated Fat 3.9g, Total Carbs 6g, Net Carbs 5g, Protein 21g, Sugar: 4g, Fiber 1g, Sodium 155mg, Potassium 533mg

168.   Pomegranate-Molasses Glazed Salmon

Preparation Time: 15 Minutes

Cooking Time: 20 Minutes

Servings: 4

Ingredients:

1 tbsp coconut oil

2 tbsp pomegranate molasses

¼ cup fresh orange juice

4 garlic cloves, crushed

1 tbsp fresh ginger, grated

4 pcs 8-oz salmon fillets

Directions:

Mix the garlic, ginger, pomegranate molasses and orange juice in a small bowl.

Pour the mixture over the salmon and marinate at room temperature for 15 minutes.

Preheat the oven to 425 degrees Fahrenheit.

Line a baking sheet with foil and grease it with coconut oil.

Place the salmon skin-side-down on the baking sheet.

Drizzle more pomegranate molasses on top of the salmon.

Bake the fillets for 15 minutes or until the salmon becomes flaky.

Nutrition:

Calories 203, Total Fat 7g, Saturated Fat 3.5g, Total Carbs 29g, Net Carbs 23g, Protein 9g, Sugar: 21g, Fiber 6g, Sodium 128mg, Potassium 472mg

169.   Quick Thai Cod Curry

Preparation Time: 15 Minutes

Cooking Time: 15 Minutes

Servings: 1

Ingredients:

1 tsp coconut oil

1 tablespoon organic Thai red curry paste

1 clove of garlic, minced

1 shallot, minced

1/4 cup coconut cream

3 tbsp water

1 cod fillet

Directions:

Place a heavy bottomed pot on medium high fire and heat pot for 2 minutes. Add oil and heat for a minute.

Sauté the curry paste, garlic, and shallots until fragrant.

Stir in coconut cream and fillet. Sauté for 3 minutes. Season with pepper and salt to taste.

Cover and bring to a boil. Once boiling, lower fire to a simmer and simmer for 10 minutes.

Adjust seasoning to taste.

Serve and enjoy.

Nutrition:

Calories 458, Total Fat 28g, Saturated Fat 4.8g, Total Carbs 10g, Net Carbs 5g, Protein 45g, Sugar: 1g, Fiber 5g, Sodium 132mg, Potassium 1268mg

170.   Salmon with Sun-Dried Tomatoes and Capers

Preparation Time: 10 Minutes
Cooking Time: 15 Minutes
Servings: 2
Ingredients:
1 salmon fillet
½ lemon, freshly squeezed
Salt and pepper to taste
¼ teaspoon cayenne pepper
½ teaspoon dried oregano
½ teaspoon dried thyme
2 cloves of garlic, minced
2 tablespoons chopped sun-dried tomatoes
1 tablespoon capers
¼ cup water
Directions:
Place a heavy bottomed pot on medium high fire and add all ingredients.

Mix well, cover and bring to a boil. Once boiling, lower fire to a simmer and simmer for 10 minutes.

Adjust seasoning to taste and continue cooking for another 5 minutes.

Serve and enjoy.

Nutrition:

Calories 265, Total Fat 8g, Saturated Fat 1.7g, Total Carbs 6g, Net Carbs 3g, Protein 41g, Sugar: 3g, Fiber 1g, Sodium 211mg, Potassium 1078g

171.   Island Style Sardines

Preparation Time: 10 Minutes
Cooking Time: 8 hours
Servings: 4
Ingredients:
2 tablespoons olive oil
1 roma tomato, diced
¼ cup sliced onion
1 clove of garlic, minced
1 teaspoon cayenne pepper flakes

½ pound sardines, gutted and scales removed
1 tablespoon lemon juice, freshly squeezed
A dash of rosemary
A dash of sage
Salt and pepper to taste
Directions:
In a slow cooker, add all ingredients and mix well.
Cover and cook on low settings for 8 hours.
Adjust seasoning if needed.
Serve and enjoy.
Nutrition:
Calories 195, Total Fat 13.5g, Saturated Fat 2g, Total Carbs 4g, Net Carbs 3g, Protein 15g, Sugar: 2g, Fiber 1g, Sodium 177mg, Potassium 366g

172. Slow Cooked Spanish Cod

Preparation Time: 10 Minutes
Cooking Time: 6 Minutes
Servings: 6
Ingredients:
1 tablespoon olive oil
¼ cup chopped onion
2 tablespoons chopped garlic
1 cup tomato sauce
15 cherry tomatoes, halved
½ cup chopped green olives
Salt and pepper to taste
6 cod fillets, sliced
Directions:
In a slow cooker, add all ingredients and mix well.
Cover and cook on low settings for 6 hours.
Adjust seasoning if needed.
Serve and enjoy.
Nutrition:
Calories 293, Total Fat 18g, Saturated Fat 3g, Total Carbs 14g, Net Carbs 10g, Protein 21g, Sugar: 4g, Fiber 7g, Sodium 428mg, Potassium 776mg

173. Multi-Spice Cod Curry

Preparation Time: 15 Minutes
Cooking Time: 20 Minutes
Servings: 6
Ingredients:
2 tablespoons olive oil
1 onion, chopped
1 teaspoon garlic paste
1 teaspoon grated ginger

2 teaspoons cumin

2 teaspoons coriander

1 teaspoon cardamom

½ teaspoon turmeric

Salt and pepper to taste

2 fresh jalapeno peppers, chopped

1 tablespoon lemon juice, freshly squeezed

1 cup tomatoes, diced

1-pound cod fillets, cut into chunks

1 cup water

¼ cup cilantro, chopped

Directions:

Place a heavy bottomed pot on medium high fire and heat pot for 2 minutes. Add oil and heat for a minute.

Sauté the onion, garlic, and ginger until fragrant.

Stir in the cumin, coriander, cardamom, turmeric, salt, and pepper. Sauté for a minute.

Pour in the rest of the ingredients and mix well.

Cover and bring to a boil. Once boiling, lower fire to a simmer and simmer for 10 minutes.

Adjust seasoning to taste and continue cooking for another 5 minutes.

Serve and enjoy.

Nutrition:

Calories 114, Total Fat 5g, Saturated Fat 0.7g, Total Carbs 5g, Net Carbs 4g, Protein 12g, Sugar: 2g, Fiber 1g, Sodium 234mg, Potassium 332mg

174.   Poached Cod Asian Style

Preparation Time: 10 Minutes

Cooking Time: 15 Minutes

Servings: 4

Ingredients:

1-pound cod, cut into chunks

6 tablespoons water

5 tablespoons soy sauce

1 thumb-size ginger, cut into thin strips

4 cloves of garlic, minced

1 tablespoon sesame oil

¾ teaspoon red pepper flakes

¼ teaspoon Chinese five spice powder

Directions:

Place a heavy bottomed pot on medium high fire and heat pot for 2 minutes. Add oil and heat for a minute.

Sauté the garlic and ginger until fragrant.

Stir in red pepper flakes and Chinese five spice. Sauté for a minute.

Pour in the rest of the ingredients and toss well.

Cover and bring to a boil. Boil for 2 minutes and then turn off fire and let it sit untouched for 5 minutes.

Serve and enjoy.

Nutrition:
Calories 175, Total Fat 8g, Saturated Fat 1.2g, Total Carbs 7g, Net Carbs 6g, Protein 19g, Sugar: 4g, Fiber 1g, Sodium 646mg, Potassium 365g

175.   Basil-Avocado Baked Salmon

Preparation Time: 10 Minutes
Cooking Time: 15 Minutes
Servings: 4
Ingredients:
1 tbsp coconut oil
4 8oz salmon fillets
1 tbsp lemon zest
1 tsp capers
1 ripe avocado
3 cloves garlic, crushed
½ cup chopped fresh basil
Directions:
Grease a baking sheet with coconut oil.
On a bowl, mash avocado until it becomes creamy. Add in the chopped garlic, capers, lemon zest and basil. Set aside.
Lay the salmon fillets on the baking sheet and spread the avocado topping on top of the salmon. Bake in a preheated 350-degree oven for 15 minutes.
Nutrition:
Calories 387, Total Fat 19g, Saturated Fat 3g, Total Carbs 5g, Net Carbs 1.5g, Protein 47g, Sugar: 0.5g, Fiber 3.5g, Sodium 133mg, Potassium 1239mg

176.   Spicy Baked Cod

Preparation Time: 15 Minutes
Cooking Time: 15 Minutes
Servings: 5
Ingredients:
2 tablespoons plain non-fat yogurt
1 teaspoon ginger, grated
2 tablespoon curry powder
1 teaspoon soy sauce
1 teaspoon rice wine vinegar
2 ½ teaspoon cayenne pepper
5 cod fillets
2 tablespoons olive oil
Directions:
In a shallow dish mix all ingredients except for oil. Let fish sit in marinade for at least an hour.
When ready, lightly grease cookie sheet with oil and preheat oven to 400oF.
Once preheated, place cod filets on prepped cookie sheet and bake to desired doneness, around 15 minutes baking time.
Serve and enjoy.

Nutrition:
Calories 254, Total Fat 8g, Saturated Fat 1g, Total Carbs 2g, Net Carbs 0.4g, Protein 42g, Sugar: 0.5g, Fiber 1.6g, Sodium 144mg, Potassium 1013mg

177. Cod Casserole Portuguese Style

Preparation Time: 10 Minutes
Cooking Time: 15 Minutes
Servings: 5
Ingredients:
2 tablespoons olive oil
2 cloves of garlic, minced
3 large onion, sliced
2 pounds cod fish, sliced into strips
4 potatoes, peeled and sliced
1 teaspoon paprika
¼ cup tablespoons tomato sauce
¼ cup water
1 ½ teaspoon crushed pepper flakes
1 tablespoon chopped parsley
Directions:
Place a heavy bottomed pot on medium high fire and heat pot for 2 minutes. Add oil and heat for a minute.
Sauté the garlic and onions until fragrant.
Stir in the cod slices and add the rest of the ingredients.
Season with salt and pepper to taste.
Cover and bring to a boil. Boil for 2 minutes and then lower fire to a simmer. Simmer for 5 minutes.
Turn off fire and let it sit untouched for 5 minutes.
Serve and enjoy.
Nutrition:
Calories 337, Total Fat 6g, Saturated Fat 1g, Total Carbs 37g, Net Carbs 31g, Protein 32g, Sugar: 7g, Fiber 6g, Sodium 747mg, Potassium 1246mg

178. Salmon with Lemon and Dill

Preparation Time: 10 Minutes
Cooking Time: 15 Minutes
Servings: 4
Ingredients:
1-pound salmon fillets
2 tablespoons olive oil
5 tablespoons lemon juice, freshly squeezed
1 tablespoon fresh dill, chopped
¼ teaspoon garlic powder
Salt and pepper to taste
Directions:
Place a trivet or steamer basket inside your pot and pour water up to an inch high. Bring to a boil.

Place the salmon fillets in a baking dish that will fit in the Pot.
Pour over the rest of the ingredients. Mix well and cover dish securely with foil.
Place the baking dish on the steam rack.
Close the lid and steam fish for 15 minutes. Turn off fire and let fish sit for another 5 minutes.
Serve and enjoy.
Nutrition:
Calories 320, Total Fat 22.1g, Saturated Fat 2.3g, Total Carbs 2.4g, Net Carbs 0.7g, Protein 25.7g, Sugar: 0g, Fiber 1.7g, Sodium 197mg, Potassium 0.3g

179.   Steamed Lemon Pepper Salmon

Preparation Time: 10 Minutes
Cooking Time: 20 Minutes
Servings: 4
Ingredients:
4 salmon fillets
2 tablespoons olive oil
2 tablespoons soy sauce
1 teaspoon lemon juice
Salt and pepper to taste
Directions:
Place a trivet or steamer basket inside your pot and pour water up to an inch high. Bring to a boil.
Place the salmon fillets in a baking dish that will fit in the Pot.
Pour over the rest of the ingredients. Mix well and cover dish securely with foil.
Place the baking dish on the steam rack.
Close the lid and steam fish for 15 minutes. Turn off fire and let fish sit for another 5 minutes.
Serve and enjoy.
Nutrition:
Calories 239, Total Fat 16.7g, Saturated Fat 3.3g, Total Carbs 0.9g, Net Carbs 0.6g, Protein 20.2g, Sugar: 0g, Fiber 0.3g, Sodium 892mg, Potassium 395mg

180.   Salmon in Parchment

Preparation Time: 15 Minutes
Cooking Time: 20 Minutes
Servings: 2
Ingredients:
2 potatoes, peeled and sliced
10 spears asparagus
2 6-oz skinless salmon fillets
Salt and pepper to taste
1 tablespoon lemon juice, freshly squeezed
1 teaspoon olive oil
Directions:
Place a steamer basket inside your pot and pour water up to an inch high. Bring to a boil.
In a large parchment paper, layer the potatoes and asparagus.
Place the salmon on top and season with salt and pepper.

Drizzle with lemon juice and olive oil.

Fold over the parchment paper to create a pocket and seal off the edges by crimping.

Place the parchment paper inside the steamer basket.

Close the lid and steam fish for 15 minutes. Turn off fire and let fish sit for another 5 minutes.

Serve and enjoy

Nutrition:

Calories 369, Total Fat 9g, Saturated Fat 1.8g, Total Carbs 33g, Net Carbs 28g, Protein 39g, Sugar: 3g, Fiber 5g, Sodium 97mg, Potassium 1565mg

181.   Minted Salmon

Preparation Time: 10 Minutes
Cooking Time: 10 Minutes
Servings: 4
Ingredients:
2 tablespoons olive oil
4 cloves of garlic, minced
1 bunch fresh mint, stems removed
1 bunch flat-leaf parsley
½ cup lemon juice, freshly squeezed
2 tablespoons honey
1 teaspoons salt
1 teaspoon ground black pepper
4 6-oz salmon fillets
Directions:

In a food processor, pulse the olive oil, garlic, mint, parsley, lemon juice, honey, salt, and pepper until smooth.

Place a heavy bottomed pan on medium high fire and heat pot for 2 minutes.

Add sauce and fish. Sauté for 2 to 3 minutes.

Add a splash of water and turn fish over. Continue cooking for another 2 minutes or until fish is pink.

Turn off fire and leave fish untouched and covered for 3 minutes to continue cooking.

Serve and enjoy.

Sauté the until fragrant.

Nutrition:

Calories 309, Total Fat 13g, Saturated Fat 2.4g, Total Carbs 12g, Net Carbs 11.6g, Protein 35g, Sugar: 9.4g, Fiber 0.4g, Sodium 668mg, Potassium 788mg

182.   Cayenne Sea Bass Mix

Preparation Time: 5 minutes
Cooking Time: 14 minutes
Servings: 4
Ingredients:
4 sea bass fillets, boneless
2 tablespoons avocado oil
4 scallions, chopped

½ cup corn
½ cup kalamata olives, pitted and cubed
1 teaspoon cayenne pepper
Juice of ½ lemon
A pinch of sea salt and black pepper
1/3 cup basil, chopped
Directions:
Heat up a pan with the oil over medium-high heat, add the scallions and sauté for 2 minutes.
Add the fish and cook it for 4 minutes on each side.
Add the rest of the ingredients, toss, cook for 4 minutes more, divide between plates and serve.
Nutrition: calories 270, fat 6, fiber 4, carbs 13, protein 15

183.   Salmon with Ginger Leeks

Preparation Time: 10 minutes
Cooking Time: 20 minutes
Servings: 4
Ingredients:
4 salmon fillets, boneless
2 tablespoons olive oil
2 leeks, sliced
1 teaspoon cumin, ground
½ teaspoon rosemary, dried
1 tablespoon ginger, grated
1 tablespoon cilantro, chopped
1 teaspoon sweet paprika
Directions:
Heat up a pan with the oil over medium heat, add the leeks and sauté for 5 minutes.
Add the fish and cook it for 5 minutes on each side.
Add the rest of the ingredients, cook the mix for 5 minutes more, divide between plates and serve.
Nutrition: calories 278, fat 3, fiber 4, carbs 14, protein 15

184.   Curry Halibut

Preparation Time: 10 minutes
Cooking Time: 14 minutes
Servings: 4
Ingredients:
4 halibut fillets, boneless
2 tablespoons olive oil
4 shallots, chopped
1 tablespoon green curry paste
¼ cup basil, chopped
2 teaspoons coconut aminos
1 red chili pepper, chopped
1 tablespoon cilantro, chopped
Directions:

Heat up a pan with the oil over medium-high heat, add the shallots, curry paste and chili pepper and sauté for 4 minutes.

Add the fish and the other ingredients, cook it for 5 minutes on each side, divide between plates and serve.

Nutrition: calories 210, fat 3, fiber 2, carbs 12, protein 16

185. Salmon and Sweet Potatoes

Preparation Time: 10 minutes
Cooking Time: 25 minutes
Servings: 4
Ingredients:
4 salmon fillets, boneless
1 garlic cloves, minced
2 tablespoons olive oil
A pinch of salt and black pepper
1 yellow onion, sliced
2 sweet potatoes, peeled and cut into wedges
1 tablespoon rosemary, chopped
1 tablespoon lime juice
Directions:
Grease a baking dish with the oil, arrange the salmon, garlic, onion and the other ingredients into the dish and bake everything at 380 degrees F for 25 minutes.
Divide the mix between plates and serve.
Nutrition: calories 260, fat 4, fiber 6, carbs 10, protein 16

186. Salmon with Herbed Sauce

Preparation Time: 5 minutes
Cooking Time: 20 minutes
Servings: 4
Ingredients:
3 tablespoons olive oil
4 salmon fillets, boneless
4 garlic cloves, minced
¼ cup coconut cream
1 tablespoon parsley, chopped
1 tablespoon rosemary, chopped
1 tablespoon basil, chopped
1 tablespoon oregano, chopped
1 tablespoon pine nuts, toasted
A pinch of salt and black pepper
Directions:
In a blender, combine the oil with the garlic and the other ingredients except the fish and pulse well.
Arrange the fish in a roasting pan, add the herbed sauce on top and cook at 380 degrees F for 20 minutes.
Divide the mix between plates and serve.

Nutrition: calories 386, fat 26.8, fiber 1.4, carbs 3.5, protein 35.6

187. Cumin Shrimp and Beans

Preparation Time: 5 minutes
Cooking Time: 12 minutes
Servings: 4
Ingredients:
1 pound shrimp, peeled and deveined
2 tablespoons olive oil
1 teaspoon cumin, ground
4 green onions, chopped
1 cup canned black beans, drained and rinsed
2 tablespoons lime juice
1 teaspoon turmeric powder
Directions:
Heat up a pan with the oil over medium heat, add the green onions and sauté for 2 minutes.
Add the shrimp and the other ingredients, toss, cook over medium heat for another 10 minutes, divide between plates and serve.
Nutrition: calories 251, fat 12, fiber 2, carbs 13, protein 16

188. Shrimp with Spinach

Preparation Time: 10 minutes
Cooking Time: 10 minutes
Servings: 4
Ingredients:
1 pound shrimp, peeled and deveined
2 tablespoons olive oil
1 tablespoon lime juice
1 cup baby spinach
A pinch of sea salt and black pepper
1 tablespoon chives, chopped
Directions:
Heat up the pan with the oil over medium heat, add the shrimp and sauté for 5 minutes.
Add the spinach and the remaining ingredients, toss, cook the mix for another 5 minutes, divide between plates and serve.
Nutrition: calories 206, fat 6, fiber 4, carbs 7, protein 17

189. Lime Cod and Peppers

Preparation Time: 10 minutes
Cooking Time: 15 minutes
Servings: 4
Ingredients:
4 cod fillets, boneless
2 tablespoons olive oil

4 spring onions, chopped
Juice of 1 lime
1 red bell pepper, cut into strips
1 green bell pepper, cut into strips
2 teaspoons parsley, chopped
A pinch of salt and black pepper
Directions:
Heat up a pan with the oil over medium heat, add the bell peppers and the onions and sauté for 5 minutes.
Add the fish and the rest of the ingredients, cook the mix for 10 minutes more, flipping the fish halfway.
Divide the mix between plates and serve.
Nutrition: calories 180, fat 5, fiber 1, carbs 7, protein 11

190.   Cod Pan

Preparation Time: 5 minutes
Cooking Time: 20 minutes
Servings: 4
Ingredients:
1 pound cod fillets, boneless and cubed
2 tablespoons avocado oil
1 avocado, peeled, pitted and cubed
1 tomato, cubed
1 tablespoon lemon juice
¼ cup parsley, chopped
1 tablespoon tomato paste
½ cup veggie stock
A pinch of sea salt and black pepper
Directions:
Heat up a pan with the oil over medium-high heat, add the fish and cook for 3 minutes on each side.
Add the rest of the ingredients, cook the mix for 14 minutes more over medium heat, divide between plates and serve.
Nutrition: calories 160, fat 2, fiber 2, carbs 4, protein 7

191.   Chili Shrimp and Zucchinis

Preparation Time: 5 minutes
Cooking Time: 8 minutes
Servings: 4
Ingredients:
1 pound shrimp, peeled and deveined
2 tablespoons avocado oil
2 zucchinis, sliced
Juice of 1 lime
A pinch of salt and black pepper
2 red chilies, chopped

3 garlic cloves, minced
1 tablespoon balsamic vinegar
Directions:
Heat up a pan with the oil over medium-high heat, add the shrimp, garlic and the chilies and cook for 3 minutes.
Add the rest of the ingredients, toss, cook everything for 5 minutes more, divide between plates and serve.
Nutrition: calories 211, fat 5, fiber 2, carbs 11, protein 15

192.   Lemon Scallops

Preparation Time: 10 minutes
Cooking Time: 10 minutes
Servings: 4
Ingredients:
2 tablespoons olive oil
1 pound sea scallops
½ teaspoon rosemary, dried
½ cup veggie stock
2 garlic cloves, minced
Juice of ½ lemon
Directions:
Heat up a pan with the oil over medium-high heat, add the garlic, the scallops and the other ingredients, cook everything for 10 minutes, divide into bowls and serve.
Nutrition: calories 170, fat 5, fiber 2, carbs 8, protein 10

193.   Crab and Shrimp Salad

Preparation Time: 5 minutes
Cooking Time: 0 minutes
Servings: 4
Ingredients:
1 cup canned crab meat, drained
1 pound shrimp, peeled, deveined and cooked
1 cup cherry tomatoes, halved
1 cucumber, sliced
2 cups baby arugula
2 tablespoons avocado oil
1 tablespoon chives, chopped
1 tablespoon lemon juice
A pinch of salt and black pepper
Directions:
In a bowl, combine the shrimp with the crab meat and the other ingredients, toss and serve.
Nutrition: calories 203, fat 12, fiber 6, carbs 12, protein 9

194.   Salmon with Zucchinis and Tomatoes

Preparation Time: 10 minutes
Cooking Time: 30 minutes
Servings: 4
Ingredients:
4 salmon fillets, boneless
2 tablespoons avocado oil
2 tablespoons sweet paprika
2 zucchinis, sliced
2 tomatoes, cut into wedges
¼ teaspoon red pepper flakes, crushed
A pinch of sea salt and black pepper
4 garlic cloves, minced
Directions:
In a roasting pan, combine the salmon with the oil and the other ingredients, toss gently and cook at 370 degrees F for 30 minutes.
Divide everything between plates and serve.
Nutrition: calories 210, fat 2, fiber 4, carbs 13, protein 10

195.   Shrimp and Mango Salad

Preparation Time: 5 minutes
Cooking Time: 0 minutes
Servings: 4
Ingredients:
1 pound shrimp, cooked, peeled and deveined
2 mangoes, peeled and cubed
3 scallions, chopped
1 cup baby spinach
1 cup baby arugula
1 jalapeno, chopped
2 tablespoons olive oil
1 tablespoon lime juice
A pinch of salt and black pepper
Directions:
In a bowl, combine the shrimp with the mango, scallions and the other ingredients, toss and serve.
Nutrition: calories 210, fat 2, fiber 3, carbs 13, protein 8

196.   Creamy Cod Bowls

Preparation Time: 5 minutes
Cooking Time: 20 minutes
Servings: 4
Ingredients:
2 tablespoons olive oil
1 pound cod fillets, boneless and cubed
2 spring onions, chopped
2 garlic cloves, minced

1 cup coconut cream
¼ cup chives, chopped
A pinch of salt and black pepper
2 tablespoons Dijon mustard
Directions:
Heat up a pan with the oil over medium heat, add the garlic and the onions and sauté for 5 minutes.
Add the fish and the other ingredients, toss, cook over medium heat for 15 minutes more, divide into bowls and serve.
Nutrition: calories 211, fat 5, fiber 5, carbs 6, protein 15

197.　　　Trout and Cilantro Sauce

Preparation Time: 5 minutes
Cooking Time: 15 minutes
Servings: 4
Ingredients:
4 trout fillets, boneless
2 tablespoons avocado oil
1 cup cilantro, chopped
2 tablespoons lemon juice
½ cup coconut cream
1 tablespoon walnuts, chopped
A pinch of salt and black pepper
3 teaspoons lemon zest, grated
Directions:
In a blender, combine the cilantro with the cream and the other ingredients except the fish and the oil and pulse well.
Heat up a pan with the oil over medium heat, add the fish and cook for 4 minutes on each side.
Add the cilantro sauce, toss gently and cook over medium heat for 7 minutes more.
Divide the mix between plates and serve.
Nutrition: calories 212, fat 14.6, fiber 1.3, carbs 2.9, protein 18

198.　　　Basil Tilapia

Preparation Time: 5 minutes
Cooking Time: 12 minutes
Servings: 4
Ingredients:
4 tilapia fillets, boneless
2 tablespoons olive oil
2 tablespoons lemon juice
1 teaspoon basil, dried
1 tablespoon cilantro, chopped
Directions:
Heat up a pan with the oil over medium heat, add the fish and cook for 5 minutes on each side.
Add the rest of the ingredients, toss gently, cook for 2 minutes more, divide between plates and serve.

Nutrition: calories 201, fat 8.6, fiber 0, carbs 0.2, protein 31.6

199. Mustard Salmon Mix

Preparation Time: 5 minutes
Cooking Time: 14 minutes
Servings: 4
Ingredients:
4 salmon fillets, boneless
½ teaspoon mustard seeds
½ cup mustard
2 tablespoons olive oil
4 scallions, chopped
Salt and black pepper to the taste
2 green chilies, chopped
¼ teaspoon cumin, ground
¼ cup parsley, chopped
Directions:
Heat up a pot with the oil over medium heat, add the scallions and the chilies and cook for 2 minutes.
Add the fish and cook for 4 minutes on each side.
Add the remaining ingredients, toss, cook everything for 4 more minutes, divide between plates and serve.
Nutrition: calories 397, fat 23.9, fiber 3.5, carbs 8,5, protein 40

200. Shrimp and Cauliflower Mix

Preparation Time: 10 minutes
Cooking Time: 10 minutes
Servings: 4
Ingredients:
2 tablespoons olive oil
1 pound shrimp, peeled and deveined
1 cup cauliflower florets
2 tablespoons lemon juice
2 tablespoons garlic, minced
1 teaspoon cumin, ground
1 teaspoon turmeric powder
Salt and black pepper to the taste
Directions:
Heat up a pan with the oil over medium-high heat, add the garlic and sauté for 2 minutes.
Add the shrimp and cook for 4 minutes more.
Add the remaining ingredients, toss, cook the mix for 4 minutes, divide between plates and serve
Nutrition: calories 200, fat 5.3, fiber 3, carbs 11, protein 6

201. Salmon with Broccoli

Preparation Time: 5 minutes
Cooking Time: 15 minutes
Servings: 4
Ingredients:
4 salmon fillets, boneless
1 teaspoon coriander, ground
1 cup broccoli florets
2 tablespoons lemon juice
2 tablespoons avocado oil
1 tablespoon lemon zest, grated
A pinch of salt and black pepper
2 tablespoons cilantro, chopped
Directions:
Heat up a pan with the oil over medium heat, add the fish and cook for 4 minutes on each side.
Add the broccoli and the other ingredients, cook the mix for 7 more minutes, divide between plates and serve.
Nutrition: calories 210, fat 4.7, fiber 2, carbs 11, protein 17

202.   Salmon with Mushrooms

Preparation Time: 10 minutes
Cooking Time: 20 minutes
Servings: 4
Ingredients:
4 salmon fillets, boneless
2 tablespoons olive oil
1 cup mushrooms, sliced
3 green onions, chopped
1 tablespoon lime juice
¼ teaspoon nutmeg, ground
¼ cup almonds, toasted and chopped
A pinch of salt and black pepper
Directions:
Heat up a pan with the oil over medium-high heat, add the green onions and sauté for 5 minutes.
Add the mushrooms and cook for 5 minutes more.
Add the fish and the other ingredients, cook it for 5 minutes on each side, divide between plates and serve.
Nutrition: calories 250, fat 10, fiber 3.3, carbs 7, protein 20

203.   Shrimp with Rice

Preparation Time: 10 minutes
Cooking Time: 25 minutes
Servings: 4
Ingredients:
1 pound shrimp, peeled and deveined
1 cup black rice

2 cups chicken stock
4 scallions, chopped
1 teaspoon chili powder
1 teaspoon sweet paprika
2 tablespoons avocado oil
A pinch of salt and black pepper
Directions:
Heat up a pan with the oil over medium-high heat, add the scallions and sauté for 5 minutes.
Add the rice and the other ingredients except the shrimp, and cook the mix for 15 minutes.
Add the shrimp, cook everything for another 5 minutes, divide into bowls and serve.
Nutrition: calories 240, fat 7, fiber 6, carbs 8, protein 14

204. Dill Sea Bass

Preparation Time: 5 minutes
Cooking Time: 12 minutes
Servings: 4
Ingredients:
4 sea bass fillets, boneless
2 tablespoons olive oil
3 spring onions, chopped
2 tablespoons lemon juice
Salt and black pepper to the taste
2 tablespoons dill, chopped
Directions:
Heat up a pan with the oil over medium heat, add the onions and sauté for 2 minutes.
Add the fish and the other ingredients, cook everything for 5 minutes on each side, divide the mix between plates and serve.
Nutrition: calories 214, fat 12, fiber 4, carbs 7, protein 17

205. Trout with Tomato Sauce

Preparation Time: 4 minutes
Cooking Time: 15 minutes
Servings: 4
Ingredients:
4 trout fillets, boneless
2 spring onions, chopped
2 tablespoons olive oil
1 cup tomatoes, peeled and crushed
¼ cup coconut cream
1 tablespoon chives, chopped
A pinch of salt and black pepper
Directions:
Heat up a pan with the oil over medium heat, add the spring onions, tomatoes and the cream and cook for 5 minutes.

Add the fish and the rest of the ingredients, toss, cook everything for 10 minutes more, divide between plates and serve.

Nutrition: calories 200, fat 5, fiber 6, carbs 12, protein 12

206.   Breakfast Avocado and Tuna Balls

Servings: 4
Preparation Time: 5minutes
Ingredients
1 can tuna
1 avocado, pitted and peeled
1/2 cup onion, chopped
1/2 teaspoon dried dill
3 ounces sunflower seed
1/2 teaspoon freshly ground black pepper
1/2 teaspoon smoked paprika
Salt, to taste
Directions
Add all ingredients in a mixing dish and mix thoroughly. Roll the mixture into 8 balls. Serve properly chilled and enjoy!

Nutrition: Calories 316 ,Protein 17.4g Protein 24: 4g ,Carbs 5.9g ,Sugar 1.4g

207.   Smoked Tilapia Pie

Servings: 6
Preparation Time: 45minutes
Ingredients
For the Crust:
3 tablespoons flaxseed meal
1/2 teaspoon baking powder
2 teaspoons ground psyllium husk powder
1/2 teaspoon kosher salt
1/2 teaspoon baking soda
1 cup almond flour
1/2 stick butter
2 tablespoons water
2 eggs
For the Filling:
1 teaspoon dried rosemary
1 ½ cups Cheddar cheese,shredded
1/2 teaspoon dried basil
1/2 cup mayonnaise
2 eggs
1/2 cup sour cream
10 ounces smoked tilapia, chopped
Salt and ground black pepper, to taste
1 teaspoon Dijon mustard

Directions

Beforehand, heat your oven to 3600F. Add all the crust ingredients in your food processor and mix. Line the baking pan with parchment paper and press the mixture into it.

Put the crust in the middle of the preheated oven and bake for approximately 13 minutes. Then, mix all the ingredients for the filling. Spread the mixture over the pie crust.

Bake for additional 30 minutes or until the pie is golden at the sides.

Enjoy!

Nutrition: Calories 416 ,Protein 19.5g ,Fat 34.2g ,Carbs 5.5g ,Sugar 1.7g

208. Spring Shrimp Salad

Servings: 6

Preparation Time: 10minutes

Ingredients

1/2 teaspoon freshly ground black pepper

1 tablespoon wine vinegar

4 spring onions, chopped

1/2 cup sour cream

1/2 teaspoon yellow mustard

1 ½ cups radishes, sliced

1/2 cup mayonnaise

1 medium-sized lime, cut into wedges

1 tablespoon hot sauce

2 cucumbers, sliced

1 tablespoon Marsala wine

2 pounds shrimp

Directions

Pour lime wedges and salt into a large pot; Boil over high heat. After this, peel and devein the shrimp. Pour the shrimp and cook for 2 to 3 minutes until they are no longer transparent. Drain and rinse the shrimp under running water. Then, peel your shrimp.

Put the remaining ingredients into a mixing dish and mix thoroughly. Add the shrimp and stir gently to mix evenly.

Place in the refrigerator until it is chill and ready to serve.

Enjoy!

Nutrition: Calories 209 ,Protein 20.2g ,Fat 9.5g ,Carbs 6.8g ,Sugar 2.1g

209. Salmon with Pine Nuts Sauce and Sautéed Brussels Sprouts

Servings: 4

Preparation Time: 25minutes

Ingredients

1/2 pounds Brussels sprouts

1 tablespoon lime juice

1/2 cup chicken broth

1/3 cup fresh cilantro

1 pound salmon

1/3 cup pine nuts, chopped

Sea salt and freshly ground black pepper, to taste
1/4 cup olive oil
2 garlic cloves, crushed
1 teaspoon dried marjoram
1 medium-sized tomato, cut into slices
Directions
Rub black pepper, salt and marjoram on the salmon on all sides; set aside.
Now, beat pine nuts, lemon juice, cilantro, olive oil, garlic in your food processor until it becomes a smooth paste.
Heat up a nonstick skillet over moderately high heat. Spritz the base of the skillet with a nonstick cooking spray and fry the salmon on each side for 2 to 4 minutes; reserve.
In the same skillet, place Brussels sprouts and chicken broth; sauté for 4 to 6 minutes or until Brussels sprouts are as tender as you want; reserve.
In the same skillet, sear tomato slices for 2 minutes on each side.
Serve warm salmon with cilantro sauce and tomato slice topping, garnished with sautéed Brussels sprouts. Bon appétit!
Nutrition: Calories 372 ,Protein 26.5g ,Fat 27.8g ,Carbs 5.6g ,Sugar 2.6g

210.   Aromatic Red Snapper Soup

Servings: 4
Preparation Time: 20minutes
Ingredients
1/4 cup fresh cilantro, chopped
1 pound red snapper, chopped
2 garlic cloves, minced
2 cups shellfish stock
1/4 cup dry white wine
 Sea salt and ground black pepper, to taste
 2 tomatoes, pureed
 2 onions, finely chopped
1/2 stick butter, melted
2 rosemary sprigs, chopped
2 thyme sprigs, chopped
1/2 teaspoon dried dill weed
1 cup water
Directions
Preheat stockpot over moderate heat and melt the butter into the pot. Sauté the onions and garlic for 3 minutes or until aromatic.
Add the fresh cilantro and cook for 1 to 2 minutes more.
Add pureed tomatoes, fish, wine, water and stock; bring to a boil.
Reduce the heat and let it simmer until the fish is properly cooked about 15 minutes.
Add the remaining seasonings and serve warm.
Nutrition: Calories 316 ,Protein 32.7g ,Fat 14.3g ,Carbs 6.6g ,Sugar 2.1g

211.   Easy Fried Tiger Prawns

Servings: 4
Preparation Time: 10minutes
Ingredients
1 teaspoon dried rosemary
2 tablespoons dry sherry
1/2 stick butter, at room temperature
1/2 teaspoon mustard seeds
1 ½ tablespoons fresh lime juice
1 tablespoon garlic paste
1 ½ pounds tiger prawns, peeled and deveined
1 teaspoon red pepper flakes, crushed
Salt and ground black pepper, to taste
Directions
Place a mustard seed, dry sherry, lime juice,flakes, rosemary, garlic paste and red pepper in a mixing bowl and mix thoroughly.
Add the prawns to the mixture in the mixing dish and leave to marinate for 1 hour in the refrigerator.
Preheat skillet over medium-high heat and melt the butter in it. Dispose of the marinade and fry prawns for 3 to 5 minutes turning once or twice.
Season with salt and pepper to taste.
Serve warm and enjoy!
Nutrition: Calories 294 ,Protein 34.6g ,Fat 14.3g ,Carbs 3.6g ,Sugar 0.1g

212.   Saucy Chilean Sea Bass with Dijon Sauce

Servings: 4
Preparation Time: 15minutes
Ingredients
1 cup scallions, chopped
1/2 cup dry sherry wine
1/2 teaspoon paprika
1 teaspoon Dijon mustard
2 cloves garlic, minced
1 pound wild Chilean sea bass, cubed
1/4 teaspoon ground black pepper
1 tablespoon avocado oil
1 cup double cream
2 Poblano pepper, chopped
Sea salt, to taste
Directions
Toss the fish, garlic, peppers, salt, wine, paprika and scallion in a mixing bowl. Leave in the refrigerator for 2 hours to marinate.
Warm avocado oil in a cast-iron skillet over a medium heat.
Cook the fish and marinade until it is thoroughly cooked, about 5 minutes; reserve cooked fish.
In the same skillet, add the double cream, ground black pepper and Dijon mustard.
Bring to a boil, and then, reduce the heat.
Continue cooking until everything is heated through, approximately 3 minutes.

Add the fish back to the skillet, remove from heat and serve immediately.
Nutrition: Calories 228 ,Protein 13.7g ,Fat 13g ,Carbs 6.5g ,Sugar 2.1g

213.   Two-Cheese and Smoked Salmon Dip

Servings: 10
Preparation Time: 10minutes
Ingredients
10 ounces smoked salmon, chopped
5 ounces Cottage cheese
5 ounces Feta cheese
4 hard-boiled egg yolks, finely chopped
Salt and freshly ground black pepper, to your liking
1/2 teaspoon smoked paprika
1/4 cup fresh chives, chopped
Directions
Place all ingredients, except for chopped chives into a mixing dish.
Stir well until the mixture is evenly mixed.
Put in a mound on a dish.
Garnish with fresh chopped chives and serve well-chilled. Bon appétit!
Nutrition: Calories 109 ,Protein11.4g ,Fat 6.3g ,Carbs 1.3g ,Sugar 0.8g

214.   Halibut Steaks for Two

Servings: 2
Preparation Time: 35 minutes
Ingredients
1 teaspoon dry thyme
1/3 cup fresh cilantro, chopped
1/3 cup fresh lime juice
2 teaspoons olive oil
1/3 teaspoon salt
2 halibut steaks
1/3 teaspoon pepper
1 teaspoon garlic, finely minced
1 teaspoon dry dill weed
Directions
In a mixing bowl, combine fresh lime juice with olive oil, salt, pepper, dill, thyme and garlic. Add halibut steak and let it marinate about 20 minutes.
Now, grill your fish steaks approximately 13 minutes, turning once or twice; make sure to baste them with the reserved marinade.
Garnish with fresh cilantro leaves. Serve warm with your favorite salad. Enjoy!
Nutrition: Calories 308 ,Protein 46.5g ,Fat 10.9g ,Carbs 2g ,Sugar 0.2g

215.   Tuna and Avocado Salad with Mayo Dressing

Servings: 4

Preparation Time: 5 minutes
Ingredients
1 teaspoon deli mustard
1/2 cup Kalamata olives, pitted and sliced
2 bell peppers, deveined and sliced
2 cans tuna chunks in spring water
1 head arugula
1 red onion, chopped
1 avocado, pitted, peeled and diced
Salt and ground black pepper, to taste
2 tablespoons fresh lime juice
1 cup cherry tomatoes, halved or quartered
1/4 cup mayonnaise
Directions
Combine tuna, avocado, bell peppers, cherry tomato, arugula and onion in a salad bowl.
In a small mixing bowl, whisk the mayonnaise with mustard, salt, pepper and lime juice. Dress the salad and gently toss to combine.
Top with Kalamata olives and serve well-chilled. Bon appétit!
Nutrition: Calories 244 ,Protein 23.4g ,Fat 12.7g ,Carbs 5.3g ,Sugar 2.8g

216.   Pan-Seared Fish Fillets with Mesclun Salad

Servings: 4
Preparation Time: 15 minutes
Ingredients
4 white fish fillets
1 tablespoon butter, softened
2 tablespoons fresh coriander, chopped
2 garlic cloves, minced
2 tablespoons fresh lime juice
Salt and ground black pepper, to taste
2 tablespoons fresh chives, chopped
For Mesclun Salad:
Salt and ground black pepper, to your liking
1 cup arugula
1 head Romaine lettuce
1/4 cup extra-virgin olive oil
2 tablespoons basil, chiffonade
1 cup chicory
2 tablespoons dandelion
1/2 cup apple cider vinegar
Directions
Toss white fish fillets with garlic, salt, lime juice, chives, pepper, and coriander; permit it to marinate at least 1 hour in the refrigerator.
Dissolve the butter in a pan over a normal heat; sear the fish fillets on each side for about 4 minutes. Now, use the marinade as a basting sauce.
Meanwhile, place Romaine lettuce, arugula, chicory, basil and dandelion in a salad container.

Then, make a dressing for your salad by whisking the remaining ingredients. Now, dress the salad and serve with warm fish fillets. Bon appétit!

Nutrition: Calories 425 ,Protein 38.3g ,Fat 27.2g ,Carbs 6.1g ,Sugar 4.1g

217. Mediterranean-Style Snapper Salad

Servings: 4
Preparation Time: 15 minutes
Ingredients
4 cups baby spinach
4 snapper fillets
2 tablespoons butter, melted
12 grape tomatoes, halved
1/2 cup ripe olives, pitted and sliced
2 shallots, thinly sliced
1 teaspoon ground sumac
Sea salt and ground black pepper, to taste
6 ounces Halloumi cheese, crumbled
For the Vinaigrette:
1 teaspoon red pepper flakes, crushed
2 tablespoons fresh mint, finely chopped
1/2 tablespoon brown mustard
1 clove garlic, smashed
Sea salt and ground black pepper, to taste
1/3 cup extra-virgin olive oil
1 lemon, juiced and zested
1 teaspoon dried oregano
Directions
Place the fish fillets on a clean board and spray both sides with salt, pepper and sumac.
Then, warm the butter in a pan that is preheated over a normal flame. Fry the fish for about 5 minutes on each side.
In a nice salad container, tomatoes, toss baby spinach, shallots, cheese and olives. Then top with chopped fish.
Thoroughly merge all ingredients for the vinaigrette in your blender. Then, dress the salad and serve well-chilled. Bon appétit!

Nutrition: Calories 507 ,Protein 24.4g ,Fat 42.8g ,Carbs 6g ,Sugar 2.2g

218. Prawn Cocktail Salad

Servings: 6
Preparation Time: 10 minutes
Ingredients
2 pounds prawns, peeled leaving tails intact
1/2 cup mayonnaise
1/4 cup chopped fresh dill
Sea salt and freshly ground black pepper, to taste
1 teaspoon deli mustard

Juice from 1 fresh lemon
1/2 cup cucumber, chopped
1 cup scallions, chopped
1/2 head Romaine lettuce, torn into pieces
Directions
Start a pot of salted water to a boil; Heat the prawns for 3 minutes. Drain and pour in a mixing bowl; permit them to cool completely.
Toss carefully with the remaining ingredients. Put it in the refrigerator until ready to serve. Bon appétit!
Nutrition: Calories 196 ,Protein 21.4g ,Fat 8.3g ,Carbs 6.5g ,Sugar 2.3g

219.   Halibut en Persillade

Servings: 4
Preparation Time: 20 minutes
Ingredients
1/2 cup scallions, sliced
2 cloves garlic, finely minced
1 ½ tablespoons olive oil
2 tablespoons fresh cilantro, chopped
4 halibut steaks
1 teaspoon garlic
Salt and ground black pepper, to taste
1/4 cup fresh parsley, finely chopped
3 tablespoons clam juice
1 tablespoon fresh lime juice
2 tablespoons coconut oil, at room temperature
1 tablespoon Worcestershire sauce
1/2 teaspoon fresh ginger, grated
1 tablespoon oyster sauce
1/2 fresh lemon, zested and juiced
Directions
Heat the oil in a cast-iron skillet over a hot flame until it begins to smoke.
Fry halibut until golden brown, approximate time of 7 minutes. Turn and fry on the other side for an additional 4 minutes. Reserve.
Heat the scallions and garlic in pan drippings until tender. Include the remaining ingredients along with reserved halibut steaks, cover and heat for 5 minutes more.
Share among four plates.
Now, whisk the remaining ingredients to make Persillade sauce. Spoon over halibut steaks on the plates and enjoy.
Nutrition: Calories 273 ,Protein 22.6g ,Fat 19.2g ,Carbs 4.3g ,Sugar 1.6g

220.   Hearty Pollock Chowder

Servings: 4
Preparation Time: 30 minutes
Ingredients

2 shallots, chopped
3 cups boiling water
3 teaspoons butter
1/4 cup dry white wine
1 celery with leaves, chopped
Sea salt and ground black pepper, to taste
1/2 cup full-fat milk
1 teaspoon Old Bay seasonings
1 ¼ pounds pollock fillets, skin removed
1/2 cup clam juice
Directions
Slice pollock fillets into bite-sized pieces.
Warm the butter in a pan over an average-high flame. Heat the vegetables until they're softened. Season with pepper, salt, and Old Bay seasonings.
Mix in chopped fish and heat for 12 to 15 minutes more. Include the boiling water and clam juice. Now, pour in the white wine and milk.
Now, bring it to a boil. Decrease the heat and cook for an additional 15 minutes. Bon appétit!
Nutrition: Calories 170 ,Protein 20g ,Fat 5.8g ,Carbs 5.7g ,Sugar 2.2g

221.   Summer Fish Cakes

Servings: 6
Preparation Time: 30 minutes
Ingredients
2 tablespoons flax meal
1 tablespoon fresh chives, chopped
2 tablespoons olive oil
2 eggs, lightly beaten
1 ½ pounds cod, boned and flaked
1 tablespoon fresh cilantro, chopped
2 teaspoons Dijon mustard
1/2 cup Ricotta cheese, at room temperature
1/3 cup almond flour
Sea salt and freshly ground black pepper, to taste
Directions
Preheat your oven to 3900F. Pat the fish dry and put it in a mixing bowl.
Include the eggs; gradually include the flour and flax meal and mix to merge well. Include the remaining ingredients and mix to merge well.
Shape the mixture into 120 patties and position them on a lightly greased baking pan.
Bake for the duration of 20 to 25 minutes turning once.
Nutrition: Calories 234 ,Protein 31.2g ,Fat 10.6g ,Carbs 2.5g ,Sugar 0.2g

222.   Lemon-Rosemary Shrimps

Preparation Time: 3 Minutes
Cooking Time: 11 Minutes
Servings: 4

5 Ingredients:
½ cup lemon juice, freshly squeezed
1 ½ lb. shrimps, peeled and deveined
2 tbsp fresh rosemary
¼ cup coconut aminos
Pepper to taste
1 tsp oil
Directions:
Place a nonstick saucepan on medium high fire and heat oil for 2 minutes.
Stir in shrimps and coconut aminos. Season with pepper. Sauté for 5 minutes.
Add remaining ingredients and cook for another 5 minutes while stirring frequently.
Serve and enjoy.
Nutrition:
Calories: 184; Fat: 2.4g; Carbs: 3.7g; Protein: 35.8g

223.   Golden Pompano in Microwave

Preparation Time: 20 Minutes
Cooking Time: 11 Minutes
Servings: 2
5 Ingredients:
½-lb pompano
1 tbsp soy sauce, low sodium
1-inch thumb ginger, diced
1 lemon, halved
1 stalk green onions, chopped
¼ cup water
1 tsp pepper
Directions:
In a microwavable casserole dish, mix well all ingredients except for pompano, green onions and lemon.
Squeeze a half of the lemon in dish and slice into thin circles the other half.
Place pompano in dish and add lemon circles on top of fish.
Cover top of casserole dish with a microwave safe plate.
Microwave for 5 minutes.
Remove from microwave, turn over fish, sprinkle green onions, top with microwavable plate.
Return to microwave and cook for another 3 minutes.
Let it rest for 3 minutes more.
Serve and enjoy.
Nutrition:
Calories: 244.5; Fat: 14.5g; Carbs: 6.3g; Protein: 22.2g

224.   Grilled Salmon Teriyaki Steaks

Preparation Time: 5 Minutes
Cooking Time: 10 Minutes
Servings: 2

5 Ingredients:
1-lb salmon fillet, skin on
1 tbsp teriyaki sauce
1 tbsp honey
1 tsp sesame seeds
2 cups spinach
½ tsp pepper
Directions:
Preheat grill to 400oF.
In a small bowl, whisk well pepper, honey, and teriyaki sauce.
Grease grate and place salmon filet. Brush tops with sauce.
Grill for 5 minutes and brush tops with sauce again. Sprinkle top with sesame seeds.
Continue grilling for 2 to 4 minutes or until desired doneness is reached.
Serve on a bed of spinach leaves and enjoy.
Nutrition:
Calories: 416.2; Fat: 14.2g; Carbs: 11.3g; Protein: 60.8g

225.   Salmon and Rice Pilaf

Preparation Time: 5 Minutes
Cooking Time: 25 Minutes
Servings: 4
5 Ingredients:
½ cup Jasmine rice
¼ cup dried vegetable soup mix
1 cup chicken broth
1 pinch saffron
1-lb wild salmon fillets
Pepper and salt to taste
Directions:
Place a heavy bottomed pot on medium high fire and add all ingredients and mix well.
Cover, bring to a boil, lower fire to a simmer, and simmer for 10 minutes.
Turn off fire, fluff rice, shred salmon, adjust seasoning to taste.
Let it rest for 5 minutes.
Fluff again, serve and enjoy.
Nutrition:
Calories: 578.5; Fat: 8.5g; Carbs: 93.7g; Protein: 31.8g

226.   Lemon Chili Halibut

Preparation Time: 5 Minutes
Cooking Time: 15 Minutes
Servings: 2
5 Ingredients:
1-lb halibut fillets
1 lemon, sliced
1 tablespoon chili pepper flakes

Pepper and salt to taste

Directions:

In a heat-proof dish that fits inside saucepan, place fish. Top fish with chili flakes, lemon slices, salt, and pepper. Cover dish with foil

Place a large saucepan on medium high fire. Place a trivet inside saucepan and fill pan halfway with water. Cover and bring to a boil.

Place dish on trivet.

Cover pan and steam for 10 minutes. Let it rest in pan for another 5 minutes.

Serve and enjoy topped with pepper.

Nutrition:

Calories: 216.4; Fat: 3.2g; Carbs: 4.2g; Protein: 42.7g

227. Chipotle Salmon Asparagus

Preparation Time: 25 Minutes

Cooking Time: 15 Minutes

Servings: 2

5 Ingredients:

1-lb salmon fillet, skin on

2 teaspoon chipotle paste

A handful of asparagus spears, trimmed

1 lemon, sliced thinly

Salt to taste

Directions:

In a heat-proof dish that fits inside saucepan, add asparagus spears on bottom of dish. Place fish, top with rosemary and lemon slices. Season with chipotle paste and salt. Cover dish with foil.

Place a large saucepan on medium high fire. Place a trivet inside saucepan and fill pan halfway with water. Cover and bring to a boil.

Place dish on trivet.

Cover pan and steam for 10 minutes. Let it rest in pan for another 5 minutes.

Serve and enjoy topped with pepper.

Nutrition:

Calories: 161.1; Fat: 1.1g; Carbs: 2.8g; Protein: 35.0g

228. Fish Filet in Sweet Orange Sauce

Preparation Time: 15 Minutes

Cooking Time: 15 Minutes

Servings: 4

5 Ingredients:

1 ½-lbs white fish fillets

Juice and zest of 2 oranges

1 thumb-size ginger, grated

1 tbsp honey

4 spring onions, chopped

Pepper and salt to taste

Directions:

In a heat-proof dish that fits inside saucepan, whisk well orange juice, orange zest, ginger, honey, and pepper. Place fish and marinate for 10 minutes. Top with green onions and cover dish with foil
Place a large saucepan on medium high fire. Place a trivet inside saucepan and fill pan halfway with water. Cover and bring to a boil.
Place dish on trivet.
Cover pan and steam for 10 minutes. Let it rest in pan for another 5 minutes.
Serve and enjoy topped with pepper.
Nutrition:
Calories: 141.9; Fat: 1.1g; Carbs: 6.5g; Protein: 26.5g

229.   Enchilada Sauce on Mahi Mahi

Preparation Time: 5 Minutes
Cooking Time: 15 Minutes
Servings: 2
5 Ingredients:
2 Mahi Mahi fillets, fresh
¼ cup commercial enchilada sauce
Pepper to taste
Directions:
In a heat-proof dish that fits inside saucepan, place fish and top with enchilada sauce.
Place a large saucepan on medium high fire. Place a trivet inside saucepan and fill pan halfway with water. Cover and bring to a boil.
Cover dish with foil and place on trivet.
Cover pan and steam for 10 minutes. Let it rest in pan for another 5 minutes.
Serve and enjoy topped with pepper.
Nutrition:
Calories: 143.1; Fat: 15.9g; Carbs: 8.9g; Protein: 19.8g

230.   Simply Steamed Alaskan Cod

Preparation Time: 10 Minutes
Cooking Time: 15 Minutes
Servings: 2
5 Ingredients:
1-lb fillet wild Alaskan Cod
1 cup cherry tomatoes, halved
1 tbsp balsamic vinegar
1 tbsp fresh basil chopped
Salt and pepper to taste
Directions:
In a heat-proof dish that fits inside saucepan, add all ingredients except for basil. Mix well.
Place a large saucepan on medium high fire. Place a trivet inside saucepan and fill pan halfway with water. Cover and bring to a boil.
Cover dish with foil and place on trivet.
Cover pan and steam for 10 minutes. Let it rest in pan for another 5 minutes.
Serve and enjoy topped with fresh basil.

Nutrition:
Calories: 195.2; Fat: 1.6g; Carbs: 4.2g; Protein: 41.0g

231. Steamed Ginger Scallion Fish

Preparation Time: Minutes
Cooking Time: Minutes
Servings:
5 Ingredients:
3 tablespoons soy sauce, low sodium
2 tablespoons rice wine
1 teaspoon minced ginger
1 teaspoon garlic
1-pound firm white fish
Pepper to taste
Directions:
In a heat-proof dish that fits inside saucepan, add all ingredients. Mix well.
Place a large saucepan on medium high fire. Place a trivet inside saucepan and fill pan halfway with water. Cover and bring to a boil.
Cover dish with foil and place on trivet.
Cover pan and steam for 10 minutes. Let it rest in pan for another 5 minutes.
Serve and enjoy.
Nutrition:
Calories: 409.5; Fat: 23.1g; Carbs: 5.5g; Protein: 44.9g

232. Sweet and Spicy Dolphinfish Filets

Preparation Time: 10 Minutes
Cooking Time: 15 Minutes
Servings: 2
5 Ingredients:
2 Dolphinfish filets
2 cloves of garlic, minced
1 thumb-size ginger, grated
2 tablespoons honey
2 tablespoons sriracha
Pepper to taste
Directions:
In a heat-proof dish that fits inside saucepan, add all ingredients. Mix well.
Place a large saucepan on medium high fire. Place a trivet inside saucepan and fill pan halfway with water. Cover and bring to a boil.
Cover dish with foil and place on trivet.
Cover pan and steam for 10 minutes. Let it rest in pan for another 5 minutes.
Serve and enjoy.
Nutrition:
Calories: 348.4; Fat: 2.2g; Carbs: 22.3g; Protein: 38.6g

233.   Sautéed Savory Shrimps

Preparation Time: 5 Minutes
Cooking Time: 15 Minutes
Servings: 8
5 Ingredients:
2 pounds shrimp, peeled and deveined
4 cloves garlic, minced
2 cups frozen sweet corn kernels
½ cup chicken stock, low sodium
1 tablespoon lemon juice
Pepper
1 tablespoon oil
Directions:
Place a heavy bottomed pot on medium high fire and heat pot for 3 minutes.
Once hot, add oil and stir around to coat pot with oil.
Sauté the garlic and corn for 5 minutes.
Add remaining ingredients and mix well.
Cover, bring to a boil, lower fire to a simmer, and simmer for 5 minutes.
Serve and enjoy.
Nutrition:
Calories: 180.6; Fat: 3.8g; Carbs: 11.4g; Protein: 25.2g

234.   Coconut Milk Sauce over Crabs

Preparation Time: 10 Minutes
Cooking Time: 20 Minutes
Servings: 6
5 Ingredients:
2-pounds crab quartered
1 can coconut milk
1 thumb-size ginger, sliced
1 onion, chopped
3 cloves of garlic, minced
Pepper and salt to taste
Directions:
Place a heavy bottomed pot on medium high fire and add all ingredients.
Cover, bring to a boil, lower fire to a simmer, and simmer for 20 minutes.
Serve and enjoy.
Nutrition:
Calories: 244.1; Fat: 11.3g; Carbs: 6.3g; Protein: 29.3g

235.   Steamed Asparagus and Shrimps

Preparation Time: 15 Minutes
Cooking Time: 15 Minutes
Servings: 6

5 Ingredients:

1-pound shrimps, peeled and deveined

1 bunch asparagus, trimmed

½ tablespoon Cajun seasoning

1 teaspoon oil

Salt and pepper to taste

Directions:

In a heat-proof dish that fits inside saucepan, add all ingredients. Mix well.

Place a large saucepan on medium high fire. Place a trivet inside saucepan and fill pan halfway with water. Cover and bring to a boil.

Cover dish with foil and place on trivet.

Cover pan and steam for 10 minutes. Let it rest in pan for another 5 minutes.

Serve and enjoy.

Nutrition:

Calories: 79.8; Fat: 1.8g; Carbs: 0.4g; Protein: 15.5g

236.   Tasty Corn and Clam Stew

Preparation Time: Minutes

Cooking Time: Minutes

Servings:

5 Ingredients:

1-lb clam

1 cup frozen corn

4 cloves garlic

1 tsp celery seeds

1 tsp Cajun seasoning

1 tsp oil

½ cup water

Directions:

Place a nonstick saucepan on medium high fire and heat pot for 3 minutes.

Once hot, add oil and stir around to coat pot with oil.

Sauté the garlic for a minute.

Add remaining ingredients, except for clams and mix well. Cook for 3 minutes.

Stir in clams.

Cover, bring to a boil, lower fire to a simmer, and simmer for 5 minutes.

Serve and enjoy. Discard any unopened clam.

Nutrition:

Calories: 120; Fat: 2.0g; Carbs: 23.2g; Protein: 2.3g

237.   Yummy Shrimp Fried Rice

Preparation Time: 10 Minutes

Cooking Time: 20 Minutes

Servings: 6

5 Ingredients:

4 tablespoons butter, divided

4 large eggs, lightly beaten
3 cups cold cooked rice
1 package (16 ouncesfrozen mixed vegetables
1-pound uncooked medium shrimp, peeled and deveined
1/2 teaspoon salt
1/4 teaspoon pepper
Directions:
In a large skillet, melt 1 tablespoon butter over medium-high heat.
Pour eggs into skillet. As eggs set, lift edges, letting uncooked portion flow underneath. Remove eggs and keep warm.
Melt remaining butter in the skillet. Add the rice, vegetables and shrimp; cook and stir for 5 minutes or until shrimp turn pink.
Meanwhile, chop eggs into small pieces. Return eggs to the pan; sprinkle with salt and pepper. Cook until heated through, stirring occasionally. Sprinkle with bacon if desired.
Nutrition:
Calories: 332; Fat: 12g; Carbs: 33g; Protein: 21g

238. Cod with Balsamic Tomatoes

Preparation Time: 5 Minutes
Cooking Time: 30 Minutes
Servings: 4
5 Ingredients:
4 center-cut bacon strips, chopped
4 cod fillets (5 ounces each
2 cups grape tomatoes, halved
2 tablespoons balsamic vinegar
1/2 teaspoon salt
1/4 teaspoon pepper
Directions:
In a large skillet, cook bacon over medium heat until crisp, stirring occasionally.
Remove with a slotted spoon; drain on paper towels.
Sprinkle fillets with salt and pepper. Add fillets to bacon drippings; cook over medium-high heat until fish just begins to flake easily with a fork, 4-6 minutes on each side. Remove and keep warm.
Add tomatoes to skillet; cook and stir until tomatoes are softened, 2-4 minutes. Stir in vinegar; reduce heat to medium-low. Cook until sauce is thickened, 1-2 minutes longer.
Serve cod with tomato mixture and bacon.
Nutrition:
Calories: 178; Fat: 6g; Carbs: 5g; Protein: 26g

239. Buttery Almond Lemon Tilapia

Preparation Time: 5 Minutes
Cooking Time: 10 Minutes
Servings: 4
5 Ingredients:
4 tilapia fillets (4 ounces each

1/4 cup butter, cubed
1/4 cup white wine or chicken broth
2 tablespoons lemon juice
1/4 cup sliced almonds
1/2 teaspoon salt
1/4 teaspoon pepper
1 tablespoon olive oil
Directions:
Sprinkle fillets with salt and pepper. In a large nonstick skillet, heat oil over medium heat.
Add fillets; cook until fish just begins to flake easily with a fork, 2-3 minutes on each side. Remove and keep warm.
Add butter, wine and lemon juice to same pan; cook and stir until butter is melted.
Serve with fish; sprinkle with almonds.
Nutrition:
Calories: 269; Fat: 19g; Carbs: 2g; Protein: 22g

240.   Clam Chowder

Preparation Time: 5 Minutes
Cooking Time: 15 Minutes
Servings: 5
5 Ingredients:
1 can (10-3/4 ouncescondensed cream of celery soup, undiluted
1 can (10-3/4 ouncescondensed cream of potato soup, undiluted
2 cups half-and-half cream
2 cans (6-1/2 ounces eachminced/chopped clams, drained
1/4 teaspoon ground nutmeg
1 teaspoon salt
Pepper
Directions:
In a large saucepan, combine all ingredients.
Cook and stir over medium heat until heated through.
Serve and enjoy.
Nutrition:
Calories: 251; Fat: 14g; Carbs: 18g; Protein: 10g

241.   Cilantro Shrimp

Preparation Time: 5 Minutes
Cooking Time: 10 Minutes
Servings: 4
5 Ingredients:
1/2 cup reduced-fat Asian sesame salad dressing
1-pound uncooked shrimp (31-40 per pound, peeled and deveined
Lime wedges
1/4 cup chopped fresh cilantro
Hot cooked brown rice, optional

Salt

Pepper

Directions:

In a large nonstick skillet, heat 1 tablespoon dressing over medium heat. Add shrimp; cook and stir 1 minute.

Stir in remaining dressing; cook, uncovered, until shrimp turn pink, 1-2 minutes longer.

To serve, squeeze lime juice over top; sprinkle with cilantro, pepper, and salt. If desired, serve with rice.

Nutrition:

Calories: 153; Fat: 4g; Carbs: 9g; Protein: 20g

242.   Pomegranate Orange Salmon

Preparation Time: 10 Minutes

Cooking Time: 25 Minutes

Servings: 4

5 Ingredients:

1 small red onion, thinly sliced

1 skinned salmon fillet (about 2 pounds

1 medium navel orange, thinly sliced

1 cup pomegranate seeds

1 tablespoon minced fresh dill

1/2 teaspoon salt

2 tablespoons extra virgin olive oil

Directions:

Preheat oven to 375°. Place a 28x18-in. piece of heavy-duty foil in a 15 x 10 x1 inch baking pan.

Place onion slices in a single layer on foil. Top with salmon; sprinkle with salt. Arrange orange slices over top. Sprinkle with pomegranate seeds; drizzle with oil. Top with a second piece of foil.

Bring edges of foil together on all sides and crimp to seal, forming a large packet.

Bake until fish just begins to flake easily with a fork, 25-30 minutes.

Remove to a platter; sprinkle with dill.

Nutrition:

Calories: 307; Fat: 19g; Carbs: 8g; Protein: 26g

243.   Shrimp Spread

Preparation Time: 10 Minutes

Cooking Time: 0 Minutes

Servings: 20

5 Ingredients:

1 package (8 ouncescream cheese, softened

1/2 cup sour cream

1 cup seafood cocktail sauce

12 ounces frozen cooked salad shrimp, thawed

1 medium green pepper, chopped

Pepper

Directions:

In a large bowl, beat the cream cheese, and sour cream until smooth.
Spread mixture on a round 12-in. platter.
Top with seafood sauce.
Sprinkle with shrimp and green peppers. Cover and refrigerate.
Serve with crackers.
Nutrition:
Calories: 136; Fat: 10g; Carbs: 4g; Protein: 8g

244.   Coconut Shrimp

Preparation Time: 5 Minutes
Cooking Time: 20 Minutes
Servings: 6
5 Ingredients:
1-pound uncooked jumbo shrimp (about 12, peeled and deveined
1/4 cup all-purpose flour
2 large egg whites, lightly beaten
1-1/3 cups sweetened shredded coconut
1 jar (12 ouncespineapple preserves
Oil for deep-fat frying
Directions:
Starting with the tail, make a slit down the inner curve of each shrimp; press lightly to flatten.
In three separate shallow bowls, place the flour, egg whites and coconut.
Coat the shrimp with flour; dip into egg whites, then coat with the coconut.
In an electric skillet or deep-fat fryer, heat oil to 375°F. Fry shrimp, a few at a time, for 1 to 1-1/2 minutes on each side or until golden brown.
Drain on paper towels.
Nutrition:
Calories: 204; Fat: 8g; Carbs: 26g; Protein: 7g

245.   Blue Cheese Shrimps

Preparation Time: 5 Minutes
Cooking Time: 15 Minutes
Servings: 6
5 Ingredients:
3 ounces cream cheese, softened
2/3 cup minced fresh parsley, divided
1/4 cup crumbled blue cheese
1/2 teaspoon Creole mustard
24 cooked jumbo shrimp, peeled and deveined
Pepper and salt to taste
Directions:
In a small bowl, beat cream cheese until smooth. Beat in 1/3 cup parsley, blue cheese, and mustard.
Season with pepper and salt as desired. Refrigerate at least 1 hour.
Make a deep slit along the back of each shrimp to within 1/4-1/2 in. of the bottom. Stuff with cream cheese mixture; press remaining parsley onto cream cheese mixture.

Nutrition:
Calories: 43; Fat: 2g; Carbs: 0g; Protein: 6g

246.   Honey Lime Shrimps

Preparation Time: 5 Minutes
Cooking Time: 3 Minutes
Servings: 4
5 Ingredients:
6 thin slices pancetta
18 uncooked large shrimp, peeled and deveined
1/4 cup honey
2 tablespoons lime juice
1 tablespoon minced fresh cilantro
1 teaspoon hot water
Directions:
Preheat oven to 375°F.Cut each slice of pancetta into three strips. Wrap one strip around each shrimp; secure with a toothpick. Place in a foil-lined 15 x 10 x1 inch baking pan.
In a small bowl, whisk honey, lime juice and water until blended; reserve 2 tablespoons for brushing cooked shrimp.
Brush half the remaining honey mixture over shrimp. Bake 5 minutes. Turn shrimp; brush with remaining half of the honey mixture.
Bake 4-6 minutes longer or until pancetta is crisp and shrimp turns pink.
Remove from oven; brush with reserved 2 tablespoons honey mixture. Sprinkle with cilantro.
Nutrition:
Calories: 89; Fat: .3g; Carbs: 18.4g; Protein: 4.4g

247.   Garlicky Mackerel Fillets

Preparation Time: 15 minutes
Servings: 2
Nutrition: 481 Calories; 14.5g Fat; 1.1g Carbs; 80g Protein; 0.1g Fiber
Ingredients
2 mackerel fillets
1 tablespoon olive oil
1/2 teaspoon thyme
1 teaspoon rosemary
2 garlic cloves, minced
Directions
In a frying pan, heat the oil over medium-high heat.
Sear the fish fillets for about 5 minutes per side until crisp.
Add in the garlic, thyme, and rosemary and continue to cook for 30 seconds more. Enjoy!

248.   Fisherman's Tilapia Burgers

Preparation Time: 50 minutes
Servings: 5
Nutrition: 238 Calories; 10.9g Fat; 2.6g Carbs; 32.9g Protein; 1.2g Fiber
Ingredients
1 ½ pounds tilapia fish, broken into chunks
1 tablespoon Cajun seasoning mix
1/2 cup shallots, chopped
1/2 cup almond flour
2 eggs, whisked
Directions
In a mixing bowl, thoroughly combine all ingredients. Form the mixture into 10 patties; refrigerate for 30 to 35 minutes.
Spritz a nonstick skillet and place it over medium-high flame. Fry your burgers for about 4 minutes per side until golden brown.
Garnish with lemon slices and enjoy!

249. Hearty Fisherman's Stew

Preparation Time: 30 minutes
Servings: 4
Nutrition: 271 Calories; 19.5g Fat; 4.8g Carbs; 18.5g Protein; 1g Fiber
Ingredients
1 pound halibut, cut into bite-sized chunks
1 ripe fresh tomato, pureed
1 tablespoon tallow, room temperature
1 red onion, chopped
2 garlic cloves, smashed
Directions
Melt the tallow in a soup pot over medium-high heat. Then, sauté the onion for 3 to 4 minutes until just tender and fragrant; stir in the garlic and continue to sauté for 30 seconds more until fragrant.
Add in tomato and continue to cook for 7 to 8 minutes, stirring periodically. Pour in 3 cups of shellfish stock or water. Add in halibut and season with the salt and black pepper to taste.
Reduce temperature to a simmer and continue to cook, partially covered, for 15 to 18 minutes longer. Ladle into individual bowls and serve hot.

250. Thai Salmon Curry

Preparation Time: 20 minutes
Servings: 4
Nutrition: 246 Calories; 16.2g Fat; 4.9g Carbs; 20.3g Protein; 0.6g Fiber
Ingredients
3/4 pound salmon, cut into bite-sized chunks
6 ounces full-fat coconut milk, canned
1 tablespoon coconut oil
1/2 cup leeks, chopped

1 teaspoon turmeric powder
Directions
Melt coconut oil in a heavy-bottomed pot over medium-high flame. Sauté the leeks for about 3 minutes or until tender and fragrant.

Add in turmeric powder and coconut milk; pour in 2 cups of water or fish stock. Fold in salmon chunks.

Reduce temperature to medium-low and continue to simmer for 10 to 12 minutes more. Serve hot!

251.   Bay Shrimp and Mushrooms

Preparation Time: 35 minutes
Servings: 6
Nutrition: 297 Calories; 18.3g Fat; 5.5g Carbs; 28g Protein; 1.3g Fiber
Ingredients
1 ½ pounds large-sized button mushroom cups
6 tablespoons mayonnaise
8 ounces ricotta cheese, softened
1 cup cheddar cheese, shredded
16 ounces fresh Bay shrimp, chopped
Directions
Bake the mushrooms in the preheated oven at 380 degrees F for 15 minutes until they are just tender.

Melt 1 tablespoon of butter in a saucepan over medium-high heat. Cook Bay shrimp for 1 to 2 minutes.

Add in mayonnaise and ricotta cheese; stir to combine well.

Divide the shrimp mixture between mushroom cups; bake for about 10 minutes. Top with cheddar cheese and continue to bake for 7 to 8 minutes until hot and bubbly. Enjoy!

252.   Catfish and Cauliflower Bake

Preparation Time: 30 minutes
Servings: 4
Nutrition: 510 Calories; 40g Fat; 5.5g Carbs; 1.6g Fiber; 31.3g Protein;
Ingredients
24 ounces catfish, cut into pieces
2 ounces butter, cold
11 ounces cauliflower
1 cup cream cheese
1 egg
Directions
Begin by preheating your oven to 385 degrees F. Then, spritz a baking dish with a nonstick cooking spray.

Heat 1 tablespoon of sesame oil in a saucepan over medium-high flame; cook the cauliflower for about 5 minutes.

Place the cauliflower in the prepared baking dish. Sprinkle with salt and black pepper. Place catfish on top.

In a bowl, combine cream cheese and egg. Spread this mixture on the cauliflower.

Top with butter and bake for about 20 minutes or until heated through. Bon appétit!

253.   Snapper and Vegetable Mélange

Preparation Time: 20 minutes
Servings: 4
Nutrition: 151 Calories; 3g Fat; 5.8g Carbs; 1.5g Fiber; 24.4g Protein;
Ingredients
1 teaspoon sesame oil
1/2 cup scallions, thinly sliced
1/2 teaspoon garlic, crushed
1 pound snapper, cut into bite-sized pieces
2 ripe tomatoes, crushed
Directions
Heat sesame oil in a heavy-bottomed pot over medium-high heat. Sauté the scallions until they have softened or about 3 minutes.

Now, sauté the garlic for 30 seconds more.

Add in snapper and tomatoes and reduce the heat to simmer. Continue to cook for 13 to 15 minutes or until the fish flakes easily and the sauce has thickened slightly. Bon appétit!

254.   Tuna and Ham Wraps

Preparation Time: 10 minutes + chilling time
Servings: 3
Nutrition: 308 Calories; 19.9g Fat; 4.3g Carbs; 27.8g Protein; 2.5g Fiber
Ingredients
1/2 pound ahi tuna steak
1/2 Hass avocado, peeled, pitted and sliced
6 slices of ham
6 lettuce leaves
1/2 cup dry white wine
Directions
Pour 1/2 cup of water into a saucepan; add in wine and bring to a boil. Add in tuna steak and simmer for 3 to 5 minutes.

Cut tuna into bite-sized chunks. Place tuna pieces on the ham.

Top with avocado; drizzle with fresh lemon juice, if desired. Roll them up and serve on lettuce leaves. Enjoy!

255.   Tuna with Sriracha Sauce

Preparation Time: 25 minutes
Servings: 4
Nutrition: 389 Calories; 17.9g Fat; 3.5g Carbs; 50.3g Protein; 0.3g Fiber
Ingredients
4 tuna fillets
4 tablespoons mayonnaise
1/2 cup sour cream
1 teaspoon Sriracha sauce
2 scallions, chopped
Directions
Start by preheating your oven to 380 degrees F. Brush tuna fillets with 1 tablespoon of peanut oil and season with salt and pepper. Top with chopped scallions.
Wrap tuna fillets in foil, making the packet.
Bake for 18 to 20 minutes or until opaque and fork-tender.
Mix mayonnaise, sour cream, and Sriracha sauce in a bowl. Serve warm tuna with the sauce on the side and enjoy!

256.   Asian-Style Scallops and Mushrooms

Preparation Time: 15 minutes
Servings: 4
Nutrition: 236 Calories; 12.5g Fat; 5.9g Carbs; 27g Protein; 2.4g Fiber
Ingredients
1 pound bay scallops
1/2 cup enoki mushrooms
1/2 cup yellow onion, sliced
1 cup asparagus spears, sliced
1/2 cup dry roasted peanuts, roughly chopped
Directions
In a wok, warm 1 teaspoon of the sesame oil over medium-high heat. Cook the onion until tender and fragrant; set aside.
In the same wok, warm another teaspoon of the sesame oil; fry your asparagus for 2 to 3 minutes until crisp-tender; set aside.
Heat another teaspoon of the sesame oil and sauté enoki mushrooms for 1 to 2 minutes until they begin to soften; reserve.
Heat the remaining teaspoon of sesame oil and cook bay scallops until they are opaque.
Stir all ingredients into the wok and serve with roasted peanuts. Enjoy!

257.   Classic Louisiana-Style Gumbo

Preparation Time: 30 minutes
Servings: 6
Nutrition: 530 Calories; 40.5g Fat; 5.1g Carbs; 31.8g Protein; 1g Fiber
Ingredients
1 pound andouille sausage, sliced

1 red onion, chopped
2 tomatoes, pureed
2 pounds halibut, cut into bite-sized chunks
1 pound lump crabmeat
Directions
Melt 1 teaspoon of the butter in a stockpot over moderate heat. Cook andouille sausage for about 3 minutes; set aside.
Melt the 2 teaspoons of butter and sauté the onion until tender and fragrant or about 3 to 4 minutes.
Now, stir in tomatoes and halibut' pour in 4 cups of water or beef broth; bring to a rapid boil. Turn the heat to simmer, partially covered, and continue to cook for 13 to 15 minutes.
Add in the Cajun seasoning blend if desired; return the reserved sausage to the stockpot. Continue to cook for about 5 minutes or until thoroughly cooked. Enjoy!

258.   One-Skillet Mackerel with Clam

Preparation Time: 15 minutes
Servings: 3
Nutrition: 379 Calories; 8.7g Fat; 3.7g Carbs; 60.1g Protein; 0.1g Fiber
Ingredients
2 mackerel fillets, patted dry
9 littleneck clams, scrubbed
1/2 cup dry white wine
1 shallot, finely chopped
2 cloves garlic, minced
Directions
In a cast-iron skillet, heat 1 teaspoon of the olive oil and swirl to coat well. Cook your fish for about 6 minutes; reserve.
Heat another teaspoon of olive oil and sauté the shallot and garlic until tender and fragrant about 2 minutes.
Add in the wine to scrape up the browned bits that stick to the bottom of the skillet. Add in Cajun seasoning blend and cook for 4 to 5 minutes more.
Stir in the clams and continue to cook for about 6 minutes or until they open. Add the fish back to the skillet, gently stir and serve warm.

259.   Sea Bass in Dijon Sauce

Preparation Time: 20 minutes
Servings: 3
Nutrition: 314 Calories; 23.2g Fat; 1.4g Carbs; 24.2g Protein; 0.3g Fiber
Ingredients
3 sea bass fillets
2 tablespoons olive oil
3 tablespoons butter
2 cloves garlic, minced
1 tablespoon Dijon mustard

Directions

Pat dry the sea bass fillets. Heat olive oil in a frying pan over medium-high flame.

Cook the fish fillets for 4 to 5 minutes on each side until they are opaque. Season with red pepper and salt to taste.

In another saucepan, melt the butter over low flame; sauté the garlic for 30 seconds. Add in mustard and continue to simmer for 2 to 3 minutes.

Serve warm fish fillets with Dijon sauce and enjoy!

260.   Spicy Tiger Prawns

Preparation Time: 15 minutes
Servings: 6
Nutrition: 219 Calories; 6.5g Fat; 2.7g Carbs; 39g Protein; 0.6g Fiber
Ingredients
2 ½ pounds tiger prawns, deveined
2 bell peppers, chopped
2 scallions, chopped
1/2 cup Marsala wine
3 tablespoons olive oil
Directions
In a saucepan, heat olive oil until sizzling. Cook the peppers and scallions for about 4 minutes or until tender and fragrant.

Stir in tiger prawns and cook for 2 minutes or until they are cooked all the way through.

Pour in wine, reduce the heat to simmer, and continue to cook for 5 to 6 minutes. Bon appétit!

261.   Creole Fish Stew

Preparation Time: 20 minutes
Servings: 4
Nutrition: 216 Calories; 9.4g Fat; 8.1g Carbs; 24.2g Protein; 1.4g Fiber
Ingredients
16 ounces haddock steak, cut into bite-sized chunks
4 ounces turkey smoked sausage, sliced
1 onion, chopped
2 tomatoes, pureed
1 celery stalk, chopped
Directions
Melt 2 tablespoons of butter in a stockpot over medium-high heat. Sauté the onion and celery for 2 to 3 minutes until they have softened.

Add in the sausage and pureed tomatoes; season with Creole seasoning blend.

Add in 2 cups of water or fish broth and bring to a rolling boil. Turn the heat to medium-low.

Stir in haddock steak, partially cover, and continue to cook for 13 to 15 minutes. Serve in individual bowls and enjoy!

262.   Shrimp and Sea Scallop Medley

Preparation Time: 15 minutes
Servings: 2
Nutrition: 305 Calories; 8.8g Fat; 2.7g Carbs; 47.3g Protein; 0.7g Fiber
Ingredients
1/2 pound shrimp, deveined
1/2 pound sea scallops
1/2 cup scallions, chopped
1/2 cup fish broth
1 garlic clove, minced
Directions
In a saucepan, heat 1 tablespoon of olive oil. Once hot, cook the scallions and garlic for 2 to 3 minutes or until they are fragrant.
Cook the shrimp and sea scallops for about 3 minutes or until they are opaque. You can add a splash of rum to deglaze the pan.
Pour in the fish broth; season with Cajun spice mix. Serve in individual bowls and enjoy!

263.   Halibut Steaks with Herbs

Preparation Time: 20 minutes
Servings: 2
Nutrition: 502 Calories; 19.1g Fat; 5.7g Carbs; 72g Protein; 1g Fiber
Ingredients
2 halibut steaks
2 tablespoons olive oil
1 teaspoon fish seasoning mix
1 red bell pepper, sliced
1 yellow onion, sliced
Directions
Begin by preheating an oven to 380 degrees F.
Brush the halibut steaks with olive oil and transfer them to a lightly-greased baking dish.
Top with the bell peppers and onion. Sprinkle fish seasoning mix over everything. Bake in the preheated oven for about 15 minutes. Bon appétit!

264.   Warm Shrimp and Vegetable Salad

Preparation Time: 10 minutes
Servings: 4
Nutrition: 268 Calories; 8g Fat; 3.5g Carbs; 46.3g Protein; 0.6g Fiber
Ingredients
2 pounds large shrimp, peeled and deveined
1 red onion, sliced
2 garlic cloves, sliced
2 Italian peppers, sliced

1 cup arugula
Directions
Pat the shrimp dry with a kitchen towel. In a preheated grill, cook the shrimp for 3 to 4 minutes until they are cooked all the way through.
Place the prepared shrimp in a salad bowl. Stir in the onion, garlic, Italian peppers, and arugula. Then, toss the ingredients with 2 tablespoons of olive oil and fresh lime juice. Serve and enjoy!

265.   White Sea Bass Chowder

Preparation Time: 20 minutes
Servings: 4
Nutrition: 257 Calories; 17.8g Fat; 3.8g Carbs; 21.3g Protein; 0.4g Fiber
Ingredients
3/4 pound sea bass, broken into chunks
2 teaspoons butter, at room temperature
1 cup double cream
1/2 white onion, chopped
1 tablespoon Old Bay seasoning
Directions
In a soup pot, melt the butter over medium-high heat. Sauté the onion until just tender.
Stir in Old Bay seasoning along with 3 cups of water; bring to a boil. Turn the heat to medium-low and allow it to simmer for about 10 minutes.
Now, stir in the sea bass and double cream; continue to simmer for about 5 minutes until cooked through. Serve in individual bowls.

266.   Sardine Burgers with Romano Cheese

Preparation Time: 15 minutes
Servings: 3
Nutrition: 267 Calories; 21.3g Fat; 6.1g Carbs; 13.5g Protein; 3.3g Fiber
Ingredients
2 tablespoons butter
1 egg, beaten
1/2 onion, chopped
2 (5.5-ouncescanned sardines, drained
2 ounces Romano cheese, preferably freshly grated
Directions
In a mixing dish, combine sardines, cheese, egg, and onion; season with Italian spice blend. Shape the mixture into six equal patties.
Melt the butter in a nonstick skillet over medium-high heat. Once hot, cook your burgers for about 5 minutes per side. Bon appétit!

267.   Creamed Shrimp Chowder

Preparation Time: 30 minutes
Servings: 4
Nutrition: 253 Calories; 18.8g Fat; 2.9g Carbs; 19g Protein; 0.4g Fiber
Ingredients
1 cup broccoli, broken into small florets
12 ounces shrimp, peeled and deveined
2 tablespoons coconut oil
1 shallot, chopped
1 cup double cream
Directions
Melt the coconut oil in a stockpot over medium-high flame. Cook the shallot for about 3 minutes or until tender and translucent.
Stir in the broccoli florets along with 4 cups of water or fish broth; bring to a boil. Reduce the heat to medium-low, partially cover, and let it simmer for about 10 minutes.
Fold in shrimp and double cream. Continue to simmer an additional 4 minutes just until the shrimp are done.
Taste and adjust the seasonings. Bon appétit!

268.   Cod Fillets with Greek Mustard Sauce

Preparation Time: 10 minutes
Servings: 4
Nutrition: 166 Calories; 8.2g Fat; 2.6g Carbs; 19.8g Protein; 0.3g Fiber
Ingredients
4 Alaskan cod fillets
1/2 cup Greek-style yogurt
3 tablespoons cream cheese
1 garlic clove, minced
1 teaspoon yellow mustard
Directions
Heat 1 tablespoon of coconut oil in a saucepan over a moderate heat. Sear cod fillets for about 3 minutes; flip them over and cook an additional 3 minutes on the other side.
Season with salt and ground black pepper to your liking.
To make the sauce, whisk yellow mustard, cream cheese, Greek yogurt, and garlic until well combined.
Top cod fillets with the sauce and serve immediately!

269.   One-Pan Scallops and Veggies

Preparation Time: 15 minutes
Servings: 5
Nutrition: 217 Calories; 3.5g Fat; 4.8g Carbs; 23.5g Protein; 1.2g Fiber
Ingredients
2 medium Italian peppers, deveined and sliced
1 teaspoon garlic, minced

2 pounds sea scallops
1 cup chicken broth
2 cups cauliflower florets
Directions
Melt 1 tablespoon of butter in a frying pan over a moderate heat.
Once hot, sauté Italian peppers, cauliflower, and garlic for 3 to 4 minutes or until the vegetables are tender.
Stir in the sea scallops and continue to cook for 3 minutes; stir to coat.
Pour in chicken broth and let it simmer, partially covered, for 4 minutes more. Bon appétit!

270.   Monkfish Fillets in Cheddar Sauce

Preparation Time: 20 minutes
Servings: 6
Nutrition: 229 Calories; 12.5g Fat; 2.2g Carbs; 25.9g Protein; 0.1g Fiber
Ingredients
6 monkfish fillets
1/2 cup cheddar cheese, shredded
2 green onions, sliced
1/2 cup sour cream
2 tablespoons olive oil
Directions
Heat the olive oil in a saucepan over medium-high heat. Then, sear the monkfish for 3 to 4 minutes per side or until it is golden brown.
Season with salt and black pepper to taste.
Place the monkfish fillets in a lightly greased baking dish. Add in the green onions.
Then, thoroughly combine the sour cream and cheddar cheese; add in Cajun seasoning mix.
Spoon the cheese mixture into the baking dish. Bake in the preheated oven at 365 degrees F for about 15 minutes until cooked through.
Bon appétit!

271.   Shrimp Mushrooms

Preparation Time: 15 minutes
Cooking Time: 7 minutes
Serving: 2
Ingredients:
1 tablespoon vegetable oil
1 cup coconut cream
10 white button mushrooms, quartered
2 cloves of garlic, peeled and minced
1/2 lb of shrimp, deveined and peeled
Salt and pepper, to taste
Directions:
Start by sautéing the shrimp with garlic in the vegetable oil for 2 minutes.

Toss in mushrooms, salt, black pepper, and coconut cream.
Cook for 5 minutes then garnish as desired.
Serve warm.
Nutrition:
Calories 211
Total Fat 18.5 g
Saturated Fat 11.5 g
Cholesterol 173 mg
Sodium 280 mg
Total Carbs 0.5 g
Sugar 0.3 g
Fiber 0.2 g
Protein 11.5 g

272.   Coconut Shrimp

Preparation Time: 15 minutes
Cooking Time: 6 minutes
Serving: 2
Ingredients:
3 tablespoons of coconut flour
1 medium egg, whisked
½ cup of coconut flakes
7oz of raw peeled shrimp
Salt and freshly ground black pepper
Directions:
Start by adding coconut flour to a bowl, whisk the egg in another and coconut flakes in another.
Season the shrimp with salt and ground black pepper
Now dip the shrimp in flour then in egg and then coat them with flakes.
Place the shrimp in a baking sheet.
Bake them for 6 minutes until golden brown.
Serve warm and fresh.
Nutrition:
Calories 489
Total Fat 43.3 g
Saturated Fat 15.2 g
Cholesterol 128 mg
Sodium 662 mg
Total Carbs 5 g
Sugar 0.1 g
Fiber 2 g
Protein 22.2 g

273.   Shrimp Cocktail

Preparation Time: 15 minutes
Cooking Time: 0 minute

Serving: 2
Ingredients:
2 tablespoons sugar-free tomato ketchup
2 tablespoons mayo
8 oz cooked, peeled prawns
1 cup iceberg lettuce, shredded
1/2 large avocado, diced
Salt and black pepper, to taste
Directions:
Whisk tomato ketchup with salt, pepper, and mayo in a suitable bowl.
Add prawn to this sauce and mix well to coat.
Toss in lettuce, and avocado then mix well.
Serve fresh.
Nutrition:
Calories 139
Total Fat 10.1 g
Saturated Fat 5 g
Cholesterol 216 mg
Sodium 238 mg
Total Carbs 2.3 g
Sugar 1.5 g
Fiber 0.2 g
Protein 10.1 g

274.   Shrimp and Cucumber

Preparation Time: 15 minutes
Cooking Time: 0 minute
Serving: 6
Ingredients:
2 cucumbers, chopped into 1.5 pieces
12 shrimps, boiled
1/4 onion, diced
1 tomato, diced
Salt and black pepper, to taste
Directions:
Scoop some flesh out of the center of the cucumber pieces.
Mix the onion with tomato, salt, black pepper and olive oil in a bowl.
Divide the mixture into the cucumber pieces.
Place the shrimp on top of each piece.
Serve fresh and warm.
Nutrition:
Calories 231
Total Fat 17.6 g
Saturated Fat 7.6 g
Cholesterol 383 mg
Sodium 244 mg

Total Carbs 3.1 g
Sugar 1.3 g
Fiber 0.8 g
Protein 15.7 g

275.   Asian Miso Soup

Preparation Time: 15 minutes
Cooking Time: 7 minutes
Serving: 4
Ingredients:
2.5 cups of chicken broth
1 tablespoon of tahini sauce
½ lb of shrimp peeled
2 green onions, sliced at an angle
1 cup of spinach, thinly sliced
Salt and black pepper to taste
Directions:
Start by adding broth, and tahini sauce to a saucepan.
Warm up the mixture then add green onions, spinach, salt, and black pepper.
Toss in shrimp and cook for at most 5 minutes approximately.
Serve fresh and warm.
Nutrition:
Calories 111
Total Fat 8.3 g
Saturated Fat 4.9 g
Cholesterol 69 mg
Sodium 896 mg
Total Carbs 1.9 g
Sugar 0.8 g
Fiber 0.6 g
Protein 7.4 g

276.   Shrimp Fried Rice

Preparation Time: 15 minutes
Cooking Time: 4 minutes
Serving: 4
Ingredients:
1/2 head of cauliflower, cut into florets
1 carrot, diced
1/2 lb of shrimp, deveined and peeled
1 teaspoon of sesame oil
2 spring onions, chopped for garnish
Salt and black pepper to taste
Directions:
Start by heating oil in a suitable skillet over medium heat.

Toss in shrimp and stir cook until al dente.
Transfer the seared shrimp to a plate and keep it aside.
Add the cauliflower florets to a food processor and pulse to chop it finely.
Transfer these cauliflower rice to a cooking pan.
Stir in spring onions, carrot, salt, and black pepper.
Sauté for 2 minutes then add shrimp.
Cook for 2 minutes with occasional stirring.
Serve fresh and warm.
Nutrition:
Calories 321
Total Fat 9 g
Saturated Fat 4.9 g
Cholesterol 108 mg
Sodium 184 mg
Total Carbs 10.8 g
Sugar 8.2 g
Fiber 3.2 g
Protein 24.3 g

277.   Garlic Shrimp

Preparation Time: 15 minutes
Cooking Time: 10 minutes
Serving: 4
Ingredients:
1 lb shrimp, peeled and deveined
8 cloves garlic, minced
2 bell peppers, chopped
4 mushrooms
1 zucchini, chopped
Salt and black pepper to taste
Directions:
Season the shrimp pieces with salt, pepper, and garlic.
Thread the shrimp, mushrooms, zucchini and bell peppers on a skewer.
Grill the shimp skewers for 5 minutes per side.
Serve fresh and warm.
Nutrition:
Calories 207
Total Fat 15 g
Saturated Fat 5.2 g
Cholesterol 64 mg
Sodium 252 mg
Total Carbs 5.4 g
Sugar 0.2 g
Fiber 1.8 g
Protein 11.1 g

278. Coconut Soup

Preparation Time: 15 minutes
Cooking Time: 12 minutes
Serving: 8
Ingredients:
2 cups of coconut cream
1-quart (32 ozchicken stock
16 Shrimp
3 large button mushrooms sliced
3 tablespoons fish sauce
Salt and black pepper, to taste
Directions:
Start by adding mushrooms, salt, and black pepper to a saucepan.
Sauté for 2 minutes then add the stock, cream and fish sauce.
Mix well and cook for 5 minutes approximately.
Stir in shrimp and continue cooking for 5 minutes until well done.
Serve fresh and warm.
Nutrition:
Calories 434
Total Fat 36.4 g
Saturated Fat 17.1 g
Cholesterol 257 mg
Sodium 1038 mg
Total Carbs 2.5 g
Sugar 0.9 g
Fiber 0.2 g
Protein 24.2 g

279. Caesar Shrimp

Preparation Time: 15 minutes
Cooking Time: 10 minutes
Serving: 4
Ingredients:
1 lb shrimp, shell removed
2 tablespoons olive oil
1 tablespoon lemon juice
3 tablespoons garlic powder
1 tablespoon onion powder
Salt and pepper, to taste
Directions:
Start by preheating your oven at 400 degrees F.
Toss the shrimp with oil, lemon juice, garlic powder, onion powder, salt and black pepper in a mixing bowl.
Spread the shrimp in a baking sheet and bake them for 10 minutes.
Serve fresh and warm.

Nutrition:
Calories 282
Total Fat 4.6 g
Saturated Fat 1.4 g
Cholesterol 75 mg
Sodium 560 mg
Total Carbs 11.1 g
Sugar 2.1 g
Fiber 1.6 g
Protein 22.2 g

280.   Mini Fish Cakes

Preparation Time: 15 minutes
Cooking Time: 25 minutes
Serving: 4
Ingredients:
1 lb white fish, raw and blended
2 cups almond flour
4 eggs, whisked
2 tablespoons scallions or chives, finely chopped
1 tablespoon garlic powder
Salt and pepper to taste
Directions:
Start by mixing the white fish with almond flour, eggs, scallions, garlic powder, salt and black pepper in a bowl.
Divide the mixture into a muffin tray lined with muffin liners.
Bake them for 25 minutes until they are golden.
Serve fresh and warm.
Nutrition:
Calories 487
Total Fat 37.4 g
Saturated Fat 8.8 g
Cholesterol 71 mg
Sodium 501 mg
Total Carbs 10.6 g
Sugar 1.2 g
Fiber 9.2 g
Protein 28.1 g

281.   Salmon Salad with Poached Egg

Preparation Time: 15 minutes
Cooking Time: 4 minutes
Serving: 4
Ingredients:
1 large handful of salad greens

2 tablespoons olive oil
1 teaspoon freshly squeezed lemon juice
4 smoked salmon slices
2 tablespoons pistachios, crushed
1 poached egg
Directions:
Start by tossing the salad greens with olive oil, and lemon juice in a bowl.
Top the greens with smoked salmon over the greens.
Add a poached egg on top and garnish with pistachios.
Serve fresh and warm.
Nutrition:
Calories 355
Total Fat 15 g
Saturated Fat 1.4 g
Cholesterol 128 mg
Sodium 1271 mg
Total Carbs 11.8 g
Sugar 2.5 g
Fiber 2.7 g
Protein 44.2 g

282.   Salmon Curry

Preparation Time: 15 minutes
Cooking Time: 10 minutes
Serving: 4
Ingredients:
1/2 medium onion, finely chopped
2 cups green beans, diced
1 (14-ozcan of coconut milk
2 cups bone broth
1 lb of raw salmon, diced
Salt and pepper, to taste
Directions:
Sauté onion in a cooking pan until soft.
Stir in green beans, broth, and coconut milk.
Continue cooking it to a boil then add salmon, salt and pepper.
Cook for 5 minutes approximately.
Serve fresh and warm.
Nutrition:
Calories 455
Total Fat 34.4 g
Saturated Fat 3.4 g
Cholesterol 64 mg
Sodium 58 mg
Total Carbs 10.8 g
Sugar 1.7 g

Fiber 5.2 g
Protein 29.6 g

283.   Lemon Garlic Salmon

Preparation Time: 15 minutes
Cooking Time: 20 minutes
Serving: 2
Ingredients:
1 tablespoon ghee
2 salmon filets, with skin on
4 cloves garlic, minced
2 teaspoons lemon juice
Salt and black pepper to taste
Directions:
Start by preheating your oven at 400 degrees F.
Season the salmon with ghee, garlic, lemon juice, salt, and black pepper.
Wrap the salmon fillet in an aluminum foil.
Place the fish in a baking sheet and bake them for 10 minutes.
Flip the salmon and bake for another 10 minutes.
Serve fresh and warm.
Nutrition:
Calories 364
Total Fat 13.2 g
Saturated Fat 3.4 g
Cholesterol 141 mg
Sodium 274 mg
Total Carbs 10.8 g
Sugar 2.8g
Fiber 5.7 g
Protein 47.7 g

284.   Salmon Dill Cakes

Preparation Time: 15 minutes
Cooking Time: 12 minutes
Serving: 8
Ingredients:
3 cans of salmon, drained and flaked
2 tablespoons of fresh dill, chopped finely
3 medium eggs, whisked
1/4 cup of coconut flour
1/4 cup of coconut oil
Salt and pepper, to taste
Directions:
Start by mixing the salmon with dill, eggs, coconut flour, salt, and pepper.
Mix well then make 8 patties out of this mixture.

Sear the patties in coconut oil while cooking in batches.
Cook each salmon patty for 3 minutes per side.
Serve fresh and warm.
Nutrition:
Calories 202
Total Fat 9.5g
Saturated Fat 2 g
Cholesterol 62 mg
Sodium 526 mg
Total Carbs 11.5 g
Sugar 5.8 g
Fiber 2.6 g
Protein 22 g

285.   Bacon-Wrapped Salmon

Preparation Time: 15 minutes
Cooking Time: 20 minutes
Serving: 2
Ingredients:
2 filets of salmon, fresh
4 slices of bacon
1 tablespoon of olive oil
2 tablespoons of Basil Pesto
Salt and freshly ground black pepper
Directions:
Start by preheating your oven at 350 degrees F.
Pat the salmon dry then wrap each fillet with bacon.
Place the wrapped fillets in a baking sheet.
Drizzle the olive oil liberally over the fillets and bake them for 20 minutes until al dente.
Top the fillets with pesto, salt, and black pepper.
Serve fresh and warm.
Nutrition:
Calories 449
Total Fat 28.7 g
Saturated Fat 14.9 g
Cholesterol 163 mg
Sodium 744 mg
Total Carbs 8.4 g
Sugar 2.6 g
Fiber 1.9 g
Protein 39.3 g

286.   Creamy Salmon Pasta

Preparation Time: 15 minutes
Cooking Time: 6 minutes

Serving: 2
Ingredients:
2 tablespoons of coconut oil
8 oz of smoked salmon, diced
2 zucchinis, spiralized
1/4 cup of mayo
Directions:
Start by heating coconut oil in a skillet over medium-high heat.
Add smoked salmon and sauté for 3 minutes.
Toss in zucchini noodles and stir cook for 2 minutes.
Add mayo and mix well then serve the pasta.
Serve warm and fresh.
Nutrition:
Calories 225
Total Fat 17.7 g
Saturated Fat 3.2 g
Cholesterol 5 mg
Sodium 386 mg
Total Carbs 11.3 g
Sugar 7.1 g
Fiber 4.5 g
Protein 7.4 g

287.   Baked Rosemary Salmon

Preparation Time: 15 minutes
Cooking Time: 30 minutes
Serving: 2
Ingredients:
2 salmon fillets
1 tablespoon fresh rosemary leaves
1/4 cup olive oil
1 teaspoon salt
Directions:
Start by rubbing the salmon fillets with oil, rosemary, and salt.
Wrap each fillet with aluminum foil.
Place the wrapped fillets in a baking sheet.
Bake them for 30 minutes until well done.
Serve fresh and warm.
Nutrition:
Calories 266
Total Fat 26.4 g
Saturated Fat 4 g
Cholesterol 13 mg
Sodium 455 mg
Total Carbs 5.4 g
Sugar 2 g

Fiber 1.6 g
Protein 20.6 g

288. Peppercorn Smoked Salmon

Preparation Time: 15 minutes
Cooking Time: 0 minute
Serving: 2
Ingredients:
1 handful of arugula salad leaves
1 teaspoon of pink peppercorns, lightly crushed
4 olives
2 oz. smoked salmon
1 slice of lemon
Directions:
Toss the arugula leaves with olives in a bowl.
Place the salmon on the arugula mixture.
Add a drizzle of peppercorns, and lemon slice.
Serve fresh.
Nutrition:
Calories 371
Total Fat 3.7 g
Saturated Fat 2.7 g
Cholesterol 168 mg
Sodium 121 mg
Total Carbs 4 g
Fiber 1.5 g
Sugar 0.3 g
Protein 26.5 g

289. Curried Tuna Salad

Preparation Time: 15 minutes
Cooking Time: 0 minute
Serving: 2
Ingredients:
1 can of tuna, drained and flaked
3 tablespoons mayo
2 teaspoons curry powder
1 teaspoon dried parsley
Salt and pepper, to taste
Directions:
Start by tossing the tuna with mayo, curry powder, parsley, salt and black pepper in a bowl.
Mix well then serve fresh.
Nutrition:
Calories 213
Total Fat 23.4 g

Saturated Fat 6.1 g
Cholesterol 102 mg
Sodium 86 mg
Total Carbs 4.5 g
Sugar 2.1 g
Fiber 1.5 g
Protein 33.2 g

290.   Coconut Tuna Cakes

Preparation Time: 15 minutes
Cooking Time: 10 minutes
Serving: 4
Ingredients:
2 cans (6 oz cansof tuna
1 jalapeno, finely diced
2 eggs, whisked
2 tablespoons coconut flour
2 tablespoons olive oil
Salt and black pepper, to taste
Directions:
Start by whisk egg in a bowl.
Stir in jalapeno, coconut flour, olive oil, tuna, salt and black pepper in a bowl.
Make 4 patties out of this mixture.
Place the patties on a baking sheet.
Bake them for 5 minutes per side at 350 degrees F.
Serve fresh and warm.
Nutrition:
Calories 392
Total Fat 40.4 g
Saturated Fat 6 g
Cholesterol 20 mg
Sodium 423 mg
Total Carbs 7.2 g
Sugar 3 g
Fiber 4.2 g
Protein 21 g

291.   Italian Tuna Salad

Preparation Time: 15 minutes
Cooking Time: 5 minutes
Serving: 2
Ingredients:
1 rib of celery, diced finely
1/2 tablespoon lemon juice
5 oz canned tuna

1/2 garlic clove, minced
5 sun-dried tomatoes
Salt and black pepper to taste
Directions:
Add tomatoes to hot water and let them soften in 30 minutes.
Pat the tomatoes dry and chop it finely.
Toss the tuna with tomatoes, celery, garlic, salt, lemon juice and black pepper in a bowl.
Serve fresh.
Nutrition:
Calories 238
Total Fat 23.2 g
Saturated Fat 13 g
Cholesterol 61 mg
Sodium 115 mg
Total Carbs 6.8 g
Sugar 0.2 g
Fiber 0.9 g
Protein 22.3 g

292.   Lemon Pepper Tuna

Preparation Time: 15 minutes
Cooking Time: 0 minute
Serving: 2
Ingredients:
1/3 cucumber, diced small
1/2 small avocado, diced small
1 teaspoon lemon juice
1 can (4-6 ozof tuna
1 tablespoon mustard
Salt and black pepper to taste
Directions:
Start by tossing the cucumber with lemon juice and avocado in a mixing bowl.
Stir in mustard, salt, pepper, and tuna.
Mix well then serve fresh.
Nutrition:
Calories 349
Total Fat 31.9 g
Saturated Fat 15 g
Cholesterol 46 mg
Sodium 237 mg
Total Carbs 6.6 g
Sugar 1.4 g
Fiber 3.4 g
Protein 11 g

293.   Cauliflower Broccoli Tuna

Preparation Time: 15 minutes
Cooking Time: 20 minutes
Serving: 4
Ingredients:
1 broccoli head, cut into small florets
1 lemon
1 cauliflower head, cut into florets
Salt and black pepper, to taste
1 5-oz can of tuna (packed in brine or olive oil
Directions:
Start by preheating your oven at 400 degrees F.
Toss the broccoli and cauliflower florets with olive oil, lemon juice, salt and black pepper in a baking tray.
Roast the veggies for 20 minutes in the oven then transfer them to a bowl.
Stir in tuna and mix well.
Serve fresh.
Nutrition:
Calories 269
Total Fat 11.9 g
Saturated Fat 5.5 g
Cholesterol 36 mg
Sodium 437 mg
Total Carbs 8.6 g
Sugar 1.4 g
Fiber 3.4 g
Protein 15 g

294.   Sardines with Olives

Preparation Time: 15 minutes
Cooking Time: 5 minutes
Serving: 2
Ingredients:
1 can (3.5 ozsardines in olive oil
5 black olives, sliced
1 tablespoon garlic flakes
1 teaspoon parsley flakes
1 tablespoon olive oil, to cook with
Directions:
Start by adding 1 tablespoon olive oil to a skillet.
Add olives, sardines, garlic, and parsley flakes.
Sauté for 5 minutes approximately.
Serve fresh and warm.
Nutrition:
Calories 376
Total Fat 21.9 g
Saturated Fat 7.8 g

Cholesterol 110 mg
Sodium 345 mg
Total Carbs 14.7 g
Sugar 4.6 g
Fiber 5.7 g
Protein 33.2 g

295.   Sardines and Onions

Preparation Time: 15 minutes
Cooking Time: 0 minute
Serving: 4
Ingredients:
2 teaspoons vinegar
1/2 red onion, sliced thinly
2 cans (3.5 ozsardines in olive oil
2 tablespoons olive oil
Salt, to taste
Directions:
Toss the onions with olive oil and vinegar in a bowl.
Top the onions with sardines and salt.
Serve fresh.
Nutrition:
Calories 335
Total Fat 5.4 g
Saturated Fat 3.3 g
Cholesterol 16 mg
Sodium 708 mg
Total Carbs 2.1 g
Sugar 0.7 g
Fiber 0.4 g
Protein 18.5 g

296.   Sardines Salad

Preparation Time: 15 minutes
Cooking Time: 0 minute
Serving: 2
Ingredients:
1 can (4-5 ozsardines in olive oil or brine, drained
1/4 lb salad greens
1/10 lb deli meat, chopped
1 tablespoon olive oil
1 tablespoon lemon juice
Salt to taste
Directions:
Toss the salad greens with lemon juice and olive oil.

Stir in deli meat and toss well.
Top the mixture with sardines and salt.
Serve fresh to enjoy.
Nutrition:
Calories 238
Total Fat 9.5 g
Saturated Fat 2.7 g
Cholesterol 103 mg
Sodium 403 mg
Total Carbs 1.8 g
Sugar 0.2 g
Fiber 0.2 g
Protein 34.2 g

297.   Baked Salmon with Pesto

Preparation Time: 15 minutes
Cooking Time: 30 minutes
Serving: 4
Ingredients:
4 oz. green pesto
1 cup mayonnaise
½ cup Greek yogurt
30 oz. salmon
salt and pepper, to taste
Directions:
Place the salmon fish fillets on a baking dish with their skin side down.
Spread 2 oz pesto over the fillet and drizzle salt and black pepper over the fish.
Bake the fillet for 30 minutes approximately at 400-degrees F.
Whisk mayonnaise, pesto, and yogurt in a large bowl.
Toss in flaky salmon and mix well.
Serve fresh and enjoy.
Nutrition:
Calories 287
Total Fat 29.5 g
Saturated Fat 3 g
Cholesterol 743 mg
Sodium 388 mg
Total Carbs 5.9 g
Sugar 1.4g
Fiber 4.3 g
Protein 4.2 g

298.   Prosciutto-wrapped salmon skewers

Preparation Time: 15 minutes
Cooking Time: 6 minutes

Serving: 4

Ingredients:

¼ cup fresh basil, finely chopped

1 lb salmon, frozen in pieces

1 pinch ground black pepper

3½ oz. prosciutto, in slices

1 tablespoon olive oil

Directions:

Start by tossing the basil, salmon, black pepper, and olive oil in a bowl.

Thread the salmon and prosciutto on the skewers.

Prepare and preheat a grill on medium heat.

Grill the skewers for 2-3 minutes per side.

Serve fresh and warm.

Nutrition:

Calories 324

Total Fat 20.7 g

Saturated Fat 6.7 g

Cholesterol 45 mg

Sodium 241 mg

Total Carbs 8.6 g

Sugar 1.4 g

Fiber 0.5 g

Protein 15.3 g

299.   Smoked Salmon and Avocado

Preparation Time: 15 minutes

Cooking Time: 0 minutes

Serving: 4

Ingredients:

7 oz. smoked salmon

2 avocados

½ cup mayonnaise

salt and pepper

Directions:

Start by slicing the avocados in halves and remove the pits.

Scoop out the avocado flesh from the center and mash this flesh in a bowl.

Stir in mayonnaise, salmon, salt and black pepper.

Mix well then divide the mixture in the avocado shells.

Serve fresh to enjoy.

Nutrition:

Calories 245

Total Fat 16g

Saturated Fat 10 g

Cholesterol 16 mg

Sodium 111 mg

Total Carbs 2 g

Sugar 1 g
Fiber 1 g
Protein 32 g

300. Seared Scallops in Butter Sauce

Preparation Time: 15 minutes
Cooking Time: 7 minutes
Serving: 4
Ingredients:
1.1 lb fresh scallops, trimmed
5 tablespoon butter
1 clove garlic, minced
salt and pepper, to taste
juice and zest 1 lemon
4 tablespoon fresh chopped parsley
Directions:
Start by heating 1 tablespoon butter in a pan.
Sear the scallops for 3 minutes per side then transfer them to a plate.
Add remaining butter, and garlic to the same pan.
Sauté for 30 seconds then add lemon zest, juice, parsley, salt, and black pepper.
Mix well then pour the garlic sauce over the scallops.
Serve warm and fresh.
Nutrition:
Calories 216
Total Fat 21.7 g
Saturated Fat 6.1 g
Cholesterol 16 mg
Sodium 111 mg
Total Carbs 7.1 g
Sugar 2.4 g
Fiber 0.6 g
Protein 28.9 g

Poultry

301. Herbed Chicken Salad

Preparation Time: 15 Minutes
Cooking Time: 10 Minutes
Servings: 4
Ingredients:
6 pitted kalamata olives, halved
1 cup grape tomatoes, halved
1 cup peeled and chopped English cucumbers
8 cups chopped romaine lettuce
1 tsp bottled minced garlic
2 tsp sesame seed paste or tahini
1 cup plain fat-free yogurt
5 tsp fresh lemon juice, divided
1-pound skinless, boneless chicken breast, cut into 1-inch cubes
Cooking spray
½ tsp salt
¾ tsp black pepper, divided
½ tsp garlic powder
1 tsp ground oregano
Directions:
In a bowl, mix together ¼ tsp salt, ½ tsp pepper, garlic powder and oregano. Then on medium high heat place a skillet and coat with cooking spray and sauté together the spice mixture and chicken until chicken is cooked. Before transferring to bowl, drizzle with juice.
In a small bowl, mix thoroughly the following: garlic, tahini, yogurt, ¼ tsp pepper, ¼ tsp salt, and 2 tsp juice.
In another bowl, mix together olives, tomatoes, cucumber and lettuce.
To Serve salad, place 2 ½ cups of lettuce mixture on plate, topped with ½ cup chicken mixture, 3 tbsp yogurt mixture and 1 tbsp of cheese.
Nutrition:
Calories 291, Total Fat 8g, Saturated Fat 2g, Total Carbs 17g, Net Carbs 14g, Protein 40g, Sugar: 12g, Fiber 3g, Sodium 965mg, Potassium 942mg

302. Chicken in Pita Bread

Preparation Time: 10 Minutes
Cooking Time: 10 Minutes
Servings: 4
Ingredients:
½ cup diced tomato
2 cups shredded lettuce
4 pcs of 6-inch pitas, cut in half
1 ½ tsp chopped fresh oregano
½ cup plain low-fat yogurt
1 tbsp olive oil

2 tsp grated lemon rind, divided
1 lb. ground chicken
2 large egg whites, lightly beaten
½ tsp coarsely ground black pepper
1 tbsp Greek or Moroccan seasoning blend
½ cup chopped green onions
Directions:
Mix thoroughly the ground chicken, 1 tsp lemon rind, egg whites, black pepper, Greek or Moroccan seasoning and green onions. Equally separate into eight parts and shaping each part into ¼ inch thick patty.
Turn fire on medium high and place a large nonstick skillet. Fry the patties until browned or for two mins each side. Then slow the fire to medium, cover the skillet and continue cooking for another four minutes.
In a small bowl, mix thoroughly the oregano, yogurt and 1 tsp lemon rind.
To serve, spread the mixture on the pita, add cooked patty, 1 tbsp tomato and ¼ cup lettuce.
Nutrition:
Calories 408, Total Fat 15g, Saturated Fat 4g, Total Carbs 41g, Net Carbs 35g, Protein 30g, Sugar: 4g, Fiber 6g, Sodium 560mg, Potassium 952mg

303.   Greek Chicken Stew

Preparation Time: 10 Minutes
Cooking Time: 40 Minutes
Servings: 8
Ingredients:
1 ½ cups chicken stock or more if needed
2 bay leaves
1 pinch dried oregano or to taste
Salt and ground black pepper to taste
2 tbsp chopped fresh parsley
1 cup tomato sauce
½ cup water
2 cloves garlic, finely chopped
1 pc, 2lbs whole chicken cut into pieces
1 tbsp olive oil
10 small shallots, peeled
Directions:
Bring to a boil a small pot of lightly salted water. Mix in the shallots and let boil uncovered until tender for around three minutes. Then drain the shallots and dip in cold water until no longer warm.
In another large pot over medium fire, heat olive oil for a minute. Then sauté in the chicken and shallots for 15 minutes or until chicken is cooked and shallots are soft and translucent. Then add the chopped garlic and cook for three mins more.
Then add bay leaves, oregano, salt and pepper, parsley, tomato sauce and the water. Let simmer for a minute before adding the chicken stock. Stir before covering and let cook for 20 minutes on medium-low fire or until chicken is tender.
Nutrition:

Calories 129, Total Fat 3g, Saturated Fat 0.6g, Total Carbs 10g, Net Carbs 7g, Protein 13g, Sugar: 5g, Fiber 3g, Sodium 651mg, Potassium 336mg

304.   Easy Stir-Fried Chicken

Preparation Time: 10 Minutes
Cooking Time: 12 Minutes
Servings: 3
Ingredients:
1 tbsp soy sauce
1 tbsp virgin coconut oil
¼ medium onion, sliced thinly
¼ lb. brown mushrooms
1 large orange bell pepper
2 7-oz skinless and boneless chicken breast
Directions:
On medium high fire, place a nonstick saucepan and heat coconut oil.
Add soy sauce, onion powder, mushrooms, bell pepper and chicken.
Stir fry for 8 to 10 minutes.
Remove from pan and serve.
Nutrition:
Calories 277, Total Fat 10g, Saturated Fat 2g, Total Carbs 4g, Net Carbs 3g, Protein 44g, Sugar: 2g, Fiber 1g, Sodium 146mg, Potassium 689mg

305.   African Chicken Stew

Preparation Time: 10 Minutes
Cooking Time: 85 Minutes
Servings: 8
Ingredients:
1 lime cut into wedges
2 lbs. bone in, skin on drumsticks and chicken thighs
¼ tsp ground allspice
½ tsp salt
½ tsp pepper
2 bay leaves
1 jalapeno pepper, seeds removed, diced
6 cloves garlic, minced
4 onions, sliced
1 tbsp zest of lemon
¼ cup lemon juice
¼ cup apple cider vinegar
2 tbsp olive oil
¼ cup water
Directions:
In wide and shallow bowl with lid, combine allspice, salt, pepper, bay leaves, jalapeno, garlic, lemon zest, lemon juice, vinegar and oil. Mix well.

Add chicken, cover and marinate in the ref. Ensuring to turn chicken in two hours. Chicken is best left overnight or for at least 4 hours.

Once you are done marinating, grease a roasting pan and preheat oven to 400oF.

Remove chicken from marinade and arrange on prepared pan. Pop in the oven and bake until juices run clear around 35-40 minutes.

Meanwhile, discard 3/4s of the marinade while reserving onions. Then place a nonstick pan on low fire and add remaining marinade with bay leaves and onions. Sauté for 45 minutes until caramelized while stirring every once in a while.

To serve, place baked chicken on a plate drizzled with caramelized onion sauce and lime wedges on the side.

Also best eaten with plain white rice.

Nutrition:

Calories 543, Total Fat 54g, Saturated Fat 6g, Total Carbs 4g, Net Carbs 3.7g, Protein 11g, Sugar: 1.5g, Fiber 0.3g, Sodium 205mg, Potassium 189mg

306.   Roasted Chicken

Preparation Time: 10 Minutes
Cooking Time: 60 Minutes
Servings: 8
Ingredients:
1 bay leaf
4 tbsp orange peel, chopped coarsely
3 cloves garlic
½ tsp thyme
½ tsp black pepper
½ tbsp. salt
1 whole chicken (3 lbs. preferred
Directions:
Prepare chicken by placing in room temperature for at least an hour.

With paper towels, pat dry chicken inside and out.

As you begin preparing chicken seasoning, preheat oven to 450oF.

In a small bowl, mix thyme, pepper and salt.

Get 1/3 of the seasoning and wipe inside the chicken. Also place inside of the chicken the bay leaf, citrus peel and garlic.

Tuck the wing tips and tie chicken legs together. Spread remaining seasoning all over and around the chicken. Then place on a roasting pan.

Pop in the oven and bake for 50-60 minutes or until chicken is a golden brown, juices run clear or chicken things or breasts register a 160oF temperature.

Remove from oven and let it sit for 15 minutes more before cutting up and the roasted chicken.

Nutrition:

Calories 270, Total Fat 6g, Saturated Fat 1.6g, Total Carbs 1g, Net Carbs 0.6g, Protein 49g, Sugar: 0g, Fiber 0.4g, Sodium 615mg, Potassium 581mg

307.   Turkey Meatballs

Preparation Time: 10 Minutes

Cooking Time: 25 Minutes
Servings: 4
Ingredients:
1 tsp oil
Pepper and salt to taste
1 tsp dried parsley
4 tbsp fresh basil, finely chopped
¼ yellow onion, finely diced
1 14-oz can of artichoke hearts, diced
1 lb. ground turkey
Directions:
Grease a cookie sheet and preheat oven to 350oF.
On medium fire, place a nonstick medium saucepan and sauté artichoke hearts and diced onions for 5 minutes or until onions are soft.
Remove from fire and let cool.
Meanwhile, in a big bowl, mix with hands parsley, basil and ground turkey. Season to taste.
Once onion mixture has cooled add into the bowl and mix thoroughly.
With an ice cream scooper, scoop ground turkey and form into balls, makes around 6 balls.
Place on prepped cookie sheet, pop in the oven and bake until cooked through around 15-20 minutes.
Remove from pan, serve and enjoy.
Nutrition:
Calories 306, Total Fat 14g, Saturated Fat 3.6g, Total Carbs 12g, Net Carbs 6g, Protein 34g, Sugar: 2g, Fiber 6g, Sodium 197mg, Potassium 770mg

308.   Chicken Breasts with Stuffing

Preparation Time: 10 Minutes
Cooking Time: 40 Minutes
Servings: 8
Ingredients:
8 pcs of 6-oz boneless and skinless chicken breasts
1 tbsp minced fresh basil
2 tbsp finely chopped, pitted Kalamata olives
¼ cup crumbled feta cheese
1 large bell pepper, halved and seeded
Directions:
In a greased baking sheet place bell pepper with skin facing up and pop into a preheated broiler on high. Broil until blackened around 15 minutes. Remove from broiler and place right away into a re-sealable bag, seal and leave for 15 minutes.
After, peel bell pepper and mince. Preheat grill to medium high fire.
In a medium bowl, mix well basil, olives, cheese and bell pepper.
Form a pocket on each chicken breast by creating a slit through the thickest portion; add 2 tbsp bell pepper mixture and seal with a wooden pick. (At this point, you can stop and freeze chicken and just thaw when needed for grilling already
Season chicken breasts with pepper and salt.

Grill for six minutes per side, remove from grill and cover loosely with foil and let stand for 10 minutes before.
Nutrition:
Calories 221, Total Fat 6g, Saturated Fat 1.7g, Total Carbs 1g, Net Carbs 0.8g, Protein 39g, Sugar: 0.5g, Fiber 0.2g, Sodium 135mg, Potassium 591mg

309. Chicken-Bell Pepper Sauté

Preparation Time: 10 Minutes
Cooking Time: 30 Minutes
Servings: 6
Ingredients:
6 4-oz skinless, boneless chicken breast halves, cut in half horizontally
Cooking spray
20 Kalamata olives
1 tsp chopped fresh oregano
2 tbsp finely chopped fresh flat-leaf parsley
¼ tsp freshly ground black pepper
½ tsp salt
2 1/3 cups coarsely chopped tomato
1 large red bell pepper, cut into ¼-inch strips
1 large yellow bell pepper, cut into ¼-inch strips
3 cups onion sliced crosswise
1 tbsp olive oil
Directions:
On medium high fire, place a large nonstick fry pan and heat oil. Once oil is hot, sauté onions until soft and translucent, around 6 to 8 minutes.
Add bell peppers and sauté for another 10 minutes or until tender.
Add black pepper, salt and tomato. Cook until tomato juice has evaporated, around 7 minutes.
Add olives, oregano and parsley, cook until heated through around 1 to 2 minutes. Transfer to a bowl and keep warm.
Wipe pan with paper towel and grease with cooking spray. Return to fire and place chicken breasts. Cook for three minutes per side or until desired doneness is reached. If needed, cook chicken in batches.
When cooking the last batch of chicken is done, add back the previous batch of chicken and the onion-bell pepper mixture and cook for a minute or two while tossing chicken to coat well in the onion-bell pepper mixture.
Serve and enjoy.
Nutrition:
Calories 81, Total Fat 3g, Saturated Fat 0.4g, Total Carbs 4g, Net Carbs 3g, Protein 10g, Sugar: 1.7g, Fiber 1g, Sodium 148mg, Potassium 266mg

310. Avocado-Orange Grilled Chicken

Preparation Time: 10 Minutes
Cooking Time: 12 Minutes
Servings: 4

Ingredients:

1 small red onion, sliced thinly

2 oranges, peeled and sectioned

¼ cup fresh lime juice

1 avocado

4 pieces of 4-6oz boneless, skinless chicken breasts

Pepper and salt to taste

1 tbsp honey

2 tbsp chopped cilantro

¼ cup minced red onion

1 cup low fat yogurt

Directions:

In a large bowl mix honey, cilantro, minced red onion and yogurt.

Submerge chicken into mixture and marinate for at least 30 minutes.

Grease grate and preheat grill to medium high fire.

Remove chicken from marinade and season with pepper and salt.

Grill for 6 minutes per side or until chicken is cooked and juices run clear.

Meanwhile, peel avocado and discard seed. Chop avocados and place in bowl. Quickly add lime juice and toss avocado to coat well with juice.

Add cilantro, thinly sliced onions and oranges into bowl of avocado, mix well.

Serve grilled chicken and avocado dressing on the side.

Nutrition:

Calories 443, Total Fat 14g, Saturated Fat 3g, Total Carbs 26g, Net Carbs 20g, Protein 53g, Sugar: 17g, Fiber 6g, Sodium 815mg, Potassium 1039mg

311.   Honey Chicken Tagine

Preparation Time: 10 Minutes

Cooking Time: 1 hour and 20 Minutes

Servings: 12

Ingredients:

1 ½ tbsp honey

1 15-oz can chickpeas, rinsed

12-oz kumquats, seeded and roughly chopped

1 14-oz can vegetable broth

1/8 tsp ground cloves

½ tsp ground pepper

½ tsp salt

¾ tsp ground cinnamon

1 tsp ground cumin

1 tsp ground coriander

2 lbs. boneless, skinless chicken thighs, trimmed of fat and cut into 2-inch pieces

1 tbsp minced fresh ginger

4 cloves garlic, slivered

2 onions, thinly sliced

1 tbsp extra virgin olive oil

Directions:

Preheat oven to 375oF.

On medium fire, place a heatproof casserole and heat oil.

Add onions and sauté for 4 minutes or until soft.

Add ginger and garlic, sauté for another minute.

Add chicken and sauté for 8 minutes.

Season with cloves, pepper, salt, cinnamon, cumin, and coriander. Sauté for a minute or until aromatic.

Add honey, chickpeas, kumquats, and broth. Bring to a boil and turn off fire.

Cover casserole and pop in the oven. Bake for an hour while stirring every after 15-minute intervals.

Nutrition:

Calories 541, Total Fat 46g, Saturated Fat 6g, Total Carbs 16g, Net Carbs 10g, Protein 20g, Sugar: 6g, Fiber 4g, Sodium 521mg, Potassium 265mg

312. Brussels Sprouts and Paprika Chicken Thighs

Preparation Time: 10 Minutes

Cooking Time: 25 Minutes

Servings: 4

Ingredients:

4 large bone-in chicken thighs, skin removed

1 tsp dried thyme

1 tbsp smoked paprika

2 cloves garlic, minced

½ tsp ground pepper, divided

¾ tsp salt, divided

3 tbsp extra virgin olive oil, divided

1 lemon, sliced

4 small shallots, quartered

1 lb. Brussels sprouts, trimmed and halved

Directions:

Preheat oven to 450oF and position rack to lower third in oven.

On a large and rimmed baking sheet, mix ¼ tsp pepper, ¼ tsp salt, 2 tbsp oil, lemon, shallots, and Brussels sprouts.

With a chef's knife, mash ½ tsp salt and garlic to form a paste.

In small bowl, mix ¼ tsp pepper, 1 tbsp oil, thyme, paprika, and garlic paste. Rub all over chicken and place around Brussels sprouts in pan.

Pop in the oven and roast for 20 to 25 minutes or until chicken is cooked and juices run clear. Serve and enjoy.

Nutrition:

Calories 293, Total Fat 14g, Saturated Fat 3.2g, Total Carbs 15g, Net Carbs 10g, Protein 29g, Sugar: 4g, Fiber 5g, Sodium 992mg, Potassium 769mg

313. Chicken and Avocado Lettuce Wraps

Preparation Time: 10 Minutes

Cooking Time: 5 Minutes

Servings: 3

Ingredients:

1/8 teaspoon black pepper

1/8 teaspoon salt

2 tablespoons cilantro chopped

2 tablespoons lime juice

1 tablespoon lemon juice

½ cups avocado, pitted and mashed

1 cup cooked chicken, shredded

6 leaves of Romaine lettuce

1 cup grape tomatoes, halved

Directions:

In a mixing bowl, mix together the avocado, lime juice, lemon juice and stir to combine.

Add the chicken and cilantro. Season with salt and pepper to taste.

Spoon into the lettuce leaves and add chopped tomatoes.

Nutrition:

Calories 134, Total Fat 6g, Saturated Fat 1g, Total Carbs 7g, Net Carbs 3g, Protein 14g, Sugar: 2.4g, Fiber 4g, Sodium 136mg, Potassium 510mg

314.   Sweet Potato, Kale and Chicken Patties

Preparation Time: 20 Minutes

Cooking Time: 10 Minutes

Servings: 7

Ingredients:

2 tablespoon coconut flour

1 egg

1 tablespoon fresh rosemary, chopped

1 teaspoon Dijon mustard

1 teaspoon paprika powder

1 clove of garlic, minced

½ teaspoon sea salt

1 pound skinless and boneless chicken, chopped finely

2 ½ cups kale, chopped

½ medium sweet potato, chopped

2 green onions, chopped

Directions:

Heat oil in a large skillet and sauté the green onions for five minutes.

Add the sweet potatoes and cook for 5 minutes until almost tender.

Mix in the kale and cook until the kale has wilted. Set aside.

In a mixing bowl, mix together the chicken and season with salt, paprika, mustard, garlic and rosemary. Add the egg, coconut flour and sweet potato mix.

Cover with plastic wrap and refrigerate for 4 hours.

Make patties out of the chicken mixture.

Cook the patties in a hot skillet for 5 minutes each side.

Nutrition:

Calories 106, Total Fat 3g, Saturated Fat 0.6g, Total Carbs 4g, Net Carbs 3g, Protein 16g, Sugar: 1.7g, Fiber 1g, Sodium 225mg, Potassium 333mg

315.   Chicken Burger with Brussel Sprouts Slaw

Preparation Time: 15 Minutes
Cooking Time: 15 Minutes
Servings: 4
Ingredients:
Salt and pepper to taste
½ avocado, cubed
1/3 cup apple, sliced into strips
½ pound Brussels sprouts, shredded
1/8 teaspoon red pepper flakes, optional
1 garlic clove, minced
¼ cup apple, diced
¼ cup green onion, diced
1 tablespoon Dijon mustard
1-pound cooked ground chicken
Directions:
In a mixing bowl, combine together chicken, green onion, Dijon mustard, garlic, apple, and pepper flakes. Season with salt and pepper to taste. Mix the ingredients then form 4 burger patties.
Heat a grill pan over medium-high flame and grill the burgers. Cook for five minutes on side. Set aside.
In another bowl, toss the Brussels sprouts and apples.
In a small pan, heat coconut oil and add the Brussels sprouts mixture until everything is slightly wilted. Season with salt and pepper to taste.
Serve burger patties with the Brussels sprouts slaw.
Nutrition:
Calories 324, Total Fat 21g, Saturated Fat 3.2g, Total Carbs 11g, Net Carbs 6g, Protein 25g, Sugar: 4g, Fiber 5g, Sodium 220mg, Potassium 1104mg

316.   Grilled Veggies 'n Chicken

Preparation Time: 10 Minutes
Cooking Time: 20 Minutes
Servings: 3
Ingredients:
Salt to taste
1 teaspoon Italian seasoning
1 teaspoon rosemary
4 tablespoon extra-virgin olive oil
1-pound organic chicken breast
1 red onion
2 cups fresh cherry tomatoes, halved
1 red pepper, chopped
1 yellow squash, chopped
1 zucchini, chopped
¼ teaspoon cayenne pepper
½ teaspoon onion powder

½ teaspoon garlic granules
Pepper to taste
1 tablespoon vinegar
1 cup organic tomatoes, blended
Directions:
Marinade the chicken by mixing together 1 tablespoon of extra virgin olive oil, Italian seasoning, and rosemary. Season with salt the set aside for at least 2 hours.
In another bowl, make the salad by combining the red onion, fresh cherry tomatoes, red pepper, squash and zucchini. Add 1 tablespoon of extra virgin olive oil and season with salt and pepper to taste. Place inside a greased tinfoil then set aside.
Prepare the grill and heat it to 3500F. Cook the chicken breast and let it cook for 7 minutes on each side. Place the tinfoil with the veggies on the grill and cook it for five to 7 minutes.
Meanwhile, make the vinaigrette my combining the cayenne pepper, onion powder, garlic granules, vinegar and blended organic tomatoes in a food processor. Add 2 tablespoon of extra virgin olive oil and season with salt and pepper to taste.
Nutrition:
Calories 448, Total Fat 14g, Saturated Fat 2.8g, Total Carbs 28g, Net Carbs 22g, Protein 51g, Sugar: 19g, Fiber 6g, Sodium 523mg, Potassium 1005mg

317.   Chicken, Butternut Squash and Hazelnut Mash

Preparation Time: 10 Minutes
Cooking Time: 45 Minutes
Servings: 4
Ingredients:
¼ cup thick coconut milk
½ cup hazelnut, crushed
6 cups baby spinach leaves, chopped
1 orange, juiced
Salt and pepper to taste
1 medium-sized boneless chicken breast, sliced in half
1 medium-sized butternut squash, halved and deseeded
Directions:
Preheat the oven to 3500F.
Sprinkle the butternut squash with salt and paper and place them face down in a baking pan. Put the chicken breasts in the same baking pan. Squeeze orange juice over the chicken. Bake for 35 minutes until both squash and chicken are cooked through.
Meanwhile, sauté spinach in a skillet and cook for 3 minutes or until wilted.
In another pan, toast the crushed hazelnuts over medium heat.
Once the chicken and squash are cooked, it is time to assemble everything.
Scoop the squash and shred the chicken and put them in a mixing bowl. Add the hazelnut, spinach and coconut cream. Mix until well combined.
Place in a baking dish and cook in the broiler for 1o minutes or until the top takes on a golden brown.
Nutrition:
Calories 301, Total Fat 17g, Saturated Fat 4.5g, Total Carbs 18g, Net Carbs 8.5g, Protein 26g, Sugar: 6g, Fiber 9.5g, Sodium 209mg, Potassium 1284mg

318.   Lettuce Tacos with Chipotle Chicken

Preparation Time: 15 Minutes
Cooking Time: 20 Minutes
Servings: 4
Ingredients:
Lime wedges for garnish
Fresh tomatoes, sliced for garnish
½ avocado, sliced
2 pickled jalapenos, chopped
A handful coriander leaves
1 head lettuce, leaves separated and washed
A pinch of brown sugar
Salt and pepper to taste
½ teaspoon cumin
1 tablespoon chopped chipotle in adobo sauce
1 can tomatoes
1 red onion, sliced
1 tablespoon olive oil
1 cup skinless chicken, cut into strips
Directions:
Heat the olive oil in a skillet and fry the chicken until they are golden brown. Set aside.
In the same pan, fry the onions until they become soft. Add the canned tomatoes, chipotle, cumin and sugar. Let it simmer for 15 minutes until the tomatoes become soft and thickened.
Add the chicken to the sauce and cook for 5 minutes.
Assemble the tacos by putting the chicken inside the lettuce wraps. Garnish with lime wedges, fresh tomatoes, avocado, jalapeno and coriander leaves.
Nutrition:
Calories 187, Total Fat 10g, Saturated Fat 1.8g, Total Carbs 8g, Net Carbs 5g, Protein 12g, Sugar: 3g, Fiber 3g, Sodium 72mg, Potassium 504mg

319.   Chicken in A Bowl

Preparation Time: 15 Minutes
Cooking Time: 10 Minutes
Servings: 2
Ingredients:
½ cup cooked chicken, cut into strips
4 green onions, diced
2 garlic cloves, minced
1 tablespoon sesame oil
1/3 cup coconut aminos
1 tablespoon coconut oil
2 large carrots, cut into strips
1 head of cabbage, chopped
Directions:
Melt coconut oil in a skillet over medium high heat.

Sauté the cabbage then add the carrots. Continue sautéing until soft. If it gets too dry, add a little bit of water.

Season with sesame oil and coconut aminos.

Add the garlic and cook for five minutes.

Throw in the chicken strips and toss the green onions.

Nutrition:

Calories 280, Total Fat 15.7g, Saturated Fat 3.4g, Total Carbs 25g, Net Carbs 18g, Protein 14g, Sugar: 13g, Fiber 7g, Sodium 143mg, Potassium 933mg

320.   Creamy Chicken with Broccoli & Spinach

Servings: 4
Preparation Time: 15 minutes
Cooking Time: 13 minutes
Ingredients:
13-ounce unsweetened coconut milk
1 teaspoon fresh ginger, grated
1½ teaspoons curry powder
2 tablespoons coconut oil, divided
1-pound tender chicken, sliced thinly
1 large onion, chopped
2 cups broccoli florets
1 large bunch fresh spinach, chopped
Directions:
In a bowl, mix together coconut milk, ginger and curry powder. Keep aside.
In a big skillet, melt 1 tablespoon of coconut oil on medium-high heat.
Add chicken and stir fry for around 3-4 minutes or till golden brown.
Transfer chicken right into a plate.
In exactly the same skillet, heat remaining oil on medium-high heat.
Add onion and sauté for around 2 minutes.
Add broccoli and stir fry for about 3 minutes.
Add chicken, spinach and coconut mixture and stir fry for approximately 3-4 minute
Nutrition:
Calories: 430, Fat: 9g, Carbohydrates: 18g, Fiber: 11g, Protein: 30g

321.   Chicken with Bell Peppers & Carrot

A most suitable choice recipe if you need a really delicious meal. This meal is packed with healthy chicken, carrot and peppers.
Servings: 4
Preparation Time: fifteen minutes
Cooking Time: 24 minutes
Ingredients:
For Chicken Marinade:
2 minced garlic cloves
2 teaspoons fresh ginger, minced
1 egg, beaten

2 tablespoons tapioca starch
2 teaspoon ground turmeric
1½ teaspoons ground cumin
1 teaspoon ground coriander
1 teaspoon red chili powder
4 skinless, boneless chicken breasts, cut into thin strips

For Cooking:
2 tablespoons olive oil
1 small red onion, minced
1 tablespoon ginger paste
1 tablespoon garlic paste
2 tablespoons red chili paste
1 teaspoon red chili powder
½ teaspoon ground cumin
Salt, to taste
4 carrots, peeled and sliced
2 green bell peppers, seeded and cubed
1-2 green chilies, seeded and sliced
Directions:
For marinade inside a bowl, mix together all ingredients except chicken.
Add chicken and coat with marinade generously.
Refrigerate to marinate for about 120 minutes.
In a sizable skillet, heat oil on medium-high heat.
Add chicken and stir fry for approximately 3-4 minutes or till golden brown.
Transfer chicken right into a plate.
In the same skillet, add onion, ginger paste, garlic paste, red chili paste, chili powder, cumin and salt and sauté for approximately 2-3 minutes.
Add vegetables and stir fry for about 5 minutes.
Add chicken and cook for approximately 5-10 minutes or till desired doneness.
Serve hot.
Nutrition:
Calories: 392, Fat: 12g, Carbohydrates: 19g, Fiber: 10g, Protein: 38g

322.   Chicken with Cabbage

Servings: 4-6
Preparation Time: 15 minutes
Cooking Time: 17 minutes
Ingredients:
½ teaspoon garlic powder
½ teaspoon fresh ginger powder
Salt and freshly ground black pepper, to taste
½ teaspoon sesame oil
3 tablespoons apple cider vinegar treatment
4 skinless, boneless chicken breasts, sliced thinly
3 tablespoons coconut oil, divided
1 onion, sliced thinly
1 large head cabbage, sliced thinly
¼ cup organic honey
¼ cup coconut aminos
Directions:
In a big bowl, mix together garlic powder, ginger powder, salt, black pepper, sesame oil and vinegar.
Add chicken and coat with mixture generously whilst aside for approximately 5 minutes.

In a large skillet, melt 2 tablespoons of coconut oil on medium-high heat.
Add chicken and stir fry for about 3-4 minutes or till golden brown.
Transfer chicken into a plate.
In exactly the same skillet, melt remaining oil on medium heat.
Add onion and cabbage and cook for about 4-5 minutes.
Add chicken, honey and coconut aminos and cook for around 5-8 minutes or till desired doneness.
Nutrition:
Calories: 403, Fat: 10g, Carbohydrates: 20g, Fiber: 8g, Protein: 37g

323.   Chicken with Veggie Combo

Servings: 2
Preparation Time: 25 minutes
Cooking Time: fifteen minutes
Ingredients:

1 tbsp olive oil

1 large skinless, boneless chicken white meat, cubed

1 cup small cauliflower florets

1 cup fresh shiitake mushrooms, sliced

1 cup Bok choy, chopped

1 cup carrot, peeled and spiralized Blade C

½ teaspoon ground ginger

½ teaspoon garlic salt

1 large zucchini, spiralized Blade C

Directions:

In a big skillet, heat oil on medium-high heat.

Add chicken and stir fry approximately 2 minutes or till golden brown.

Add onion and cabbage and cook for around 4-5 minutes.

Add cauliflower whilst without stirring for around 30-45 seconds.

Cook, tossing occasionally for about2 minutes.

Add mushrooms and cook for approximately 2 minutes.

Add Bok choy, carrot, ground ginger and garlic salt and cook, tossing occasionally or about 2-3 minutes.

Add zucchini and cook for around 2-3 minutes.

Remove from heat and make aside for about 3-5 minutes before.

Nutrition:

Calories: 416, Fat: 12g, Carbohydrates: 20g, Fiber: 8g, Protein: 40g

324. Chicken with Mixed Veggies & Almonds

Delicious chicken with mixed veggies and almonds recipe.

Servings: 8-10

Preparation Time: 25 minutes

Cooking Time: 10 min

Ingredients:

2 tablespoons coconut oil
2 skinless, boneless chicken breasts, cubed
2 (8-ouncecans water chestnuts
4 cups broccoli florets
1 cup fresh mushrooms, sliced
½ cup celery stalk, chopped
1 head cabbage, shredded
½ cup green onions, chopped
4-5 garlic cloves, minced
2 tablespoons fresh ginger, minced
½ cup almonds, chopped
3 tablespoons coconut aminos
White sesame seeds, for garnishing
Directions:
In a sizable skillet, melt coconut oil on medium-high heat.
Add chicken and stir fry for approximately 3-4 minutes or till golden brown.
Add water chestnuts, broccoli, mushrooms and celery and stir fry for around 2 minutes.
Add cabbage, green onion, garlic, ginger, almonds and coconut aminos and cook for approximately 2-3 minutes.
Serve hot with the garnishing of sesame seeds.
Nutrition:
Calories: 433, Fat: 9g, Carbohydrates: 18g, Fiber: 7g, Protein: 33g

325. Chicken with Mango, Veggies & Cashews

Servings: 4
Preparation Time: 25 minutes
Cooking Time: 18 minutes
Ingredients:

2 tablespoons coconut oil
2 skinless, boneless chicken breasts, sliced
1 red onion, sliced thinly
2 minced garlic cloves
2 tablespoons fresh ginger, minced
1 ripe mango, peeled, pitted and cubed
1 bunch broccoli, cut into small florets
1 zucchini, sliced
1 cup mushrooms, sliced
1 red bell pepper, seeded and cubed
2 cups beans sprouts
3 tablespoons coconut aminos
¼ teaspoon red chili flakes, crushed
Salt and freshly ground black pepper, to taste
¼ cup cashews, toasted
Directions:
In a big skillet, melt coconut oil on medium-high heat.
Add chicken and stir fry for approximately 4-5 minutes or till golden brown.
Transfer chicken in a plate.
In the same skillet, add onion, garlic and ginger and sauté for about 1-2 minutes.
Add mango, broccoli, zucchini and bell pepper and cook for approximately 5-7 minutes.
Add chicken, beans sprouts, coconut aminos, red chili flakes, salt and black pepper and cook for approximately 3-4 minutes or till desired doneness.
Serve with the topping of cashews.
Nutrition:
Calories: 445, Fat: 10g, Carbohydrates: 28g, Fiber: 13g, Protein: 39g

326. Chicken with Strawberries, Rhubarb & Zucchini

Servings: 2
Preparation Time: twenty or so minutes
Cooking Time: 13 minutes
Ingredients:
2 zucchinis, spiralized with Blade C
Salt, to taste
1½ teaspoons olive oil
½ teaspoon fresh ginger, minced
¾ cup rhubarb, chopped
1 (8-ounceskinless, boneless chicken breasts, cubed
4 teaspoons organic honey
1 teaspoon fresh lime zest, grated finely
¼ cup plus 2 teaspoons fresh orange juice, divided
1 tablespoon fresh lime juice
2 teaspoons fresh mint leaves, minced
½ cup fresh strawberries, hulled and sliced
2 tablespoons almonds, toasted and slivered
Directions:

Arrange a sizable strainer over sink.

Place the zucchini noodles in strainer and sprinkle using a pinch of salt.

Keep aside to release the moisture.

In a sizable skillet, heat oil on medium heat.

Add ginger and rhubarb and cook for about 2-3 minutes.

Stir in chicken and cook for approximately 4-5 minutes.

Add honey, lime zest, ¼ cup of orange juice, lime juice and pinch of salt and cook and raise the heat to high.

Bring to your boil reducing heat to medium.

Simmer, stirring occasionally approximately 4-5 minutes and take off from heat.

Squeeze the moisture from zucchini and pat dry with paper towels.

In a smaller bowl, mix together remaining orange juice and mint.

Divide zucchini noodles in plates and drizzle with mint mixture.

Place chicken mixture, strawberries and almonds over zucchini noodles and gently stir to combine.

Serve immediately.

Nutrition:

Calories: 355, Fat: 10.7g, Carbohydrates: 33.8g, Fiber: 6.1g, Protein: 35.9g

327. Chicken in Spicy Gravy

Servings: 3-4

Preparation Time: 10 min

Cooking Time: 38 minutes

Ingredients:

For Marinade:

1 teaspoon garlic paste

1 teaspoon ginger paste

2 teaspoons chili powder

½ teaspoon ground turmeric

Salt, to taste

1 teaspoon freshly squeezed lemon juice

Water, as required

1-pound skinless, boneless chicken breast, cut into medium pieces

For Cooking:

5 tbsps. essential olive oil

2 large onions, sliced thinly

10 curry leaves

1½ teaspoons garlic paste

1½ teaspoons ginger paste

2 green chilies, chopped

2 teaspoons ground coriander

1 teaspoon garam masala

1 teaspoon chili powder

1 teaspoon ground turmeric

Salt and freshly ground black pepper, to taste

½ cup chicken broth

1 large tomato, chopped finely

Directions:

For marinate in a big bowl, mix together all ingredients except water and chicken.

Add enough water and mix till a paste forms.

Add chicken and coat with marinade generously.

Cover and refrigerate to marinate for around 30 minutes.

In a big skillet, heat oil on medium-high heat.

Add chicken and stir fry approximately 4-5 minutes or till golden brown.

Transfer chicken in a plate.

In a similar skillet, add onion and curry leaves on medium-low heat

Cook, covered for around 15-20 minutes till golden brown, stirring occasionally.

Add garlic ginger paste and green chilies and sauté approximately 1-2 minutes.

Stir in spices and sauté for approximately 1 minute.

Stir in chicken and cook, covered approximately 5-6 minutes.

Add broth and cook for approximately 5-6 minutes.

Add tomato and cook, stirring occasionally approximately 5 minutes more.

Nutrition:

Calories: 441, Fat: 11g, Carbohydrates: 28g, Fiber: 7g, Protein: 37g

328. Lemon Braised Chicken

Servings: 6

Preparation Time: fifteen minutes

Cooking Time: one hour

Ingredients:

2 tablespoons organic olive oil

6 bone-in chicken thighs

Salt and freshly ground black pepper, to taste

½ of onion, sliced

4 cups chicken broth

8 sprigs fresh dill

Pinch of cayenne pepper

½ teaspoon ground turmeric

2 tablespoons fresh lemon juice

2 tablespoons arrowroot starch

1 tablespoon cold water

½ tablespoon fresh dill, chopped

Directions:

In a substantial skillet, heat oil on high heat.

Sprinkle the chicken with salt and black pepper.

Place inside the skillet, skin side down and cook for about 3-4 minutes.

Transfer the thighs in a very plate.

In a similar skillet, add onion on medium heat and sauté approximately 4-5 minutes.

Return the thighs in skillet, skin side up with broth.

Place the dill sprigs over thighs and sprinkle with cayenne, turmeric and salt.

Bring to some boil reducing the warmth to medium-low.

Simmer, covered for around 40-45 minutes, coating the thighs with cooking liquid.

Meanwhile in a small bowl, mix together arrowroot starch and water.

Discard the thyme sprigs and transfer the thighs into a bowl.
Stir in freshly squeezed lemon juice in sauce.
Slowly, add arrowroot starch mixture, stirring continuously.
Cook, stirring occasionally for approximately 3-4 minutes or till desired thickness.
Serve hot using the topping of chopped dill.
Nutrition:
Calories: 462, Fat: 11g, Carbohydrates: 20g, Fiber: 6g, Protein: 35g

329.   Citrus Glazed Chicken

Servings: 6
Preparation Time: 10 min
Cooking Time: 18 minutes
Ingredients:

3 garlic cloves, minced
½ cup fresh orange juice
1 tablespoon apple cider vinegar
2 tablespoons coconut aminos
½ teaspoon orange blossom water
¼ teaspoon ground ginger
¼ teaspoon ground cinnamon
Salt, to taste
2 pound skinless, bone-in chicken thighs
Directions:
For marinate in a big bowl, mix together all ingredients except chicken.
Add chicken and coat with marinade generously.
Cover and refrigerate to marinate for around 2 hours.
Heat a sizable nonstick skillet, on medium-high heat.
Add chicken in skillet, reserving marinade.
Cook for about 5-6 minutes or till golden brown.
Flip the medial side and cook for about 4 minutes.
Add reserved marinade and provide to a boil.
Reduce heat to medium-low heat.
Cook, covered for about 6-8 minutes or till sauce becomes thick.
Serve warm.
Nutrition:
Calories: 477, Fat: 14g, Carbohydrates: 23g, Fiber: 9g, Protein: 38g

330.   Herbed Chicken with Olives

Servings: 4
Preparation Time: fifteen minutes
Cooking Time: 1 hour 45 minutes
Ingredients:

4-6 bone-in chicken legs and thighs
Salt and freshly ground black pepper, to taste
1 tablespoon fresh lemon juice
1 cup olives, pitted and sliced
¼ cup essential olive oil
2 medium yellow onions, sliced thinly
2 tablespoons fresh lemon zest, grated finely
3 garlic cloves, crushed
½ teaspoon ground ginger
¼ teaspoon saffron threads, crushed
1½ cups chicken broth
¼ cup fresh parsley leaves, chopped
¼ cup fresh cilantro leaves, chopped
Directions:
Drizzle the chicken with all the freshly squeezed lemon juice and sprinkle with salt and black pepper.
In a substantial Dutch oven, heat oil on medium-high heat.
Add chicken and cook for around 4-6 minutes per side.
Add remaining ingredients except herbs and bring to a boil.
Reduce the heat to medium-low.
Simmer for around 75 minutes.
Stir in herbs and simmer for 15 minutes more.
Serve immediately.

331.   Chicken with Chickpeas & Veggies

Servings: 4
Preparation Time: 15 minutes
Cooking Time: 36 minutes
Ingredients:

1-pound skinless, boneless chicken, cubed
Salt, to taste
2 carrots, peeled and sliced
1 onion, chopped
2 celery stalks, chopped
2 garlic cloves, chopped
1 tablespoon fresh ginger root, minced
½ teaspoon dried oregano, crushed
¾ teaspoon ground cumin
½ teaspoon paprika
¼ tsp red pepper cayenne
¼ teaspoon ground turmeric
1 cup tomatoes, crushed
1½ cups chicken broth
1 zucchini, sliced
1 cup canned chickpeas, drained
1 tablespoon freshly squeezed lemon juice
Directions:
Heat a big nonstick pan on medium heat.
Add chicken and sprinkle with salt and cook for approximately 4-5 minutes.
With a slotted spoon, transfer chicken right into a plate.
In exactly the same pan, add carrot, onion, celery and garlic and sauté for about 4-5 minutes.
Add ginger, oregano and spices and sauté for around 1 minute.
Add chicken, tomato and broth and provide to some boil.
Reduce the temperature to low and simmer for approximately 10 minutes.
Add zucchini and chickpeas and simmer, covered for approximately fifteen minutes.
Stir in fresh lemon juice and serve hot.
Nutrition:
Calories: 286, Fat: 3.7g, Carbohydrates: 27.9g, Fiber: 6.3g, Protein: 36g

332.   Chicken Chili with Zucchini

Servings: 4-5
Preparation Time: 15 minutes
Cooking Time: 35 minutes
Ingredients:
3 tablespoons organic olive oil
1 poblano pepper, seeded and chopped
½ of red onion, chopped
1 tablespoon garlic, minced
1 zucchini, halved lengthwise and sliced
2 (15-ouncecans cannellini beans, rinsed and drained
1½ cups rotisserie chicken, shredded
1 tablespoon fresh oregano, minced
1 teaspoon ground turmeric
1 teaspoon ground cumin
Salt and freshly ground black pepper, to taste

2 cups water
2 cups chicken broth
1/3 cup sharp cheddar cheese, shredded
Chopped chives, for garnishing

Directions:

In a substantial pan, heat oil on medium-low heat.

Add poblano pepper and onion and sauté for approximately 10 min.

Add garlic and zucchini and cook for around 5 minutes.

Add remaining ingredients except cheese and chives and produce to your boil.

Reduce the heat to low and simmer for around twenty minutes.

Add the cheese and stir till well combined.

Serve hot with the topping of chives.

Nutrition:

Calories: 446, Fat: 10g, Carbohydrates: 26g, Fiber: 12g, Protein: 40g

333. Chicken Chili with Sweet Potato

Servings: 6

Preparation Time: 15 minutes

Cooking Time: 35 minutes

Ingredients:

2 tablespoons extra-virgin essential olive oil

1 medium red onion, chopped

4-6 garlic cloves, minced

2 medium sweet potatoes, peeled and cubed

2 teaspoons dried oregano, crushed

2 teaspoons ground cumin

2 teaspoons ground ginger

1 teaspoon red chili powder

¼ teaspoon red pepper flakes, crushed

Salt, to taste

4 cups chicken broth

2 (15-ouncecans white beans, rinsed and drained

¾ cup mild roasted green chilis

4 cups cooked chicken, shredded

1 tablespoon fresh lime juice

2 tablespoons fresh cilantro, chopped

Directions:

In a substantial pan, heat oil on medium-high heat.

Add poblano pepper and onion and sauté for about 2-3 minutes.

Add garlic and sauté for approximately 1-2 minutes.

Add sweet potato, oregano and spices and stir to combine well.

Add broth, beans and green chilis and provide to your boil.

Reduce the warmth to low and simmer for about 25-a half-hour.

Stir in chicken and lime juice and take off from heat.

Serve hot with all the topping of cilantro.

Nutrition:

Calories: 415, Fat: 9g, Carbohydrates: 23g, Fiber: 10g, Protein: 39g

334. Chicken Chili with Two Beans & Corn

Servings: 6

Preparation Time: 15 minutes

Cooking Time: 28 minutes

Ingredients:

1 tbsp essential olive oil

1-pound skinless, boneless chicken, cubed into 1-inch size

1 cup onion, chopped

1 cup green bell pepper, seeded and chopped

1½ teaspoons dried oregano, crushed

1 teaspoon garlic powder

1 teaspoon ground cumin

1 tablespoon paprika

¼ teaspoon red pepper flakes, crushed

1 cup frozen corn

1 (14½-ouncecan diced tomatoes with liquid

1 (15-ouncecan great Northern beans, rinsed and drained

1 (15-ouncecan black beans, rinsed and drained

1 cup chicken broth
Directions:
In a substantial pan, heat oil on medium-high heat.
Add chicken, onion and bell pepper and sauté approximately 6-8 minutes.
Add oregano and spices and stir to blend well.
Add remaining ingredients and provide to your boil.
Reduce the temperature to low and simmer for about twenty minutes.
Serve hot.
Nutrition:
Calories: 188, Fat: 4g, Carbohydrates: 20g, Fiber: 6g, Protein: 18g

335.　　　Chicken & Tomato Curry

Servings: 4
Preparation Time: 15 minutes
Cooking Time: 70 minutes
Ingredients:

3 tablespoons organic olive oil
1 medium onion, chopped
1 teaspoon ginger paste
1 teaspoon garlic paste
4-6 large fresh tomatoes, chopped finely
1 teaspoon ground cumin
Pinch of ground turmeric
1½ teaspoons red chili powder
2 pounds bone-in chicken breasts, cut each breast into 2-3 pieces
2 cups water, divided
2 cardamom pods
2 tablespoons fresh cilantro, chopped
Directions:
In a big pan, heat oil on medium heat.
Add onion and sauté for about 8-9 minutes.
Add ginger and garlic and sauté for about1 minute.
Add tomatoes and spices reducing the heat to medium-low.
Cook, stirring occasionally for about 15-20 min.
Remove from heat whilst aside to chill slightly.
In a blender, add tomato mixture and pulse till smooth.
Return the mixture to pan with chicken and ½ cup from the water on medium-high heat.
Cook, stirring occasionally approximately 15-twenty minutes.
Add cardamom pods and remaining water and lower the temperature to low.
Simmer for approximately 15-20 min.
Serve top with the topping of cilantro.
Nutrition:
Calories: 470, Fat: 10g, Carbohydrates: 20g, Fiber: 13g, Protein: 36g

336.　　Chicken & Sweet Potato Curry

Increase the flavor of the traditional chicken curry with all the addition of healthy sweet potato. Curry powder and ground ginger adds a rich flavor.
Servings: 4
Preparation Time: fifteen minutes
Cooking Time: 6-10 minutes
Ingredients:
2 tablespoons organic olive oil, divided
Salt and freshly ground black pepper, to taste
1-pound skinless, boneless chicken breast, cut into chunks
½ of onion, chopped
2 minced garlic cloves
1 teaspoon ground ginger
1 teaspoon curry powder
½ cup chicken broth
2 large sweet potatoes, peeled and cubed
1 can coconut milk

Directions:

In a sizable skillet, heat 1 tablespoon of oil on medium heat.

Add chicken and sprinkle with salt and black pepper.

Stir fry approximately 3-4 minutes per side.

Transfer chicken right into a plate.

In the identical skillet, heat remaining oil on medium heat.

Add onion and sauté for about 5-7 minutes.

Add garlic, ground ginger and curry powder and sauté for around 1-2 minutes.

Add chicken and remaining ingredients and stir to mix well.

Simmer, covered for around 15-twenty minutes.

Stir in salt and black pepper and serve hot.

Nutrition:

Calories: 442, Fat: 9g, Carbohydrates: 30g, Fiber: 6g, Protein: 34g

337.   Dill Chicken Thighs

Preparation Time: 10 minutes

Cooking Time: 45 minutes

Servings: 4

Ingredients:

2 tablespoons olive oil

1 yellow onion, chopped

2 pounds chicken thighs, skinless, boneless

4 garlic cloves, minced

½ cup chicken stock

1 teaspoon turmeric powder

1 leek, sliced

A pinch of salt and black pepper

3 tablespoons dill, chopped

2 tablespoons lemon juice

Directions:

Heat up a pan with the oil over medium heat, add the onion, garlic and leek and sauté for 5 minutes.

Add the meat and brown for 5 minutes more.

Add the rest of the ingredients, toss, introduce the pan in the oven and bake at 380 degrees F for 35 minutes.

Divide everything between plates and serve.

Nutrition: calories 531, fat 24.2, fiber 1.5, carbs 8.6, protein 67.1

338.   Turkey and Berries Mix

Preparation Time: 5 minutes

Cooking Time: 8 hours

Servings: 4

Ingredients:

2 pounds turkey breast, skinless, boneless and sliced

1 cup blackberries

1 yellow onion, sliced

2 tablespoons olive oil
½ cup chicken stock
½ teaspoon chili powder
1 teaspoon sweet paprika
A pinch of salt and black pepper
4 garlic cloves, minced
1 tablespoon parsley, chopped
Directions:
In a slow cooker, combine the turkey with the blackberries and the other ingredients, toss gently, put the lid on and cook on Low for 8 hours.
Divide the mix between plates and serve.
Nutrition: calories 331, fat 11.2, fiber 4, carbs 17.2, protein 39.9

339.   Turkey and Leeks

Preparation Time: 5 minutes
Cooking Time: 30 minutes
Servings: 4
Ingredients:
2 pounds turkey breast, skinless, boneless and cubed
2 leeks, sliced
1 tablespoon olive oil
2 teaspoons coriander, chopped
A pinch of salt and black pepper
2 garlic clove, minced
2 tablespoons balsamic vinegar
2 tablespoons almonds, chopped
1 tablespoon cilantro, chopped
Directions:
Heat up a pan with the oil over medium-high heat, add the leeks and the garlic and sauté for 5 minutes.
Add the turkey and brown for 5 minutes more.
Add the rest of the ingredients, toss, cook over medium heat for 20 minutes, divide between plates and serve.
Nutrition: calories 320, fat 9, fiber 3, carbs 18, protein 40.6

340.   Chicken and Zucchini Chili

Preparation Time: 5 minutes
Cooking Time: 35 minutes
Servings: 4
Ingredients:
1 pound chicken breast, skinless, boneless and ground
1 yellow onion, chopped
2 tablespoons olive oil
2 zucchinis, sliced
2 garlic cloves, minced

2 cups tomatoes, cubed
½ cup tomato paste
1 cup chicken stock
1 teaspoon chili powder
1 teaspoon cumin, ground
1 teaspoon rosemary, dried
A pinch of salt and black pepper
1 tablespoon cilantro, chopped
Directions:
Heat up a pot with the oil over medium-high heat, add the onion and the garlic and sauté for 5 minutes.
Add the meat and brown for 5 minutes more.
Add the zucchinis and the other ingredients, toss, bring to a simmer and cook over medium heat for 25 minutes.
Divide the chili into bowls and serve.
Nutrition: calories 269, fat 10.8, fiber 4.6, carbs 17, protein 28.2

341.   Lime Creamy Turkey

Preparation Time: 10 minutes
Cooking Time: 30 minutes
Servings: 4
Ingredients:
1 pound turkey breast, skinless, boneless and cubed
1 yellow onion, chopped
2 tablespoons avocado oil
1 teaspoon chili powder
A pinch of salt and black pepper
1 cup coconut cream
1 tablespoon lime zest, grated
2 tablespoons lime juice
3 garlic cloves, minced
2 green chilies, chopped
Directions:
Heat up a pan with the oil over medium-high heat, add onion, garlic, chilies and chili powder and sauté for 5 minutes.
Add the meat and cook it for 5 minutes more.
Add the remaining ingredients, toss, bring to a simmer and cook over medium heat for 20 minutes more.
Divide everything between plates and serve.
Nutrition: calories 283, fat 17.2, fiber 3.3, carbs 12.6, protein 21.4

342.   Chicken and Oregano Squash

Preparation Time: 10 minutes
Cooking Time: 40 minutes
Servings: 4

Ingredients:
2 pounds chicken breast, skinless, boneless and sliced
1 yellow onion, chopped
2 tablespoons olive oil
2 garlic cloves, minced
1 teaspoon turmeric powder
½ teaspoon cumin, ground
½ teaspoon fennel seeds, crushed
14 ounces canned tomatoes, chopped
1 teaspoon oregano, dried
1 teaspoon chili powder
A pinch of salt and black pepper
2 cups butternut squash, peeled and cubed
2 tablespoons cilantro, chopped
Directions:
Heat up a pot with the oil over medium-high heat, add the onion and the garlic and sauté for 5 minutes.
Add the meat and brown it for 5 minutes more.
Add the cumin, turmeric, the squash and the other ingredients, toss, bring to a simmer and cook over medium heat for 30 minutes more.
Divide the whole mix between plates and serve.
Nutrition: calories 261, fat 4, fiber 8, carbs 15, protein 7

343.   Chicken with Beans

Preparation Time: 10 minutes
Cooking Time: 40 minutes
Servings: 4
Ingredients:
2 pounds chicken breasts, skinless, boneless and cubed
1 cup canned black beans, drained and rinsed
1 cup canned red kidney beans, drained and rinsed
1 yellow onion, chopped
2 tablespoons avocado oil
A pinch of salt and black pepper
1 teaspoon smoked paprika
1 teaspoon basil, dried
1 cup chicken stock
1 cup canned tomatoes, crushed
1 tablespoon parsley, chopped
Directions:
Heat up a pan with the oil over medium-high heat, add the onion and sauté for 5 minutes.
Add the meat and brown it for 5 minutes more.
Add the beans and the other ingredients, toss, reduce heat to medium and cook everything for 30 minutes more.
Divide the mix between plates and serve.
Nutrition: calories 312, fat 7, fiber 7, carbs 15, protein 15

344.   Turkey and Basil Rice

Preparation Time: 10 minutes
Cooking Time: 40 minutes
Servings: 4
Ingredients:
2 pounds turkey breast, skinless, boneless and cubed
1 yellow onion, chopped
2 tablespoons olive oil
3 garlic cloves, minced
A pinch of salt and black pepper
1 cup black rice
3 cups chicken stock
1 tablespoon basil, chopped
½ teaspoon cumin, ground
1 teaspoon chili powder
1 teaspoon rosemary, dried
1 tablespoon thyme, chopped
Directions:
Heat up a pot with the oil over medium-high heat, add the onion and the garlic and sauté for 5 minutes.
Add the meat and brown for 5 minutes more.
Add the rice, stock and the other ingredients, toss, bring to a simmer and cook over medium heat for 30 minutes.
Divide the mix between plates and serve right away.
Nutrition: calories 251, fat 4, fiber 7, carbs 13, protein 5

345.   Chicken with Mushrooms Mix

Preparation Time: 5 minutes
Cooking Time: 45 minutes
Servings: 4
Ingredients:
1 yellow onion, chopped
2 tablespoons avocado oil
2 pounds chicken breast, skinless, boneless and sliced
2 cups white mushrooms, sliced
A pinch of salt and black pepper
¼ cup mint, chopped
2 garlic cloves, minced
1 teaspoon coriander, ground
½ teaspoon cayenne pepper
1 tablespoon sweet paprika
1 tablespoon lemon juice
Directions:
Heat up a pan with the oil over medium-high heat, add the onion and the garlic and sauté for 5 minutes.

Add the mushrooms and cook them for 5 minutes more.
Add the chicken and sauté for another 5 minutes.
Add the rest of the ingredients, put the pan in the oven and bake at 380 degrees F for 30 minutes.
Divide everything between plates and serve.
Nutrition: calories 251, fat 4, fiber 6, carbs 15, protein 7

346.   Chicken and Hot Peas

Preparation Time: 10 minutes
Cooking Time: 40 minutes
Servings: 4
Ingredients:
2 pounds chicken breast, skinless, boneless and sliced
4 scallions, chopped
2 tablespoons olive oil
2 cups sugar snap peas
2 garlic cloves, minced
1 teaspoon cayenne pepper
½ teaspoon hot paprika
2 tablespoons balsamic vinegar
1 tablespoon sesame seeds, toasted
1 tablespoon cilantro, chopped
Directions:
Heat up a pan with the olive oil over medium-high heat, add the scallions and the garlic and sauté for 5 minutes.
Add the meat and brown for 5 minutes more.
Add the snap peas and the rest of the ingredients, toss, cook over medium heat for 30 minutes more, divide between plates and serve.
Nutrition: calories 261, fat 2, fiber 6, carbs 15, protein 6

347.   Turkey with Lime Chickpeas

Preparation Time: 10 minutes
Cooking Time: 35 minutes
Servings: 4
Ingredients:
1 sweet onion, chopped
4 garlic cloves, minced
1 pound turkey breast, skinless, boneless and cubed
2 tablespoons olive oil
1 cup canned chickpeas, drained and rinsed
1 cup chicken stock
2 tablespoons lemon juice
A pinch of salt and black pepper
1 tablespoon parsley, chopped
Directions:

Heat up a pan with the oil over medium-high heat, add the onion, garlic and the meat and brown for 10 minutes.

Add the rest of the ingredients, toss, cook over medium heat for 25 minutes more, divide between plates and serve.

Nutrition: calories 272, fat 5, fiber 6, carbs 15, protein 6

348.   Turkey and Cucumber Mix

Preparation Time: 5 minutes
Cooking Time: 35 minutes
Servings: 4
Ingredients:
2 pounds turkey breast, skinless, boneless and sliced
2 tablespoons olive oil
1 yellow onion, chopped
2 teaspoons Italian seasoning
1 teaspoon coriander, ground
½ teaspoon basil, dried
A pinch of salt and black pepper
2 cucumbers, sliced
1 tablespoon cilantro, chopped
Directions:
Heat up a pan with the oil over medium-high heat, add the onion and sauté for 5 minutes.
Add the meat and brown for 5 minutes more.
Add the rest of the ingredients, toss, introduce in the oven and bake at 400 degrees F for 25 minutes more.
Divide the mix between plates and serve.
Nutrition: calories 277, fat 4, fiber 4, carbs 14, protein 8

349.   Chicken with Spinach and Fennel

Preparation Time: 5 minutes
Cooking Time: 35 minutes
Servings: 4
Ingredients:
2 pounds chicken thighs, skinless, boneless and cubed
1 yellow onion, chopped
2 tablespoons olive oil
A pinch of salt and black pepper
1 cup baby spinach
1 fennel bulb, sliced
½ teaspoon fennel seeds, crushed
½ teaspoon coriander, ground
½ cup chicken stock
1 tablespoon cilantro, chopped
1 tablespoon chives, chopped
Directions:

Heat up a pan with the oil over medium-high heat, add the onion and the fennel and sauté for 5 minutes.

Add the chicken and brown for 5 minutes more.

Add the fennel seeds and the other ingredients, toss, bring to a simmer and cook over medium heat for 25 minutes more.

Divide the mix between plates and serve.

Nutrition: calories 288, fat 4, fiber 6, carbs 12, protein 7

350.   Chicken with Peppers and Olives

Preparation Time: 10 minutes
Cooking Time: 40 minutes
Servings: 4
Ingredients:
1 pound chicken breasts, skinless, boneless and sliced
1 red bell pepper, sliced
2 tablespoons olive oil
1 green bell pepper, sliced
1 yellow onion, chopped
1 cup black olives, pitted and halved
4 garlic cloves, minced
1 bay leaf
1 teaspoon black peppercorns
A pinch of salt and black pepper
1 tablespoon balsamic vinegar
Directions:
In a roasting pan, combine the chicken with the bell peppers and the other ingredients, toss a bit, introduce in the oven and bake at 380 degrees F for 40 minutes.

Divide the mix between plates and serve.

Nutrition: calories 221, fat 4, fiber 5, carbs 14, protein 11

351.   Turkey with Radish Quinoa

Preparation Time: 10 minutes
Cooking Time: 40 minutes
Servings: 4
Ingredients:
1 pound turkey breast, skinless, boneless and sliced
1 cup quinoa
3 cups chicken stock
½ cup radish, sliced
2 tablespoons olive oil
A pinch of salt and black pepper
4 scallions, chopped
¼ cup basil, torn
Directions:

Heat up a pan with the oil over medium-high heat, add the scallions and the meat and brown for 5 minutes.

Add the quinoa and the other ingredients, toss, bring to a simmer and cook over medium heat for 35 minutes.

Divide everything between plates and serve.

Nutrition: calories 213, fat 3, fiber 5, carbs 9, protein 6

352. Rosemary Chicken

Preparation Time: 10 minutes
Cooking Time: 8 hours
Servings: 4
Ingredients:
1 yellow onion, sliced
2 pounds chicken thighs, boneless and skinless
2 tablespoons olive oil
A pinch of salt and black pepper
1 rosemary bunch, torn
Juice of ½ lemon
½ cup tomatoes, cubed
Directions:
In your slow cooker, combine the chicken with the oil and the other ingredients, toss and cook on Low for 8 hours.

Divide the mix between plates and serve.

Nutrition: calories 300, fat 7, fiber 4, carbs 15, protein 20

353. Chicken and Cherries Mix

Preparation Time: 5 minutes
Cooking Time: 30 minutes
Servings: 4
Ingredients:
1 pound chicken breasts, skinless, boneless and sliced
A pinch of salt and black pepper
2 tablespoons lemon juice
1 tablespoon lemon zest, grated
2 tablespoons olive oil
1 teaspoon sweet paprika
2 cups sweet cherries, pitted and chopped
1 tablespoon cilantro, chopped
Directions:
Heat up a pan with the oil over medium heat, add the chicken and brown for 5 minutes.

Add the rest of the ingredients, toss, cook over medium heat for 25 minutes more, divide between plates and serve.

Nutrition: calories 227, fat 3, fiber 6, carbs 15, protein 9

354. Duck and Cauliflower Mix

Preparation Time: 10 minutes
Cooking Time: 35 minutes
Servings: 4
Ingredients:
1 yellow onion, chopped
1 pound duck breast, boneless and skin scored
2 tablespoons olive oil
2 tablespoons parsley, chopped
4 garlic cloves, minced
A pinch of salt and black pepper
Juice of 1 lemon
½ pound cauliflower florets
1 teaspoon chili powder
½ teaspoon red pepper, crushed
Directions:
Heat up a pan with the oil over medium-high heat, add the onion and sauté for 5 minutes.
Add the duck, skin side down and cook for 5 minutes more.
Add the rest of the ingredients, toss, cook over medium heat for 25 minutes more, divide between plates and serve.
Nutrition: calories 278, fat 14, fiber 6, carbs 14, protein 27

355.   Chicken with Peaches

Preparation Time: 10 minutes
Cooking Time: 30 minutes
Servings: 4
Ingredients:
1 yellow onion, chopped
2 tablespoons olive oil
1 pound chicken breast, skinless, boneless and sliced
1 cup peaches, peeled and cubed
3 tablespoons lime juice
A pinch of salt and black pepper
1 tablespoon lime zest, grated
1 tablespoon cilantro, chopped
Directions:
Heat up a pan with the oil over medium-high heat, add the onion and sauté for 5 minutes.
Add the meat and brown for 5 minutes more.
Add the rest of the ingredients, toss, cook over medium heat for 20 minutes, divide between plates and serve.
Nutrition: calories 271, fat 4, fiber 8, carbs 16, protein 8

356.   Simple and Delicious Chicken Drumettes

Servings 4
Preparation Time: 30 minutes
Ingredients

2 tablespoons tallow
Salt to taste
4 chicken drumettes
2 cloves minced garlic
1/2 cup chopped leeks
1 rosemary sprig
1 thyme sprig
1 teaspoon mixed peppercorns
1 tablespoon Worcestershire sauce
2 crushed tomatoes
1 cup turkey stock
1/2 teaspoon mustard seeds
1 teaspoon dried marjoram
1 teaspoon cayenne pepper
Directions
Put a pan on medium-high heat and melt the tallow. Put the salt onto the chicken drumettes.
Cook the chicken drumettes until they are slightly browned on both sides. Put to one side.
Cook the garlic and leeks over a moderate heat in the pan drippings.
Add the rosemary, thyme, peppercorns, Worcestershire sauce, tomatoes, turkey stock, mustard seeds, marjoram and cayenne pepper. Simmer for 15 – 20 minutes partially covered. Serve hot.
Nutrition: 165 Calories; 12.4g Protein; 9.8g Fat; 7.7g Carbs; 3.9g Sugar

357.   Creamy Chicken Salad with Cheese

Servings 6
Preparation Time: 20 minutes
Ingredients
2 chicken breasts
2 sliced medium-sized cucumbers
1/3 teaspoon dried basil
1/2 teaspoon dried oregano
1/4 teaspoon chili pepper flakes
1/2 teaspoon coarse salt
1/4 teaspoon ground black pepper
2 romaine hearts, leaves separated
1/4 cup finely grated Parmesan
For the dressing:
2 large egg yolks
2 minced garlic cloves
1 teaspoon mustard
1 tablespoon fresh lime juice
1/4 cup olive oil
Directions
Grill the chicken breasts and cut into cubes when cooked.
Mix the chicken with the sliced cucumber and the basil, oregano, chili pepper flakes, salt and pepper.
Place the romaine leaves in a salad bowl and add the chicken and cucumber.

Whisk together the egg yolks, garlic cloves, mustard, lime juice and olive oil and pour this over the chicken and cucumber.

Sprinkle the parmesan on top and serve. Delicious.

Nutrition: Calories 183 ,Protein 16.3g ,Fat 12.5g ,Carbs 1.7g ,Sugar 0.3g

358.   The Best Chicken Stew Ever

Servings 6
Preparation Time: 1 hour
Ingredients
2 tablespoons tallow at room temperature
2 sliced garlic cloves
2 medium finely chopped shallots
1 quart chicken broth
1 teaspoon dried marjoram
1 sprig rosemary
1 pound chicken drumsticks
2 chopped ripe tomatoes
1 chopped poblano pepper
1 chopped celery
1 chopped bell pepper
1/2 teaspoon smoked paprika
1/2 teaspoon ground black pepper
1 teaspoon salt
Directions
Preheat a heavy pot over a medium flame. Melt the tallow and cook the garlic and shallots until tender and fragrant.

Turn the heat up to moderate-high and mix in the rosemary, marjoram, chicken broth and chicken drumsticks. Bring to the boil.

Add the tomatoes, poblano pepper, celery, bell pepper, smoked paprika, salt and pepper. Reduce the heat to medium-low and simmer for 50 minutes.

Take out the chicken bones and chop the chicken. Serve the dish hot.

Nutrition: Calories 239 ,Protein 25.6g ,Fat 14.7g ,Carbs 2.5g ,Sugar 1.9g

359.   Chicken, Rutabaga and Taro Leaf Soup

Servings 4
Preparation Time: 45 minutes
Ingredients
1 pound chicken thighs
1/2 cup cubed rutabaga
2 celery stalks
1/2 cup chopped leeks
1/2 cup roughly chopped taro leaves
1/4 teaspoon granulated garlic
1/4 teaspoon ground cloves
1 tablespoon chopped fresh parsley

Salt and black pepper, to taste
3 cups water
1 cup canned chicken consommé
1 teaspoon cayenne pepper
Directions
Put all of the ingredients apart from the cayenne pepper into a stockpot and bring to the boil on high heat.
Turn the heat down to moderate-low and let it simmer for 35 minutes. Partially cover the pot.
Take the vegetables and the chicken out of the pot. Add the cayenne pepper to the broth and simmer for 8 minutes.
Cut the chicken meat off the bone when cool enough and put back in the pot. Simmer for a few minutes and enjoy.
Nutrition: Calories 256 ,Protein 3.5g ,Fat 12.9g ,Carbs 3.2g ,Sugar 1.4g

360.   Keto Flat bread and Chicken Liver Pâté

Servings 4
Preparation Time: 2 hours
Ingredients
10 ounces chicken livers
1 teaspoon granulated garlic
1 finely chopped white onion
2 teaspoons Italian seasoning blend
4 tablespoons olive oil
For Flat bread:
1 1/4 cups almond flour
1/2 cup flax meal
1 1/2 tablespoons psyllium husks
Salt, to taste
1/2 stick butter
1 cup lukewarm water
1/2 teaspoon minced fresh ginger
1/2 teaspoon turmeric powder
Directions
In a food processor blend the chicken livers, garlic, onion, Italian seasoning and olive oil until it is all well mixed. Refrigerate.
To make the flat bread, mix together the dry ingredients in one bowl and the wet in another. Then combine the two and mix well.
Leave the dough to rest at room temperature for a couple of hours. Then divide the dough into 8 pieces and roll out until each is very thin.
Preheat a skillet to a moderate-high heat and cook the flat bread for a minute on each side. Serve these with the chicken liver pate. Enjoy!
Nutrition: Calories 395 ,Protein 17.9g ,Fat 30.2g ,Carbs 3.6g ,Sugar 1.4g

361.   Turkey Meatballs Chinese- Style

Servings 4

Preparation Time: 20 minutes
Ingredients
For the Meatballs:
3/4 pound ground turkey
3 teaspoon Five-spice powder
3 teaspoon black pepper
1/3 cup freshly grated cheddar
1 egg
For the Sauce:
1 1/3 cups water
2 tablespoons Worcestershire sauce
1/2 cup sugar-free tomato puree
1/3 cup red wine vinegar
1/2 teaspoon cayenne pepper
3/4 cup erythritol
Directions
Combine the ground turkey with the five-spice powder, black pepper, grated cheddar and egg. Form the mixture into about 28 meatballs.
Heat a skillet over moderate heat and brown the meatballs on all sides. Take the meatballs out of the skillet.
Put the water, Worcestershire sauce, tomato puree, vinegar, cayenne pepper and erythritol in the skillet and whisk.
Put in the meatballs and simmer for about 10 minutes until the meatballs are cooked. Serve with a lettuce salad.
Nutrition: Calories 244 ,Protein 27.6g ,Fat 13.7g ,Carbs 5g ,Sugar 3.2g

362.   Chicken Meatballs for Kids

Servings 6
Preparation Time: 20 minutes
Ingredients
For the Meatballs:
2 lightly beaten eggs
3/4 cup grated Parmesan cheese
1 teaspoon onion powder
1 tablespoon chopped fresh parsley leaves
1 tablespoon chopped sage leaves
1/3 teaspoon dried rosemary
2 minced garlic cloves
Salt and ground black pepper, to taste
1/2 teaspoon crushed red pepper flakes
1 1/4 pounds ground chicken
For the sauce:
2 ½ tablespoons bacon fat
3 ripe chopped tomatoes
1 peeled and chopped white onion
1 cup chicken stock

Directions

Combine the ingredients for the meatballs and shape them to the size you want.

Heat up 1 tablespoon of bacon fat in a skillet over medium heat and cook the meatballs for 2 –4 minutes. Put them to one side and keep warm.

Heat the rest of the fat and sauté the onions until soft. Stir in the chicken stock and tomatoes and cook for another 4 minutes.

Put in the meatballs and cook on medium-low for 6 minutes. Then it's ready to serve. Enjoy!

Nutrition: Calories 252 ,Protein 34.2g ,Fat 9.7g ,Carbs 5.3g ,Sugar 2.7g

363.   Chicken and Prosciutto with Cottage Cheese

Servings 2
Preparation Time: 35 minutes
Ingredients
1 boneless, skinless and flattened chicken breast
Salt and ground black pepper to taste
1 teaspoon smoked paprika
1/2 cup Cottage cheese
1 tablespoon fresh cilantro, chopped
4 slices of prosciutto
Directions
Preheat your oven to 3900F. Line a baking pan with parchment paper.

Put the salt, ground pepper and smoked paprika on the chicken breast. Then put on the cottage cheese and sprinkle the cilantro on top.

Cut the chicken into 4 pieces and wrap each piece with prosciutto Secure with a toothpick.

Put the chicken into a baking pan and cook for about half an hour. Serve hot.

364.   Superb Chicken and Broccoli

Servings 4
Preparation Time: 50 minutes
Ingredients
1 pound chicken wings
1 teaspoon garlic paste
1 cup chopped scallions
1 pound broccoli florets
3 tablespoons olive oil
1 teaspoon Italian seasoning mix
2 cups Colby cheese, shredded
Directions
Put the oven on at 3900F. Grease a baking sheet.

Roast the chicken wings for about 35 minutes until they are cooked all the way through. Add the garlic paste, scallions and broccoli.

Put the Italian seasoning mix on the broccoli and chicken. Pour the olive oil on them.

Roast for another 13 – 15 minutes Sprinkle the cheese on top and serve hot. Bon appétit!

Nutrition: Calories 450 ,Protein 25.1g ,Fat 35.5g ,Carbs 4.6g ,Sugar 2.1g

365. Zingy Chicken with Avocado-Mayo Sauce

Servings 4
Preparation Time: 20 minutes
Ingredients
1/3 cup almond meal
1/4 teaspoon chili flakes
1/3 teaspoon ground cumin
1 teaspoon cayenne pepper
1 teaspoon lime zest
1 teaspoon shallot powder
Salt and pepper to taste
2 eggs
8 chicken thighs cut into small chunks
2 tablespoons olive oil
For the Sauce:
1/2 medium Has avocado
1/2 cup mayonnaise
1/2 teaspoon coarse salt
1 teaspoon garlic paste
Directions
Put the meal into a food processor together with the chili flakes, cumin, cayenne pepper, lime zest, shallot powder, salt and pepper. Blend them together.
Whisk the eggs in a small dish.
Pat the chicken thighs dry with a paper towel. Put the chicken pieces into the eggs and then into the almond meal mix.
Take a skillet and heat the oil over moderate heat. Fry the chicken for 4 – 6 minutes on each side. Put the chicken on paper towels to drain off the oil.
Make the sauce by mashing up the avocado and mixing it with the mayonnaise, salt and garlic paste. Serve the hot chicken with the sauce.
Nutrition: Calories 370 ,Protein 31.4g ,Fat 25g ,Carbs 4.1 ,Sugar 0.7g

366. Duck and Eggplant Quiche

Servings 4
Preparation Time: 45 minutes
Ingredients
1/2 teaspoon kosher salt
1 1/2 cups almond flour
8 eggs
1 pound ground duck meat
1 1/2 tablespoons melted butter
1/3 cup whipping cream
1/2 teaspoon dried basil
1/2 teaspoons celery seeds
1 teaspoon ground black pepper
1/2 pound peeled and sliced eggplant

Directions

Put the oven on at 3500F.

Mix the kosher salt in with the almond meal. Add one of the eggs and the melted butter to form a dough. Roll into a round shape.

Put the dough into a slightly-greased baking dish.

Cook the ground duck in a skillet for around 2 -3 minutes. Stir all the time.

In a mixing bowl, mix the whipping cream, basil, celery seeds and black pepper.

Mix in the duck and combine well with the cream mixture. Pour it into the baking dish. Put the eggplant slices on top.

The quiche needs to be baked for between 37 – 42 minutes. Cool a little before. Enjoy!

Nutrition: Calories 562 ,Protein 22.5g ,Fat49.5g ,Carbs 6.7g ,Sugar 2.4g

367.   Chicken Fillets Hungarian-Style

Servings 6
Preparation Time: 30 minutes
Ingredients
1 ½ pounds chicken fillet
1/2 teaspoon freshly ground black pepper
1 teaspoon coarse salt
1 teaspoon thyme
1/2 teaspoon marjoram
1 teaspoon Hungarian paprika
1 teaspoon garlic paste
1/4low-sodium soy sauce
1/2 cup homemade tomato sauce
1 large chopped onion
1 chopped and deveined bell pepper
2 tablespoons curly parsley, for garnish
Directions
Rub each chicken fillet with the black pepper, salt, thyme, marjoram, paprika and garlic paste.
Preheat a pot over a moderate flame and put in the chicken.
Cook on each side for 4 – 5 minutes.
Pour in the soy sauce and the tomato sauce and allow to boil. Add the onion and bell pepper.
Partially cover the pot, reduce the heat to moderate-low and cook for 25 minutes more. Garnish with parsley and serve hot. Bon appétit!
Nutrition: Calories 239 ,Protein 34.3g ,Fat 8.6g ,Carbs 5.5g ,Sugar 3.3g

368.   Turkey and Chinese Cabbage

Servings 4
Preparation Time: 45 minutes
Ingredients
1 tablespoon olive oil
1 teaspoon minced fresh garlic
1/2 cup chopped shallots
1 pound finely chopped Chinese cabbage

2 ripe chopped tomatoes
1/3 teaspoon fennel seeds
1/2 teaspoon mustard seeds
1/2 teaspoon dried marjoram
1/2 teaspoon dried basil
Coarse salt and ground black pepper, to taste
2 slices chopped smoked bacon
1/2 pound ground turkey
Directions
Put a pan on medium heat and heat the olive oil. Fry the garlic and shallots until fragrant.
Add the tomatoes, cabbage, fennel seeds, mustard seeds, marjoram, basil, salt and pepper. Cook until the cabbage leaves have wilted; about 5 minutes.
Mix in the bacon and turkey and cook for 35 minutes on a moderate-low heat. Crumble the meat with a spatula.
Divide the mixture between 4 bowls and serve hot.
Nutrition: Calories 282 ,Protein 11.5g ,Fat 20g ,Carbs 2g ,Sugar 0.5g

369.   Goat Cheese and Smoked Turkey Spread

Servings 6
Preparation Time: 10 minutes
Ingredients
4 ounces crumbled goat cheese
4 ounces chopped smoked turkey
2 tablespoons flaxseed meal
2 tablespoons roughly chopped fresh cilantro
2 tablespoons sunflower seeds
Directions
Put the goat cheese, smoked turkey, cilantro and flaxseed meal in a food processor. Blend until all the ingredients have combined well.
Put in a bowl and sprinkle sunflower seeds on top. Serve with vegetable sticks like peppers and cucumber.
Nutrition: Calories 212 ,Protein 10.6g ,Fat 18.8g ,Carbs 2g ,Sugar 0.5g

370.   Herby Chicken Fillets

Servings 6
Preparation Time: 15 minutes
Ingredients
1 1/2 pounds chicken fillets
1 1/2 tablespoons olive oil
1/2 teaspoon ground black pepper
1 teaspoon kosher salt
1 stick butter
2 teaspoons apple cider vinegar
1/3 cup chopped fresh cilantro
2 tablespoons finely minced shallots

1 teaspoon finely minced garlic
Directions
Preheat a skillet over moderate heat. Add the olive oil. Fry the chicken fillets for around 10 minutes until they are brown.
In a bowl mix together the salt, pepper, butter, apple cider vinegar, cilantro, shallots and garlic.
Serve the chicken fillets with the herby sauce.
Nutrition: Calories 258.6, Protein 15.2g ,Fat 20.2g ,Carbs 4g ,Sugar 1.5g

371. Turkey Meatballs with a side of Basil Chutney

Servings 6
Preparation Time: 30 minutes
Ingredients
For the Meatballs:
2 tablespoons olive oil
1 1/2 pounds ground turkey
1/4 teaspoon ground black pepper
1/2 teaspoon sea salt
½ teaspoon celery seeds
1/4 teaspoon dried thyme
1/2 teaspoon onion powder
1/2 teaspoon garlic powder
3 tablespoons flax seed meal
1/2 teaspoons paprika
½ cup grated Parmesan cheese
2 small-sized eggs, lightly beaten
For the Basil Chutney:
1/2 cup fresh basil leaves
1/2 cup coriander leaves
2 tablespoons fresh lemon juice
1 teaspoon grated fresh ginger root
2 tablespoons water
2 tablespoons olive oil
Salt and pepper, to taste
1 tablespoon minced green chili
Directions
Mix together all the meatball ingredients. Form into 16 balls and put to one side.
Preheat a skillet over medium heat and then heat the olive oil. Fry the meatballs for 7 -8 minutes, making sure that all sides are browned.
Then make the chutney. Put the basil leaves, coriander leaves, lemon juice, ginger, olive oil, salt, pepper and chili into a food processor and blend.
Serve the chutney as a side to the hot meatballs. Enjoy.
Nutrition: Calories 260 ,Protein 25.4g ,Fat 15g ,Carbs 6g ,Sugar 2.1g

372. Asian Saucy Chicken

Preparation Time: 25 minutes
Servings: 4
Nutrition: 367 Calories; 14.7g Fat; 3.5g Carbs; 51.2g Protein; 1.1g Fiber
Ingredients
1 tablespoon sesame oil
4 chicken legs
1/4 cup Shaoxing wine
2 tablespoons brown erythritol
1/4 cup spicy tomato sauce
Directions
Heat the sesame oil in a wok over medium-high heat. Fry the chicken until golden in color; reserve. Add Shaoxing wine to deglaze the pan.
Add in erythritol and spicy tomato sauce, and bring the mixture to a boil. Then, immediately reduce the heat to medium-low.
Let it simmer for about 10 minutes until the sauce coats the back of a spoon. Add the chicken back to the wok.
Continue to cook until the chicken is sticky and golden or about 4 minutes. Enjoy!

373. Duck Stew Olla Tapada

Preparation Time: 30 minutes
Servings: 3
Nutrition: 228 Calories; 9.5g Fat; 3.3g Carbs; 30.6g Protein; 1g Fiber
Ingredients
1 red bell pepper, deveined and chopped
1 pound duck breasts, boneless, skinless, and chopped into small chunks
1/2 cup chayote, peeled and cubed
1 shallot, chopped
1 teaspoon Mexican spice mix
Directions
In a clay pot, heat 2 teaspoons of canola oil over a medium-high flame. Sauté the peppers and shallot until softened about 4 minutes.
Add in the remaining ingredients; pour in 1 ½ cups of water or chicken bone broth. Once your mixture starts boiling, reduce the heat to medium-low.
Let it simmer, partially covered, for 18 to 22 minutes, until cooked through. Enjoy!

374. Cheesy Ranch Chicken

Preparation Time: 20 minutes
Servings: 4
Nutrition: 295 Calories; 19.5g Fat; 2.9g Carbs; 25.5g Protein; 0.4g Fiber
Ingredients
2 chicken breasts
1/2 tablespoon ranch seasoning mix
4 slices bacon, chopped

1/2 cup Monterey-Jack cheese, grated
4 ounces Ricotta cheese, room temperature
Directions
Preheat your oven to 360 degrees F.
Rub the chicken with ranch seasoning mix.
Heat a saucepan over medium-high flame. Now, sear the chicken for about 8 minutes. Lower the chicken into a lightly greased casserole dish.
Top with cheese and bacon and bake in the preheated oven for about 10 minutes until hot and bubbly. Serve with freshly snipped scallions, if desired.

375.   Turkey Crust Meatza

Preparation Time: 35 minutes
Servings: 4
Nutrition: 360 Calories; 22.7g Fat; 5.9g Carbs; 32.6g Protein; 0.7g Fiber
Ingredients
1/2 pound ground turkey
2 slices Canadian bacon
1 tomato, chopped
1 tablespoon pizza spice mix
1 cup Mozzarella cheese, grated
Directions
Mix the ground turkey and cheese; season with salt and black pepper and mix until everything is well combined.
Press the mixture into a foil-lined baking pan. Bake in the preheated oven at 380 degrees F for 25 minutes.
Top the crust with Canadian bacon, tomato, and pizza spice mix. Continue to bake for a further 8 minutes.
Let it rest a couple of minutes before slicing and. Bon appétit!

376.   Simple Turkey Goulash

Preparation Time: 45 minutes
Servings: 6
Nutrition: 220 Calories; 7.4g Fat; 2.7g Carbs; 35.5g Protein; 1g Fiber
Ingredients
2 tablespoons olive oil
1 large-sized leek, chopped
2 cloves garlic, minced
2 pounds turkey thighs, skinless, boneless and chopped
2 celery stalks, chopped
Directions
In a clay pot, heat 2 olive oil over a medium-high flame. Then, cook the leeks until tender and translucent.
Then, continue to sauté the garlic for 30 seconds to 1 minute.

Stir in the turkey, celery, and 4 cups of water. Once your mixture starts boiling, let it simmer, partially covered, for about 40 minutes.
Bon appétit!

377. Fajita with Zucchini

Preparation Time: 20 minutes
Servings: 4
Nutrition: 212 Calories; 9.2g Fat; 5.6g Carbs; 26g Protein; 1.2g Fiber
Ingredients
1 red onion, sliced
1 teaspoon Fajita seasoning mix
1 pound turkey cutlets
1 zucchini, spiralized
1 chili pepper, chopped
Directions
In a nonstick skillet, heat 1 tablespoon of the olive oil over a medium-high flame. Cook the turkey cutlets for 6 to 7 minutes on each side. Slice the meat into strips and reserve.
Heat another tablespoon of olive oil and sauté the onion and chili pepper until they are just tender. Sprinkle with Fajita seasoning mix.
Add in the zucchini and the reserved turkey; let it cook for 4 minutes more or until everything is cooked through. Serve with 1/2 cup of salsa, if desired. Enjoy!

378. Easiest Turkey Meatballs Ever

Preparation Time: 1 hour 20 minutes
Servings: 4
Nutrition: 366 Calories; 27.7g Fat; 3g Carbs; 25.9g Protein; 0.5g Fiber
Ingredients
1 egg, whisked
4 spring onions, finely chopped
1/2 cup parmesan cheese, grated
1 tablespoon Italian spice mix
1 pound ground turkey
Directions
Thoroughly combine all ingredients. Roll the turkey mixture into balls and place them in your refrigerator for 1 hour.
In a cast-iron skillet, heat 2 tablespoons of olive oil over medium-high heat. Sear the meatballs for 12 minutes or until nicely browned on all sides.
Bon appétit!

379. Greek-Style Chicken Drumettes

Preparation Time: 30 minutes
Servings: 2
Nutrition: 341 Calories; 14.3g Fat; 3.6g Carbs; 47g Protein; 1.1g Fiber
Ingredients
1 tablespoon olive oil
6 Kalamata olives, pitted and sliced
1 pound chicken drumettes
6 ounces tomato sauce
1 teaspoon Greek seasoning blend
Directions
Rub the chicken drumettes with Greek seasoning blend.
In a nonstick skillet, heat the olive oil over medium-high flame. Sear the chicken for about 10 minutes until nicely brown.
Add in the olives and tomato sauce. Stir and continue to cook, partially covered, for about 18 minutes until everything is thoroughly heated. Bon appétit!

380.   Chicken Tawook Salad

Preparation Time: 20 minutes
Servings: 2
Nutrition: 403 Calories; 18g Fat; 5.3g Carbs; 51.6g Protein; 1.6g Fiber
Ingredients
2 chicken breasts
4 tablespoons apple cider vinegar
1 cup grape tomatoes, halved
1 Lebanese cucumber, thinly sliced
2 tablespoons extra-virgin olive oil
Directions
Preheat a grill to medium-high and oil a grill grate. Grill the chicken for about 13 minutes, turing them over a few times.
Slice the chicken into the bite-sized chunks and transfer them to a bowl. Add in the vinegar, tomatoes, cucumber, and olive oil. Toss to combine well.
Serve at room temperature or well-chilled. Bon appétit!

381.   Greek Chicken with Peppers

Preparation Time: 20 minutes
Servings: 2
Nutrition: 403 Calories; 31.4g Fat; 5g Carbs; 24.5g Protein; 1.1g Fiber
Ingredients
2 chicken drumsticks, boneless and skinless
2 bell peppers, deveined and halved
1 small chili pepper, finely chopped
2 tablespoons Greek aioli
6 Kalamata olives, pitted

Directions

Rub the chicken with 1 tablespoon of extra-virgin olive oil. Season with salt and black pepper to taste.

Grill the chicken drumsticks for 8 to 9 minutes; add the bell peppers and grill them for a further 6 minutes.

Place the meat and peppers in a bowl; add in chili pepper and Greek aioli. Top with Kalamata olives and serve.

382.   Colorful Chicken Chowder

Preparation Time: 50 minutes
Servings: 6
Nutrition: 283 Calories; 18.9g Fat; 2.6g Carbs; 25.4g Protein; 0.5g Fiber
Ingredients
1 tablespoon olive oil
6 chicken wings
1 cup mixed frozen vegetables (celery, onions, and pepper
1 tablespoon poultry seasoning mix
1 whole egg
Directions
Heat the olive oil in a heavy-bottomed pot over medium-high heat. Then, brown the chicken for 10 minutes or until no longer pink; set them aside.

Then, cook the vegetables in the pan drippings until they are crisp-tender.

Season with poultry seasoning mix and turn the heat to medium-low; continue to simmer for a further 40 minutes or until everything is thoroughly cooked.

Chop the chicken and discard the fat and bones.

Whisk the egg into the cooking liquid. Add the reserved chicken back to the pot. Taste and adjust the seasonings. Enjoy!

383.   Chicken Frittata with Asiago Cheese and Herbs

Preparation Time: 30 minutes
Servings: 4
Nutrition: 484 Calories; 31.8g Fat; 5.8g Carbs; 41.9g Protein; 0.7g Fiber

Ingredients
1 pound chicken breasts, cut into small strips
4 slices of bacon
1 cup Asiago cheese, shredded
6 eggs
1/2 cup yogurt
Directions
Preheat an oven-proof skillet. Then, fry the bacon until crisp and reserve. Then, in the pan drippings, cook the chicken for about 8 minutes or until no longer pink.

Add the reserved bacon back to the skillet.

In a mixing dish, thoroughly combine the eggs and yogurt; season with Italian spice mix.

Pour the egg mixture over the chicken and bacon. Top with cheese and bake in the preheated oven at 380 degrees F for 22 minutes until hot and bubbly.

Let it rest a couple of minutes before slicing and. Bon appétit!

384. Stuffed Chicken with Sauerkraut and Cheese

Preparation Time: 35 minutes
Servings: 5
Nutrition: 376 Calories; 16.7g Fat; 5.8g Carbs; 47g Protein; 1g Fiber
Ingredients
5 chicken cutlets
1 cup Romano cheese, shredded
2 garlic cloves, minced
5 Italian peppers, deveined and chopped
5 tablespoons sauerkraut, for
Directions
Spritz a baking pan with 1 tablespoon of the olive oil. Brush the chicken with another tablespoon of olive oil.

Season the chicken with Italian spice mix. You can spread Dijon mustard on one side of each chicken cutlet, if desired.

Divide the garlic, peppers and Romano cheese between chicken cutlets; roll them up.

Bake at 360 degrees F for 25 to 33 minutes until nicely brown on all sides. Serve with the sauerkraut and serve. Bon appétit!

385. Cream of Chicken Soup

Preparation Time: 40 minutes
Servings: 5
Nutrition: 514 Calories; 38g Fat; 5.4g Carbs; 35.3g Protein; 0.5g Fiber
Ingredients
1/2 cup Italian peppers, deseeded and chopped
1/2 cup green cabbage, shredded
5 chicken thighs
1/2 cup celery, chopped
7 ounces full-fat cream cheese
Directions
Add Italian peppers, cabbage, chicken thighs, and celery to a large clay pot.

Pour in 5 cups of water or chicken broth.

Partially cover and let it simmer over medium-high heat approximately 30 minutes. Transfer the chicken to a cutting board,

Shred the chicken and return it to the pot. Add in full-fat cream cheese and stir until everything is well incorporated.

Ladle into bowls and enjoy!

386.   Lemony and Garlicky Chicken Wings

Preparation Time: 25 minutes + marinating time
Servings: 4
Nutrition: 131 Calories; 7.8g Fat; 1.8g Carbs; 13.4g Protein; 0.3g Fiber
Ingredients
8 chicken wings
2 garlic cloves, minced
1/4 cup leeks, chopped
2 tablespoons lemon juice
1 teaspoon Mediterranean spice mix
Directions
Place all ingredients in a ceramic dish. Cover and let it sit in your refrigerator for 2 hours.
Brush the chicken wings with melted ghee. Grill the chicken wings for 15 to 20 minutes, turning them occasionally to ensure even cooking.
Enjoy!

387.   Creamiest Chicken Salad Ever

Preparation Time: 1 hour 20 minutes
Servings: 3
Nutrition: 400 Calories; 35.1g Fat; 5.6g Carbs; 16.1g Protein; 1g Fiber
Ingredients
1 chicken breast, skinless
1/4 mayonnaise
1/4 cup sour cream
2 tablespoons Cottage cheese, room temperature
1/2 avocado, peeled and cubed
Directions
Cook the chicken in a pot of salted water. Remove from the heat and let the chicken sit, covered, in the hot water for 10 to 15 minutes.
Slice the chicken into bite-sized strips. Toss with the remaining ingredients.
Place in the refrigerator for at least one hour. Serve well chilled. Enjoy!

388.   Thai Turkey Curry

Preparation Time: 1 hour
Servings: 4
Nutrition: 295 Calories; 19.5g Fat; 2.9g Carbs; 25.5g Protein; 1g Fiber
Ingredients
1 pound turkey wings, boneless and chopped
2 cloves garlic, finely chopped
1 Thai red chili pepper, minced
1 cup unsweetened coconut milk, preferably homemade
1 cup turkey consommé

Directions

In a saucepan, warm 2 teaspoons of sesame oil. Once hot, brown turkey about 8 minutes or until it is golden brown.

Add in the garlic and Thai chili pepper and continue to cook for a minute or so.

Add coconut milk and consommé. Season with salt and black pepper to taste. Continue to cook for 40 to 45 minutes over medium heat. Serve warm and enjoy!

389.   Baked Teriyaki Turkey

Preparation Time: 15 minutes
Servings: 2
Nutrition: 410 Calories; 27.1g Fat; 6.6g Carbs; 36.5g Protein; 1g Fiber
Ingredients
3/4 pound lean ground turkey
1 brown onion, chopped
1 red bell pepper, deveined and chopped
1 serrano pepper, deveined and chopped
1/4 cup keto teriyaki sauce
Directions
Cook the ground turkey in the preheated pan over medium-high heat; cook for about 5 minutes until no longer pink.

Now, sauté the onion and peppers for 3 minutes more. Add in teriyaki sauce and bring the mixture to a boil.

Immediately remove from the heat; add in the cooked ground turkey and sautéed mixture. Serve warm and enjoy!

390.   Ranch Turkey with Greek Sauce

Preparation Time: 20 minutes
Servings: 4
Nutrition: 396 Calories; 27.5g Fat; 3.9g Carbs; 33.1g Protein; 1.9g Fiber
Ingredients
2 eggs
1 tablespoon Ranch seasoning blend
1/2 cup almond meal
1 pound turkey tenders, 1/2-inch thick
1/2 cup Greek keto sauce
Directions
In a shallow bowl, whisk the eggs with Ranch seasoning blend.

In another shallow bowl, place the almond meal. Dip the turkey tenders into the Ranch egg mixture. Then, press them into the almond meal; press to coat well.

Heat 2 tablespoons of olive oil in a pan over medium-high heat. Brown turkey tenders for 3 to 4 minutes on each side.

Serve the turkey tenders with Greek keto sauce. Enjoy!

391. Mediterranean Herbed Chicken

Preparation Time: 20 minutes
Servings: 5
Nutrition: 370 Calories; 16g Fat; 0.9g Carbs; 51g Protein; 0.2g Fiber
Ingredients
2 tablespoons butter, softened at room temperature
5 chicken legs, skinless
2 scallions, chopped
1 tablespoon Mediterranean spice mix
1 cup vegetable broth
Directions
In a saucepan, melt 1 tablespoon of butter over a medium-high flame. Now, brown the chicken legs for about 10 minutes, turning them periodically.
Add in the remaining tablespoon of butter, scallions, Mediterranean spice mix, and broth. When your mixture reaches boiling, reduce the temperature to a simmer.
Continue to simmer for 10 to 11 minutes until cooked through. Taste and adjust the seasoning. Bon appétit!

392. Saucy Chicken with Marsala Wine

Preparation Time: 20 minutes
Servings: 2
Nutrition: 347 Calories; 20.4g Fat; 4.7g Carbs; 35.3g Protein; 1.4g Fiber

Ingredients
2 chicken fillets
1/4 cup marsala wine
1 cup broccoli florets
1/4 tomato paste
1/2 cup double cream
Directions
Heat 1 tablespoon of olive oil in a sauté pan over medium-high heat. Once hot, sear the chicken for 10 minutes, flipping them over once or twice.
Add marsala wine and deglaze the pot. Add in the broccoli and tomato paste. Reduce the heat to simmer.
Continue to simmer for a further 5 to 7 minutes. Lastly, stir in the double cream. Season with paprika, salt, and black pepper to taste.
Bon appétit!

393. Chicken Mulligatawny

Preparation Time: 35 minutes
Servings: 4
Nutrition: 343 Calories; 26.7g Fat; 3.8g Carbs; 20.9g Protein; 0.2g Fiber

Ingredients
2 tablespoons ghee
1 pound chicken thighs, boneless and skinless
1 tablespoon Indian spice mix
1 celery stalk, chopped
1 cup milk
Directions
Melt the butter in a soup pot over medium-high flame. Brown the chicken thighs until nicely browned on all sides about 6 minutes.
Add in Indian spice mix and celery; stir to combine and reduce the heat to simmer; continue to simmer for 30 minutes more.
Pour in the milk and stir to combine well. Bon appétit!

394.   Naga Chicken Salad Ole

Preparation Time: 20 minutes + chilling time
Servings: 6
Nutrition: 278 Calories; 16.1g Fat; 4.9g Carbs; 27.2g Protein; 0.9g Fiber

Ingredients
1/2 cup dry white wine
1 ½ pounds chicken breasts
1 Spanish naga chili pepper, chopped
1/4 cup mayonnaise
2 cups arugula
Directions
Place the chicken breasts and wine in a deep saucepan. Then, cover the chicken with water, and bring to a boil.
When your mixture reaches boiling, reduce the temperature to a simmer.
Let it simmer, partially covered, for about 13 minutes or until cooked through.
Shred the chicken, discarding the bones and poaching liquid. Place in a salad bowl and add naga chili pepper, arugula, and mayonnaise to the bowl.
Add Spanish peppers, if desired and stir to combine well.
Serve well-chilled and enjoy!

395.   Oven-Roasted Chimichurri Chicken

Preparation Time: 40 minutes + marinating time
Servings: 5
Nutrition: 305 Calories; 14.7g Fat; 0.8g Carbs; 27.9g Protein; 0.2g Fiber
Ingredients
1 ½ pounds chicken tenders
1/2 cup fresh parsley, chopped
2 garlic cloves, minced
1/4 cup olive oil

4 tablespoons white wine vinegar
Directions
Blend the parsley, olive oil, vinegar, and garlic in your food processor until the smooth and uniform sauce forms. Pierce the chicken with a small knife.

Add chicken and 1/2 of the chimichurri sauce to a glass dosh and let them marinate for 2 hours in your refrigerator.

Spritz a baking pan with nonstick cooking spray. Place the chicken in the baking pan. Season with salt and black pepper.

Bake in the preheated oven at 360 degrees F for 35 minutes or until an internal temperature reaches about 165 degrees F.

Serve with the reserved chimichurri sauce. Bon appétit!

396.   Classic Garlicky Chicken Drumettes

Preparation Time: 40 minutes + marinating time
Servings: 5
Nutrition: 266 Calories; 19.3g Fat; 0.8g Carbs; 20.3g Protein; 0.2g Fiber
Ingredients
1/4 cup coconut aminos
1 tablespoon olive oil
1 tablespoon apple cider vinegar
2 cloves garlic, minced
5 chicken drumettes
Directions
Thoroughly combine, coconut aminos, olive oil, apple cider vinegar, and garlic in a glass dish. Allow it to marinate for 2 hours in your refrigerator

Place the chicken in a foil-lined baking dish. Season with salt and black pepper to taste.

Bake in the preheated oven at 410 degrees F for 35 minutes, basting the chicken with the reserved marinade.

Bon appétit!

397.   Barbeque Chicken Wings

Preparation Time: 15 minutes
Cooking Time: 14 minutes
Serving: 6
Ingredients:
2 lb. chicken wings
1/2 teaspoon basil; dried
3/4 cup BBQ sauce
1 teaspoon red pepper; crushed.
2 teaspoons paprika
Salt and black pepper to the taste
Directions:
Start by tossing the chicken wings with remaining ingredients in a bowl.

Prepare and preheat a grill to cook the wings.
Grill the wings for 7 minutes per side on medium low heat.
Serve fresh and warm.
Nutrition:
Calories 251
Total Fat 15.3 g
Saturated Fat 6.5 g
Cholesterol 122 mg
Sodium 366 mg
Total Carbs 3 g
Fiber 1.8 g
Sugar 0.9 g
Protein 25 g

398. Saucy Duck

Preparation Time: 15 minutes
Cooking Time: 15 minutes
Serving: 2
Ingredients:
1 duck, cut into small chunks
2 tablespoon ginger garlic paste
2 green onions; roughly chopped
4 tablespoon soy sauce
4 tablespoon sherry wine
Salt and black pepper to the taste
Directions:
Start by tossing the duck with all other ingredients in a bowl.
Marinate the meat for 4 hours in the refrigerator.
Spread the duck chunks in a baking tray.
Bake the meat for 15 minutes with occasional tossing.
Serve fresh.
Nutrition:
Calories 225
Total Fat 14.3 g
Saturated Fat 0.6 g
Cholesterol 137 mg
Sodium 538 mg
Total Carbs 2.8 g
Fiber 7 g
Sugar 0.3 g
Protein 28.2 g

399. Chicken Roux Gumbo

Preparation Time: 15 minutes
Cooking Time: 20 minutes

Serving: 2
Ingredients:
1 lb. chicken thighs; cut into halves
¼ cup 1 tablespoon vegetable oil
1/2 cup almond flour
1 cup vegetable stock
1 teaspoon Cajun spice
Salt and black pepper to the taste
Directions:
Start by toss the chicken with salt, black pepper and 1 tablespoon oil in a bowl.
Cover the thighs and refrigerate for 1 hour for marination.
Sear the marinated chicken in a sauté pan.
Cook for 5 minutes per side until golden brown.
Whisk almond flour with Cajun spice and remaining oil in a separate bowl.
Add almond mixture to a cooking pot and stir cook for 2 minutes.
Stir in stock and cook well until it thickens.
Toss in the sear chicken and cook for 4 minutes.
Serve fresh and warm.
Nutrition:
Calories 433
Total Fat 15.2 g
Saturated Fat 8.6 g
Cholesterol 179 mg
Sodium 318 mg
Total Carbs 2.7 g
Fiber 1.1 g
Sugar 1.1 g
Protein 68.4 g

400. Chunky Salsa Chicken

Preparation Time: 15 minutes
Cooking Time: 25 minutes
Serving: 2
Ingredients:
1 lb. chicken breast, skinless and boneless
1 cup chunky salsa
3/4 teaspoon cumin
A pinch of oregano
Salt and black pepper to the taste
Directions:
Pat dry the chicken and rub it with salt and pepper.
Place this chicken in the insert of the Instant Pot.
Add cumin, oregano and chunky salsa.
Mix well then seal the lid of the Instant Pot.
Cook on poultry mode for 25 minutes.
Once done, release the pressure quickly then shred meat with a fork.

Serve the meat with its salsa.

Enjoy.

Nutrition:

Calories 272

Total Fat 27 g

Saturated Fat 16 g

Cholesterol 83 mg

Sodium 175 mg

Total Carbs 7.8 g

Fiber 0.4 g

Sugar 5.2 g

Protein 5.3 g

401.   Dijon Chicken

Preparation Time: 15 minutes

Cooking Time: 20 minutes

Serving: 6

Ingredients:

2 lb. chicken thighs; skinless and boneless

1/4 cup lemon juice

2 tablespoon extra-virgin olive oil

3 tablespoon Dijon mustard

2 tablespoon Italian seasoning

Salt and black pepper to the taste

Directions:

Start by tossing chicken with all other ingredients in a bowl.

Prepare and preheat the grill on medium heat.

Grill the chicken pieces for 5 minutes per side until al dente.

Serve fresh.

Nutrition:

Calories 242

Total Fat 15.9 g

Saturated Fat 10.6 g

Cholesterol 36 mg

Sodium 421 mg

Total Carbs 4.6 g

Fiber 2 g

Sugar 1.6 g

Protein 20.8 g

402.   Chicken Thighs with Vegetables

Preparation Time: 15 minutes

Cooking Time: 30 minutes

Serving: 6s

Ingredients:

6 chicken thighs
15 oz. canned tomatoes; chopped.
1 yellow onion; chopped.
2 cups chicken stock
1/4 lb. baby carrots; cut into halves
Salt and black pepper to the taste
Directions:
Start by adding chicken and all other ingredients to a cooking pot.
Cove the pot's lid and cook for 30 minutes on medium low heat.
Mix well and serve fresh.
Nutrition:
Calories 362
Total Fat 15.9 g
Saturated Fat 9.9 g
Cholesterol 49 mg
Sodium 684 mg
Total Carbs 4.1 g
Fiber 1.4 g
Sugar 1.1 g
Protein 23.3 g

403.   Chicken Dipped in Tomatillo Sauce

Preparation Time: 15 minutes
Cooking Time: 15 minutes
Serving: 2
Ingredients:
1 lb. chicken thighs; skinless and boneless
2 tablespoon extra-virgin olive oil
1 yellow onion; thinly sliced
5 oz. tomatoes; chopped.
Salt and black pepper to the taste
15 oz. canned tomatillos; chopped.
Directions:
Start by heating olive oil in a cooking pot.
Toss in chicken, tomatillos, onion, salt, pepper, and tomatoes.
Cook for 15 minutes on medium low heat and cover the pot's lid.
Stir well and serve fresh.
Nutrition:
Calories 260
Total Fat 13 g
Saturated Fat 5 g
Cholesterol 0.3 mg
Sodium 465 mg
Total Carbs 6 g
Fiber 5.4 g
Sugar 1.3 g

Protein 26 g

404. Crispy Italian Chicken

Preparation Time: 15 minutes
Cooking Time: 10 minutes
Serving: 6
Ingredients:
6 chicken thighs
1 cup almond flour
2 eggs; whisked
1 ½ cups panko breadcrumbs
Salt and black pepper to the taste
Directions:
Start by tossing the flour with salt and black pepper in a flat plate.
Whisk the eggs in a separate bowl and spread breadcrumbs in a plate.
Coat the chicken thighs with the flour then dip in the eggs and then coat with crumbs.
Prepare and preheat the grill on medium heat.
Grill the chicken for 5 minutes per side on medium heat.
Serve fresh and warm.
Nutrition:
Calories 355
Total Fat 16.8 g
Saturated Fat 4 g
Cholesterol 150 mg
Sodium 719 mg
Total Carbs 1.4 g
Fiber 0.5 g
Sugar 0.1 g
Protein 47 g

405. Cacciatore Olive Chicken

Preparation Time: 15 minutes
Cooking Time: 20 minutes
Serving: 8
Ingredients:
28 oz. canned tomatoes and juice; crushed.
8 chicken drumsticks; bone-in
1/2 cup olives; pitted and sliced
1 cup chicken stock
1 yellow onion; chopped.
Salt and black pepper, to the taste
Directions:
Start by adding chicken and all other ingredients to a cooking pot.
Cover the pot's lid and cook for 20 minutes with occasional stirring.
Serve warm and fresh.

Nutrition:
Calories 489
Total Fat 18.7 g
Saturated Fat 3.8 g
Cholesterol 151 mg
Sodium 636 mg
Total Carbs 6.1 g
Fiber 0.5 g
Sugar 4.3 g
Protein 50 g

406. Duck and Vegetable Stew

Preparation Time: 15 minutes
Cooking Time: 40 minutes
Serving: 6
Ingredients:
1 duck; chopped into medium pieces
2 carrots; chopped
2 cups of water
1 cucumber; chopped
1-inch ginger pieces; chopped
Salt and black pepper to the taste
Directions:
Place the duck pieces in the insert of the Instant Pot
Add carrots, wine, ginger, water, salt, and pepper.
Mix well and seal the lid. Cook for 40 minutes on Poultry mode.
Once done, release the pressure quickly, then remove the lid.
Serve fresh.
Nutrition:
Calories 325
Total Fat 14.4 g
Saturated Fat 3.5 g
Cholesterol 135 mg
Sodium 552 mg
Total Carbs 2.3 g
Fiber 0.4 g
Sugar 0.5 g
Protein 44 g

407. Chicken Eggplant Curry

Preparation Time: 15 minutes
Cooking Time: 15 minutes
Serving: 4
Ingredients:
8 chicken pieces

1 eggplant; cubed
3 garlic cloves; crushed.
14 oz. canned coconut milk
2 tablespoon green curry paste
Salt and black pepper to the taste
Directions:
Start by adding chicken and all other ingredients to a cooking pot.
Cover the pot's lid and cook for 15 minutes with occasional stirring.
Serve warm and fresh.
Nutrition:
Calories 452
Total Fat 3.5 g
Saturated Fat 0.5 g
Cholesterol 181 mg
Sodium 461 mg
Total Carbs 7.5 g
Fiber 1.7 g
Sugar 1.3 g
Protein 91.8 g

408.   Mushroom Cream Goose Curry

Preparation Time: 15 minutes
Cooking Time: 25 minutes
Serving: 4
Ingredients:
12 oz. canned mushroom cream
3 goose breasts; fat trimmed off and cut into pieces
1 yellow onion; chopped.
3 ½ cups water
2 teaspoon garlic; minced.
Salt and black pepper to the taste
Directions:
Start by adding chicken and all other ingredients to a cooking pot.
Cover the pot's lid and cook for 25 minutes with occasional stirring.
Serve warm and fresh.
Nutrition:
Calories 386
Total Fat 10 g
Saturated Fat 1.7 g
Cholesterol 93 mg
Sodium 179 mg
Total Carbs 11.7 g
Fiber 0.4 g
Sugar 0.7 g
Protein 25.7 g

409.   Chicken Curry

Preparation Time: 15 minutes
Cooking Time: 25 minutes
Serving: 8
Ingredients:
3 lb. chicken drumsticks and thighs
1 yellow onion; finely chopped
1 cup chicken stock
15 oz. canned tomatoes; crushed.
1 lb. spinach; chopped.
Salt and black pepper to the taste
Directions:
Start by adding chicken and all other ingredients to a cooking pot.
Cover the pot's lid and cook for 25 minutes with occasional stirring.
Serve warm and fresh.
Nutrition:
Calories 283
Total Fat 23 g
Saturated Fat 7.9 g
Cholesterol 69 mg
Sodium 106 mg
Total Carbs 0.2 g
Fiber 0.1 g
Sugar 0 g
Protein 18 g

410.   Saucy Teriyaki Chicken

Preparation Time: 15 minutes
Cooking Time: 25 minutes
Serving: 4
Ingredients:
2 lb. chicken breasts; skinless and boneless, diced
1 cup teriyaki sauce
1/2 cup chicken stock
A handful green onions; chopped.
Salt and black pepper to the taste
Directions:
Start by adding chicken and all other ingredients to a cooking pot.
Cover the pot's lid and cook for 25 minutes with occasional stirring.
Serve warm and fresh.
Nutrition:
Calories 402
Total Fat 20.8 g
Saturated Fat 5 g
Cholesterol 130 mg

Sodium 112 mg
Total Carbs 2.9 g
Fiber 0.9 g
Sugar 0.8 g
Protein 50.5 g

411.   Chicken Shrimp Curry

Preparation Time: 15 minutes
Cooking Time: 20 minutes
Serving: 2
Ingredients:
8 oz. shrimp; peeled and deveined
8 oz. chicken breasts; skinless; boneless and chopped.
2 tablespoon extra-virgin olive oil
2 teaspoon Creole seasoning
1 cup chicken stock
2 cups canned tomatoes; chopped.
Directions:
Start by adding chicken and all other ingredients except shrimp to a cooking pot.
Cover the pot's lid and cook for 15 minutes with occasional stirring.
Toss in shrimp and cook for another 5 minutes.
Serve warm and fresh.
Nutrition:
Calories 377
Total Fat 11.4 g
Saturated Fat 1.8 g
Cholesterol 168 mg
Sodium 215 mg
Total Carbs 10.4 g
Fiber 0.2 g
Sugar 0.1 g
Protein 64 g

412.   Whole Chicken with Prunes and Capers

Preparation Time: 55 minutes
Servings: 6
Ingredients
1 whole chicken, 3 lb
½ cup pitted prunes
3 minced cloves of garlic
2 tbsp capers
2 bay leaves
2 tbsp red wine vinegar
2 tbsp olive oil
1 tbsp dried oregano

¼ cup packed brown sugar
1 tbsp chopped and fresh parsley
Salt and black pepper
Directions
In a big and deep bowl, mix the prunes, the olives, capers, garlic, olive oil, bay leaves, oregano, vinegar, salt and pepper. Spread the mixture on the bottom of a baking tray, and place the chicken. Preheat the Air Fryer to 360 F. Sprinkle a little bit of brown sugar on top of the chicken; cook for 55 minutes.

413.   White Wine Chicken with Herbs

Preparation Time: 45 minutes
Servings: 6
Ingredients
1 whole chicken, around 3 lb, cut in pieces
3 chopped cloves of garlic
½ cup olive oil
½ cup white wine
1 tbsp fresh rosemary
1 tbsp chopped fresh oregano
1 tbsp fresh thyme
Juice from 1 lemon
Salt and black pepper, to taste
Directions
In a large bowl, combine cloves of garlic, rosemary, thyme, olive oil, lemon juice, oregano, salt and pepper. Mix all ingredients very well and spread the mixture into a baking dish. Add the chicken and stir.
Preheat the Air Fryer to 380 F, and transfer in the chicken mixture. Sprinkle with wine and cook for 45 minutes.

414.   Tasty Chicken Quarters with Broccoli & Rice

Preparation Time: 60 minutes
Servings: 3
Ingredients
3 chicken leg quarters
1 package instant long grain rice
1 cup chopped broccoli
2 cups water
1 can condensed cream chicken soup
1 tbsp minced garlic
Directions
Preheat the Air Fryer to 390 F, and place the chicken quarters in the Air Fryer. Season with salt, pepper and one tbsp of oil; cook for 30 minutes. Meanwhile, in a large deep bowl, mix the rice, water, minced garlic, soup and broccoli. Combine the mixture very well.
Remove the chicken from the Air fryer and place it on a platter to drain. Spread the rice mixture on the bottom of the dish and place the chicken on top of the rice. Cook again for 30 minutes.

415. Asian-style Chicken with Vegetables

Preparation Time: 35 minutes
Servings: 4
Ingredients
1 lb chicken, cut in stripes
2 tomatoes, cubed
3 green peppers, cut in stripes
1 tbsp cumin powder
1 large onion
2 tbsp oil
1 tbsp mustard
A pinch of ginger
A pinch of fresh and chopped coriander
Salt and black pepper
Directions
Heat the oil in a deep pan. Add the mustard, the onion, the ginger, the cumin and the green chili peppers. Sauté the mixture for 2-3 minutes. Then, add the tomatoes, the coriander and salt and keep stirring.
Preheat the Air Fryer to 380 F. Coat the chicken with oil, salt and pepper and cook it for 25 minutes. Remove from the Air Fryer and pour the sauce over and around.

416. Southwest-Style Buttermilk Chicken Thighs

Preparation Time: 4 hrs 40 minutes
Servings: 6
Ingredients
1 ½ lb chicken thighs
1 tbsp cayenne pepper
3 tbsp salt divided
2 cups flour
2 tbsp black pepper
1 tbsp paprika
1 tbsp baking powder
2 cups buttermilk
Directions
Rinse and pat dry the chicken thighs. Place the chicken thighs in a bowl. Add cayenne pepper, 2 tbsp of salt, black pepper and buttermilk, and stir to coat well. Refrigerate for 4 hours. Preheat the air fryer to 350 F.
In another bowl, mix the flour, paprika, 1 tbsp of salt, and baking powder. Dredge half of the chicken thighs, one at a time, in the flour, and then place on a lined dish. Cook for 10 minutes, flip over and cook for 8 more minutes. Repeat with the other batch.

417. Coconut Crunch Chicken Strips

Preparation Time: 22 minutes
Servings: 4

Ingredients

3 ½ cups coconut flakes

4 chicken breasts cut into strips

½ cup cornstarch

¼ tsp pepper

¼ tsp salt

3 eggs, beaten

Directions

Preheat the Air fryer to 350 F. Mix salt, pepper, and cornstarch in a small bowl. Line a baking sheet with parchment paper. Dip the chicken first in the cornstarch, then into the eggs, and finally, coat with coconut flakes. Arrange on the sheet and cook for 8 minutes. Flip the chicken over, and cook for 8 more minutes, until crispy.

418. American-Style Buttermilk Fried Chicken

Preparation Time: 30 minutes

Servings: 4

Ingredients

6 chicken drumsticks, skin on and bone in

2 cups buttermilk

2 tbsp salt

2 tbsp black pepper

1 tbsp cayenne pepper

2 cups all-purpose flour

1 tbsp baking powder

1 tbsp garlic powder

1 tbsp paprika

1 tbsp salt

Directions

Rinse chicken thoroughly underwater and pat them dry; remove any fat residue. In a large bowl, mix paprika, black pepper and chicken. Toss well to coat the chicken evenly. Pour buttermilk over chicken and toss to coat.

Let the chicken chill overnight. Preheat your Air Fryer to 400 F. In another bowl, mix flour, paprika, pepper and salt. Roll the chicken in the seasoned flour. Place the chicken in the cooking basket in a single layer and cook for 10 minutes. Repeat the same steps for the other pieces.

419. Chicken With Parmesan and Sage

Preparation Time: 12 minutes

Servings: 4

Ingredients

4 chicken breasts, skinless and boneless

3 oz breadcrumbs

2 tbsp grated Parmesan cheese

2 oz flour

2 eggs, beaten

1 tbsp fresh, chopped sage

Directions

Preheat the air fryer to 370 F. Place some plastic wrap underneath and on top of the chicken breasts. Using a rolling pin, beat the meat until it becomes really thin. In a bowl, combine the Parmesan cheese, sage and breadcrumbs.

Dip the chicken in the egg first, and then in the sage mixture. Spray with cooking oil and arrange the meat in the air fryer. Cook for 7 minutes.

420. Party Chicken Tenders

Preparation Time: 25 minutes
Servings: 4
Ingredients
¾ pound chicken tenders
Prep + Cook Time2 whole eggs, beaten
½ cup seasoned breadcrumbs
½ cup all-purpose flour
1 tbsp black pepper
2 tbsp olive oil
Directions

Preheat your air fryer to 330 F. Add breadcrumbs, eggs and flour in three separate bowls (individually. Mix breadcrumbs with oil and season with salt and pepper. Dredge the tenders into flour, eggs and into the crumbs.

Add chicken tenders in the Air Fryer and cook for 10 minutes. Increase to 390 F, and cook for 5 more minutes.

421. Chicken Tenders with Pineapple Juice

Preparation Time: 4h 15 minutes
Servings: 4
Ingredients
1 lb boneless and skinless chicken tenders
4 cloves garlic, chopped
4 scallions, chopped
2 tbsp sesame seeds, toasted
1 tbsp fresh ginger, grated
½ cup pineapple juice
½ cup soy sauce
⅓ cup sesame oil
A pinch of black pepper
Directions

Skew each tender and trim any excess fat. Mix the other ingredients in one large bowl. Add the skewered chicken and place in the fridge for 4 to 24 hours. Preheat the Air Fryer to 375°F. Using a paper towel, pat the chicken until it is completely dry. Fry for 10 minutes.

422. Crispy Panko Turkey Breasts

Preparation Time: 25 minutes
Servings: 6
Ingredients
3 turkey breasts, boneless and skinless
2 cups panko1 tbsp salt
½ tsp cayenne pepper
½ tbsp black pepper
1 stick butter, melted
Directions
In a bowl, combine the panko, half of the black pepper, cayenne pepper, and half of the salt. In another small bowl, combine the melted butter with salt and pepper. Don't add salt if you use salted butter.
Brush the butter mixture over the turkey breasts. Coat the turkey with the panko mixture. Arrange them on a lined baking dish. Air fry for 15 minutes at 390 degrees F. If the turkey breasts are thinner, cook only for 8 minutes.

423.   Avocado-Mango Chicken Breasts

Preparation Time: 3 hrs 20 minutes
Servings: 2
Ingredients
2 chicken breasts, cubed
1 large mango, cubed
1 medium avocado, sliced
1 red pepper, chopped
5 tbsp balsamic vinegar
15 tbsp olive oil
4 garlic cloves, minced
1 tbsp oregano
1 tbsp parsley, chopped
A pinch of mustard powder
Salt and black pepper to taste
Directions
In a bowl, mix whole mango, garlic, oil, and balsamic vinegar. Add the mixture to a blender and blend well. Pour the liquid over chicken cubes and soak for 3 hours. Take a pastry brush and rub the mixture over breasts as well.
Preheat your Air Fryer to 360 F. Place the chicken cubes in the cooking basket, and cook for 12 minutes. Add avocado, mango and pepper and toss well. Drizzle balsamic vinegar and garnish with chopped parsley.
Turkey Nuggets with Parsley & Thyme
Preparation Time: 20 minutes
Servings: 2
Ingredients
8 oz turkey breast, boneless and skinless
1 egg, beaten
1 cup breadcrumbs
1 tbsp dried thyme

½ tbsp dried parsley
Salt and black pepper to taste
Directions
Preheat the air fryer to 350 F. Mince the turkey in a food processor; transfer to a bowl. Stir in the thyme and parsley, and season with salt and pepper.
Take a nugget-sized piece of the turkey mixture and shape it into a ball, or another form. Dip in the breadcrumbs, then egg, then in the breadcrumbs again. Place the nuggets onto a prepared baking dish, and cook for 10 minutes.

424. Korean-Style Honey Chicken Wings

Preparation Time: 15 minutes
Servings: 5
Ingredients
1 pound chicken wings
8 oz flour
8 oz breadcrumbs
3 beaten eggs
4 tbsp Canola oil
Salt and black pepper to taste
2 tbsp sesame seeds
2 tbsp Korean red pepper paste
1 tbsp apple cider vinegar
2 tbsp honey
1 tbsp soy sauce
Sesame seeds, to serve
Directions
Separate the chicken wings into winglets and drumettes. In a bowl, mix salt, oil and pepper. Preheat your Air Fryer to a temperature of 350 F. Coat the chicken with beaten eggs followed by breadcrumbs and flour.
Place the chicken in your Air Fryer's cooking basket. Spray with a bit of oil and cook for 15 minutes. Mix red pepper paste, apple cider vinegar, soy sauce, honey and ¼ cup of water in a saucepan and bring to a boil over medium heat. Transfer the chicken to sauce mixture and toss to coat. Garnish with sesame to enjoy!

425. Savory Chicken Drumsticks with Honey and Garlic

Preparation Time: 20 minutes
Servings: 3
Ingredients
2 chicken drumsticks, skin removed
2 tbsp olive oil
2 tbsp honey
½ tbsp garlic, minced
Directions

Preheat your Air Fryer to 400 F. Add garlic, oil and honey to a sealable zip bag. Add chicken and toss to coat; set aside for 30 minutes. Add the coated chicken to the Air Fryer basket, and cook for 15 minutes. Serve and enjoy!

426. Garlic-Buttery Chicken Wings

Preparation Time: 20 minutes
Servings: 4
Ingredients
16 chicken wings
¼ cup butter
¼ cup honey
½ tbsp salt
4 garlic cloves, minced
¾ cup potato starch
Directions
Preheat the air fryer to 370 F. Rinse and pat dry the wings, and place them in a bowl. Add the starch to the bowl, and mix to coat the chicken. Place the chicken in a baking dish that has been previously coated with cooking oil.
Cook for 5 minutes in the air fryer. Whisk the rest of the ingredients together in a bowl. Pour the sauce over the wings and cook for another 10 minutes.

427. Pineapple & Ginger Chicken Kabobs

Preparation Time: 20 minutes
Servings: 4
Ingredients
¾ oz boneless and skinless chicken tenders
½ cup soy sauce
½ cup pineapple juice
¼ cup sesame oil
4 cloves garlic, chopped
1 tbsp fresh ginger, grated
4 scallions, chopped
2 tbsp toasted sesame seeds
1 A pinch of black pepper
Directions
Skewer the chicken pieces into the skewers and trim any fat. In a large sized bowl, mix the remaining ingredients.
Dip the skewered chicken into the seasoning bowl. Preheat your Air Fryer to 390 F. Pat the chicken to dry using a towel and place in the Air Fryer cooking basket. Cook for 5-7 minutes.

428. Worcestershire Chicken Breasts

Preparation Time: 20 minutes
Servings: 6
Ingredients

¼ cup flour
½ tbsp flour
5 chicken breasts, sliced
1 tbsp Worcestershire sauce
3 tbsp olive oil
¼ cup onions, chopped
1 ½ cups brown sugar
¼ cup yellow mustard
¾ cup water
½ cup ketchup
Directions
Preheat your Fryer to 360 F. In a bowl, mix in flour, salt and pepper. Cover the chicken slices with flour mixture and drizzle oil over the chicken. In another bowl, mix brown sugar, water, ketchup, chopped onion, mustard, Worcestershire sauce and salt. Transfer chicken to marinade mixture; set aside for 10 minutes. Place the chicken in your Air Fryer's cooking basket and cook for 15 minutes.

429.   Sherry Grilled Chicken

Preparation Time: 25 minutes
Servings: 2
Ingredients
4 chicken breasts, cubed
2 garlic clove, minced
½ cup ketchup
½ tbsp ginger, minced
½ cup soy sauce
2 tbsp sherry
½ cup pineapple juice
2 tbsp apple cider vinegar
½ cup brown sugar
Directions
Preheat your Air Fryer to 360 F. In a bowl, mix in ketchup, pineapple Juice, sugar, cider vinegar, ginger. Heat the sauce in a frying pan over low heat. Cover chicken with the soy sauce and sherry; pour the hot sauce on top. Set aside for 15 minutes to marinate. Place the chicken in the Air Fryer cooking basket and cook for 15 minutes.

430.   Mustard Chicken with Thyme

Preparation Time: 20 minutes
Servings: 4
Ingredients
4 garlic cloves, minced
8 chicken slices
1 tbsp thyme leaves
½ cup dry wine
Salt as needed
½ cup Dijon mustard

2 cups breadcrumbs
2 tbsp melted butter
1 tbsp lemon zest
2 tbsp olive oil
Directions
Preheat your Air Fryer to 350 F. In a bowl, mix garlic, salt, cloves, breadcrumbs, pepper, oil, butter and lemon zest. In another bowl, mix mustard and wine. Place chicken slices in the wine mixture and then in the crumb mixture. Place the prepared chicken in the Air Fryer cooking basket and cook for 15 minutes.

431.   Shrimp Paste Chicken

Preparation Time: 30 minutes
Servings: 2
Ingredients
8 chicken wings, washed and cut into small portions
½ tbsp sugar
2 tbsp corn flour
½ tbsp wine
1 tbsp shrimp paste
1 tbsp ginger
½ tbsp olive oil
Directions
Preheat your Air Fryer to 360 F. In a bowl, mix oil, ginger, wine and sugar. Cover the chicken wings with the prepared marinade and top with flour. Add the floured chicken to shrimp paste and coat it. Place the prepared chicken in your Air Fryer's cooking basket and cook for 20 minutes, until crispy on the outside.

Meat

432. Beef with Carrot & Broccoli

Servings: 4
Preparation Time: fifteen minutes
Cooking Time: 14 minutes
Ingredients:
2 tablespoons coconut oil, divided
2 medium garlic cloves, minced
1-pound beef sirloin steak, trimmed and sliced into thin strips
Salt, to taste
¼ cup chicken broth
2 teaspoons fresh ginger, grated
1 tablespoon ground flax seeds
½ teaspoon red pepper flakes, crushed
¼ teaspoon freshly ground black pepper
1 large carrot, peeled and sliced thinly
2 cups broccoli florets
1 medium scallion, sliced thinly
Directions:
In a substantial skillet, heat 1 tablespoon of oil on medium-high heat.
Add garlic and sauté approximately 1 minute.
Add beef and salt and cook for approximately 4-5 minutes or till browned.
With a slotted spoon, transfer the beef in a bowl.
Remove the liquid from skillet.
In a bowl, mix together broth, ginger, flax seeds, red pepper flakes and black pepper.
In a similar skillet, heat remaining oil on medium heat.
Add carrot, broccoli and ginger mixture and cook for approximately 3-4 minutes or till desired doneness.
Stir in beef and scallion and cook for around 3-4 minutes.
Nutrition:
Calories: 412, Fat: 13g, Carbohydrates: 28g, Fiber: 9g, Protein: 35g

433. Beef with Mushroom & Broccoli

Servings: 4
Preparation Time: 15 minutes
Cooking Time: 12 minutes
Ingredients:
For Beef Marinade:
1 garlic clove, minced
1 (2-inchpiece fresh ginger, minced
Salt and freshly ground black pepper, to taste
3 tablespoons white wine vinegar
¾ cup beef broth
1-pound flank steak, trimmed and sliced into thin strips

For Vegetables:
2 tablespoons coconut oil, divided
2 minced garlic cloves
3 cups broccoli rabe, chopped
4-ounce shiitake mushrooms, halved
8-ounce cremini mushrooms, sliced

Directions:

For marinade in a substantial bowl, mix together all ingredients except beef.

Add beef and coat with marinade generously.

Refrigerate to marinate for around 15 minutes.

In a substantial skillet, heat oil on medium-high heat.

Remove beef from bowl, reserving the marinade.

Add beef and garlic and cook for about 3-4 minutes or till browned.

With a slotted spoon, transfer the beef in a bowl.

In exactly the same skillet, add reserved marinade, broccoli and mushrooms and cook for approximately 3-4 minutes.

Stir in beef and cook for about 3-4 minutes.

Nutrition:

Calories: 417, Fat: 10g, Carbohydrates: 23g, Fiber: 11g, Protein: 33g

434. Citrus Beef with Bok Choy

Servings: 4

Preparation Time: fifteen minutes

Cooking Time: 11 minutes

Ingredients:

For Marinade:

2 minced garlic cloves

1 (1-inchpiece fresh ginger, grated

1/3 cup fresh orange juice

½ cup coconut aminos

2 teaspoons fish sauce

2 teaspoons Sriracha

1¼ pound sirloin steak, trimmed and sliced thinly

For Veggies:

2 tablespoons coconut oil, divided
3-4 wide strips of fresh orange zest
1 jalapeño pepper, sliced thinly
½ pound string beans, stemmed and halved crosswise
1 tablespoon arrowroot powder
½ pound Bok choy, chopped
2 teaspoons sesame seeds
Directions:
For marinade in a big bowl, mix together garlic, ginger, orange juice, coconut aminos, fish sauce and Sriracha.
Add beef and coat with marinade generously.
Refrigerate to marinate for around couple of hours.
In a substantial skillet, heat oil on medium-high heat.
Add orange zest and sauté approximately 2 minutes.
Remove beef from bowl, reserving the marinade.
In the skillet, add beef and increase the heat to high.
Stir fry for about 2-3 minutes or till browned.
With a slotted spoon, transfer the beef and orange strips right into a bowl.
With a paper towel, wipe out the skillet.
In a similar skillet, heat remaining oil on medium-high heat.
Add jalapeño pepper and string beans and stir fry for about 3-4 minutes.
Meanwhile add arrowroot powder in reserved marinade and stir to mix.
In the skillet, add marinade mixture, beef and Bok choy and cook for about 1-2 minutes.
Serve hot with garnishing of sesame seeds.
Nutrition:
Calories: 398, Fat: 11g, Carbohydrates: 20g, Fiber: 6g, Protein: 34g

435.   Beef with Zucchini Noodles

A nutritious blend of beef, zucchini and ginger. This simple and easy, super-fast beef stir-fry is often a great method to burn up loads of summer zucchini.
Servings: 4
Preparation Time: 15 minutes
Cooking Time: 9 minutes
Ingredients:
1 teaspoon fresh ginger, grated
2 medium garlic cloves, minced
¼ cup coconut aminos
2 tablespoons fresh lime juice
1½ pound NY strip steak, trimmed and sliced thinly
2 medium zucchinis, spiralized with Blade C
Salt, to taste
3 tablespoons essential olive oil
2 medium scallions, sliced
1 teaspoon red pepper flakes, crushed
2 tablespoons fresh cilantro, chopped
Directions:

In a big bowl, mix together ginger, garlic, coconut aminos and lime juice.
Add beef and coat with marinade generously.
Refrigerate to marinate approximately 10 minutes.
Place zucchini noodles over a large paper towel and sprinkle with salt.
Keep aside for around 10 minutes.
In a big skillet, heat oil on medium-high heat.
Add scallion and red pepper flakes and sauté for about 1 minute.
Add beef with marinade and stir fry for around 3-4 minutes or till browned.
Add zucchini and cook for approximately 3-4 minutes.
Serve hot with all the topping of cilantro.
Nutrition:
Calories: 434, Fat: 17g, Carbohydrates: 23g, Fiber: 12g, Protein: 29g

436.   Beef with Asparagus & Bell Pepper'

Servings: 4-5
Preparation Time: fifteen minutes
Cooking Time: 13 minutes
Ingredients:
4 garlic cloves, minced
3 tablespoons coconut aminos
1/8 teaspoon red pepper flakes, crushed
1/8 teaspoon ground ginger
Freshly ground black pepper, to taste
1 bunch asparagus, trimmed and halved
2 tablespoons olive oil, divided
1-pound flank steak, trimmed and sliced thinly
1 red bell pepper, seeded and sliced
3 tablespoons water
2 teaspoons arrowroot powder

Directions:
In a bowl, mix together garlic, coconut aminos, red pepper flakes, crushed, ground ginger and black pepper. Keep aside.
In a pan of boiling water, cook asparagus for about 2 minutes.
Drain and rinse under cold water.
In a substantial skillet, heat 1 tablespoon of oil on medium-high heat.
Add beef and stir fry for around 3-4 minutes.
With a slotted spoon, transfer the beef in a bowl.
In a similar skillet, heat remaining oil on medium heat.
Add asparagus and bell pepper and stir fry for approximately 2-3 minutes.
Meanwhile in the bowl, mix together water and arrowroot powder.
Stir in beef, garlic mixture and arrowroot mixture and cook for around 3-4 minutes or till desired thickness.
Nutrition:
Calories: 399, Fat: 17g, Carbohydrates: 27g, Fiber: 8g, Protein: 35g

437.   Spiced Ground Beef

Servings: 5
Preparation Time: 10 min
Cooking Time: 22 minutes
Ingredients:
2 tablespoons coconut oil
2 whole cloves
2 whole cardamoms
1 (2-inchpiece cinnamon stick
2 bay leaves
1 teaspoon cumin seeds
2 onions, chopped
Salt, to taste
½ tablespoon garlic paste
½ tablespoon fresh ginger paste
1-pound lean ground beef
1½ teaspoons fennel seeds powder
1 teaspoon ground cumin
1½ teaspoons red chili powder
1/8 teaspoon ground turmeric
Freshly ground black pepper, to taste
1 cup coconut milk
¼ cup water
¼ cup fresh cilantro, chopped
Directions:
In a sizable pan, heat oil on medium heat.
Add cloves, cardamoms, cinnamon stick, bay leaves and cumin seeds and sauté for about 20-a few seconds.
Add onion and 2 pinches of salt and sauté for about 3-4 minutes.
Add garlic-ginger paste and sauté for about 2 minutes.

Add beef and cook for about 4-5 minutes, entering pieces using the spoon.
Cover and cook approximately 5 minutes.
Stir in spices and cook, stirring for approximately 2-2½ minutes.
Stir in coconut milk and water and cook for about 7-8 minutes.
Season with salt and take away from heat.
Serve hot using the garnishing of cilantro.
Nutrition:
Calories: 444, Fat: 15g, Carbohydrates: 29g, Fiber: 11g, Protein: 39g

438. Ground Beef with Cabbage

Servings: 6
Preparation Time: 10 minutes
Cooking Time: 15 minutes
Ingredients:

1 tbsp. olive oil
1 onion, sliced thinly
2 teaspoons fresh ginger, minced
4 garlic cloves, minced
1-pound lean ground beef
1½ tablespoons fish sauce
2 tablespoons fresh lime juice
1 small head purple cabbage, shredded
2 tablespoons peanut butter
½ cup fresh cilantro, chopped
Directions:
In a large skillet, heat oil on medium heat.
Add onion, ginger and garlic and sauté for about 4-5 minutes.
Add beef and cook for approximately 7-8 minutes, getting into pieces using the spoon.
Drain off the extra liquid in the skillet.
Stir in fish sauce and lime juice and cook for approximately 1 minute.
Add cabbage and cook approximately 4-5 minutes or till desired doneness.
Stir in peanut butter and cilantro and cook for about 1 minute.
Serve hot.
Nutrition:
Calories: 402, Fat: 13g, Carbohydrates: 21g, Fiber: 10g, Protein: 33g

439.   Ground Beef with Veggies

A colorful presentation of your beef and mixed veggies. This colorful meal is super delicious and hearty as well.
Servings: 2-4
Preparation Time: 15 minutes
Cooking Time: twenty or so minutes
Ingredients

1-2 tablespoons coconut oil
1 red onion, sliced
2 red jalapeño peppers, seeded and sliced
2 minced garlic cloves
1-pound lean ground beef
1 small head broccoli, chopped
½ of head cauliflower, chopped
3 carrots, peeled and sliced
3 celery ribs, sliced
Chopped fresh thyme, to taste
Dried sage, to taste
Ground turmeric, to taste
Salt and freshly ground black pepper, to taste
Directions:
In a large skillet, melt coconut oil on medium heat.
Add onion, jalapeño peppers and garlic and sauté for about 5 minutes.
Add beef and cook for around 4-5 minutes, entering pieces using the spoon.
Add remaining ingredients and cook, stirring occasionally for about 8-10 min.
Serve hot.
Nutrition:
Calories: 453, Fat: 17g, Carbohydrates: 26g, Fiber: 8g, Protein: 35g

440.   Ground Beef with Cashews & Veggies

Servings: 4
Preparation Time: 15 minutes
Cooking Time: 15 minutes
Ingredients:

1½ pound lean ground beef
1 tablespoon garlic, minced
2 tablespoons fresh ginger, minced
¼ cup coconut aminos
Salt and freshly ground black pepper, to taste
1 medium onion, sliced
1 can water chestnuts, drained and sliced
1 large green bell pepper, seeded and sliced
½ cup raw cashews, toasted
Directions:
Heat a nonstick skillet on medium-high heat.
Add beef and cook for about 6-8 minutes breaking into pieces with all the spoon.
Add garlic, ginger, coconut aminos, salt and black pepper and cook approximately 2 minutes.
Add vegetables and cook approximately 5 minutes or till desired doneness.
Stir in cashews and immediately remove from heat.
Serve hot.
Nutrition:
Calories: 452, Fat: 20g, Carbohydrates: 26g, Fiber: 9g, Protein: 36g

441.   Ground Beef with Greens & Tomatoes

Servings: 4
Preparation Time: fifteen minutes
Cooking Time: 15 minutes
Ingredients:
1 tbsp. organic olive oil
½ of white onion, chopped
2 garlic cloves, chopped finely
1 jalapeño pepper, chopped finely
1-pound lean ground beef
1 teaspoon ground coriander
1 teaspoon ground cumin
½ teaspoon ground turmeric
½ teaspoon ground ginger
½ teaspoon ground cinnamon
½ teaspoon ground fennel seeds
Salt and freshly ground black pepper, to taste
8 fresh cherry tomatoes, quartered
8 collard greens leaves, stemmed and chopped
1 teaspoon fresh lemon juice
Directions:
In a big skillet, heat oil on medium heat.
Add onion and sauté for approximately 4 minutes.
Add garlic and jalapeño pepper and sauté for approximately 1 minute.
Add beef and spices and cook approximately 6 minutes breaking into pieces while using spoon.
Stir in tomatoes and greens and cook, stirring gently for about 4 minutes.
Stir in lemon juice and take away from heat.

Nutrition:
Calories: 432, Fat: 16g, Carbohydrates: 27g, Fiber: 12g, Protein: 39g

442. Beef & Veggies Chili

Servings: 6-8
Preparation Time: 15 minutes
Cooking Time: one hour
Ingredients:
2 pounds lean ground beef
½ head cauliflower, chopped into large pieces
1 onion, chopped
6 garlic cloves, minced
2 cups pumpkin puree
1 teaspoon dried oregano, crushed
1 teaspoon dried thyme, crushed
1 teaspoon ground cumin
1 teaspoon ground turmeric
1-2 teaspoons chili powder
1 teaspoon paprika
1 teaspoon cayenne pepper
¼ teaspoon red pepper flakes, crushed
Salt and freshly ground black pepper, to taste
1 (26-ouncecan tomatoes, drained
½ cup water
1 cup beef broth
Directions:
Heat a substantial pan on medium-high heat.
Add beef and stir fry for around 5 minutes.
Add cauliflower, onion and garlic and stir fry for approximately 5 minutes.
Add spices and herbs and stir to mix well.
Stir in remaining ingredients and provide to a boil.
Reduce heat to low and simmer, covered approximately 30-45 minutes.
Serve hot.
Nutrition:
Calories: 453, Fat: 10g, Carbohydrates: 20g, Fiber: 8g, Protein: 33g

443. Ground Beef & Veggies Curry

Servings: 6-8
Preparation Time: 15 minutes
Cooking Time: 36 minutes
Ingredients:
2-3 tablespoons coconut oil
1 cup onion, chopped
1 garlic clove, minced
1-pound lean ground beef

1½ tablespoons curry powder
1/8 teaspoon ground ginger
1/8 teaspoon ground cinnamon
1/8 teaspoon ground turmeric
Salt, to taste
2½-3 cups tomatoes, chopped finely
2½-3 cups fresh peas, shelled
2 sweet potatoes, peeled and chopped
Directions:
In a sizable pan, melt coconut oil on medium heat.
Add onion and garlic and sauté for around 4-5 minutes.
Add beef and cook for about 4-5 minutes.
Add curry powder and spices and cook for about 1 minute.
Stir in tomatoes, peas and sweet potato and bring to your gentle simmer.
Simmer, covered approximately 25 minutes.
Nutrition:
Calorie: 432, Fat: 16g, Carbohydrates: 21g, Fiber: 11g, Protein: 36g

444. Spicy & Creamy Ground Beef Curry

Servings: 4
Preparation Time: 15 minutes
Cooking Time: 32 minutes
Ingredients:

1-2 tablespoons coconut oil
1 teaspoon black mustard seeds
2 sprigs curry leaves
1 Serrano pepper, minced
1 large red onion, chopped finely
1 (1-inchpiece fresh ginger, minced
4 garlic cloves, minced
1 teaspoon ground coriander
1 teaspoon ground cumin
½ teaspoon ground turmeric
¼ teaspoon red chili powder
Salt, to taste
1-pound lean ground beef
1 potato, peeled and chopped
3 medium carrots, peeled and chopped
¼ cup water
1 (14-ouncecan coconut milk
Salt and freshly ground black pepper, to taste
Chopped fresh cilantro, for garnishing
Directions:
In a big pan, melt coconut oil on medium heat.
Add mustard seeds and sauté for about thirty seconds.
Add curry leaves and Serrano pepper and sauté approximately half a minute.
Add onion, ginger and garlic and sauté for about 4-5 minutes.
Add spices and cook for about 1 minute.
Add beef and cook for about 4-5 minutes.
Stir in potato, carrot and water and provide with a gentle simmer.
Simmer, covered for around 5 minutes.
Stir in coconut milk and simmer for around fifteen minutes.
Stir in salt and black pepper and remove from heat.
Serve hot while using garnishing of cilantro.
Nutrition:
Calories: 432, Fat: 14g, Carbohydrates: 22g, Fiber: 8g, Protein: 39g

445.   Curried Beef Meatballs

Servings: 6
Preparation Time: twenty minutes
Cooking Time: 22 minutes
Ingredients:
For Meatballs:
1-pound lean ground beef
2 organic eggs, beaten
3 tablespoons red onion, minced
¼ cup fresh basil leaves, chopped
1 (1-inchfresh ginger piece, chopped finely
4 garlic cloves, chopped finely

3 Thai bird's eye chilies, minced
1 teaspoon coconut sugar
1 tablespoon red curry paste
Salt, to taste
1 tablespoon fish sauce
2 tablespoons coconut oil
For Curry:
1 red onion, chopped
Salt, to taste
4 garlic cloves, minced
1 (1-inchfresh ginger piece, minced
2 Thai bird's eye chilies, minced
2 tablespoons red curry paste
1 (14-ouncecoconut milk
Salt and freshly ground black pepper, to taste
Lime wedges, for
Directions:
For meatballs in a large bowl, add all ingredients except oil and mix till well combined.
Make small balls from mixture.
In a large skillet, melt coconut oil on medium heat.
Add meatballs and cook for about 3-5 minutes or till golden brown all sides.
Transfer the meatballs right into a bowl.
In the same skillet, add onion as well as a pinch of salt and sauté for around 5 minutes.
Add garlic, ginger and chilies and sauté for about 1 minute.
Add curry paste and sauté for around 1 minute.
Add coconut milk and meatballs and convey to some gentle simmer.
Reduce the warmth to low and simmer, covered for around 10 minutes.
Serve using the topping of lime wedges.
Nutrition:
Calories: 444, Fat: 15g, Carbohydrates: 20g, Fiber: 2g, Protein: 37g

446.   Beef Meatballs in Tomato Gravy

Servings: 4
Preparation Time: 20 minutes
Cooking Time: 37 minutes
Ingredients:
For Meatballs:

1-pound lean ground beef
1 organic egg, beaten
1 tablespoon fresh ginger, minced
1 garlic oil, minced
2 tablespoons fresh cilantro, chopped finely
2 tablespoons tomato paste
1/3 cup almond meal
1 tablespoon ground cumin
Pinch of ground cinnamon
Salt and freshly ground black pepper, to taste
¼ cup coconut oil
For Tomato Gravy:
2 tablespoons coconut oil
½ of small onion, chopped
2 garlic cloves, chopped
1 teaspoon fresh lemon zest, grated finely
2 cups tomatoes, chopped finely
Pinch of ground cinnamon
1 teaspoon red pepper flakes, crushed
¾ cup chicken broth
Salt and freshly ground black pepper, to taste
¼ cup fresh parsley, chopped
Directions:
For meatballs in a sizable bowl, add all ingredients except oil and mix till well combined.
Make about 1-inch sized balls from mixture.
In a substantial skillet, melt coconut oil on medium heat.
Add meatballs and cook for approximately 3-5 minutes or till golden brown all sides.
Transfer the meatballs in to a bowl.
For gravy in a big pan, melt coconut oil on medium heat.
Add onion and garlic and sauté approximately 4 minutes.
Add lemon zest and sauté approximately 1 minute.
Add tomatoes, cinnamon, red pepper flakes and broth and simmer approximately 7 minutes.
Stir in salt, black pepper and meatballs and reduce the warmth to medium-low.
Simmer for approximately twenty minutes.
Serve hot with all the garnishing of parsley.
Nutrition:
Calories: 404, Fat: 11g, Carbohydrates: 27g, Fiber: 4g, Protein: 38g

447.   Honey Glazed Beef

Servings: 2-3
Preparation Time: 15 minutes
Cooking Time: 12 minutes
Ingredients:

2 tablespoons arrowroot flour

Salt and freshly ground black pepper, to taste

1-pound flank steak, cut into ¼-inch thick slices

½ cup plus 1 tablespoon coconut oil, divided

2 minced garlic cloves

1 teaspoon ground ginger

Pinch of red pepper flakes, crushed

1/3 cup organic honey

½ cup beef broth

½ cup coconut aminos

3 scallions, chopped

Directions:

In a bowl, mix together arrowroot flour, salt and black pepper.

Coat beef slices in arrowroot flour mixture evenly after which get rid of excess mixture.

Keep aside for about 10-15 minutes.

For sauce in a pan, melt 1 tablespoon of coconut oil on medium heat.

Add garlic, ginger powder and red pepper flakes and sauté for about 1 minute.

Add honey, broth and coconut aminos and stir to mix well.

Increase the heat to high and cook, stirring continuously for around 3 minutes.

Remove from heat and keep aside.

In a large skillet, melt remaining coconut oil on medium heat.

Add beef and stir fry approximately 2-3 minutes.

Transfer the beef onto a paper towel lined plate to drain.

Remove the oil from skillet and return the beef into skillet.

Stir fry for around 1 minute.

Stir in honey sauce and cook approximately 3 minutes.

Stir in scallion and cook approximately 1 minute more.

Serve hot.

Nutrition:

Calories: 399, Fat: 15g, Carbohydrates: 28g, Fiber: 7g, Protein: 38g

448.   Pan Grilled Flank Steak

Servings: 3-4

Preparation Time: 10 minutes

Cooking Time: 12-16 minutes

Ingredients:

8 medium garlic cloves, crushed

1 (5-inchpiece fresh ginger, sliced thinly

1 tablespoon organic honey

¼ cup organic olive oil

Salt and freshly ground black pepper, to taste

1½ pound flank steak, trimmed

Directions:

In a large sealable bag, mix together all ingredients except steak.

Add steak and coat with marinade generously.

Seal the bag and refrigerate to marinate for approximately one day.

Remove from refrigerator and in room temperature approximately 15 minutes.

Lightly, grease a grill pan as well as heat to medium-high heat.

Discard the surplus marinade from steak and place in grill pan.

Cook for about 6-8 minutes from each party.

Remove from grill pan and keep side for around 10 min before slicing.

With a clear, crisp knife cut into desired slices and serve.

Nutrition:

Calories: 432, Fat: 16g, Carbohydrates: 26g, Fiber: 5g, Protein: 35g

449.   Mediterranean Roast Beef

Preparation Time: 2 hours 35 minutes

Servings: 8

Nutrition: 353 Calories; 18.2g Fat; 3.7g Carbs; 43g Protein; 0.5g Fiber

Ingredients

2 ½ pounds beef chuck roast, cut into bite-sized pieces

1 cup condensed cream of mushroom soup

1 Italian pepper, deseeded and sliced

1 celery stalk, sliced

1/2 cup leeks, sliced

Directions

Begin by preheating an oven to 330 degrees F.

Heat 1 tablespoon of olive oil in a saucepan. Brown beef chuck roast over medium-high flame. Place the beef chuck roast in a large roasting pan.

Scatter the leeks, pepper and celery around the beef.

Add in the cream of mushroom soup along with 1 cup of water. Sprinkle with salt and black pepper.

Bake approximately 2 hours 20 minutes or until the meat is fall-apart. Bon appétit!

450.   Old-Fashioned Steak

Preparation Time: 8 hours 15 minutes

Servings: 6

Nutrition: 448 Calories; 36.1g Fat; 1.6g Carbs; 28.2g Protein; 0.1g Fiber

Ingredients

2 tablespoons peanut oil

2 pounds bone-in rib eye steaks (1 1/2-inch thick

2 cloves garlic, pressed
1/2 cup rice wine
1 cup cream of mushroom soup
Directions
In your slow cooker, heat the oil in until sizzling; now, sear the steaks for about 3 minutes per side.
Stir in the garlic, rice wine, and cream of mushroom soup. Set the cooker on Low, cover, and cook for 7 to 8 hours.
Preheat your broiler for 5 minutes and position the oven rack.
Broil the meat for 8 to 9 minutes. Check doneness using an instant-read thermometer and enjoy!

451.   Meatballs with French Sauce

Preparation Time: 45 minutes
Servings: 6
Nutrition: 434 Calories; 25.2g Fat; 5.2g Carbs; 44.4g Protein; 1g Fiber
Ingredients
4 ounces bacon, diced
2 pounds ground beef
1/2 cup Parmigiano-Reggiano cheese, grated
1/2 cup tomato puree
1/2 cup French onion soup
Directions
Mix the bacon, ground beef, and Parmigiano-Reggiano cheese until well combined.
Cook your meatballs in a lightly greased grill pan over medium-high heat for about 6 minutes.
Then, in a mixing bowl, whisk tomato puree and French onion soup. Pour the sauce over the meatballs.
Reduce the heat to medium-low and let it simmer, partially covered, for 30 to 33 minutes or until cooked through. Bon appétit!

452.   American-Style BBQ Ribs

Preparation Time: 1 hour 45 minutes
Servings: 2
Nutrition: 481 Calories; 41g Fat; 5.9g Carbs; 19.9g Protein; 1.3g Fiber
Ingredients
1/2 pound beef ribs
1 teaspoon American-style mustard
1 leek, sliced
1/4 teaspoon stevia powder
3/4 cup vegetable broth
Directions
In a grill pan, heat 1 tablespoon of olive oil over medium-high flame. Cook the ribs for about 4 minutes per side; stir in the leek and continue to sauté for 3 to 4 minutes.
Add a splash of wine to scrape up the browned bits that stick to the bottom of the pot, if desired. Then, add in broth and stir to combine well.

Reduce the temperature to medium-low, partially cover, and let it simmer for 35 to 40 minutes longer. Season with the salt and black pepper to taste.

Place the ribs along with the cooking liquid in a foil-lined baking dish.

Add in stevia and American-style mustard. Bake in the preheated oven at 310 degrees F for 50 to 55 minutes, flipping them occasionally.

Garnish with fresh chives if desired. Bon appétit!

453.   Mini Spinach Meatloaves

Preparation Time: 35 minutes
Servings: 2
Nutrition: 439 Calories; 18.4g Fat; 8.4g Carbs; 40.1g Protein; 5g Fiber
Ingredients
1 bunch spinach, chopped
1/2 pound lean ground beef
2 tablespoons tomato paste
1/4 cup almond meal
1 egg, beaten
Directions
Thoroughly combine the ingredients until everything is well incorporated.

Divide the meat mixture into lightly greased muffin cups. Bake in the preheated oven at 365 degrees F for 25 minutes.

Bon appétit!

454.   Buttery Steak with Broccoli

Preparation Time: 15 minutes + marinating time
Servings: 3
Nutrition: 331 Calories; 24.7g Fat; 4.5g Carbs; 24.1g Protein; 2.8g Fiber
Ingredients
2 tablespoons butter, room temperature
1/2 pound broccoli, cut into florets
1/2 cup steak marinade
1/2 pound skirt steak, sliced into pieces
1/2 cup scallions, chopped
Directions
Place the steak marinade and beef in a ceramic bowl; let it marinate in your refrigerator for 3 hours.

In a frying pan, melt 1 tablespoon of butter over medium-high heat. Then, sauté the broccoli for 2 to 3 minutes or until it is crisp-tender; reserve.

Heat the remaining tablespoon of butter in the pan. Now, sauté the scallions until tender for 2 to 3 minutes; reserve.

Brown skirt steak, adding a small amount of the reserved marinade.

Stir in the reserved vegetables and continue to cook until everything is thoroughly warmed. Bon appétit!

455.   French-Style Beef with Onion Gravy

Preparation Time: 1 hour 25 minutes
Servings: 8
Nutrition: 532 Calories; 34.6g Fat; 3.2g Carbs; 45.8g Protein; 0.8g Fiber
Ingredients
3 tablespoons peanut oil
1/2 cup of red wine
4 garlic cloves, halved
4 pounds beef sirloin
1 onion, sliced
Directions
Rub the garlic halves all over the beef; season with the salt and black pepper. Add in 2 tablespoons of peanut oil and let it to marinate in your refrigerator for 3 hours.
Then, heat the remaining tablespoon of peanut oil in a sauce pan over medium-high heat. Now, sear the meat until nicely browned all sides.
Place the beef sirloin in a lightly greased baking pan; pour in 1 cup of water or vegetable broth. Bake in the preheated oven at 365 degrees F for about 55 minutes.
In the meantime, heat a sauce pan over a low heat and sweat the onion for 15 minutes until caramelized.
Now, whisk in red wine and let it simmer until the sauce has reduced by half. Spoon the sauce over the beef and enjoy!

456.   Chunky Beef and Cheese Casserole

Preparation Time: 30 minutes
Servings: 6
Nutrition: 534 Calories; 43.5g Fat; 6.9g Carbs; 30.5g Protein; 1g Fiber
Ingredients
1 yellow onion, chopped
1 ½ pounds ground chuck
2 cups double cream
1 ¼ cups Monterey Jack cheese, shredded
1 cup marinara sauce
Directions
In a saucepan, melt 1 teaspoon of butter over medium-high flame. Cook the onion and beef until the onion is tender and translucent and the beef is no longer pink.
Add in marinara sauce and stir to combine; let it cook approximately 5 minutes. Transfer the onion/beef mixture to a buttered baking dish.
Spread double cream over the meat mixture.
Bake in the preheated oven at 390 degrees F for 15 minutes. Top with the Monterey Jack cheese and continue to bake for 6 minutes more or until nicely brown around edges. Bon appétit!

457.   Festive Chuck Roast

Preparation Time: 1 hour 35 minutes
Servings: 5
Nutrition: 267 Calories; 11.4g Fat; 2.4g Carbs; 37.8g Protein; 0.4g Fiber
Ingredients
2 pounds chuck eye roast
1 tablespoon steak spice mix
1/3 cup cream of mushroom soup
1 tablespoon Dijon mustard
1/4 cup apple cider vinegar
Directions
Preheat your oven to 360 degrees F.
Spritz a large frying pan with cooking oil; preheat the frying pan over medium-high heat and sear the roast for about 4 minutes per each side until nicely brown. Lower the roast into a baking dish.
In a bowl, whisk the vinegar, cream of mushroom soup, mustards, and spices. Pour the sauce over the beef roast.
Cover with a piece of aluminum foil and roast for 1 hour 35 minutes. Let your roast sit for 10 minutes before slicing.
To serve, spoon the sauce over the chuck roast and enjoy!

458.   Easy Short Loin

Preparation Time: 30 minutes
Servings: 3
Nutrition: 313 Calories; 11.6g Fat; 0.1g Carbs; 52g Protein; 0.1g Fiber
Ingredients
1 ½ pounds beef short loin
Sea salt and ground black pepper, to taste
1 teaspoon garlic powder
2 thyme sprigs, chopped
1 rosemary sprig, chopped
Directions
Place all ingredients in a re-sealable bag. Shake until the beef is well coated on all sides.
Grill for 10 minutes; turn over and cook for 10 minutes more.
Bon appétit!

459.   Home-Style Burgers

Preparation Time: 30 minutes
Servings: 5
Nutrition: 297 Calories; 23.6g Fat; 0.7g Carbs; 20.2g Protein; 0.1g Fiber
Ingredients
1 tablespoon olive oil
1 ½ pounds ground beef
8 ounces cheddar cheese, shredded
Sea salt and freshly cracked black pepper, to season

1 egg, beaten
Directions
Mix ground beef, 4 ounces of cheese, salt, black pepper, and egg. Form the beef mixture into 5 patties.
Warm the olive oil in a frying pan over a moderate heat. Fry your burgers for 6 minutes.
Place the remaining cheddar cheese on top of your patties; fry them for a further 6 minutes.
Serve on lettuce leaves and enjoy!

460.   Famous New York Steak

Preparation Time: 15 minutes + marinating time
Servings: 5
Nutrition: 441 Calories; 23.1g Fat; 5.8g Carbs; 52.4g Protein; 1.9g Fiber
Ingredients
2 pounds New York strip, cut into bite-sized chunks
1/2 cup steak marinade
2 cloves garlic, pressed
1 bell pepper, deseeded and sliced
1/2 pound Brussels sprouts, trimmed and halved
Directions
Place the New York strip and marinade in a large ceramic dish. Let it sit in your refrigerator for 2 hours.
Heat 1 tablespoon of the peanut oil in a frying pan. Brown the beef over moderate heat for 10 to 12 minutes; reserve.
Pour in a splash of the reserved marinade to deglaze the pan.
Heat 1 tablespoon of peanut oil. Now, cook the garlic, bell pepper and Brussels sprouts for 4 to 5 minutes until they have softened.
Season with salt and black pepper; return the beef to the frying pan and let it cook for about 3 minutes until cooked through. Bon appétit!

461.   Mexican Taco Soup

Preparation Time: 1 hour 10 minutes
Servings: 4
Nutrition: 201 Calories; 4.8g Fat; 8.9g Carbs; 26.4g Protein; 2.5g Fiber
Ingredients
1 pound beef shoulder, cut into small chunks
1 cup celery, chopped
1 red bell pepper, chopped
1 cup tomato puree
1/2 (1.25-ouncepackage taco seasoning mix
Directions
Melt 1 tablespoon of avocado oil in a large heavy-bottomed pot over medium-high heat. Brown the beef shoulder for about 5 minutes until nicely browned.

Add in the celery, pepper, tomato puree and taco seasoning mix. Reduce the temperature to medium-low. Pour in 4 cups of water or vegetable broth; stir to combine well.

Continue to simmer, partially covered, for 50 to 55 minutes. Enjoy!

462.   Dad's Ragù with a Twist

Preparation Time: 30 minutes
Servings: 4
Nutrition: 335 Calories; 23g Fat; 6.1g Carbs; 22.7g Protein; 1.1g Fiber
Ingredients
1/2 cup shallots, chopped
2 cups button mushrooms, sliced
1 pound ground beef
1 cup tomato sauce with onion and garlic
1 cup cream of onion soup
Directions
Melt 1 tablespoon of lard in a pot over a moderate heat. Once hot, cook the shallots and mushrooms, stirring periodically, until just tender for 3 to 4 minutes.

Stir in the ground beef; continue to cook for 4 to 5 minutes, falling apart with a fork or spatula. Pour in tomato sauce and cream of onion soup.

Stir and partially cover. Allow it to simmer for 20 to 25 minutes more and serve warm. Bon appétit!

463.   Aromatic Roast Beef with Herbs

Preparation Time: 1 hour 10 minutes
Servings: 2
Nutrition: 316 Calories; 13.2g Fat; 2.6g Carbs; 47.2g Protein; 0.5g Fiber
Ingredients
1 pound rump roast, boneless
1 tablespoon yellow mustard
1 tablespoon Mediterranean spice mix
1/2 cup beef bone broth
2 yellow onions, quartered
Directions
Pat the roast dry with kitchen towels. Then, place the roast, yellow mustard and spices in a resealable bag. Shake to coat your roast on all sides.

Place the roast in a baking pan and pour in the broth. Scatter the onions around the roast.

Roast in the preheated oven at 360 degrees F for 30 to 35 minutes. Then reduce the heat to 300 degrees F and cook the roast for 35 minutes longer. Enjoy !

464.   Italian Meatloaf with Marinara Sauce

Preparation Time: 1 hour 15 minutes
Servings: 6

Nutrition: 342 Calories; 21.2g Fat; 5.9g Carbs; 30.4g Protein; 0.9g Fiber
Ingredients
1/2 cup leeks, chopped
1 ½ pounds ground chuck
1 egg, whisked
1/2 cup full-fat milk
1/2 cup low-carb marinara sauce
Directions
Preheat your oven to 330 degrees F.
Melt 1 teaspoon of tallow in a pan over moderate heat; cook the leeks and ground chuck for 5 to 6 minutes, stirring periodically.
Then, add in the egg and milk; season with the salt and black pepper to taste and mix to combine well.
Spoon the meat mixture in a lightly greased loaf pan. Bake in the preheated oven for 45 to 50 minutes.
Afterwards, top your meatloaf with the marinara sauce and continue to bake for another 8 to 10 minutes. Bon appétit!

465.   Saucy Beef with Herbs

Preparation Time: 50 minutes
Servings: 4
Nutrition: 421 Calories; 35.7g Fat; 5.9g Carbs; 19.7g Protein; 1g Fiber
Ingredients
1 tablespoon olive oil
1 pound rib eye, cut into strips
1 tablespoon Italian herb mix
2 chipotle peppers in adobo sauce, chopped
1 cup tomato sauce with garlic and onions
Directions
Heat the oil in a saucepan over a moderate heat. Sear the beef for about 7 minutes or until no longer pink.
Add in the remaining ingredients along with 1/2 cup of beef bone broth. Then, reduce the temperature to medium-low; continue to simmer for 40 to 45 minutes.
Shred the beef with two forks and serve topped with cooking juice. Bon appétit!

466.   Aromatic Beef Stew

Preparation Time: 55 minutes
Servings: 6
Nutrition: 277 Calories; 21.5g Fat; 2.7g Carbs; 17.4g Protein; 0.8g Fiber
Ingredients
1 ½ pounds top chuck, cut into bite-sized cubes
1/2 cup onions, chopped
2 Italian peppers, chopped

1 celery stalk, chopped
1 cup tomato sauce with garlic
Directions
In a heavy-bottomed pot, melt 1 teaspoon of lard over medium-high heat. Sear the top chuck for about 10 minutes until brown; reserve.
In the pan drippings, sauté the onion, Italian peppers, and celery for 5 to 6 minutes until they have softened.
Return the beef to the pot along with tomato sauce. Season with salt and black pepper.
Let it simmer, partially covered, for 35 to 40 minutes. Bon appétit!

467. Double-Cheese Meatloaf

Preparation Time: 1 hour
Servings: 4
Nutrition: 361 Calories; 23.1g Fat; 5.6g Carbs; 32.2g Protein; 0.8g Fiber
Ingredients
1 pound ground beef
2 teaspoons sunflower oil
1 egg, whisked
1 cup marinara sauce
1 Swiss cheese, grated
Directions
In a frying pan, heat the oil over medium-high heat. Cook ground beef until no longer pink or 4 to 5 minutes. Season with onion powder, salt, and black pepper to taste.
Add in the cheese and egg; mix until everything is well incorporated. Press the mixture into a lightly greased baking pan.
Bake in the preheated oven at 380 degrees F.for 40 minutes. Now, spoon marinara sauce over the meatloaf.
Continue to bake an additional 10 minutes or until cooked through. Enjoy!

468. Steak Salad with Avocado

Preparation Time: 20 minutes
Servings: 4
Nutrition: 231 Calories; 17.1g Fat; 6g Carbs; 13.8g Protein; 3.4g Fiber
Ingredients
8 ounces flank steak, salt-and-pepper-seasoned
1 ripe avocado, peeled and sliced
1 cucumber, sliced
2 medium-sized heirloom tomatoes, sliced
1/2 cup onions, finely sliced
Directions
Heat 1 tablespoon of olive oil in a frying pan over a moderate flame. Brown the flank steak for 5 to 7 minutes, turning periodically to ensure even cooking.
One the meat is cool enough to handle, slice it thinly across the grain. Place the meat in a bowl.

Add the remaining ingredients and toss with 1 tablespoon of olive oil and lemon juice. Serve at room temperature or well chilled. Enjoy!

469. Harvest Vegetable and Hamburger Soup

Preparation Time: 35 minutes
Servings: 2
Nutrition: 299 Calories; 15.1g Fat; 6.5g Carbs; 32g Protein; 2.7g Fiber
Ingredients
1/2 pound lean ground beef
1 cup green cabbage, shredded
1/2 cup celery stalks, chopped
1 vine-ripe tomato, pureed
1/2 cup scallions, chopped
Directions
Heat 1 teaspoon of olive oil in a soup pot over medium-high heat. Now, cook the beef and celery for 4 to 5 minutes.
Add in scallions and continue to sauté an additional 2 to 3 minutes or until it is tender.
Then, stir in the cabbage and tomato; turn the temperature to simmer and continue to cook, partially covered, for 35 to 40 minutes longer. Bon appétit!

470. Italian Meatballs in Asiago Sauce

Preparation Time: 15 minutes
Servings: 3
Nutrition: 458 Calories; 35.8g Fat; 4.3g Carbs; 28.2g Protein; 0.2g Fiber
Ingredients
1 teaspoon Italian spice mix
1/2 pound ground beef
1 egg
3 ounces Asiago cheese, grated
1/4 cup mayonnaise
Directions
In a mixing bowl, thoroughly combine Italian slice mix, beef, and egg. Mix until everything is well combined. Roll the mixture into meatballs.
In another bowl, mix Asiago cheese and mayonnaise.
Heat 1 tablespoon of olive oil in a frying pan over a moderate heat. Then, sear the meatballs for about 5 minutes, turning them occasionally to ensure even cooking. Bon appétit!

471. Meatloaf with a Sweet Sticky Glaze

Preparation Time: 1 hour
Servings: 2
Nutrition: 517 Calories; 32.3g Fat; 8.4g Carbs; 48.5g Protein; 6.5g Fiber

Ingredients
3/4 pound ground chuck
1/4 cup flaxseed meal
2 eggs, beaten
1/2 cup tomato sauce with garlic and onion
1 teaspoon liquid monk fruit
Directions
In a mixing bowl, combine the ground chuck, flaxseed meal, and eggs; season with the salt and black pepper.
In a separate mixing bowl, combine the tomato sauce and liquid monk fruit; add 1 teaspoon of mustard and whisk until well combined.
Spoon the mixture into the foil-lined loaf pan and smooth the surface. Bake in the preheated oven at 365 degrees F for about 25 minutes.
Spoon the tomato mixture on top of the meatloaf and continue to bake for a further 25 minutes or until thoroughly cooked.
Allow your meatloaf to rest for 10 minutes before slicing and. Bon appétit!

472.   Pork Chops with Shallots

Preparation Time: 10 minutes
Cooking Time: 40 minutes
Servings: 4
Ingredients:
1 cup shallots, chopped
½ cup vegetable stock
2 pounds pork stew meat, roughly cubed
2 garlic cloves, minced
A pinch of salt and black pepper
2 tablespoons olive oil
1 tablespoon cilantro, chopped
Directions:
Heat up a pan with the oil over medium-high heat, add the shallots and sauté for 10 minutes.
Add the meat and the other ingredients, toss, cook over medium heat for 30 minutes, divide between plates and serve.
Nutrition: calories 250, fat 12, fiber 2, carbs 13, protein 17

473.   Mint Pork

Preparation Time: 10 minutes
Cooking Time: 40 minutes
Servings: 4
Ingredients:
4 pork chops
1 cup mint leaves
2 tablespoons balsamic vinegar
1 tablespoon almonds, chopped

2 tablespoons olive oil
2 garlic cloves, minced
Salt and black pepper to the taste
¼ teaspoon red pepper flakes
Directions:
In a blender, combine the mint with the vinegar and the other ingredients except the pork chops and pulse well.
Heat up a pan with the mint mix over medium heat, add the pork chops, toss, introduce in the oven and bake at 390 degrees F for 40 minutes.
Divide everything between plates and serve.
Nutrition: calories 260, fat 6 fiber 1, carbs 8, protein 23

474.   Pork with Spiced Zucchinis

Preparation Time: 10 minutes
Cooking Time: 40 minutes
Servings: 4
Ingredients:
2 pounds pork stew meat, roughly cubed
2 zucchinis, sliced
2 tablespoons olive oil
1 teaspoon nutmeg, ground
1 teaspoon cinnamon powder
1 teaspoon cumin, ground
2 tablespoons lime juice
2 garlic cloves, minced
A pinch of sea salt and black pepper
Directions:
In a roasting pan, combine the meat with the zucchinis, the nutmeg and the other ingredients, toss and bake at 390 degrees F for 40 minutes.
Divide everything between plates and serve.
Nutrition: calories 200, fat 5, fiber 2, carbs 10, protein 22

475.   Pork and Cumin Pinto Beans

Preparation Time: 10 minutes
Cooking Time: 1 hour
Servings: 4
Ingredients:
2 pounds pork stew meat, roughly cubed
1 cup canned pinto beans, drained and rinsed
4 scallions, chopped
2 tablespoons olive oil
1 tablespoon chili powder
2 teaspoons cumin, ground
A pinch of sea salt and black pepper
2 garlic cloves, minced

1 cup vegetable stock
A handful parsley, chopped
Directions:
Heat up a pan with the oil over medium-high heat, add the scallions and the garlic and sauté for 5 minutes.
Add the meat and brown for 5 minutes more.
Add the beans and the other ingredients, toss, introduce the pan in the oven and cook everything at 380 degrees F for 50 minutes.
Divide the mix between plates and serve.
Nutrition: calories 291, fat 4, fiber 10, carbs 15, protein 24

476.   Pork and Veggies Pan

Preparation Time: 10 minutes
Cooking Time: 40 minutes
Servings: 4
Ingredients:
1 tablespoon olive oil
2 spring onions, chopped
2 pounds pork stew meat, cut into strips
1 zucchini, cubed
1 red bell pepper, cut into strips
1 green bell pepper, cut into strips
2 tomatoes, cubed
1 teaspoon coriander, ground
1 teaspoon oregano, dried
A pinch of salt and black pepper
1 teaspoon ginger, grated
Directions:
Heat up a pan with the oil over medium-high heat, add the spring onions, ginger and the meat and brown for 10 minutes stirring from time to time.
Add the rest of the ingredients, toss, cook over medium heat for 30 minutes more, divide between plates and serve.
Nutrition: calories 270, fat 3, fiber 6, carbs 8, protein 15

477.   Pork and Green Chilies Mix

Preparation Time: 10 minutes
Cooking Time: 45 minutes
Servings: 4
Ingredients:
1 yellow onion, chopped
2 pounds pork stew meat, roughly cubed
2 tablespoons olive oil
1 cup canned green chilies, chopped
1 red bell pepper, chopped
¼ cup vegetable stock

A pinch of salt and black pepper
1 tablespoon chili powder
Directions:
Heat up a pan with the oil over medium heat, add the onion and the meat and brown for 10 minutes.
Add the rest of the ingredients, toss, cook over medium heat for 35 minutes more, divide between plates and serve.
Nutrition: calories 600, fat 30.4, fiber 4.3, carbs 12.8, protein 68.2

478.   Pork and Brown Rice

Preparation Time: 10 minutes
Cooking Time: 40 minutes
Servings: 4
Ingredients:
1 pound pork stew meat, cubed
2 tablespoons avocado oil
1 yellow onion, chopped
1 cup brown rice
3 cups vegetable stock
2 teaspoons sweet paprika
1 teaspoon fennel seeds, crushed
A pinch of salt and black pepper
1 tablespoon parsley, chopped
Directions:
Heat up a pan with the oil over medium-high heat, add the onion and the meat and brown for 10 minutes.
Add the rest of the ingredients, toss, cook over medium heat for 30 minutes more, divide between plates and serve.
Nutrition: calories 440, fat 13.9, fiber 3.2, carbs 40.6, protein 37.4

479.   Caraway and Dill Pork

Preparation Time: 10 minutes
Cooking Time: 45 minutes
Servings: 4
Ingredients:
2 pounds pork meat, cubed
1 yellow onion, chopped
2 tablespoons olive oil
1 cup vegetable stock
1 teaspoon caraway seeds
A pinch of salt and black pepper
2 tablespoons dill, chopped
Directions:
Heat up a pan with the oil over medium heat, add the onion and sauté for 5 minutes.
Add the meat and brown for 5 minutes more.

Add the rest of the ingredients, toss, cook over medium heat for 35 minutes, divide between plates sand serve.

Nutrition: calories 300, fat 12.8, fiber 6, carbs 12, protein 16

480.　　Pork with Corn and Peas

Preparation Time: 10 minutes
Cooking Time: 40 minutes
Servings: 4
Ingredients:
2 pounds pork stew meat, cut into strips
½ cup corn
½ cup green peas
2 tablespoons olive oil
½ cup yellow onion, chopped
3 tablespoons coconut aminos
½ cup vegetable stock
A pinch of salt and black pepper
Directions:
Heat up a pan with the oil over medium heat, add the meat and the onion and brown for 10 minutes.
Add the corn and the other ingredients, toss, cook over medium heat for 30 minutes more, divide between plates and serve.
Nutrition: calories 250, fat 4, fiber 6, carbs 9.7, protein 12

481.　　Pork with Carrots

Preparation Time: 10 minutes
Cooking Time: 1 hour
Servings: 4
Ingredients:
1 pound pork meat, cubed
2 carrots, sliced
2 tablespoons avocado oil
1 yellow onion, chopped
A pinch of salt and black pepper
¼ teaspoon smoked paprika
½ cup tomato sauce
Directions:
Heat up a pan with the oil over medium-high heat, add the onion and the meat and brown for 10 minutes.
Add the rest of the ingredients, toss, put the pan in the oven and bake at 390 degrees F for 50 minutes.
Divide everything between plates and serve.
Nutrition: calories 300, fat 7, fiber 6, carbs 12, protein 20

482.　　Pork and Creamy Leeks

Preparation Time: 10 minutes
Cooking Time: 55 minutes
Servings: 4
Ingredients:
2 pounds pork stew meat, cubed
3 leeks, sliced
2 tablespoons olive oil
1 teaspoon black peppercorns
1 tablespoon parsley, chopped
2 cups coconut cream
1 teaspoon rosemary, dried
A pinch of salt and black pepper
Directions:
Heat up a pan with the oil over medium heat, add the leeks and the meat and brown for 5 minutes.
Add the rest of the ingredients, toss, put the pan in the oven and bake at 390 degrees F for 50 minutes.
Divide everything into bowls and serve.
Nutrition: calories 280, fat 5, fiber 7, carbs 12, protein 18

483.   Tarragon Pork Roast

Preparation Time: 10 minutes
Cooking Time: 1 hour
Servings: 4
Ingredients:
2 pounds pork loin roast, sliced
1 tablespoon tarragon, chopped
A pinch of salt and black pepper
4 garlic cloves, chopped
1 teaspoon red pepper, crushed
¼ cup olive oil
Directions:
In a roasting pan, combine the roast with the tarragon and the other ingredients, toss and bake at 390 degrees F for 1 hour.
Divide the mix between plates and serve.
Nutrition: calories 281, fat 5, fiber 7, carbs 8, protein 10

484.   Roast with Onions and Potatoes

Preparation Time: 10 minutes
Cooking Time: 1 hour
Servings: 4
Ingredients:
2 pounds pork roast, sliced
2 sweet potatoes, peeled and sliced
2 tablespoons olive oil
1 teaspoon rosemary, dried

1 teaspoon turmeric powder
2 yellow onions, sliced
½ cup veggie stock
A pinch of salt and black pepper
Directions:
In a roasting pan, combine the pork slices with the sweet potatoes, the onions and the other ingredients, toss and bake at 400 degrees F for 1 hours.
Divide everything between plates and serve.
Nutrition: calories 290, fat 4, fiber 7, carbs 10, protein 17

485. Pork with Pineapple and Mango

Preparation Time: 10 minutes
Cooking Time: 40 minutes
Servings: 4
Ingredients:
4 pork chops
2 tablespoons olive oil
½ cup vegetable stock
4 scallions, chopped
1 cup pineapple, peeled and cubed
1 mango, peeled and cubed
4 tablespoons lime juice
1 handful basil, chopped
A pinch of salt and cayenne pepper
Directions:
Heat up a pan with the oil over medium heat, add the scallions and the meat and brown for 5 minutes.
Add the pineapple and the other ingredients, toss, cook over medium heat for 35 minutes more, divide between plates and serve.
Nutrition: calories 250, fat 5, fiber 6, carbs 8, protein 17

486. Pork with Celery and Sprouts

Preparation Time: 10 minutes
Cooking Time: 40 minutes
Servings: 4
Ingredients:
2 pounds pork stew meat, roughly cubed
2 tablespoons olive oil
2 tablespoons lemon juice
5 garlic cloves, minced
2 stalks celery, chopped
1 cup Brussels sprouts, trimmed and halved
A pinch of salt and black pepper
½ teaspoon cinnamon powder
2 tablespoons parsley, chopped

Directions:

Heat up a pan with the oil over medium-high heat, add the garlic and the meat and brown for 5 minutes.

Add the celery and the other ingredients, toss, introduce the pan in the oven and cook at 400 degrees F for 35 minutes more.

Divide the mix between plates and serve.

Nutrition: calories 284, fat 4, fiber 4, carbs 9, protein 15

487. Smoked Beef Sausage Bake with Broccoli

Servings: 4
Preparation Time: 45 minutes
Ingredients
1 red bell pepper, thinly sliced
2 shallots, chopped
1 cup broccoli, broken into florets
4 smoked beef sausages, sliced
1 green bell pepper, thinly sliced
2 tablespoons fresh parsley, roughly chopped
2 garlic cloves, minced
1/2 teaspoon ground bay leaf
Salt and black pepper, to taste
1 teaspoon marjoram
6 eggs, whisked
Directions
Begin by preheating your oven to 3700F.

Heat up a nonstick skillet using a moderate flame; now, Heat the sausage for 3 minutes, stirring regularly.

Include the peppers, shallots, broccoli, and garlic; continue cooking for about 5 minutes. Season with marjoram, salt, pepper and ground bay leaf.

Move the sausage mixture to a previously greased baking dish. Pour the whisked eggs over it. Bake for 35 minutes. Enjoy garnished with fresh parsley.

Nutrition: Calories 289 ,Protein 19.8g ,Fat 19.7g ,Carbs 6.3g ,Sugar 2.4g

488. Keto Tacos with Bacon Sauce

Servings: 4
Preparation Time: 30 minutes
Ingredients
1 ½ cups ground beef
2 jalapeno peppers, minced
2 Campari tomatoes, crushed
1/2 teaspoon ground cumin
6 slices bacon, chopped
2 teaspoon champagne vinegar
1/2 teaspoon onion powder
1/2 teaspoon celery salt

1 ½ cups Cotija cheese, shredded
Salt and ground black pepper, to taste
1/2 cup bone broth
3 tablespoons tomato paste
Directions
Begin by preheating your oven to 3900F. Spritz a baking pan with the aid of a nonstick cooking spray.
Spread 6 (sixpiles of Cotija cheese on the baking pan; bake for about 15 minutes; allow taco shells to cool down for some minutes.
In a nonstick skillet, brown the beef for the duration of about 4 to 5 minutes crumbling with a spatula. Include crushed pepper, tomatoes, salt, celery salt, onion powder, and ground cumin. Heat until everything is cooked through.
Now, make the sauce by cooking the bacon for the duration of 2 to 3 minutes stirring continually. Include the remaining ingredients and heat until everything comes together.
After the above, assemble your tacos. Share the meat mixture among 6 taco shells; top with the bacon sauce. Bon appétit!
Nutrition: Calories 258 ,Protein 16.3g ,Fat 19.3g ,Carbs 5g ,Sugar 2.9g

489.   Broccoli and Ground Beef Delight

Servings: 4
Preparation Time: 20 minutes
Ingredients
1 head broccoli, cut into small florets
1 cup red onion, sliced
1/2 ground black pepper
1 teaspoon garlic, minced
1/2 teaspoon turmeric
1 pound ground beef
2 tablespoons Marsala wine
2 teaspoons avocado oil
1/2 teaspoon salt
1/2 cup beef bone broth
1/4 teaspoon cayenne pepper
1/2 teaspoon dill weed
Directions
Heat 1 teaspoon of avocado oil in a pan which has been preheated over a moderate flame. After that, cook the broccoli for about 3 to 4 minutes, stirring often.
Suceeding the above step, stir in the garlic and onion; heat until aromatic and just tender, or rather about 2 minutes. Reserve.
Now, heat another teaspoon of avocado oil. Stir in the beef and heat until it is well browned.
Include the reserved broccoli mixture, reduce the heat and include the remaining ingredients. Cook, shut the lid, until everything is heated through, or probably about 10 minutes.
Now, Serve with a dollop of sour cream. Enjoy!
Nutrition: Calories 241 ,Protein 36g ,Fat 7.6g ,Carbs 6g ,Sugar 1.9g

490.   Burgundy Beef Soup with Pancetta

Servings: 4
Preparation Time: 2 hours 10 minutes
Ingredients
1 shallot, chopped
2 tablespoons fresh parsley, roughly chopped
1 small-sized ripe tomato, crushed
2 bay leaves
4 ounces pancetta, chopped
2 cloves garlic, minced
1 sprig rosemary
1 pound beef, cubed
2 sprigs thyme
2 tablespoons olive oil
2 tablespoons dry red wine
1 tablespoon soy sauce
1 celery rib, chopped
1/2 tablespoon bouillon granules
4 cups water
1 tablespoon flax seed meal
Directions
Begin by preheating your oven to 3200F.
Heat 1 tablespoon of oil in a stock pot that is preheated over a normal flame. After those mentioned above, fry the pancetta for about 3 to 4 minutes while crumbling it with a fork; reserve.
In the next step, heat another tablespoon of olive oil; sauté the shallots and garlic for 3 minutes or until they are softened. Stir in beef and heat until it browns.
Include the remaining ingredients, leaving out flaxseed and parsley, bringing to a rolling boil.
Reduce the heat, close the lid of the pot, and let your soup simmer for an additional 2 hours.
Remove the lid and mix in 1 tablespoon of flax seed meal that has been dissolved in 2 tablespoons of cold water.
Stir to merge well and cook for an additional 3 minutes or rather, until thoroughly warmed. Enjoy garnished with fresh parsley and crumbled pancetta. Bon appétit!
Nutrition: Calories 340 ,Protein 30.2g ,Fat 19.6g ,Carbs 6.5g ,Sugar 1.2g

491.   Beef Sausage and Colby Dip

Servings: 8
Preparation Time: 20 minutes
Ingredients
1 cup cream cheese, at room temperature
1 onion, finely chopped
2 tablespoons fresh chives, roughly chopped
1 ½ cups Colby cheese, shredded
1 tablespoon lard, at room temperature
1 ½ cups smoked beef sausages, crumbled
2 garlic cloves, minced
Directions
Begin by preheating an oven to 3300F.

Dissolve the lard in a pan over moderately high heat. Now, sweat the onion for about 3 to 4 minutes. Stir in the garlic and commence on sautéing until aromatic.

Include the sautéed onion and garlic to a mixing dish. Include the Colby cheese, sausage, cream cheese; mix to merge well.

Move the mixture to a baking dish; bake for about 15 minutes. Garnish it using fresh chives and serve with veggie sticks. Bon appétit!

Nutrition: Calories 333 ,Protein 14.7g ,Fat 29.2g ,Carbs 2.9g ,Sugar 0.8g

492.   Bacon-Wrapped Meatballs with Parsley Sauce

Servings: 6
Preparation Time: 30 minutes
Ingredients
1/2 cup crushed pork rinds
2 cloves garlic, smashed
1/2 pound bacon slices
1 egg, beaten
Toothpicks
1/2 teaspoon cayenne pepper
1 pound ground beef
1 ½ tablespoons olive oil
1/4 cup fresh cilantro, chopped
Sea salt and ground black pepper, to your liking
For the Parsley Sauce:
Sea salt and black pepper, to taste
1 tablespoon almonds, toasted
1 cup fresh parsley
1 tablespoon sunflower seeds, soaked
1/2 tablespoon olive oil
Directions
Foreheat your oven to 3900F.
Now, in a mixing container, thoroughly merge the olive oil, ground beef, garlic, egg, crushed pork rinds, cilantro, salt, black pepper, and cayenne pepper.
Shape and mold the mixture into 1.5-inch meatballs. Wrap each of the shaped balls with a slice of bacon and secure with a toothpick.
Organize the meatballs on a baking sheet; bake in the preheated oven for the duration of about 25 to 30 minutes.
Meanwhile, make the parsley sauce. Pulse all ingredients in a food processor till they become uniform and smooth.
Now, Serve warm meatballs with parsley sauce on the side. Enjoy!
Nutrition: Calories 399 ,Protein 37.7g ,Fat 27g ,Carbs 1.8g ,Sugar 0.2g

493.   Sunday Flank Steak

Servings: 6
Preparation Time: 20 minutes
Ingredients

1 tablespoon lime lemon juice
1 teaspoon garlic paste
A bunch of scallions, chopped
2 tablespoons soy sauce
1/4 cup dry red wine
2 pounds flank steak
Salt and cayenne pepper, to taste
2 tablespoons olive oil
1/2 teaspoon black peppercorns, crushed
Directions
In a mixing container, thoroughly merge the garlic paste, oil, soy sauce, lemon juice, scallions, and red wine.
After that, season the flank steak with cayenne pepper, salt and black peppercorns. Put the meat in a marinade; cover and refrigerate for about 6 hours.
Foreheat a nonstick skillet over a moderately high flame. Fry your steaks for about 10 minutes while turning once. Bon appétit!
Nutrition: Calories 350 ,Protein 42.7g ,Fat 17.3g ,Carbs 2.1g ,Sugar 0.6g

494. Father's Day Stuffed Avocado

Servings: 6
Preparation Time: 20 minutes
Ingredients
1 tablespoon avocado oil
3/4 pound beef, ground
1/3 cup beef broth
1/2 cup shallots, sliced
Salt and black pepper, to taste
3 ripe avocados, pitted and halved
2 small-sized tomatoes, chopped
3/4 cup Colby cheese, shredded
3 tablespoons Kalamata olives, pitted and sliced
1/2 cup mayonnaise
Directions
Preheat an oven to 3400F.
Heat avocado oil in a pan over moderate heat; now, brown the ground beef for 2 to 3 minutes crumbling it with a wooden spatula.
Add the broth and shallots. Cook until the shallots turn translucent. Season with salt and pepper.
Then, scoop out some of the middle of each avocado. Mash the avocado flesh that you scooped out along with chopped tomatoes.
Add the reserved beef mixture and stuff your avocado. Afterward, top with shredded cheese and sliced olives.
Place stuffed avocado on a roasting pan. Bake for 8 to 10 minutes in the preheated oven. Serve with mayonnaise and enjoy!
Nutrition: Calories 407 ,Protein 23.4g Fat 28.8g ,Carbs 16.4g ,Sugar 2.4g

495. Beef Sausage and Vegetable Skillet

Servings: 4
Preparation Time: 40 minutes
Ingredients
2 spring garlic, minced
2 rosemary sprigs
2 ripe tomatoes, pureed
1/4 cup dry red wine
2 shallots, chopped
1 ½ cups beef bone broth
2 tablespoons ketchup, sugar-free
Salt2 bell peppers, deveined and chopped
 and pepper, to taste
4 beef sausages, sliced
2 thyme sprigs
Directions
Heat the oil in a deep skillet over a normal heat. Heat the sausage for about 2 to 3 minutes, stirring occasionally.
Stir in the bell peppers, shallots and garlic; season with pepper and salt. Heat approximately 7 minutes.
Include the remaining ingredients and bring it to a boil. Decrease the heat to medium-low. Allow it simmer for 25 minutes. Enjoy warm.
Nutrition: Calories 250 ,Protein 6.8g ,Fat 17.5g ,Carbs 5.4g ,Sugar 2.7g

496.   Hamburger Soup with Cabbage

Servings: 4
Preparation Time: 35 minutes
Ingredients
Seasoned salt and ground black pepper, to taste
1 cup sour cream
1 tomato, pureed
2 cloves garlic, minced
6 cups chicken broth
1 cup cabbage, shredded
1 bay leaf
2 tablespoons lard, melted
1 celery with leaves, diced
1/2 cup scallions, chopped
3/4 pound ground chuck
Directions
Dissolve the lard in a stockpot. Heat the chuck until it is no longer pink; reserve.
Now, heat the cabbage, scallions, garlic and celery in the pan drippings, stirring continually.
Stir in the other ingredients and the reserved chuck, bringing to a rapid boil. Then, turn the heat to a simmer. Heat another 27 minutes partially covered.
Suceeding the above, taste and adjust the seasonings. Ladle into individual bowls; enjoy dolloped with full-fat sour cream.
Nutrition: Calories 307 ,Protein 14.8g ,Fat 23.6g ,Carbs 5.4g ,Sugar 2.2g

497.   Ultimate Thai Beef Salad

Servings: 4
Preparation Time: 15 minutes
Ingredients
1 teaspoon soy sauce
2 tablespoons olive oil
1 garlic clove, minced
1 tablespoon fresh lime juice
1/3 teaspoon freshly cracked black pepper
1/4 cup pumpkin seeds
1 teaspoon minced Thai chili
2 tablespoons rice vinegar
1/2 pound beef rump steak, cut into strips
2 avocados, pitted, peeled and sliced
1 bunch fresh Thai basil, leaves picked
1/2 teaspoon sea salt
1 b1 red onion, peeled and sliced
unch fresh mint
2 cucumbers, sliced
Directions
Merge the beef with the salt, pepper and soy sauce.
Foreheat the oil in a nonstick skillet over medium-low heat. Now, sauté the onion and garlic until they become tender and aromatic, about 4 minutes.
Heat the beef on a grill pan for 5 minutes or rather, until cooked to your liking.
Organize fresh mint, cucumber, avocado slices, Thai basil, and Thai chili in a nice salad bowl. Top with the beef slices. Include the onion-garlic mixture.
Drizzle with lime juice and rice vinegar. Spray with pumpkin seeds and serve.
Nutrition: Calories 404 ,Protein 12.8g ,Fat 32.9g ,Carbs 6.3g ,Sugar 3.3g

498.   Hungarian Beef Stew

Servings: 4
Preparation Time: 1 hour 25 minutes
Ingredients
2 tablespoons olive oil
1 ¼ pounds chuck-eye roast, diced
Celery salt and ground black pepper, to taste
1 tablespoon Hungarian paprika
1 tablespoon pear cider vinegar
1/2 cup Cabernet Sauvignon
4 cups water
2 tablespoons beef bouillon granules
1/4 teaspoon ground bay leaf
2 onions, peeled and chopped
1 celery with leaves, chopped
1 tablespoon flaxseed meal

Directions

Heat the oil in a heavy-bottomed pot. Then, cook the meat until no longer pink, for 3 to 4 minutes; work in batches and set aside. Season with celery salt, pepper, and Hungarian paprika.

Now, pour the vinegar and Cabernet Sauvignon to deglaze the bottom of the pot. Add the water, beef bouillon granules and reserved beef to the pot.

Stir in the ground bay leaf, onions, celery and cook an additional 1 hour 15 minutes over medium-low heat.

Add the flaxseed meal to thicken the liquid; constantly stir for 3 minutes. Serve in individual bowls and enjoy!

Nutrition: Calories 357 ,Protein 40.2g ,Fat 15.8g ,Carbs 5g ,Sugar 1.2g

499.   Za'atar Strip Steaks with Cabbage

Servings: 4
Preparation Time: 20 minutes
Ingredients
1 yellow onion, chopped
Sea salt and ground black pepper, to taste
2 tablespoons olive oil
1 pound New York strip steaks, cut into bite-sized pieces
1 tablespoon fresh lemon juice
2 garlic cloves, chopped
1 cup cabbage, shredded
1 tablespoon hoisin sauce
1 bell pepper, chopped
1 teaspoon Za'atar
Directions
Put strip steaks with black pepper, hoisin sauce, fresh lemon juice, salt, and Za'atar seasoning.

Marinate in the refrigerator for a minimum duration of 3 hours.

Heat the oil in a skillet that is preheated over a normal high heat. After that, brown strip steaks for the duration of 3 to 4 minutes while stirring occasionally.

Include the onions to the same skillet and heat until it is translucent. Include the cabbage, garlic and bell pepper and set the temperature to medium-low.

Simmer for another 10 minutes and serve warm. Bon appétit!

Nutrition: Calories 321 ,Protein 36.7g ,Fat 14g ,Carbs 5.3g ,Sugar 1.3g

500.   Old-Fashioned Beef Stew

Servings: 6
Preparation Time: 40 minutes
Ingredients
1 cup leeks, thinly sliced
Salt and black pepper, to taste
4 cubes beef bouillon, crumbled
2 garlic cloves, chopped
1 teaspoon cayenne pepper
1 bay leaf

1 teaspoon dried marjoram
1 egg, lightly whisked
4 cups water
1 tablespoon tallow, at room temperature
1 tablespoon cremini mushrooms, thinly sliced
1 ½ pounds beef stew meat, cubed
1/4 teaspoon smoked paprika
Directions
Dissolve the tallow in your pot that is preheated over a moderate flame.
Suceeding the above step, sear the beef until it is just browned; ensure to stir periodically. Set aside.
In pan drippings, heat the leeks and garlic for the duration of 1 to 1 minute 30 seconds or until aromatic. Mix in the mushrooms; heat until they're tender and fragrant.
Include the remaining ingredients, shut the lid and heat for 30 to 40 minutes. Include the whisked egg in hot soup and stir for 1 minute. Now, serve in individual bowls and enjoy!
Nutrition: Calories 259 ,Protein 35.7g ,Fat 10.1g ,Carbs 4.1g ,Sugar 1.4g

501.　　Filet Mignon Steaks with Wine Sauce

Servings: 4
Preparation Time: 30 minutes
Ingredients
1 cup scallions, chopped
2 tablespoons lard, room temperature
Celery salt and freshly ground pepper, to taste
1/2 cup dry red wine
1 thyme sprigs
4 (6-ouncefilet mignon steaks
2 rosemary sprigs
2 garlic cloves, minced
1 tablespoon deli mustard
1 red bell pepper, deveined and chopped
Directions
Wiper filet mignon steaks with mustard. Spray filet mignon steaks with the pepper, salt, rosemary and thyme.
Cook the lard in a heavy-bottomed skillet over moderate heat. Heat filet mignon steaks for 10 minutes on each side or probably until a thermometer registers 1200F.
Suceeding the above step, cook the scallions, garlic, and pepper in pan drippings for about 3 minutes. Put in the wine to scrape up any browned bits from the bottom of the skillet.
Heat until the liquid is reduced by half. Serve immediately.
Nutrition: Calories 451 ,Protein 29.7g ,Fat 34.4g ,Carbs 3.6g ,Sugar 1.2g

502.　　Mini Meatloaf Muffins with Cremini Mushrooms

Servings: 4
Preparation Time: 40 minutes
Ingredients
1/4 cup pine nuts, ground

3/4 cup Romano cheese, grated

1 teaspoon cayenne pepper

1/2 pound Cremini mushrooms, chopped

Salt and ground black pepper, to taste

1 yellow onion, chopped

1/2 teaspoon granulated garlic

1 ¼ pounds ground beef

1/2 cup tomato puree

1 tablespoon olive oil

2 eggs, lightly beaten

1/2 cup crushed chicharrones

Directions

Start by preheating your oven to 3900F.

Heat the oil in a pan that is preheated over a normal high heat. After that, sauté the onion until it is translucent and aromatic.

Stir in the mushrooms and heat an additional 4 minutes or probably until almost all of the liquid has evaporated.

Include the eggs, granulated garlic, cheese, crushed chicharrones, pine nuts and ground beef.

Suceeding the above, mix until everything is well incorporated.

Share the meatloaf mixture among lightly greased muffin cups. Bake for 25 minutes.

In the meantime, mix tomato puree with salt, black pepper and cayenne pepper. Now, Spread the tomato mixture over meatloaves.

Bake until a thermometer registers 1650F, and about 5 to 10 minutes more. Permit your meatloaves to cool for a couple of minutes before removing from the pan. Bon appétit!

Nutrition: Calories 404 ,Protein 44g ,Fat 22.8g ,Carbs 6.2g ,Sugar 2.8g

503.   Crock Pot Beef Brisket with Blue Cheese

Servings: 6

Preparation Time: 8 hours

Ingredients

1 cup water

1/2 tablespoon garlic paste

1/4 cup soy sauce

1 ½ pounds corned beef brisket

1/3 teaspoon ground coriander

1/4 teaspoon cloves, ground

2 tablespoons olive oil

1 shallot, chopped

6 ounces blue cheese, crumbled

Directions

Heat a sauté pan with the olive oil over normal heat. Heat the shallot until it is softened.

Include garlic paste and heat an additional minute; move to your Crock pot that is previously greased with a nonstick cooking spray.

Now, Sear the brisket until it has a golden-brown crust. Move to the Crock pot. Include the remaining ingredient, except for blue cheese.

Shut the lid and cook on Low heat setting for 6 to 8 hours or until the meat is very tender. Now, Serve topped with blue cheese. Enjoy!
Nutrition: Calories 397 ,Protein 23.5g ,Fat 31.4g ,Carbs 3.9g ,Sugar 2.3g

504.   Sriracha and Scallion Chuck

Servings: 4
Preparation Time: 50 minutes
Ingredients
1 tablespoon garlic paste
1 teaspoon mustard seeds
2 tablespoons soy sauce
1/4 teaspoon cumin
1 bunch scallions,chopped
Salt and crushed mixed peppercorns, to taste
1/4 teaspoon celery seeds
1 teaspoon Sriracha sauce
1 tablespoon fresh parsley, roughly chopped
1/2 teaspoon dried marjoram
1/2 tablespoon tallow
1 ½ pounds chuck pot roast, cubed
Directions
Whisk the Sriracha sauce, soy sauce and garlic paste in a mixing bowl. Include the marjoram, salt, crushed peppercorns, mustard seeds, and scallions.
Include the cubed beef and allow it marinate for 40 minutes in your refrigerator.
Dissolve the tallow a frying pan over moderately high heat. Heat marinated beef for 5 to 6 minutes, stirring constantly; work in batches to heat beef cubes through evenly.
Now, season with cumin and celery seeds. Serve garnished with fresh parsley. Enjoy!
Nutrition: Calories 292 ,Protein 14.3g 36.9g ,Fat ,Carbs 3.9g ,Sugar 1.7g

505.   Beef Casserole with Sour Cream Sauce

Servings: 4
Preparation Time: 25 minutes
Ingredients
1 pound ground beef
1 tablespoon olive oil
1 teaspoon Italian seasoning
2 ounces sun-dried tomatoes, chopped
1 cup cheddar cheese
1 teaspoon minced garlic
2 ripe tomatoes, chopped
1/4 teaspoon ground black pepper
1/2 teaspoon salt
1/2 tablespoon dill relish
1/2 teaspoon chili powder
3/4 cup sour cream

1/2 cup shallots, finely chopped
Directions
Preheat the oven to 4000F.
Now, heat the oil in a nonstick skillet that is preheated over a moderate flame.
Suceeding the above, Brown the ground beef in butter, crumbling it with a large spatula. Include the tomatoes, dill relish and seasonings.
Put the beef mixture in a baking dish. Top with cheese and bake for about 18 minutes.
In the meantime, thoroughly combine the sour cream with the garlic and shallots. Enjoy with your casserole dish.
Nutrition: Calories 509 ,Protein 45.2g ,Fat 29.6g ,Carbs 6.1g ,Sugar 2.4g

506.   Buttery Roasted Chuck with Horseradish Sauce

Servings: 6
Preparation Time: 2 hours
Ingredients
1/3 cup dry red wine
1 tablespoon Italian seasoning mix
1/2 teaspoon cayenne pepper, or more to taste
1/4 teaspoon black pepper, to taste
2 bay leaves
1 teaspoon sea salt
1/4 cup olive oil
1 ½ pounds chuck
1 ½ tablespoons whole grain mustard
1 garlic clove, minced
For the Sauce:
2 tablespoons mayonnaise
2 tablespoons prepared horseradish
1/4 cup sour cream
Directions
Put the chuck with Italian seasoning, bay leaves, olive oil, garlic, mustard, red wine, salt, black pepper and cayenne pepper.
Allow it marinate overnight in the refrigerator. Put your chuck in a baking dish that is lined with a piece of foil; put the marinade over it.
Now, wrap with the foil. Bake at 3750F for about 2 hours or until a thermometer registers 1250F.
Meanwhile, mix all ingredients for the sauce. Slice your chuck across the grain and enjoy with the sauce on the side.
Nutrition: Calories 493 ,Protein 27.9g ,Fat 39.4g ,Carbs 2.9g ,Sugar 0.8g

507.   Italian-Style Holiday Meatloaf

Servings: 6
Preparation Time: 50 minutes
Ingredients
2 tablespoons fresh pureed tomato
Seasoned salt and ground black pepper

1 tablespoon mustard
2 shallots, chopped
1 ½ teaspoons coconut aminos
Nonstick cooking spray
1 egg, slightly beaten
2 tablespoons flax seed meal
1 teaspoon Italian seasonings
1/3 cup almond flour
1/3 cup full-fat milk
1 tablespoon garlic paste
1/4 teaspoon ground sage
2 pounds ground chuck
For the Tomato Sauce:
Salt and black pepper, to taste
1 tablespoon cilantro, minced
2 ripe tomatoes, crushed
Directions
Begin by preheating your oven 3600F. After that, lightly grease a loaf pan with a nonstick cooking spray.
In a mixing container, thoroughly merge all the meatloaf ingredients.
Press the meatloaf mixture into the prepared meatloaf.
Include all ingredients for the sauce to a pan that is preheated over medium-low heat. Simmer for about 2 to 3 minutes, stirring periodically.
Now, spread the sauce over the top of your meatloaf. Bake for about 45 minutes. Allow it cool down for a couple of minutes before slicing and. Bon appétit!
Nutrition: Calories 163 ,Protein 12.2g ,Fat 8.4g ,Carbs 5.6g ,Sugar 2.1g

508.   Royal Keto Lasagna

Servings: 6
Preparation Time: 1 hour 30 minutes
Ingredients
For the Lasagna Sheets:
1 cup Colby cheese, shredded
3 eggs, whisked
1/2 teaspoon cumin powder
6 ounces mascarpone cheese, at room temperature
1/2 teaspoon dried oregano
1/2 cup Parmesan cheese, grated
1/2 teaspoon onion powder
For the Filling:
1/4 cup fresh parsley, finely chopped
2 garlic cloves, minced
1 cup tomato sauce
1 ½ pounds ground chuck
1 cup mascarpone cheese
1/2 teaspoon dried basil

2 slices bacon, chopped
1 tablespoon olive oil
1 onion, chopped
1/2 teaspoon oregano
2 cups sour cream
Directions
Begin by preheating your oven to 3700F. Coat a baking pan with a sheet of parchment paper or a Silpat mat.

After that, thoroughly combine the eggs and 6 ounces of mascarpone cheese with a hand mixer. Include the other ingredients for the lasagna sheets; mix to merge well.

Now, press the mixture onto the baking pan, creating an even layer. Bake approximately for 20 minutes.

Refrigerate the "sheet" for 30 minutes. Now, Cut into lasagna sheets and set aside.

Heat the oil in a pan that is preheated over moderate heat. After Brown ground beef for 3 to 4 minutes.

Include the onion, garlic and bacon and cook an additional 3 minutes stirring regularly. Stir in tomato sauce, oregano and basil; heat an additional 13 minutes.

Suceeding the above, pour 1/4 cup of the sauce into the bottom of a previously greased casserole dish. Top with the first lasagna sheet. Now, repeat these steps 3 times.

After the above, top with sour cream and 1 cup of mascarpone cheese. Spray fresh parsley over the top. Bake for 15 to 22 minutes longer. Serve warm and enjoy!

Nutrition: Calories 494 ,Protein 24.1g ,Fat 41g ,Carbs 3.8g ,Sugar 2.2g

509.   Cabbage, Beef and Cheese Casserole

Servings: 6
Preparation Time: 55 minutes
Ingredients
1 cup salsa, preferably homemade
1/2 pound ground turkey
1 teaspoon dried oregano
8 slices American cheese
1/2 pound ground chuck
2 slices bacon, chopped
1 leek, chopped
2 eggs
1 head of cabbage, cut into quarters
1 teaspoon dried basil
1/2 teaspoon dried marjoram
Salt and black pepper, to taste
1 ½ cups cream cheese, crumbled
Directions
At first, boil cabbage approximately 5 minutes; drain. Now, preheat your oven to 4000F.

Preheat a pan over a normal high heat; heat ground beef and turkey, breaking with a spatula, for 4 to 5 minutes.

Include the leeks and bacon; cook for a further 3 minutes stirring frequently.

Stir in the marjoram, salt, basil, oregano, pepper and salsa; bring it to a boil. Set the heat to medium-low; cook an additional 6 minutes.

Include 1/2 of this mixture to the bottom of a lightly greased baking dish. Include a layer of boiled cabbage leaves. Repeat layers one more time.

In a mixing container, merge cream cheese, American cheese, and eggs. Top your casserole with the cheese layer and bake for 30 minutes or until everything is thoroughly cooked.

Permit your casserole to cool down for a couple of minutes before slicing and.

Nutrition: Calories 467 ,Protein 27.1g ,Fat 37g ,Carbs 4.9g ,Sugar 3.9g

510.   Top Round Steak with Marsala Sauce

Servings: 6
Prep Time + Cook Time:1 hour 40 minutes
Ingredients
2 tablespoons olive oil
1 shallot, chopped
1 cup broth
1/2 teaspoon dried basil
1/4 teaspoon freshly ground black pepper
1 tablespoon dried sage, crushed
1 ½ pounds top round steak, cut into 4-size pieces
1 teaspoon ground bay leaf
1 garlic clove, pressed
1 ½ cups Brussels sprouts, quartered
1/2 teaspoon sea salt
For the Sauce:
3/4 teaspoon Dijon mustard
1/4 teaspoon freshly grated nutmeg
1/2 cup Marsala wine
1 cup double cream
1/2 cup chicken broth
Directions
Start by preheating your oven to 3400F. Flatten each top round steak using a meat tenderizer.

Heat olive oil in an oven-safe pan over average-high heat. Cook the steak until just browned; reserve.

Heat the shallots and garlic in pan drippings in the same pan until they're softened. Now, heat Brussels sprouts until tender and smell good.

Include the round steak back to the pan. Season with sage, ground bay leaf, basil, salt, and pepper. Put in 1 cup of broth. Wrap with foil and roast for 1 hour 10 minutes.

Include the wine, 1/2 cup chicken cup of broth and nutmeg to the same roasting pan. Let it simmer for a duration of 15 to 18 minutes or until the sauce is reduced to half.

Stir in the mustard and double cream; heat an additional 15 minutes or probably until everything is heated thoroughly.

Share top round steak among four plates; now, ladle the sauce over them and serve warm.

Nutrition: Calories 339 ,Protein 35g ,Fat 21.7g ,Carbs 5.2g ,Sugar 1.2g

511.   Skirt Steak and Eggs Skillet

Servings: 6
Preparation Time: 30 minutes;
Ingredients
1 bell pepper, chopped
1 ½ pounds skirt steak, cut into cubes
1 teaspoon garlic, minced
2 tablespoons olive oil
1/2 cup spring onions onion, chopped
1/2 teaspoon red pepper flakes
Celery salt and ground black pepper, to taste
6 eggs
1 serrano pepper, chopped
Directions
Heat the oil in a nonstick pot over moderately high heat.
Boil beef cubes for 10 minutes or until it is no longer pink, stirring occasionally. Season with salt, red pepper flakes, black pepper and set aside. Cook spring onion and garlic in the same skillet for 3 to 4 minutes until aromatic Add the peppers and leave to cook for 3 minutes more.
Now, make six holes in the mixture to expose the bottom of your pan. Crack an egg into each hole. Cover and cook for 4 to 6 minutes or until the eggs are set.
Serve immediately!
Nutrition: Calories 429 ,Protein 1g ,Fat 27.8g ,Carbs 3.2g ,Sugar 39.1.6g

512.   Spicy Indian Pork

Servings 8
Preparation Time: 1 hour 15 minutes
Ingredients
1 tablespoon olive oil
2 pounds pork belly, cubed
1/2 teaspoon ground coriander
Salt and freshly ground pepper
1/2 tablespoon ground cloves
1/2 tablespoon curry powder
2 minced garlic cloves
A bunch of chopped scallions
2 cups bone broth
1/2 cup unsweetened coconut milk
1/2 teaspoon fennel seeds
1 deveined and chopped Thai chili
1 deveined and chopped bell pepper
2 tomatoes, pureed
Directions
Put a pan on medium heat and warm the olive oil.
Put the coriander, salt and pepper on the pork belly and cook for 10 minutes, stirring often. Put the pork to one side.
Cook the cloves, curry powder, garlic and scallions in the pan drippings.

Put the mixture into the slow cooker and add the bone broth, coconut milk, fennel seeds, Thai chili, bell pepper and tomatoes. Scrape the mixture into the slow cooker.

Cook the pork for 1 hour over a low heat. Serve hot.

Nutrition: 369 Calories; 41.3g Protein; 20.2g Fat; 2.9g Carbs; 1.5g Sugar

513.   Pork Rib and Spinach

Servings 6
Preparation Time: 25 minutes + marinating time
Ingredients
1 ½ pounds pork rib chops
Sea salt and ground black pepper, to taste
1 tablespoon garlic paste
1/4 cup champagne
1 tablespoon fresh lime juice
1 tablespoon cider vinegar
2 tablespoons oyster sauce
2 teaspoons olive oil
1 chopped bell pepper
1 sliced celery stalk
1 sliced red onion
2 cups spinach
Directions
Sprinkle salt and pepper over the pork rib chops.

Make the marinade by whisking together the garlic paste, champagne, lime juice, cider vinegar and oyster sauce.

Put the pork in the marinade and leave for a minimum of 2 hours.

Preheat a pan on a medium flame and cook the pepper, celery and onion in 1 tablespoon of oil for 5 minutes. Stir often and then set aside.

Put the other tablespoon of oil in the pan and cook the pork with the marinade. The pork needs 4 minutes cooking each side.

Add the vegetables to the pan together with the spinach and cook for 6 minutes by which time the spinach leaves should be wilted. Serve hot. Bon appétit!

Nutrition: 234 Calories; 29.8g Protein; 11g Fat; 2g Carbs; 0.6g Sugar

514.   Pork Meatloaf with Tomato Sauce

Servings 6
Preparation Time: 45 minutes
Ingredients
Nonstick cooking spray
1 teaspoon mustard powder
Sea salt and ground black pepper
1 large egg
3 cloves finely minced garlic
2 chopped shallots
1/3 cup flaxseed meal

1/4 cup crushed pork rinds
1 1/2 pounds ground pork
For the Sauce:
1 teaspoon fresh parsley
1/2 teaspoon dried thyme
1 tablespoon cider vinegar
1 1/2 tablespoons Swerve
2 tablespoon tomato ketchup
2 pureed ripe plum tomatoes
Directions
Put your oven on at 3600F. Spray a loaf pan with nonstick cooking spray.
Mix together the mustard powder, salt, black pepper, egg, garlic, shallots, flaxseed meal, pork rinds and ground pork.
Put the meatloaf mixture into the loaf pan.
Next, cook the parsley, thyme, cider vinegar, Swerve, ketchup and tomatoes over medium heat and pour over the meatloaf. Bake in the oven for 40 minutes.
Cool the meatloaf for a couple of minutes and then slice and serve.
Nutrition: 251 Calories; 34.6g Protein; 7.9g Fat; 6.5g Carbs; 3g Sugar

515.   Pork with a Blue Cheese Sauce

Servings 6
Preparation Time: 30 minutes
Ingredients
1 1/2 pounds boneless pork shoulder, cut into 6 pieces
1 teaspoon dried thyme
Salt and freshly cracked black peppercorns, to taste
1 tablespoon butter
2 chopped garlic cloves
1 chopped onion
1/3 cup homemade broth
1/3 cup dry sherry wine
1/3 cup double cream
6 ounces blue cheese
1 tablespoon soy sauce
1 teaspoon dried hot chili flakes
Directions
Put the thyme, salt and pepper on each piece of the pork shoulder.
Heat the butter in a pan over medium-high heat and cook the pork until it is browned. This should take about 18 minutes. Put the meat to one side.
Sauté the garlic and onions in the pan drippings until they are soft and aromatic. Add the broth and wine and stir.
Put the heat down to medium and add the double cream, blue cheese, soy sauce and chili flakes. Simmer until the mixture has thickened.
Pour the sauce over the pork and serve. Bon appétit!
Nutrition: 495 Calories; 33.4g Protein; 36.9g Fat; 3.6g Carbs; 1.1g Sugar

516.   Easy Meatballs

Servings 6
Preparation Time: 30 minutes
Ingredients
For the Meatballs:
1/2pound ground beef
1 pound ground pork
2 small eggs
1 tablespoon beef bouillon granules
1 tablespoon Montreal steak seasoning
2 minced cloves of garlic
For the Sauce:
3 teaspoons butter
1 cup bone broth
1 cup heavy whipping cream
1/2 teaspoon dried thyme
Salt and pepper, to taste
Directions
Put your oven on at 3600F.
Mix together the ground beef, ground pork, eggs, beef bouillon granules, Montreal steak seasoning and garlic. With oiled hands form this mixture into 20 balls.
Grease a baking sheet with nonstick cooking spray and place the meatballs on it.
Cook in the oven for 18 – 22 minutes and then place the meatballs under the broiler for 2 minutes to get a brown and crispy crust.
While the meatballs are cooking, make the sauce. Melt the butter over medium heat. Slowly add in the bone broth, whipping cream, thyme, salt and pepper. Whisk all the time.
Bring the sauce to boil and simmer until the sauce is thick. Serve the sauce with the meatballs.
Nutrition: Calories 284 ,Protein 34.4g ,Fat 14.8g ,Carbs 1.3g ,Sugar 0.3g

517.   Peppered Pork with Avocado and Blue Cheese

Servings 2
Preparation Time: 20 minutes
Ingredients
1/2 pound ground pork
1 tablespoon bacon grease
1 deveined and chopped jalapeno pepper
1 deveined and chopped bell pepper
1/4 cup beef bone broth
1/4 teaspoon marjoram
Kosher salt and black pepper, to taste
1 small head of Romaine lettuce leaves separated
1 pitted, peeled and diced avocado
1/2 cup trimmed and sliced radicchio
2 teaspoons fresh lemon juice
2 diced tomatoes

2 chopped shallots

1/2 cup crumbled blue cheese

1/2 cup Greek yogurt

Directions

In a saucepan warm the bacon grease over moderate heat. Put in the ground pork and brown for around 8 minutes. Stir all the time using a wooden spatula. While doing this, break up the meat.

Mix in the peppers and cook until they are soft and fragrant. This should take 3 minutes. Pour In the bone broth and sprinkle in the marjoram, salt and pepper. Cook for 4 – 5 minutes and put it to one side.

Put lettuce leaves on to two plates and put the meat mixture on top of them.

Place slices of avocado and radicchio around the mixture and sprinkle on some lemon juice.

Put the tomatoes and shallots on top of the meat and garnish with blue cheese and Greek yogurt. Bon appétit!

Nutrition: Calories 431 ,Protein 42.4g ,Fat 22.0g ,Carbs 5.2g ,Sugar 2g

518.   Pork Belly with a Tasty Barbecue Sauce

Servings 8

Preparation Time: 2 hours

Ingredients

2 pounds pork belly

2 halved garlic cloves

2 tablespoons olive oil

1/2 teaspoon freshly ground black pepper

1 teaspoon salt

For the Barbecue Sauce:

1/2 cup tomato puree

1 teaspoon Dijon mustard

1 teaspoon hot sauce

1/3 teaspoon ground cumin

1/3 teaspoon smoked paprika

A few drops of liquid smoke

Directions

Put your oven on at 4200F.

Rub the pork belly with garlic and oil.

Put the pork belly in the oven and cook for 18 – 22 minutes. Lower the heat to 3300F and cook for another 1 hour 30 minutes.

While the pork is roasting, prepare the barbecue sauce. Combine the tomato puree, mustard, hot sauce, cumin, paprika and liquid smoke.

Take the pork belly out of the oven and remove the crackling. Slice the pork belly and serve with the barbecue sauce.

Nutrition: Calories 561 ,Protein 52.7g ,Fat 34g ,Carbs 4.7g ,Sugar 2.5g

519.   Pork Cutlets in the Oven with Vegetables

Servings 4

Preparation Time: 30 minutes + marinating time

Ingredients

2 tablespoons cider vinegar

1/2 teaspoon freshly ground black pepper

1/2 teaspoon sea salt

1 teaspoon garlic paste

1 tablespoon yellow mustard

2 tablespoons melted lard

4 pork cutlets

1 cup sliced leeks

1 diced celery stalk

Directions

Combine the cider vinegar, pepper, salt, garlic paste and mustard in a bowl. Put the pork cutlets in this mixture and leave them to marinate for 2 hours.

In an oven-safe pan, melt the lard over medium heat. Cook the pork cutlets for 5 minutes on each side until they are brown. Add the leeks and celery.

Cook for 5 more minutes stirring every now and then.

Put the pan in the oven and cook the pork and vegetables for 13 minutes. Serve with the pan juices. Bon appétit!

Nutrition: Calories452 ,Protein26.3g ,Fat 34.8g ,Carbs 4.7g ,Sugar 2.5g

520.   Succulent Pork Medallions and Scallions

Servings 4

Preparation Time: 20 minutes

Ingredients

1 pound pork tenderloin, cut crosswise into 12 medallions

1/2 teaspoon crushed red pepper flakes

1/2 teaspoon garlic powder

Coarse salt and ground black pepper to your liking

1 tablespoon butter

1 minced thyme sprig

2 minced rosemary sprigs

1 bunch of roughly chopped scallions

1 teaspoon crushed dried sage

Directions

Take each pork medallion and season with red pepper flakes, garlic powder, salt and pepper.

In a saucepan, melt the butter over moderate-high heat. Put the pork medallions in the pan and cook for 3 minutes on each side.

Add the thyme, rosemary and scallions and cook for an extra 3 minutes. Sprinkle the dried sage on top and serve. Bon appétit!

Nutrition: Calories 192 ,Protein 29.8g ,Fat 6.9g ,Carbs 0.9g ,Sugar 0.4g

521.   Slow Cooker Peppery Pork Ribs

Servings 4

Preparation Time: 8 hours

Ingredients

1 tablespoon lard
1 pound pork ribs
1 thinly sliced bell pepper
1 teaspoon minced Anchor chilies
1/4 cup dry red wine
1/4 cup Worcestershire sauce
1/2 teaspoon ground cloves
1/2 teaspoon ground oregano
1 crushed garlic clove
1/2 teaspoon smoked cayenne pepper
1 teaspoon grated lime peel
Directions
Rub the inside of your slow cooker with the melted lard. Put the pork ribs, the bell pepper and the chilies on the bottom.
Pour over the wine and Worcestershire sauce. Sprinkle the cloves, oregano, garlic and cayenne pepper on the pork.
Cook on low for 8 hours. When ready to serve, garnish the pork ribs with grated lime peel.
Nutrition: Calories 192 ,Protein 29.8g ,Fat 6.9g ,Carbs 0.9g ,Sugar 0.4g

522.   Stuffed Peppers with Pork and a Chive and Yogurt Sauce

Servings 4
Preparation Time: 40 minutes
Ingredients
6 deveined bell peppers
1 tablespoon olive oil
1 minced garlic clove
1 small chopped yellow onion
1/3 pound ground veal
1/2 pound ground pork
1 ripe tomato, chopped
1 teaspoon paprika
1/2 teaspoon sea salt
1/4 teaspoon ground black pepper, to taste
1/2 teaspoon ground coriander
2 tablespoons chopped chives
1/2 cup Greek yogurt
Directions
Fill a pan with salted water and parboil the peppers for 4 – 6 minutes.
Preheat a pan over a medium flame and heat the oil. Sauté the garlic and onions until soft and fragrant.
Mix in the ground pork and veal and crumble with a spatula. Cook for 5 – 6 minutes until the meat is brown. Add the tomato and cook for another 4 minutes.
Season the meat with paprika, salt, pepper and coriander. Put the oven on at 3600F.
Stuff the peppers with the meat mixture and put them in a baking dish. Cook for about 22 minutes.
Combine the chopped chives with the Greek yogurt. Put the peppers on plates and serve with a spoonful of the chive and yogurt sauce.

Nutrition: Calories 330 ,Protein 27.1g ,Fat 20.8g ,Carbs 3.6g ,Sugar 1.8g

523.   Leeks with Rolled Pork Loin

Servings 6
Preparation Time: 1 hour + marinating time
Ingredients
1 1/2 pounds butterflied boneless pork loin
2 pressed garlic cloves
1/2 teaspoon celery seeds
1 teaspoon mustard seeds
1 chopped thyme sprig
1 chopped rosemary sprig
1 tablespoon butter
1 cup bone broth
1/2 cup Burgundy wine
1 thinly sliced leek
1 teaspoon whole black peppercorns
Directions
Take the pork and pour boiling water over it so it gets a crispy crackling. Spray a pan with nonstick cooking spray.
Combine the garlic, celery seeds, mustard seeds, thyme and rosemary with the butter.
Spread the butter/herb mixture all over the cut side of the unfolded pork loin. Roll the loin again and secure it with string. Put in the roasting pan and marinate for 2 hours in the fridge.
Put your oven on at 4000F.
Add the broth, wine and leeks to the pork. Sprinkle whole peppercorns around the meat. Roast for about an hour when the juices should run clear. Serve with a salad Bon appétit!
Nutrition: Calories 220 ,Protein 33.3g ,Fat 6g ,Carbs 3g ,Sugar 0.8g

524.   Pork Stew like Grandma Used to Make

Servings 8
Preparation Time: 45 minutes
Ingredients
2 tablespoons lard, at room temperature
2 pounds pork shoulder, cut into 3/4-inch cubes
1 teaspoon sea salt
1 teaspoon freshly cracked mixed peppercorns
1 chopped celery stalk
1 large chopped red onion
1 minced chili pepper
2 finely minced garlic cloves
2 tablespoons dry red wine
3 cups homemade beef stock
1 cup sliced fresh button mushrooms
1 teaspoon dried marjoram
1 1/2 teaspoons dried sage

2 chopped ripe tomatoes
1 bay leaf
1/2 teaspoon dried basil
1/2 cup fresh cilantro, chopped
Directions
Preheat a stockpot over medium heat and melt the lard. Brown the meat and then season with salt and the peppercorns. Put to one side.
Put the celery, onion and chili pepper in the stockpot and cook until soft. Deglaze the bottom of your pot with the wine.
Add the pork, beef stock, mushrooms, marjoram, sage, tomatoes, bay leaf and basil. Partially cover the pot and cook for 40 minutes. Top with cilantro and serve hot.
Nutrition: Calories 390 ,Protein 28.3g ,Fat 27.8g ,Carbs 4.7g ,Sugar 2/3g

525. Pork Chops in a Sauce of Ancho Chilies

Servings 6
Preparation Time: 30 minutes
Ingredients
1 tablespoon olive oil
6 pork chops
For the Sauce:
1/2 cup bone broth
2 chopped Ancho chilies
1/2 teaspoon crushed red pepper flakes
1 teaspoon dried basil
2 minced garlic cloves
1/2 teaspoon ground cumin
Salt and ground black pepper, to taste
2 teaspoons olive oil
Directions
Preheat a saucepan over a medium-high flame and heat 1 tablespoon of olive oil. Cook the pork chops until they are brown and the juices run clear.
While they are cooking, make the sauce. Boil the bone broth and Ancho chilies for a couple of minutes. Take the pot off the heat and leave the chilies in hot water for 15 – 25 minutes.
Put the chilies and the liquid into a blender together with the crushed red pepper flakes, basil, garlic, cumin, salt and pepper.
Blend until smooth and creamy. Serve the pork chops with the sauce poured over.
Nutrition: Calories 347 ,Protein 20.2g ,Fat 27.8g ,Carbs 0.2g ,Sugar 0.2g

526. Slow Cooker Spare Ribs

Servings 4
Preparation Time: 4 hours 30 minutes
Ingredients
1 tablespoon lard, at room temperature
1 1/2 pounds spare ribs
3/4 cup homemade vegetable stock

1/2 teaspoon ground cumin

Salt to taste

A bunch of chopped scallions

2 teaspoons Swerve

2 cloves chopped garlic

1 chopped Serrano pepper

2 bay leaves

1 teaspoon whole black peppercorns

Directions

In a pan, melt the lard over medium heat. Fry the spare ribs for 8 minutes turning now and then. While the spare ribs are cooking whisk together the stock, cumin, salt, scallions, Swerve, garlic and Serrano pepper.

Put the spare ribs in your slow cooker and pour in the stock mixture. Add the bay leaves and black peppercorns.

Cook on a low heat for 4 hours 30 minutes. This goes well with cauliflower rice. Bon appétit!

Nutrition: Calories 412 ,Protein 46.3g ,Fat 22g ,Carbs 3g ,Sugar 1g

527.   Pork Stuffed Tomatoes

Preparation Time: 50 minutes

Servings: 4

Nutrition: 300 Calories; 21.9g Fat; 9g Carbs; 14.3g Protein; 2g Fiber

Ingredients

4 ounces pork sausage, sliced

1 onion, chopped

1 garlic clove, minced

4 tomatoes

6 ounces Colby cheese, shredded

Directions

Brown the pork sausage over medium-high heat for 5 to 6 minutes, breaking the meat apart with a spatula.

Add in the onion and garlic and continue to sauté cook for 3 to 4 minutes more. Season with salt and black pepper to taste.

Now, slice a thin piece off the top of each tomato using a sharp kitchen knife. Scoop out the pulp and divide the filling between tomatoes.

Arrange the stuffed tomatoes in a foil-lined baking pan. Bake in the preheated oven at 350 degrees F for about 35 to 40 minutes.

Top with Colby cheese and continue to bake an additional 5 minutes. Bon appétit!

528.   Favorite Pork Shoulder with Broccoli

Preparation Time: 50 minutes

Servings: 6

Nutrition: 476 Calories; 31.4g Fat; 4.5g Carbs; 40.5g Protein; 0.9g Fiber

Ingredients

2 pounds pork shoulder, cut into slices

2 cups broccoli florets
2 bell peppers, deseeded and quartered
4 cloves garlic, halved
1 yellow onion, quartered
Directions
Heat 2 tablespoons of olive oil in a saucepan over medium-high flame. Now, brown the pork for 5 minutes.
Add vegetables and turn the heat to medium-low; Add in 1/2 cup of water or chicken broth. Season with the salt and pepper to taste. Add red pepper flaked if desired.
Let it cook, partially covered, for 35 to 40 minutes (the pork must reach an internal temperature of 145 degrees F.
Serve the pork shoulder with the cooking juices and enjoy!

529. Puerto Rican Sancocho

Preparation Time: 40 minutes
Servings: 6
Nutrition: 305 Calories; 17.7g Fat; 2.8g Carbs; 31.4g Protein; 0.8g Fiber
Ingredients
1/2 pound Chorizo sausage, sliced
1 ½ pounds pork stew meat, cut into bite-sized pieces
1/2 cup shallots, chopped
1 chipotle pepper, deseeded and minced
2 ripe tomatoes, crushed
Directions
Melt 1 tablespoon of lard in a stockpot over medium-high flame. Then, brown Chorizo sausage and pork for 5 to 7 minutes; reserve.
Then, stir in the shallots and chipotle pepper; continue to sauté for 3 to 4 minutes or until tender and aromatic.
Season with salt and black pepper to taste. Add in tomatoes along with the reserved pork and Chorizo sausage.
Cover with 4 cups of water and reduce the heat to simmer. Partially cover and continue to simmer for 30 to 35 minutes.
Serve with pimento olives if desired.

530. Paprika Pork with Romano Cheese

Preparation Time: 15 minutes
Servings: 6
Nutrition: 454 Calories; 21.5g Fat; 1.1g Carbs; 60.7g Protein; 0.4g Fiber
Ingredients
2 tablespoons sesame oil
6 pork cutlets
1 cup Romano cheese, preferably freshly grated
2 eggs, whisked

1 tablespoon paprika
Directions
Season the pork with salt and black pepper to taste.
Dip each pork cutlet into the eggs, then roll in the cheese mixture, pressing to coat well. Season with paprika.
Warm the sesame oil in a saucepan over a medium-high heat.
Cook for 4 to 5 minutes on each side. Serve immediately.

531. Mediterranean Ground Pork Salad

Preparation Time: 15 minutes
Servings: 5
Nutrition: 455 Calories; 38.2g Fat; 2.7g Carbs; 23.7g Protein; 0.7g Fiber
Ingredients
1 ½ pounds ground pork
2 scallions, sliced
2 bell peppers, deveined and sliced
1 cucumber, sliced
1 tablespoon Mediterranean herb mix
Directions
Heat 1 tablespoon of the olive oil in a cast-iron skillet over moderate flame. Then, brown the ground pork for 5 to 6 minutes or until no longer pink; transfer the browned pork to a salad bowl. Add in the scallions, peppers, and cucumber. Season with Mediterranean herb mix. Toss your salad with about 2 tablespoons of olive oil and balsamic vinegar to taste.
Serve immediately.

532. Tuscan Meatballs with cheese

Preparation Time: 45 minutes
Servings: 4
Nutrition: 263 Calories; 13.8g Fat; 4.7g Carbs; 30g Protein; 0.5g Fiber
Ingredients
1 pound lean ground pork
1/2 cup Romano cheese, grated
1 egg
1 Italian pepper, chopped
1 tablespoon Italian seasoning blend
Directions
Thoroughly combine all ingredients until everything is well incorporated. Roll the mixture into 16 balls.
Melt 1 tablespoon of lard in a nonstick skillet over medium-high heat.
Cook the meatballs until well browned on all sides or 9 to 14 minutes; work in batches. Bon appétit!

533. Pork Carnitas with Herbs

Preparation Time: 3 hours | 4
Nutrition: 338 Calories; 21.2g Fat; 4.4g Carbs; 30.8g Protein; 1.2g Fiber
Ingredients
1 cup tomato sauce
3 tablespoons apple cider vinegar
1 tablespoon Taco seasoning blend
1/2 teaspoon chipotle powder
1 ½ pounds Boston butt
Directions
Start by preheating your oven to 310 degrees F.
Place tomato sauce, apple cider vinegar, seasonings and Boston butt in a lightly greased baking dish.
Bake for about 2 hours 40 minutes, turning occasionally to ensure even cooking.
Then, shred the pork and serve with cooking juices. Enjoy!

534.   Easy Roasted Pork Shoulder

Preparation Time: 4 hours + marinating time
Servings: 4
Nutrition: 609 Calories; 40.1g Fat; 0.6g Carbs; 57g Protein; 0.1g Fiber
Ingredients
2 pounds pork shoulder
2 tablespoons coconut aminos
1/2 cup red wine
1 tablespoon Dijon mustard
1 tablespoon Mediterranean spice mix
Directions
Place the ingredients a ceramic dish. Allow it to marinate in your refrigerator for at least 2 hours.
Put the rack into a roasting pan. Lower the marinated pork onto the rack. Roast in the preheated oven at 410 degrees F for 30 minutes.
Turn the heat to 340 degrees F. Continue to roast an additional 3 hours, basting with the marinade. Bon appétit!

535.   Thai Pork Chop Salad

Preparation Time: 20 minutes + marinating time
Servings: 6
Nutrition: 296 Calories; 14.2g Fat; 6g Carbs; 35.3g Protein; 1.4g Fiber
Ingredients
2 pounds pork rib chops
1 cup pork marinade
6 cups lettuce, torn into small pieces
1 bell pepper, deseeded and sliced
1/2 cup sour cream, for garnish
Directions

Place the marinade and pork in a ceramic dish. Let it marinate in your refrigerator for at least 2 hours.

Heat 1 tablespoon of olive oil in an oven-proof skillet over a moderate flame. Sear the pork rib chops for about 10 minutes, flipping them over to ensure even cooking.

Season with salt and black pepper. Transfer the skillet to the preheated oven and roast the pork for 15 minutes or until thoroughly cooked.

Transfer pork chops to a cutting board.

Shred the pork chops and transfer to a salad bowl. Add the lettuce, bell pepper, and sour cream. Toss to combine and serve well-chilled.

Enjoy!

536.   Buttery Pork Chops with Mushrooms

Preparation Time: 20 minutes
Servings: 2
Nutrition: 494 Calories; 39.8g Fat; 5.3g Carbs; 28.6g Protein; 2g Fiber
Ingredients
1/3 pound pork loin chops
1/2 stick butter, room temperature
1/2 cup Swiss cheese, shredded
1/2 cup white onion, chopped
4 ounces button mushrooms, sliced
Directions
Warm 1/4 of the butter stick in a saucepan over moderate heat. Now, sauté the onions and mushrooms until the onions are caramelized and the mushrooms are aromatic, about 5 to 6 minutes. Set aside.

Warm the remaining 1/4 of the butter stick. Once hot, cook the pork for about 10 to 12 minutes. \ Add the onion mixture back to the skillet. Afterwards, top pork chops with Swiss cheese, cover and let it sit in the residual heat until cheese has melted. Enjoy!

537.   Asian Pork Bowl

Preparation Time: 20 minutes
Servings: 6
Nutrition: 538 Calories; 41.9g Fat; 4.9g Carbs; 34.1g Protein; 1.6g Fiber
Ingredients
6 eggs
2 pounds ground pork
1 teaspoon ginger-garlic paste
1 red onion, chopped
1/2 Chinese cabbage, shredded
Directions
Heat 2 tablespoons of the sesame oil in a skillet over medium-high flame. Once hot, fry the eggs for about 5 minutes; set aside.

In the same skillet, heat another 2 tablespoons of sesame oil. Now, cook the ground pork, breaking the meat apart with a fork.

Add in the ginger-garlic paste, onion, and Chinese cabbage; continue to cook for a further 6 to 7 minutes or until the vegetables are tender.

Remove from heat and add 4 tablespoon of rice wine if desired. Stir to combine and top with fried eggs.

Serve garnished with 1/2 cup of roasted peanuts if desired.

538.   Indian Spicy Pork

Preparation Time: 15 minutes
Servings: 4
Nutrition: 478 Calories; 34.7g Fat; 2.2g Carbs; 36.4g Protein; 0.1g Fiber
Ingredients
1 pound pork shoulder, sliced
2 dried Kashmiri red chillies, roasted
1/2 cup ground pork rinds
1/2 cup parmesan cheese, grated
2 eggs
Directions
Season the pork shoulder with salt and ground black pepper to taste.

Then, mix Kashmiri red chillies, pork rinds and parmesan cheese. In another shallow bowl, whisk the eggs.

Now, dip the pork into the egg; then, dredge the pork in the pork rind mixture, pressing to coat well.

Melt 2 tablespoons of tallow in a nonstick skillet over medium-high flame. Cook the pork slices for about 7 minutes, flipping them over to ensure even cooking. Bon appétit!

539.   Authentic Mexican Pork

Preparation Time: 45 minutes
Servings: 4
Nutrition: 477 Calories; 16.2g Fat; 5.7g Carbs; 67.7g Protein; 2.2g Fiber
Ingredients
2 pounds pork butt, cut into 2-inch cubes
1/2 cup dry red wine
1 tablespoons Taco seasoning mix
1/2 cup tomato sauce
4 tablespoons scallions, chopped
Directions
Preheat a lightly greased Dutch oven with nonstick cooking spray over medium-high heat; now, sear the pork until no longer pink.

Now, add the remaining ingredients to the stockpot. Add 1/2 cup of chicken broth and stir to combine well.

Wrap in a piece of foil and bake at 360 degrees F for 30 to 35 minutes.

Afterwards, place the pork under the preheated broil for 8 minutes, until the top is slightly crisp. Enjoy!

540. Winter Pork Stew

Preparation Time: 40 minutes
Servings: 4
Nutrition: 351 Calories; 22.7g Fat; 2.7g Carbs; 32.3g Protein; 2g Fiber
Ingredients
1/4 cup leeks, chopped
1 bell pepper, seeded and chopped
1 pound pork stew meat, cubed
2 garlic cloves, minced
1/4 cup of creme fraiche
Directions
Melt 2 tablespoons of lard in a heavy-bottomed pot over medium heat. Then, cook the leeks, garlic, and peppers for 4 to 5 minutes.
Add the pork to the pot and cook an additional 5 minutes, stirring periodically.
Pour in 2 cups of water or vegetable broth. Continue to cook over low-medium heat for 25 to 30 minutes.
Stir in creme fraiche, cover with the lid, and let it sit in the residual heat. Serve warm.

541. Pork Belly with Peppers

Preparation Time: 20 minutes
Servings: 4
Nutrition: 607 Calories; 60g Fat; 4.4g Carbs; 11.4g Protein; 1.5g Fiber
Ingredients
1 pound skinless pork belly, poke holes with fork
2 bell peppers, seeded and sliced
2 cloves garlic, pressed
1/2 cup shallots, sliced
1 teaspoon dried Mediterranean herb mix
Directions
Rub Mediterranean herb mix all over the pork belly; sprinkle with the salt and black pepper to taste.
Lower the pork into a foil-lined baking dish. Top the pork with garlic, shallots, and peppers.
Roast in the preheated oven at 380 degrees F for 15 to 20 minutes. Serve warm.

542. Classic Italian Meatloaf

Preparation Time: 1 hour
Servings: 5
Nutrition: 426 Calories; 28.1g Fat; 5.2g Carbs; 34.6g Protein; 0.9g Fiber
Ingredients

1 1/3 pound ground pork
1/2 cup yellow onions, chopped
1 egg
1 cup parmesan cheese, preferably freshly grated
1 tablespoon Italian seasoning mix
Directions
Mix all ingredients until everything is well incorporated.
Scrape the mixture into a lightly greased baking pan.
Bake in the preheated oven at 360 degrees F for 50 to 55 minutes. Serve warm.

543.   Pork with Dijon Sauce

Preparation Time: 20 minutes
Servings: 4
Nutrition: 343 Calories; 17.5g Fat; 5.4g Carbs; 40g Protein; 1g Fiber
Ingredients
1 pound pork fillets
2 scallions, chopped
2 cloves garlic, minced
1/2 cup dry white wine
2 tablespoons whole-grain Dijon mustard
Directions
Melt 2 tablespoon of butter in a nonstick skillet over a moderate flame. Now, sear the pork for 3 to 4 minutes per side; reserve.
Next, sauté the scallions and garlic in the pan drippings for 1 to 2 minutes. Pour in white wine to scrape up the browned bits that stick to the bottom of the skillet.
Add in Dijon mustard along with the reserved pork; partially cover and cook for a further 12 minutes or until the sauce has reduced by half.
Serve the pork fillets garnished with the sauce. Bon appétit!

544.   Greek Hoirino me Selino

Preparation Time: 20 minutes
Servings: 6
Nutrition: 214 Calories; 11.5g Fat; 2.6g Carbs; 24.7g Protein; 0.7g Fiber
Ingredients
1 ½ pounds pork shoulder, and cut into small chunks
1 cup tomato puree
1/2 cup shallots, chopped
5 cups chicken stock
1 tablespoon Greek seasoning mix
Directions
Heat 1 tablespoon of olive oil in a soup pot over medium-high heat. Once hot, brown the pork for 4 to 5 minutes.
Stir in the shallots and continue to sauté for 4 minutes more or until it has softened.

Stir in Greek seasoning mix, chicken stock, and tomato puree. When the mixture reaches boiling, immediately reduce the heat to simmer.

Cover and continue to simmer for 10 to 15 minutes or until everything is thoroughly cooked.

Serve with a dollop of Greek yogurt, if desired.

545. Pork in Sherry Sauce

Preparation Time: 20 minutes
Servings: 4
Nutrition: 288 Calories; 17.3g Fat; 1.1g Carbs; 29.9g Protein; 0.9g Fiber
Ingredients
1 pound pork cutlets
2 tablespoons sherry
1/4 cup sour cream
1/4 cup beef bone broth
1 teaspoon mustard
Directions
Season the pork cutlets with salt and black pepper to taste.

Melt 1 tablespoon of lard in a saucepan over medium-high flame; once hot, cook pork cutlets for 3 to 4 minutes per each side. Set aside, keeping them warm.

Deglaze the saucepan with sherry. Stir in the cream, beef broth, and mustard. Partially cover and let it simmer until the sauce has thickened and reduced slightly, approximately 10 minutes.

Stir in the reserved pork and let it simmer for 5 minutes more. Serve warm.

546. Cheeseburger and Mushroom Bowl

Preparation Time: 20 minutes
Servings: 4
Nutrition: 463 Calories; 60g Fat; 4.7g Carbs; 36.2g Protein; 1g Fiber
Ingredients
2 slices Canadian bacon, chopped
1/2 cup shallots, sliced
1 pound ground pork
6 ounces Cremini mushrooms, sliced
1/2 cup cream cheese
Directions
Preheat a frying pan over medium heat. Then, fry the bacon for 3 to 4 minutes, crumbling with a fork; reserve.

Sauté the shallots in the bacon fat for about 3 minutes. Stir in the ground pork and continue to cook for 4 to 5 minutes more, stirring frequently.

Season the pork with salt and black pepper. Add in mushrooms along with 1/2 cup of water or broth. Cook, covered, for 10 minutes longer over medium-low heat.

Remove from heat and fold in cream cheese; stir to combine well, top with the reserved bacon and serve!

547.   Classic Mexican Tacos

Preparation Time: 20 minutes
Servings: 4
Nutrition: 330 Calories; 26.3g Fat; 4.9g Carbs; 17.9g Protein; 1.1g Fiber
Ingredients
1 tablespoon lard
8 ounces mixed ground meat (pork and turkey
4 tablespoons sour cream
12 lettuce leaves
4 tablespoons roasted tomatillo salsa
Directions
Place the ground meat in a bowl and season with the salt and black pepper to taste.
In a saucepan, warm the lard over medium-high heat. Now, cook the ground meat for 5 to 6 minutes, stirring continuously and crumbling with a spatula.
Fold in the roasted tomatillo salsa and stir again. Remove from heat.
Afterwards, divide the meat mixture between lettuce leaves. Top with sour cream and serve.

548.   French Pork Daube

Preparation Time: 50 minutes
Servings: 4
Nutrition: 615 Calories; 61g Fat; 2.7g Carbs; 12.9g Protein; 0.8g Fiber
Ingredients
1 pound pork belly, cut into bite-sized chunks
1/2 pound ripe tomatoes, pureed
2 scallions, chopped
1 teaspoon garlic, minced
1 tablespoon Herbes de Provence
Directions
Heat up a soup pot over medium-high heat. Now, sear the pork for about 5 minutes, stirring frequently to ensure even cooking.
Add in pureed tomatoes, scallions, garlic, and Herbes de Provence. Pour in 2 cups of water or broth and bring to a rapid boil.
Then, immediately reduce the heat to medium-low. Continue to simmer for 35 to 40 minutes or until everything is cooked through.
Divide among soup bowls and garnish with 8 niçoise olives if desired. Enjoy!

549.   Rich Ground Pork Casserole

Preparation Time: 40 minutes
Servings: 6
Nutrition: 620 Calories; 50g Fat; 5.7g Carbs; 33.9g Protein; 0.7g Fiber
Ingredients
2 pounds ground pork

1 bell pepper, deseeded and chopped
1 leek, chopped
2 eggs, beaten
1 1/2 cups cream cheese, at room temperature
Directions
In a nonstick skillet, warm 1 tablespoon of butter over moderate flame. Then, brown the ground pork until no longer pink or about 4 minutes.

Stir in the peppers and leek and continue to sauté for 6 to 7 minutes, stirring frequently.

Pour in 1/2 cup of water or chicken bone broth; continue to cook for 6 to 7 minutes. Scrape the mixture into a greased casserole dish.

Then, whisk the eggs and cream cheese until well combined. Pour the egg mixture into the prepared casserole dish.

Bake in the preheated oven at 340 degrees F for about 9 minutes until bubbly and golden brown on the top. Let it sit for 10 minutes before slicing and.

550.   Pork and Mushroom Skillet

Preparation Time: 20 minutes
Servings: 3
Nutrition: 364 Calories; 17.3g Fat; 4.6g Carbs; 45g Protein; 0.9g Fiber
Ingredients
1 onion, sliced
2 cups button mushrooms, sliced
3 pork medallions
1 tomato, sliced
1 bell pepper, deveined and sliced
Directions
In a cast-iron skillet, heat 2 tablespoon of olive oil over medium-high heat. Once hot, sweat the onions until they are just tender and translucent.

Stir in the mushrooms and continue to cook for 2 minutes more or until they are tender and aromatic.

Add in the pork medallions tomato, and bell pepper; season with the salt and pepper and let it cook for about 13 minutes.

Garnish with fresh parsley if desired. Bon appétit!

Vegetables

551. Nutty and Fruity Garden Salad

Preparation Time: 10 Minutes
Cooking Time: 0 Minutes
Servings: 2
Ingredients:
6 cups baby spinach
½ cup chopped walnuts, toasted
1 ripe red pear, sliced
1 ripe persimmon, sliced
1 teaspoon garlic minced
1 shallot, minced
1 tablespoon extra-virgin olive oil
2 tablespoons fresh lemon juice
1 teaspoon whole grain mustard
Directions:
Mix well garlic, shallot, oil, lemon juice and mustard in a large salad bowl.
Add spinach, pear and persimmon. Toss to coat well.
To serve, garnish with chopped pecans.
Nutrition:
Calories 332, Total Fat 21g, Saturated Fat 2g, Total Carbs 37g, Net Carbs 28g, Protein 7g, Sugar: 20g, Fiber 9g, Sodium 75mg, Potassium 864mg

552. Creamy Cauliflower-Broccoli Soup

Preparation Time: 15 Minutes
Cooking Time: 15 Minutes
Servings: 6
Ingredients:
Pepper and salt to taste
4 cups chicken broth
1 teaspoon dried basil
1 teaspoon dried oregano
½ cup onion, roughly chopped
2 cups carrots, cubed
3 cups cauliflower florets
2 cups broccoli florets
Directions:
In a large soup pot, bring to a boil chicken broth, basil, oregano and onions. Once boiling, lower fire to a simmer.
Meanwhile, dice cauliflower and broccoli florets. And add to pot. Add carrots, cover and simmer for 10 minutes. Season with pepper and salt to taste.
Turn off fire and allow soup to cool.

Place veggies into a blender while ensuring that liquid is reserved. Puree veggies along with 1 cup of reserved liquid. If you want a thick soup, then 1 cup liquid is enough. If you desire a less thick soup, add more reserved liquid until desired consistency is reached.

Return pureed soup to empty pot and simmer until heated through. Adjust seasoning if needed before.

Nutrition:

Calories 39, Total Fat 0.3g, Saturated Fat 0.1g, Total Carbs 8g, Net Carbs 5g, Protein 2g, Sugar: 4g, Fiber 3g, Sodium 47mg, Potassium 348mg

553.   Nutty and Fruity Amaranth Porridge

Preparation Time: 10 Minutes
Cooking Time: 30 Minutes
Servings: 2
Ingredients:
1 medium pear, chopped
½ cup blueberries
1 tsp cinnamon
1 tbsp raw honey
¼ cup pumpkin seeds
2 cups filtered water
2/3 cups whole-grain amaranth
Directions:
In a nonstick pan with cover, boil water and amaranth. Slow fire to a simmer and continue cooking until liquid is absorbed completely, around 25-30 minutes.
Turn off fire.
Mix in cinnamon, honey and pumpkin seeds. Mix well.
Pour equally into two bowls.
Garnish with pear and blueberries.
Serve and enjoy.
Nutrition:
Calories 416, Total Fat 12g, Saturated Fat 2g, Total Carbs 68g, Net Carbs 61g, Protein 14g, Sugar: 23g, Fiber 7g, Sodium 48mg, Potassium 481mg

554.   Korean Barbecue Tofu

Preparation Time: 10 Minutes
Cooking Time: 15 Minutes
Servings: 3
Ingredients:
1 tbsp olive oil
2 tsp onion powder
4 garlic cloves, minced
2 tsp dry mustard
3 tbsp brown sugar
½ cup soy sauce
1 ½ lbs. firm tofu, sliced to ¼-inch cubes

Directions:

In a re-sealable bag, mix all ingredients except for tofu and oil. Mix well until sugar is dissolved. Add sliced tofu and slowly turn bag to mmix. Seal bag and place flatly inside the ref for an hour. After an hour, turn bag to the other side and marinate for another hour.

To cook, in a nonstick fry pan, heat oil on medium high fire. Add tofu and stir fry until sides are browned.

Serve and enjoy.

Nutrition:

Calories 437, Total Fat 25g, Saturated Fat 3g, Total Carbs 23g, Net Carbs 15g, Protein 40g, Sugar: 8g, Fiber 6g, Sodium 1600mg, Potassium 724mg

555.   Fruit Bowl with Yogurt Topping

Preparation Time: 15 Minutes
Cooking Time: 0 Minutes
Servings: 6
Ingredients:
¼ cup golden brown sugar
2/3 cup minced fresh ginger
1 16-oz Greek yogurt
¼ tsp ground cinnamon
2 tbsp honey
½ cup dried cranberries
3 navel oranges
2 large tangerines
1 pink grapefruit, peeled
Directions:
Into sections, break tangerines and grapefruit.

Slice tangerine sections in half and grapefruit sections into thirds. Place all sliced fruits and its juices in a large bowl.

Peel oranges, remove pith, slice into ¼-inch thick rounds and then cut into quarters. Transfer to bowl of fruit along with juices.

In bowl, add cinnamon, honey and ¼ cup of cranberries. Place in the ref for an hour.

In a medium bowl mix ginger and yogurt. Place on top of fruit bowl, drizzle with remaining cranberries and brown sugar.

Serve and enjoy.

Nutrition:

Calories 171, Total Fat 1g, Saturated Fat 0.1g, Total Carbs 35g, Net Carbs 32g, Protein 9g, Sugar: 28g, Fiber 3g, Sodium 31mg, Potassium 400mg

556.   Mushroom, Spinach and Turmeric Frittata

Preparation Time: 10 Minutes
Cooking Time: 40 Minutes
Servings: 6
Ingredients:
½ tsp pepper

½ tsp salt
1 tsp turmeric
5-oz firm tofu
4 large eggs
6 large egg whites
¼ cup water
1 lb. fresh spinach
6 cloves freshly chopped garlic
1 large onion, chopped
1 lb. button mushrooms, sliced
Directions:
Grease a 10-inch nonstick and oven proof skillet and preheat oven to 350oF.
Place skillet on medium high fire and add mushrooms. Cook until golden brown.
Add onions, cook for 3 minutes or until onions are tender.
Add garlic, sauté for 30 seconds.
Add water and spinach, cook while covered until spinach is wilted, around 2 minutes.
Remove lid and continue cooking until water is fully evaporated.
 In a blender, puree pepper, salt, turmeric, tofu, eggs and egg whites until smooth. Pour into skillet once liquid is fully evaporated.
Pop skillet into oven and bake until the center is set around 25-30 minutes.
Remove skillet from oven and let it stand for ten minutes before inverting and transferring to a plate.
Cut into 6 equal wedges, serve and enjoy.
Nutrition:
Calories 358, Total Fat 6g, Saturated Fat 1.6g, Total Carbs 65g, Net Carbs 52g, Protein 21g, Sugar: 4g, Fiber 12g, Sodium 371mg, Potassium 1809mg

557.   Roasted Root Vegetables

Preparation Time: 10 Minutes
Cooking Time: 1 hour and 30 Minutes
Servings: 6
Ingredients:
2 tbsp olive oil
1 head garlic, cloves separated and peeled
1 large turnip, peeled and cut into ½-inch pieces
1 medium sized red onion, cut into ½-inch pieces
1 ½ lbs. beets, trimmed but not peeled, scrubbed and cut into ½-inch pieces
1 ½ lbs. Yukon gold potatoes, unpeeled, cut into ½-inch pieces
2 ½ lbs. butternut squash, peeled, seeded, cut into ½-inch pieces
Directions:
Grease 2 rimmed and large baking sheets. Preheat oven to 425oF.
In a large bowl, mix all ingredients thoroughly.
Into the two baking sheets, evenly divide the root vegetables, spread in one layer.
Season generously with pepper and salt.
Pop into the oven and roast for 1 hour and 15 minute or until golden brown and tender.
Remove from oven and let it cool for at least 15 minutes before.

Nutrition:
Calories 278, Total Fat 5g, Saturated Fat 1g, Total Carbs 57g, Net Carbs 47g, Protein 6g, Sugar: 15g, Fiber 10g, Sodium 124mg, Potassium 1598mg

558.   Tropical Fruit Parfait

Preparation Time: 10 Minutes
Cooking Time: 10 Minutes
Servings: 1
Ingredients:
1 tbsp toasted sliced almonds
¼ cup plain soy yogurt
½ cup of fruit combination cut into ½-inch cubes (pineapple, mango and kiwi
Directions:
Prepare fresh fruit by peeling and slicing into ½-inch cubes.
Place cubed fruit in a bowl and top with a dollop of soy yogurt.
Garnish with sliced almonds and if desired, refrigerate for an hour before.
Nutrition:
Calories 119, Total Fat 2g, Saturated Fat 0.1g, Total Carbs 25g, Net Carbs 24g, Protein 2g, Sugar: 21g, Fiber 1g, Sodium 9mg, Potassium 161mg

559.   Cinnamon Chips with Avocado-Strawberry Salsa

Preparation Time: 10 Minutes
Cooking Time: 10 Minutes
Servings: 6
Ingredients:
3/8 tsp salt
2 tsp fresh lime juice
1 tsp minced seeded jalapeno pepper
2 tbsp minced fresh cilantro
1 cup finely chopped strawberries
1 ½ cups finely chopped, peeled and ripe avocado
½ tsp ground cinnamon
2 tsp sugar
6 6-inch brown rice tortillas
2 tsp olive oil
Directions:
Preheat oven to 350oF.
Prepare the cinnamon chips by brushing olive oil all over the brown rice tortilla.
In a small bowl, mix together cinnamon and sugar.
Sprinkle cinnamon-sugar mixture evenly all over each of the brown rice tortilla.
Cut up each tortilla into 12 wedges, evenly and place on a baking sheet. If needed you can bake tortilla in two batches.
Pop the tortillas into the oven and bake until crisped, around 10 minutes. Remove from oven and keep warm.
Meanwhile, prepare salsa by mixing the remaining ingredients in a medium bowl. Stir to mix well.

To enjoy, dip crisped tortillas into bowl of salsa and eat or, you can spread the fruity salsa all over one tortilla chip and enjoy.

Nutrition:

Calories 213, Total Fat 11g, Saturated Fat 3g, Total Carbs 25g, Net Carbs 18g, Protein 5g, Sugar: 4g, Fiber 7g, Sodium 362mg, Potassium 337mg

560. Stir Fried Brussels Sprouts and Carrots

Preparation Time: 10 Minutes
Cooking Time: 15 Minutes
Servings: 6
Ingredients:
1 tbsp cider vinegar
1/3 cup water
1 lb. Brussels sprouts, halved lengthwise
1 lb. carrots cut diagonally into ½-inch thick lengths
3 tbsp olive oil, divided
2 tbsp chopped shallot
½ tsp pepper
¾ tsp salt
Directions:
On medium high fire, place a nonstick medium fry pan and heat 2 tbsp oil.
Ass shallots and cook until softened, around one to two minutes while occasionally stirring.
Add pepper salt, Brussels sprouts and carrots. Stir fry until vegetables starts to brown on the edges, around 3 to 4 minutes.
Add water, cook and cover.
After 5 to 8 minutes, or when veggies are already soft, add remaining butter.
If needed season with more pepper and salt to taste.
Turn off fire, transfer to a platter, serve and enjoy.
Nutrition:
Calories 98, Total Fat 4g, Saturated Fat 2g, Total Carbs 14g, Net Carbs 9g, Protein 3g, Sugar: 5g, Fiber 5g, Sodium 357mg, Potassium 502mg

561. Curried Veggies and Poached Eggs

Preparation Time: 10 Minutes
Cooking Time: 50 Minutes
Servings: 4
Ingredients:
4 large eggs
½ tsp white vinegar
1/8 tsp crushed red pepper – optional
1 cup water
1 14-oz can chickpeas, drained
2 medium zucchinis, diced
½ lb. sliced button mushrooms
1 tbsp yellow curry powder

2 cloves garlic, minced

1 large onion, chopped

2 tsp extra virgin olive oil

Directions:

On medium high fire, place a large saucepan and heat oil.

Sauté onions until tender around four to five minutes.

Add garlic and continue sautéing for another half minute.

Add curry powder, stir and cook until fragrant around one to two minutes.

Add mushrooms, mix, cover and cook for 5 to 8 minutes or until mushrooms are tender and have released their liquid.

Add red pepper if using, water, chickpeas and zucchini. Mix well to combine and bring to a boil.

Once boiling, reduce fire to a simmer, cover and cook until zucchini is tender around 15 to 20 minutes of simmering.

Meanwhile, in a small pot filled with 3-inches deep of water, bring to a boil on high fire.

Once boiling, reduce fire to a simmer and add vinegar.

Slowly add one egg, slipping it gently into the water. Allow to simmer until egg is cooked, around 3 to 5 minutes.

Remove egg with a slotted spoon and transfer to a plate, one plate one egg.

Repeat the process with remaining eggs.

Once the veggies are done cooking, divide evenly into 4 and place one per plate of egg.

Serve and enjoy.

Nutrition:

Calories 254, Total Fat 9g, Saturated Fat 2g, Total Carbs 30g, Net Carbs 21g, Protein 16g, Sugar: 7g, Fiber 9g, Sodium 341mg, Potassium 480mg

562.   Braised Kale

Preparation Time: 10 Minutes

Cooking Time: 15 Minutes

Servings: 3

Ingredients:

2 to 3 tbsp water

1 tbsp coconut oil

½ sliced red pepper

2 stalk celery (sliced to ¼-inch thick

5 cups of chopped kale

Directions:

Heat a pan over medium heat.

Add coconut oil and sauté the celery for at least five minutes.

Add the kale and red pepper.

Add a tablespoon of water.

Let the vegetables wilt for a few minutes. Add a tablespoon of water if the kale starts to stick to the pan.

Serve warm.

Nutrition:

Calories 61, Total Fat 5g, Saturated Fat 1g, Total Carbs 3g, Net Carbs 2g, Protein 1g, Sugar: 1g, Fiber 1g, Sodium 20mg, Potassium 185mg

563.   Braised Leeks, Cauliflower and Artichoke Hearts

Preparation Time: 10 Minutes
Cooking Time: 10 Minutes
Servings: 4
Ingredients:
2 tbsp coconut oil
2 garlic cloves, chopped
1 ½ cup artichoke hearts
1 ½ cups chopped leeks
1 ½ cups cauliflower flowerets
Directions:
Heat oil in a skillet over medium high heat.
Add the garlic and sauté for one minute. Add the vegetables and stir constantly until the vegetables are cooked.
Serve with roasted chicken, fish or pork.
Nutrition:
Calories 111, Total Fat 7g, Saturated Fat 1g, Total Carbs 12g, Net Carbs 8g, Protein 3g, Sugar: 2g, Fiber 4g, Sodium 65mg, Potassium 305mg

564.   Celery Root Hash Browns

Preparation Time: 10 Minutes
Cooking Time: 10 Minutes
Servings: 4
Ingredients:
4 tbsp coconut oil
½ tsp sea salt
2 to 3 medium celery roots
Directions:
Scrub the celery root clean and peel it using a vegetable peeler.
Grate the celery root in a food processor or a manual grater.
In a skillet, add oil and heat it over medium heat.
Place the grated celery root on the skillet and sprinkle with salt.
Let it cook for 10 minutes on each side or until the grated celery turns brown.
Serve warm.
Nutrition:
Calories 160, Total Fat 14g, Saturated Fat 3g, Total Carbs 10g, Net Carbs 7g, Protein 1.5g, Sugar: 0g, Fiber 3g, Sodium 314mg, Potassium 320mg

565.   Zucchini Pasta with Avocado Sauce

Preparation Time: 10 Minutes
Cooking Time: 10 Minutes
Servings: 1
Ingredients:
A squeeze of lemon juice

Salt and pepper to taste
1 tbsp coconut milk
½ ripe avocado
1 medium zucchini cut into noodles
2 tbsp olive oil
Directions:
Heat the oil in a skillet over medium heat and add the zucchini noodles. Sauté for three minutes or until the noodles have softened.
While the zucchini is cooking, mash the avocado together with the coconut milk, lemon juice and salt and pepper.
Add the sauce to the zucchini noodles and sauté. Serve warm.
Nutrition:
Calories 471, Total Fat 43g, Saturated Fat 6g, Total Carbs 23g, Net Carbs 14g, Protein 6g, Sugar: 10g, Fiber 9g, Sodium 33mg, Potassium 1221mg

566. Blueberry Chia Pudding

Preparation Time: 10 Minutes
Cooking Time: 10 Minutes
Servings: 2
Ingredients:
½ cup chia seeds
½ of frozen banana
5 dates (soaked in water
2/3 cup almond milk
2 cups frozen blueberries
Directions:
Combine the milk, blueberries, dates and bananas in a blender. Process until the mixture becomes smooth.
Transfer the blueberry to a bowl and add the chia seeds.
Refrigerate for 30 minutes or overnight if necessary, until the chia seeds forms mucilage.
Serve with your favorite fruit or nut toppings.
Nutrition:
Calories 343, Total Fat 13g, Saturated Fat 3g, Total Carbs 55g, Net Carbs 39g, Protein 9g, Sugar: 32g, Fiber 16g, Sodium 42mg, Potassium 529mg

567. Roasted Veggies

Servings: 12
Preparation Time: 25 minutes
Cooking Time: 55 minutes
Ingredients:

1½ cups pecans

1 small butternut squash, peeled, seeded and cut into ¼-thick slices

1 medium head cauliflower, cut into florets

1-pound Brussels sprouts, trimmed and halved

2 large parsnips, peeled and cut into ¼-thick slices

4 medium carrots, peeled and cut into ¼-thick slices

¼ teaspoon nutmeg, grated freshly

Salt and freshly ground black pepper, to taste

½ cup extra-virgin organic olive oil

2 tablespoons fresh ginger, minced

1/3 cup raw honey

Directions:

Preheat the oven to 425 degrees F.

In a pie plate, put the pecans.

Roast approximately 6 minutes or till toasted.

Remove from heat and keep aside to cool down the.

In a big bowl, add all vegetables, nutmeg, salt, black pepper and oil and toss to coat well.

In 2 large rimmed baking sheets, spread the vegetable mixture evenly.

Roast for about thirty minutes.

Remove the baking sheets from oven.

Sprinkle the vegetables with ginger and pecans e and drizzle with honey evenly.

Roast approximately 25 minutes.

Serve warm.

Nutrition:

Calories: 265.8, Fat: 19.3g, Carbohydrates: 23.9g, Fiber: 510.1, Protein: 4.1g

568. Grilled Veggies

A platter of summer vegetables that's great for entertaining the guests. Grilling brings out their natural sweetness, in a nice way.

Servings: 6

Preparation Time: 20 or so minutes

Cooking Time: 12 minutes

Ingredients:

¼ cup essential olive oil

4 teaspoons balsamic vinegar

2tablespoons raw honey

1 teaspoon dried oregano, crushed

1 teaspoon ground cumin

12 teaspoon garlic powder

Salt and freshly ground black pepper, to taste

3 small carrots, peeled and halved lengthwise

1 medium yellow squash, cut into ½-inch slices

1 large red bell pepper, seeded and cut into1-inch strips

1-pound fresh as asparagus, trimmed

1 medium red onion, cut into wedges

Directions:

In a tiny bowl, mix together all ingredients except vegetables.

In a substantial bowl, add 3 tablespoons of marinade, reserving the residual.

Add vegetables and toss to coat well.

Keep aside, covered approximately 1½ hours.

Preheat the grill to medium heat. Grease the grill grate.

Place the vegetables over grill grate inside a single layer and arrange in the grill rack.

Grill, covered approximately 8-12 minutes, flipping occasionally.

Nutrition:

Calories: 144, Fat: 9g, Carbohydrates: 15g, Fiber: 3g, Protein: 2g

569.   Grilled Veggie Skewers

A really yummy strategy to take advantage of the vegetables in what you eat. These grilled veggie skewers are popular for lunch or dinner as well.

Servings: 5

Preparation Time: 20 minutes

Cooking Time: 15 minutes

Ingredients:

For Marinade Mixture:

3 garlic cloves, chopped
1 (1-inchpieces fresh ginger, chopped
1 teaspoon ground cumin
1 teaspoon ground coriander
1teaspoon sweet paprika
1/8 teaspoon red chili powder
Salt and freshly ground black pepper, to taste
¼ cup fresh lemon juice
¼ cup organic olive oil
½ lot of fresh cilantro
½ couple of fresh parsley
For Vegetables:
2 medium red bell pepper, seeded and cut into 1-inch pieces
2 medium zucchinis, cut into 1/3-inch thick round slices
1-pound small mushrooms
1 large yellow onion, sliced into 1-inch pieces
1 large eggplant, quartered lengthwise and cut into ½-inch thick slices diagonally
Directions:
For marinade mixture in the blender, add all ingredients except herbs and pulse till well combined.
Add fresh herbs and pulse till smooth.
In a sizable bowl, add vegetables and marinade and toss to coat well.
Refrigerate, covered approximately 4 hours.
Preheat the grill to medium-low heat. Grease the grill grate.
Thread the skewers for around 15 minutes, flipping occasionally.
Nutrition:
Calories: 254, Fat: 5g, Carbohydrates: 25g, Fiber: 6g, Protein: 27g

570.   Mushrooms with Broccoli & Bell Pepper

A satisfying and flavorful satisfying dish of mushroom, bell pepper and broccoli. This marinade produces a perfect balance of savory, citrusy, and sweet in veggies.
Servings: 2-3
Preparation Time: 15 minutes
Cooking Time: 12 minutes
Ingredients:
For Mushroom Marinade:
2 teaspoons fresh ginger, minced
2 minced garlic cloves
3-4 tablespoons organic honey
3-4 tablespoons coconut aminos
3 tablespoons fresh lime juice
1 tablespoon sesame oil
1 tablespoon water
2 Portobello mushrooms, sliced into thin strips

For Vegetables:
1 tablespoon sesame seeds
1 cup broccoli, chopped
1 red bell pepper, seeded and sliced thinly
1 cup scallion, chopped
Directions:
For mushrooms in a big bowl, add all ingredients except mushrooms and mix till well combined.
Add mushrooms and coat with marinade generously.
Keep aside for about 10-12 minutes.
In a big nonstick skillet, heat sesame oil on medium heat.
Remove the mushrooms from marinade and add inside skillet in 2 batches and sauté for approximately 2-4 minutes per side.
Transfer the mushrooms in a very bowl and cover which has a foil paper to maintain warm.
In exactly the same skillet, add broccoli and bell pepper and sauté for about 2-3 minutes.
Add scallion and then for any remaining marinade from the bowl and sauté approximately 1 minute.
Remove from heat and immediately mix with mushrooms.
Serve immediately.
Nutrition:
Calories: 161, Fat: 5g, Carbohydrates: 26.5g, Fiber: 4g, Protein: 6.1g

571. Three Mushrooms Medley

Servings: 3
Preparation Time: 15 minutes
Cooking Time: 17 minutes
Ingredients:
3 tablespoons extra-virgin extra virgin olive oil
3 portabella mushrooms, sliced
6-ounce shiitake mushrooms, stemmed and sliced
7½-ounce baby beech mushrooms
1 tablespoon fresh ginger, minced
5 garlic cloves, minced
1 dried red chili, crushed
2 teaspoons coconut aminos
1 teaspoon sesame oil
Directions:
In a skillet, heat 1 tablespoon of essential olive oil on medium heat.
Add portabella mushrooms and cook stirring occasionally for approximately 4-5 minutes.
Transfer the mushrooms in a large bowl.
In a similar skillet, heat 1 tablespoon of extra virgin olive oil on medium heat.
Add shiitake mushrooms and cook for approximately 4-5 minutes.
Transfer the mushrooms in to the large bowl with portabella mushrooms.
In a similar skillet, heat ½ tablespoon from the organic olive oil on medium heat.
Add baby beech mushrooms and cook approximately 3-4 minutes.
Transfer the mushrooms to the large bowl with portabella mushrooms.
In exactly the same skillet, heat remaining extra virgin olive oil on medium heat.
Add ginger, garlic and red chili and sauté for around 1 minute.

Add the mushroom mixture, coconut aminos and sesame oil and stir till well combined. Cook for around 1-2 minutes.
Serve hot.
Nutrition:
Calories: 261, Fat: 6g, Carbohydrates: 25g, Fiber: 8g, Protein: 11g

572.   Mushroom with Spinach

Servings: 2
Preparation Time: 15 minutes
Cooking Time: 13 minutes
Ingredients:
1 teaspoon coconut oil
5-6 button mushrooms, sliced
2 tablespoons olive oil
½ of red onion, sliced
1 garlic oil, minced
½ teaspoon fresh lemon rind, grated finely
¼ cup cherry tomatoes, halved
Salt and freshly ground black pepper, to taste
Pinch of ground nutmeg
3 cups fresh spinach, torn
½ tablespoon fresh lemon juice
Directions:
I a skillet, melt coconut oil on medium heat.
Add mushrooms and sauté for around 3-4 minutes.
Transfer the mushrooms in a bowl and make aside.
In a similar skillet, heat olive oil on medium heat.
Add onion and sauté for about 2-3 minutes.
Add garlic, lemon rind and tomatoes, salt and black pepper and cook approximately 2-3 minutes, revealing the tomatoes slightly which has a spatula.
Stir inside spinach and cook for approximately 2-3 minutes.
Stir in mushrooms and freshly squeezed lemon juice and take off from heat.
Serve hot.
Nutrition:
Calories: 261, Fat: 4g, Carbohydrates: 20g, Fiber: 7g, Protein: 10g

573.   Nutty Spinach

A vegetarian friendly version of a healthy dish of spinach with almonds. Almonds offer a delicious crunch to healthy spinach.
Servings: 4
Preparation Time: 15 minutes
Cooking Time: 23 minutes
Ingredients:

3 tablespoons coconut oil
1½ tablespoons coconut sugar
½ teaspoon cumin seeds
1 tablespoon black mustard seeds
¼ teaspoon fenugreek seeds
2-pounds fresh spinach, trimmed
1 tablespoon green chili, minced
½ tablespoon fresh ginger, grated
2/3 cup almonds, soaked in warm water for 4 hours and drained
1/3 cup coconut, shredded
Salt and freshly ground black pepper, to taste
2 tablespoons water
1/8 teaspoon ground nutmeg
Directions:
In a big skillet, melt coconut oil on medium heat.
Add brown sugar, cumin seeds, mustard seeds and fenugreek seeds and sauté for around 1 minute.
Stir in spinach, green chili, ginger, almonds, coconut, salt and black pepper.
Reduce the heat to low and simmer, covered approximately 10 minutes.
Uncover and stir in water and simmer approximately 10 min.
Stir within the nutmeg and simmer for about 1-2 minutes more.
Nutrition:
Calories: 344.9, Fat: 25.9g, Carbohydrates: 23.3g, Fiber: 8.3g, Protein: 12.2g

574. Mixed Root Vegetables & Kale

Enjoy the flavor of root vegetables within your dinner. Tender and long-leafed kale enhances the flavor of root vegetables.
Servings: 6-8
Preparation Time: 15 minutes
Cooking Time: 20 minutes
Ingredients:
2 tablespoons essential olive oil
1 large sweet onion, chopped
1 medium parsnip, peeled and chopped
2 minced garlic cloves
3 tablespoons tomato paste
1 teaspoon ground cumin
½ teaspoon ground cinnamon
½ teaspoon ground ginger
¼ tsp cayenne
Salt and freshly ground black pepper, to taste
2 medium carrots, peeled and chopped
2 medium purple potatoes, peeled and chopped
2 medium sweet potatoes, peeled and chopped
4 cups vegetable broth
2 cups fresh kale, trimmed and chopped roughly
2 tablespoons fresh lemon juice

¼ cup fresh cilantro, chopped
Directions:
In a sizable soup pan, heat oil on medium-high heat.
Add onion and sauté approximately 5 minutes.
Add parsnip and cook approximately 3 minutes.
Add garlic, tomato paste and spices and sauté for approximately 2 minutes.
Add carrots, potatoes, sweet potatoes and broth and bring with a boil.
Reduce the warmth to medium-low and simmer for about 20 min, stirring occasionally.
Stir in kale and freshly squeezed lemon juice and simmer approximately 2-3 minutes.
Garnish with cilantro and serve.
Nutrition:
Calories: 277, Fat: 6g, Carbohydrates: 22g, Fiber: 7g, Protein: 11g

575.   Mixed Vegetables Stew

Servings: 4
Preparation Time: 20 minutes
Cooking Time: 52 minutes
Ingredients:
2 tablespoons organic olive oil
1¼ cups yellow onion, chopped
1 tablespoon garlic, minced
1 tablespoon chile paste
1½ tablespoons fresh turmeric, grated
1½ teaspoons ground cumin
1 teaspoon ground cinnamon
1 cup carrots, peeled and chopped roughly
1 cup cauliflower, chopped roughly
2 cups broccoli, chopped roughly
4 cups green cabbage, chopped roughly
1 cup coconut water
2 cups canned crushed tomatoes
¾ cup frozen peas, thawed
Salt and freshly ground black pepper, to taste
Directions:
In a sizable pan, heat poi on medium heat.
Add onion and garlic and sauté approximately 10 min.
Add chile paste, turmeric, cumin and cinnamon and sate for around 1 minute.
Stir in carrots and cook for around 3-4 minutes.
Stir in cauliflower and broccoli and cook for about 2-3 minutes.
Stir in cabbage reducing heat to low.
Simmer for about 4 minutes.
Add coconut water and tomatoes and produce to some boil on medium-high heat.
Reduce heat to low and simmer, covered for approximately thirty minutes.
Stir in peas, salt and black pepper and remove from heat.
Serve hot.
Nutrition:

Calories: 299, Fat: 2g, Carbohydrates: 16 g, Fiber: 12g, Protein: 26g

576.   Veggie Curry

This healthy, vegetarian Thai green curry is full of flavors. This delicious curry is easy enough for weeknight dinners.

Servings: 2-4
Preparation Time: 15 minutes
Cooking Time: 22 minutes
Ingredients:
2 teaspoons coconut oil
1 small white onion, chopped
2 garlic cloves, chopped finely
1 tablespoon fresh ginger, chopped finely
Salt, to taste
3 carrots, peeled and cut into ¾-inch round slices
2 cups asparagus, trimmed and cut into 2-inch pieces
2 tablespoons green curry paste
1½ teaspoons coconut sugar
1 (14-ouncecan coconut milk
½ cup water
2 cups fresh baby spinach, chopped roughly
1½ teaspoons coconut aminos
1½ teaspoons balsamic vinegar
Crushed red pepper flakes, to taste
Directions:
In a substantial deep skillet, melt coconut oil on medium heat.
Add onion, garlic, ginger as well as a pinch of salt and sauté for around 5 minutes.
Add carrots and asparagus and cook, stirring occasionally for around 3 minutes.
Stir inside the curry paste and cook, stirring occasionally for approximately 2 minutes.
Add coconut sugar, coconut milk and water and provide to a gentle simmer.
Cook for about 5-10 minutes or till desired doneness of vegetables.
Stir within the spinach and cook for approximately 1 minute.
Stir in coconut aminos, vinegar, salt and red pepper flakes and take away from heat.
Serve hot.
Nutrition:
Calories: 301, Fat: 2g, Carbohydrates: 23g, Fiber: 9g, Protein: 16g

577.   Veggies Curry in Pumpkin Puree

Servings: 4
Preparation Time: 15 minutes
Cooking Time: 30 minutes
Ingredients:

1 tablespoon coconut oil
1 green bell pepper, seeded and chopped
1 onion, chopped
1 cup homemade pumpkin puree
1 tablespoon curry powder
1 teaspoon ground cinnamon
¼ teaspoon ground ginger
Salt, to taste
1 (14-ouncecan coconut milk
1 cup water
1 sweet potato, peeled and cut into 1-inch cubes
1 head broccoli, cut into florets
Directions:
In a big pan, melt coconut oil on medium heat.
Add onion and sauté for about 8 minutes.
Add pumpkin puree, curry powder, cinnamon, ginger, salt, coconut milk and water and stir to blend well.
Stir in pumpkin and broccoli and bring with a gentle simmer.
Simmer, covered approximately 15-twenty minutes.
Serve hot.
Nutrition:
Calories: 271, Fat: 6g, Carbohydrates: 18g, Fiber: 8g, Protein: 20g

578. Spicy Mixed Veggies

A really delicious dish of spicy vegetables. The combo of spices enhances the flavor of mixed vegetables inside a great way.
Servings: 6
Preparation Time: 25 minutes
Cooking Time: 35 minutes
Ingredients:

2 tablespoons extra virgin olive oil
1 teaspoon mustard seeds
2 onions, chopped finely
2 fresh green chilies, seeded and chopped
1 bunch curry leaves
½ teaspoon garam masala
½ teaspoon ground cumin
½ teaspoon ground coriander
¼ teaspoon ground turmeric
¼ teaspoon red chili powder
6 tomatoes, chopped
1 eggplant, cubed
2 potatoes, peeled and cubed
2 sweet potatoes, peeled and cubed
½ cup coconut milk
½ cup okra, trimmed and chopped
½ cup French beans
½ cup fresh peas, shelled
Salt and freshly ground black pepper, to taste
Directions:
In a sizable pan, heat oil on medium heat.
Add mustard seeds and sauté for about 1 minute.
Add onion, green chilies, curry leaves and spices and sauté for approximately 4-5 minutes.
Add tomatoes and cook approximately 2-3 minutes.
Stir in eggplant, potatoes, sweet potatoes and coconut milk and provide to some gentle simmer.
Reduce the warmth to medium-low.
Simmer, covered for about 15-twenty minutes or till desired doneness.
Stir in the remaining ingredients and cook for around 5 minutes.
Serve hot.
Nutrition:
Calories: 265, Fat: 4g, Carbohydrates: 15g, Fiber: 11g, Protein: 26g

579.   Stuffed Zucchini

One associated with an awesome recipe of stuffed zucchini. This salted filling balances the sweetness of zucchini nicely.
Servings: 6
Preparation Time: 20 minutes
Cooking Time: 30 minutes
Ingredients:

6 medium zucchinis, halved lengthwise
Salt, to taste
1½ baking potatoes, peeled and cubed
4 teaspoons olive oil
2½ cups onion, chopped
1 Serrano chile, mined
2 minced garlic cloves
1½ tablespoons fresh ginger, minced
2 tablespoons chickpea flour
1 teaspoon ground coriander
¼ teaspoon ground cumin
¼ teaspoon ground turmeric
Freshly ground black pepper, to taste
1½ cups frozen green peas, thawed
2 tablespoons fresh cilantro, chopped
Directions:
Preheat the oven to 375 degrees F.
With a scooper, scoop your pulp from zucchini halves, leaving about ¼-inch thick shell.
In a shallow roasting pan, arrange the zucchini halves, cut side up.
Sprinkle the zucchini halves which has a little salt.
In a pan of boiling water, cook the potatoes for around 2 minutes.
Drain well whilst aside.
In a nonstick skillet, heat oil on medium-high heat.
Add onion, Serrano, garlic and dinger and sauté for around 3 minutes.
Reduce the heat to medium-low.
Stir in chickpea flour and spices and cook for about 5 minutes.
Sir in cooked potato, green peas and cilantro and take off from heat.
With a paper towel, pat dry the zucchini halves.
Stuff the zucchini halves with all the veggie mixture evenly,
Bake, covered for about twenty or so minutes.
Nutrition:
Calories: 145, Fat: 3.5g, Carbohydrates: 24.9g, Fiber: 6g, Protein: 5.7g

580.   Stuffed Bell Peppers

A delicious recipe of stuffed sweet peppers that looks beautiful too. Your family would love to enjoy these stuffed bell peppers.
Servings: 4
Preparation Time: 15 minutes
Cooking Time: 23 minutes (plus time of brown rice
Ingredients:

1 cup brown rice, rinsed and drained
2 cups vegetable broth
1 tablespoon coconut oil
1 small can unsweetened sweet corn
1 (15-ouncecan kidney beans, rinsed and drained
2 teaspoons ground cumin
1 teaspoon ground turmeric
1 teaspoon garlic powder
1 teaspoon red chili powder
Salt and freshly ground black pepper, to taste
2 tablespoons fresh parsley, chopped
4 large peppers, tops and seeds removed
Directions:
Preheat the oven to 375 degrees F. Grease a large baking sheet.
Prepare the brown rice as outlined by package's directions in vegetable broth.
In a substantial nonstick skillet, melt coconut oil on medium heat.
Add cooked rice, corns, beans and spices and cook for around 2-3 minutes.
Stir in parsley and take off from heat.
Stuff the sweet peppers with rice mixture evenly.
Arrange the bell peppers in prepared baking sheet.
Bake for around 15-20 minutes.
Nutrition:
Calories: 199, Fat: 3g, Carbohydrates: 24g, Fiber: 5g, Protein: 10g

581. Veggies with Red Lentils

A filling dish that will satisfy you well. This dish gets its exotic flavors from spices, coconut oil and coconut milk.
Servings: 6
Preparation Time: 20 or so minutes
Cooking Time: 35 minutes
Ingredients:
2 tablespoons coconut oil
12 fresh curry leaves
1 teaspoon cumin seeds
1 teaspoon brown mustard seeds
1 medium onion, chopped finely
4 garlic cloves, chopped finely
3 tablespoons fresh ginger, minced
1 Serrano chile, chopped finely
1½ cups red lentils
1 teaspoon ground turmeric
Salt, to taste
(1 (14-ouncecan coconut milk
4½ cups water
2 cups cauliflower, cut into 1-inch florets
2½ cups butternut squash, peeled and cubed

1 large Yukon gold potato, peeled and cut into ½-inch cubes
2 tablespoons fresh lime juice
1 tablespoon garam masala
Directions:
In a sizable pan, melt coconut oil on medium-high heat.
Add curry leaves, cumin seeds and mustard seeds and sauté for around a few seconds.
Add onion and sauté approximately 5 minutes.
Add garlic, ginger and Serrano chile and sauté for approximately half a minute.
Add lentils, turmeric, salt, coconut milk and water and produce to your boil, stirring occasionally.
Stir inside the vegetables and again bring to your boil.
Reduce heat to low and simmer, covered for around 20-25 minutes or till desired doneness.
Stir in lime juice and garam masala and immediately, remove from heat.
Serve hot.
Nutrition:
Calories: 340, Fat: 10g, Carbohydrates: 47g, Fiber: 10g, Protein 12

582.   Veggies with Green Lentils

A vibrant, healthy and satisfying one-pot vegetables and lentil recipe. This one-pot meal is just delicious.
Servings: 4
Preparation Time: 20 minutes
Cooking Time: 37 minutes
Ingredients:
1 tbsp. extra virgin olive oil
1 onion, chopped
2 minced garlic cloves
1 teaspoon fresh ginger, minced
1 russet potato, peeled and chopped
1 large carrot, peeled and chopped
2celery stalks, chopped
1 zucchini, chopped
1½ cups green lentils, soaked for about 15 minutes and drained
3 cups canned tomatoes
1 teaspoon ground cumin
1 teaspoon ground coriander
1 teaspoon ground turmeric
½ teaspoon cayenne
Salt and freshly ground black pepper, to taste
2½ cups water
½ cup fresh parsley, chopped

Directions:

In a large pan, heat oil on medium heat.

Add onion, garlic and ginger and sauté for about 4-5 minutes.

Add vegetables and cook for about 5-7 minutes.

Stir in lentils, tomatoes, spices and water and bring to some boil.

Boil for around 5 minutes, stirring occasionally.

Reduce heat to low and simmer, covered for about twenty or so minutes.

Stir in parsley and remove from heat.

Nutrition:

Calories: 265, Fat: 4g, Carbohydrates: 21g, Fiber: 6g, Protein: 23g

583.   Veggies with Chickpeas

This dish is loaded using the delish flavors of chickpeas, vegetables and spices. Definitely whole family will want to eat this dish.

Servings: 2

Preparation Time: 20 minutes

Cooking Time: 25 minutes

Ingredients:

¼ cup onion, chopped

1 (1-inchfresh piece ginger, chopped

4 garlic cloves, chopped

2-3 tablespoons water

1 teaspoon organic olive oil

½ teaspoon ground coriander

½ teaspoon ground cumin

½ teaspoon ground turmeric

¼ teaspoon ground cardamom

¼ teaspoon ground cinnamon

1/3 teaspoon red pepper cayenne

½ cup coconut milk

3 tablespoons almond butter

¾ cup vegetable broth

1 (15-ouncecan chickpeas, rinsed and drained

½ cup zucchini, sliced

½ cup carrot, peeled and sliced

½ of red bell pepper, seeded and sliced

Crushed red pepper flakes, to taste

Salt and freshly ground black pepper, to taste

1 teaspoon fresh lime juice

¼ cup fresh cilantro, chopped

Directions:

In blender, add onion, ginger, garlic and water and pulse till smooth.

In a pan, heat oil on medium heat.

Add spices and sauté for about 30 seconds.

Reduce the temperature to medium-low.

Add onion mixture and sauté for about 7-9 minutes.

Add coconut milk and almond butter and stir to blend well.

Increase heat to medium-high.

Stir in broth, chickpeas, vegetables, red pepper flakes, salt and black pepper and bring to your boil for about 4 minutes.

Reduce the warmth to medium-low and simmer for approximately 5 minutes.

Stir in lime juice and cilantro and simmer for approximately 3-4 minutes.

Nutrition:

Calories: 188, Fat: 5g, Carbohydrates: 26g, Fiber: 14g, Protein: 36g

Salad Recipes

584. Nutty and Fruity Garden Salad

Preparation Time: 10 Minutes
Cooking Time: 10 Minutes
Servings: 2
Ingredients:
6 cups baby spinach
½ cup chopped walnuts, toasted
1 ripe red pear, sliced
1 ripe persimmon, sliced
1 teaspoon garlic minced
1 shallot, minced
3 tablespoons extra virgin olive oil
2 tablespoons fresh lemon juice
1 teaspoon whole grain mustard
Directions:
Mix well garlic, shallot, oil, lemon juice and mustard in a large salad bowl.
Add spinach, pear and persimmon. Toss to coat well.
To serve, garnish with chopped pecans.
Nutrition:
Calories 354, Total Fat 22g, Saturated Fat 3g, Total Carbs 37g, Net Carbs 28g, Protein 6.82g, Sugar: 20g, Fiber 9g, Sodium 225mg, Potassium 871mg

585. Salad Greens with Pear and Persimmon

Preparation Time: 10 Minutes
Cooking Time: 10 Minutes
Servings: 2
Ingredients:
6 cups baby spinach
½ cup chopped pecans, toasted
1 ripe red pear, sliced
1 ripe persimmon, sliced
1 tsp minced garlic
1 shallot, minced
3 tbsps extra virgin olive oil
2 tbsps fresh lemon juice
1 tsp whole grain mustard
Directions:
In a big mixing bowl, mix garlic, olive oil, lemon juice and mustard.
Once thoroughly mixed, add remaining ingredients.
Toss to coat.
Equally divide into two bowls, serve and enjoy.
Nutrition:

Calories 220, Total Fat 16g, Saturated Fat 3g, Total Carbs 12g, Net Carbs 8g, Protein 7g, Sugar: 2g, Fiber 5g, Sodium 368mg, Potassium 285mg

586. Salad Greens with Goat Cheese and Oregano Dressing

Preparation Time: 10 Minutes
Cooking Time: 0 Minutes
Servings: 4
Ingredients:
1/3 cup chopped red onion
¾ cup crumbled soft fresh goat cheese
1 ½ cups diced celery
1 ½ large red bell peppers, diced
4 cups baby spinach leaves, coarsely chopped
1 tbsp chopped fresh oregano
2 tbsps fresh lemon juice
2 tbsps extra virgin olive oil
Directions:
In a large salad bowl, mix oregano, lemon juice and oil.
Add pepper and salt to taste.
Mix in red onion, goat cheese, celery, bell peppers and spinach.
Toss to coat well, serve and enjoy.
Nutrition:
Calories 131, Total Fat 8g, Saturated Fat 1g, Total Carbs 12g, Net Carbs 6g, Protein 6.7g, Sugar: 3g, Fiber 6g, Sodium 151mg, Potassium 746mg

587. Delicious Herbed Kale and Flaxseed Salad

Preparation Time: 10 Minutes
Cooking Time: 10 Minutes
Servings: 4
Ingredients:
¼ cup Kalamata olives
1 garlic clove, minced
1 small cucumber, sliced thinly
2 tbsps green onion, chopped
2 tbsps red onion, minced
1 ½ tbsps flaxseeds
1 tbsp extra virgin olive oil
A pinch of salt
A pinch of dried basil
½ of a lemon
6 cups dinosaur kale, chopped
Directions:
Bring a medium pot, half-filled with water to a boil.
Rinse kale and cut into small strips. Place in a steamer and put on top of boiling water and steam for 5 – 7 minutes.

Transfer steamed kale to a salad bowl.

Season kale with oil, salt, basil and lemon. Toss to coat well.

Add remaining ingredients into salad bowl, toss to mix.

Serve and enjoy.

Nutrition:

Calories 90, Total Fat 5g, Saturated Fat 1g, Total Carbs 11.7g, Net Carbs g, Protein 3g, Sugar: 5g, Fiber 4g, Sodium 149mg, Potassium 304mg

588. Detox Salad

Preparation Time: 10 Minutes

Cooking Time: 0 Minutes

Servings: 4

Ingredients:

4 cups mixed greens

2 tbsps lemon juice

2 tbsps pumpkin seed oil

1 tbsps chia seeds

2 tbsps almonds, chopped

1 large apple, diced

1 large carrot, coarsely grated

1 large beet, coarsely grated

Directions:

In a medium salad bowl, except for mixed greens, combine all ingredients thoroughly.

Into 4 salad plates, divide the mixed greens.

Evenly top mixed greens with the salad bowl mixture.

Serve and enjoy.

Nutrition:

Calories 126, Total Fat 8g, Saturated Fat 1g, Total Carbs 15g, Net Carbs 11g, Protein 2g, Sugar: 9g, Fiber 4g, Sodium 137mg, Potassium 458mg

589. Grilled Egg Plant Salad

Preparation Time: 15 Minutes

Cooking Time: 15 Minutes

Servings: 4

Ingredients:

Parsley sprigs for garnish

1 lemon, zested

Freshly ground black pepper

Salt

Olive oil

Honey

1 tbsp coarsely chopped oregano leaves

1 tsp Dijon mustard

1 tbsp red wine vinegar

1 avocado, halved, pitted, peeled and cubed

Canola oil

1 large red onion, cut into rounds

1 Italian eggplant, cut into 1-inch thick slices

Directions:

With canola oil, brush onions and eggplant and place on grill.

Grill on high until onions are slightly charred and eggplants are soft around 5 minutes for onions and 8 to 12 minutes for eggplant.

Remove from grill and let cool for 5 minutes.

Roughly chop eggplants and onions and place in salad bowl.

Add avocado and toss to mix.

Whisk oregano, mustard and red wine vinegar in a small bowl.

Whisk in olive oil and honey to taste. Season with pepper and salt to taste.

Pour dressing to eggplant mixture, toss to mix well.

Garnish with parsley sprigs and lemon zest before.

Nutrition:

Calories 153, Total Fat 10g, Saturated Fat 1g, Total Carbs 17g, Net Carbs 9g, Protein 3g, Sugar: 8g, Fiber 8g, Sodium 23mg, Potassium 685mg

590. Ginger Yogurt Dressed Citrus Salad

Preparation Time: 15 Minutes

Cooking Time: 0 Minutes

Servings: 6

Ingredients:

2/3 cup minced crystallized ginger

1 16-oz Greek yogurt

¼ tsp ground cinnamon

2 tbsps honey

½ cup dried cranberries

3 navel oranges

2 large tangerines, peeled

1 pink grapefruit, peeled

Directions:

Into sections, break tangerines and grapefruit.

Cut tangerine sections into half.

Into thirds, slice grapefruit sections.

Cut orange pith and peel in half and slice oranges into ¼ inch thick rounds, then quartered.

In a medium bowl, mix oranges, grapefruit, tangerines and its juices.

Add cinnamon, honey and ½ cup of cranberries.

Cover and place in the ref for an hour.

In a small bowl, mix ginger and yogurt.

To serve, add a dollop of yogurt dressing onto a of fruit and sprinkle with cranberries.

Nutrition:

Calories 155, Total Fat 1g, Saturated Fat 0g, Total Carbs 31g, Net Carbs 28g, Protein 9g, Sugar: 24g, Fiber 3g, Sodium 31mg, Potassium 400mg

591. Goat Cheese 'n Red Beans on Salad

Preparation Time: 15 Minutes
Cooking Time: 0 Minutes
Servings: 6
Ingredients:
1 1/2 cups red grape tomatoes, halved
1 bunch parsley, chopped
1/2 teaspoon salt
1/2 teaspoon white pepper
2 cans of Red Kidney Beans, drained and rinsed well
3 cloves garlic, minced
3 tablespoons lemon juice
3 tablespoons olive oil
6 ounces goat cheese, crumbled
Water or vegetable broth to cover beans
Directions:
In a large bowl, combine beans, parsley, tomatoes and garlic.
Add olive oil, lemon juice, salt and pepper.
Mix well and refrigerate until ready to serve.
Spoon into individual dishes top with crumbled goat cheese.
Nutrition:
Calories 262, Total Fat 20g, Saturated Fat 4g, Total Carbs 12g, Net Carbs g, Protein 11g, Sugar: 7g, Fiber 1g, Sodium 414mg, Potassium 482mg

592.   Simple Greek Salad

Preparation Time: 10 Minutes
Cooking Time: 0 Minutes
Servings: 8
Ingredients:
½ red onion, sliced
1/3 cup diced oil packed dried tomatoes, oil drained and reserved
3 cups diced roma tomatoes
1 cup black olives, pitted and sliced
1 ½ cups crumbled feta cheese, optional
3 cucumbers, seeded and ribbon cut
Directions:
Mix thoroughly the red onion, 2 tbsp of reserved sun-dried tomato oil, sundried tomatoes, roma tomatoes, olives, feta cheese and cucumbers in a large salad bowl.
Serve and enjoy.
Nutrition:
Calories 123, Total Fat 9g, Saturated Fat 1g, Total Carbs 7g, Net Carbs g, Protein 5g, Sugar: 4g, Fiber 2g, Sodium 398mg, Potassium 326mg

593.   Blue Cheese, Fig and Arugula Salad

Preparation Time: 10 Minutes
Cooking Time: 0 Minutes

Servings: 4
Ingredients:
Pepper and salt to taste
3 tbsp olive oil
1 tsp Dijon mustard
3 tbsp Balsamic Vinegar
¼ cup crumbled blue cheese
2 bags arugula
1-pint fresh figs, quartered
Directions:
Whisk thoroughly together pepper, salt, olive oil, Dijon mustard, and balsamic vinegar to make the dressing. Set aside in the ref for at least 30 minutes to marinate and allow the spices to combine.
On four plates, evenly arrange arugula and top with blue cheese and figs.
Drizzle each plate of salad with 1 ½ tbsp of prepared dressing.
Serve and enjoy.
Nutrition:
Calories 143, Total Fat 13g, Saturated Fat 3g, Total Carbs 5g, Net Carbs g, Protein 3g, Sugar: 4g, Fiber 1g, Sodium 117mg, Potassium 127mg

594.   Veggie Slaw

Preparation Time: 10 Minutes
Cooking Time: 10 Minutes
Servings: 6
Ingredients:
2 tsp salt
2 tbsp Bavarian seasoning
½ cup lightly packed fresh mint leaves
½ cup fresh lemon juice
½ cup roasted and shelled pistachios, roughly chopped
6 oz dried cranberries
4 bacon strips, cooked to a crisp (keep rendered fatand chopped to bits
1/3 cup extra virgin olive oil (use rendered fat from bacon to reach ½ cup
2 lbs. Brussels sprouts, cleaned and trimmed of large stem pieces
Directions:
Shred Brussels sprouts in a food processor. Transfer into a large salad bowl.
In a small bowl mix salt, Bavarian seasoning, mint and lemon juice. Then slowly add oil while whisking continuously and vigorously. Add more seasoning to taste if needed.
Pour half of dressing into the salad bowl, toss to mix and add more if needed.
Top salad with bacon pieces, dried cranberries and pistachios before.
Nutrition:
Calories 272, Total Fat 18g, Saturated Fat 2g, Total Carbs 24g, Net Carbs 17g, Protein 8g, Sugar: 9g, Fiber 7g, Sodium 1070mg, Potassium 757mg

595.   Cucumber and Tomato Salad

Preparation Time: 10 Minutes

Cooking Time: 0 Minutes
Servings: 4
Ingredients:
Ground pepper to taste
Salt to taste
1 tbsp fresh lemon juice
1 onion, chopped
1 cucumber, peeled and diced
2 tomatoes, chopped
4 cups spinach
Directions:
In a salad bowl, mix onions, cucumbers and tomatoes.
Season with pepper and salt to taste.
Add lemon juice and mix well.
Add spinach, toss to coat, serve and enjoy.
Nutrition:
Calories 41, Total Fat 0g, Saturated Fat 0g, Total Carbs 9g, Net Carbs g, Protein 2g, Sugar: 4g, Fiber 2g, Sodium 29mg, Potassium 468mg

596. Grilled Eggplant Caprese

Preparation Time: 10 Minutes
Cooking Time: 10 Minutes
Servings: 4
Ingredients:
1 eggplant aubergine, small/medium
1 tomato large
2 basil leaves or a little more as needed
4-oz mozzarella
good quality olive oil
Pepper and salt to taste
Directions:
Cut the ends of the eggplant and then cut it lengthwise into ¼-inch thick slices. Discard the smaller pieces that's mostly skin and short.
Slice the tomatoes and mozzarella into thin slices just like the eggplant.
On medium-high the fire, place a griddle and let it heat up.
Brush eggplant slices with olive oil and place on grill. Grill for 3 minutes. Turnover and grill for a minute. Add a slice of cheese on one side and tomato on the other side. Continue cooking for another 2 minutes.
Sprinkle with basil leaves. Season with pepper and salt.
Fold eggplant in half and skewer with a cocktail stick.
Serve and enjoy.
Nutrition:
Calories 82, Total Fat 0g, Saturated Fat 0g, Total Carbs 11g, Net Carbs 6g, Protein 11g, Sugar: 7g, Fiber 5g, Sodium 216mg, Potassium 216mg

597. Caesar Salad Supreme

Preparation Time: 10 Minutes
Cooking Time: 0 Minutes
Servings: 2
Ingredients:
1 head romaine lettuce, torn into bite sized pieces
Ground black pepper to taste
Salt to taste
1 tbsp lemon juice
1 tsp Dijon mustard
1 tsp Worcestershire sauce
6 tbsps low-fat Parmesan cheese, grated and divided
5 anchovy filets, minced
½ cup low-fat mayonnaise
3 cloves garlic, peeled and minced
Directions:
In a small bowl, whisk well lemon juice, mustard, Worcestershire sauce, 2 tbsp Parmesan cheese, anchovies, mayonnaise, and minced garlic. Season with pepper and salt to taste. Set aside in the ref. In large bowl, place lettuce and pour in dressing. Toss well to coat. Top with remaining Parmesan cheese.
Serve, and enjoy.
Nutrition:
Calories 199, Total Fat 9g, Saturated Fat 2g, Total Carbs 15g, Net Carbs g, Protein 17g, Sugar: 6g, Fiber 7g, Sodium 708mg, Potassium 983mg

598.   Sunflower Seed, Grape, and Arugula Salad

Preparation Time: 10 Minutes
Cooking Time: 0 Minutes
Servings: 4
Ingredients:
¼ tsp ground black pepper
¼ tsp salt
1 tsp chopped fresh thyme
2 tbsps toasted sunflower seed kernels
2 cups red grapes, halved
7 cups loosely packed baby arugula
2 tsps grapeseed oil
½ tsp stone-ground mustard
1 tsp maple syrup
1 tsp honey
3 tbsps red wine vinegar
Directions:
In a small bowl, whisk well mustard, syrup, honey, and vinegar. Slowly add oil while whisking continuously.
In large salad bowl, mix thyme, seeds, grapes, and arugula.
Pour mustard mixture into bowl of salad and toss well to coat evenly with dressing.
Nutrition:

Calories 75, Total Fat 1g, Saturated Fat 1g, Total Carbs 18g, Net Carbs 17g, Protein 2g, Sugar: 15g, Fiber 1g, Sodium 157mg, Potassium 291mg

599. Spinach and Cranberry Salad

Preparation Time: 15 Minutes
Cooking Time: 5 Minutes
Servings: 4
Ingredients:
½ cup olive oil
¼ cup cider vinegar
¼ cup white wine vinegar
¼ tsp paprika
2 tsps minced onion
¼ cup honey
1 cup dried cranberries
1 lb spinach, rinsed and torn into bite sized pieces
½ cup pumpkin seeds
Directions:
Toast pumpkin seeds by placing in a nonstick saucepan on medium fire. Stir frequently and toast for at least 3 to 5 minutes. Remove from fire and set aside.
In a medium bowl, mix well olive oil, cider vinegar, white wine vinegar, paprika, onion, and honey. Whisk well until mixture is uniform.
In a large salad bowl, add torn spinach.
Drizzle with dressing and toss well to coat.
Garnish with cooled and toasted pumpkin seeds and dried cranberries.
Serve and enjoy.
Nutrition:
Calories 508, Total Fat 35g, Saturated Fat 5g, Total Carbs 45g, Net Carbs 40g, Protein 9g, Sugar: 34g, Fiber 5g, Sodium 145mg, Potassium 991mg

600. Fresh Carrot Salad

Preparation Time: 20 Minutes
Cooking Time: 0 Minutes
Servings: 4
Ingredients:
1 large avocado, diced
1 cup cherry tomatoes, halved
1 bunch scallions, sliced
4 cups carrots, spiralized
salt to taste
¼ tsp chipotle powder
1 tbsp chili powder
2 tbsps olive oil
1 tbsp lemon juice
3 tbsps lime juice

Directions:

In a salad bowl, mix and arrange avocado, cherry tomatoes, scallions and spiralized carrots. Set aside.

In a small bowl, whisk salt, chipotle powder, chili powder, olive oil, lemon juice and lime juice thoroughly.

Pour dressing over noodle salad. Toss to coat well.

Serve and enjoy at room temperature.

Nutrition:

Calories 25, Total Fat 8g, Saturated Fat 2g, Total Carbs 25g, Net Carbs 17g, Protein 3g, Sugar: 11g, Fiber 8g, Sodium 142mg, Potassium 747mg

601.   Winter Persimmon Salad

Preparation Time: 20 Minutes
Cooking Time: 0 Minutes
Servings: 2
Ingredients:
½ cup sweet potato, spiralized
2 fuyu persimmon, sliced
1 red bell pepper, julienned
4 cups mixed greens
salt to taste
3 tbsp lime juice
a pinch of chipotle powder
1 tbsp chili powder
1 ripe fuyu persimmon, diced
1 red bell pepper, diced
½ cup coarsely chopped pistachio
Directions:

In a salad bowl, mix and arrange persimmons, bell pepper and sweet potatoes. Set aside.

In a food processor, puree salt, lime juice, chipotle powder, chili powder, diced persimmon and diced bell pepper until smooth and creamy.

Pour over salad, toss to mix.

Serve and enjoy.

Nutrition:

Calories 346, Total Fat 15g, Saturated Fat 2g, Total Carbs 52g, Net Carbs 37g, Protein 11g, Sugar: 27g, Fiber 15g, Sodium 293mg, Potassium 1459mg

602.   Arugula Garden Salad

Preparation Time: 15 Minutes
Cooking Time: 0 Minutes
Servings: 2
Ingredients:
1 large avocado, sliced into ½ inch cubes
¼ cup grated parmesan cheese
Black pepper, freshly ground
Salt to taste

1 tbsp rice vinegar
2 tbsps olive oil or grapeseed oil
¼ cup pine nuts
1 cup cherry tomatoes, halved
4 cups young arugula leaves, rinsed and dried
Directions:
Get a bowl with cover, big enough to hold the salad and mix together the parmesan cheese, vinegar, oil, pine nuts, cherry tomatoes and arugula.
Season with pepper and salt according to how you like it. Place the lid and jiggle the covered bowl to combine the salad.
Serve the salad topped with sliced avocadoes.
Nutrition:
Calories 375, Total Fat 30g, Saturated Fat 5g, Total Carbs 24g, Net Carbs 15g, Protein 9g, Sugar: 11g, Fiber 9g, Sodium 242mg, Potassium 751mg

603. Tuna Salad Mediterranean Style

Preparation Time: 10 Minutes
Cooking Time: 10 Minutes
Servings: 3
Ingredients:
1 head lettuce
1 tbsp small capers, rinsed and drained
2 green onions, sliced
¼ cup drained and chopped roasted red peppers
¼ cup chopped pitted ripe olives
¼ cup Mayonnaise dressing with olive oil
2 pcs of 6 oz cans of tuna, drained and flaked
Directions:
With the exception of salad greens or bread, mix together all of the ingredients in a bowl. If desired, you can arrange it on top of salad greens.
Nutrition:
Calories 110, Total Fat 9g, Saturated Fat 1g, Total Carbs 3g, Net Carbs 2g, Protein 5g, Sugar: 1g, Fiber 1g, Sodium 354mg, Potassium 190mg

604. Grilled Vegetable Salad

Preparation Time: 15 Minutes
Cooking Time: 10 Minutes
Servings: 3
Ingredients:
¼ cup feta cheese
¼ cup fresh basil leaves
Pepper and salt to taste
¼ cup extra virgin olive oil, for brushing
1 red bell pepper, quartered, seeds and ribs removed
1 yellow bell pepper, quartered, seeds and ribs removed

1 medium onion, cut into ½ inch rings

1-pint cherry tomatoes

½ bunch asparagus, trimmed and cut into bite-size pieces

Directions:

Toss olive oil and vegetables in a big bowl. Season with salt and pepper.

Frill vegetables in a preheated griller for 5-7 minutes or until charred and tender.

Transfer veggies to a platter, add feta and basil.

In a separate small bowl, mix olive oil, balsamic vinegar, garlic seasoned with pepper and salt.

Drizzle dressing over vegetables and serve.

Nutrition:

Calories 231, Total Fat 21g, Saturated Fat 4g, Total Carbs 9g, Net Carbs 7g, Protein 4g, Sugar: 3g, Fiber 2g, Sodium 119mg, Potassium 312mg

605.   Coleslaw Asian Style

Preparation Time: 10 Minutes

Cooking Time: 10 Minutes

Servings: 10

Ingredients:

½ cup chopped fresh cilantro

6 green onions, chopped

2 carrots, julienned

2 red bell peppers, thinly sliced

2 cups shredded napa cabbage

2 cups thinly sliced red cabbage

5 cups thinly sliced green cabbage

1 ½ tbsps minced garlic

2 tbsps minced fresh ginger root

3 tbsps brown sugar

3 tbsps soy sauce

5 tbsps creamy peanut butter

6 tbsps vegetable oil

6 tbsps rice wine vinegar

Directions:

Mix thoroughly the following in a medium bowl: garlic, ginger, brown sugar, soy sauce, peanut butter, oil and rice vinegar.

In a separate bowl, blend well cilantro, green onions, carrots, bell pepper, napa cabbage, red cabbage and green cabbage. Pour in the peanut sauce above and toss to mix well.

Serve and enjoy.

Nutrition:

Calories 59, Total Fat 2g, Saturated Fat 0g, Total Carbs 10g, Net Carbs 7g, Protein 2g, Sugar: 4g, Fiber 3g, Sodium 237mg, Potassium 349mg

606.   Fennel and Pears Salad

Preparation Time: 10 Minutes

Cooking Time: 10 Minutes

Servings: 6
Ingredients:
2 tbsp olive oil
3 tbsp fresh lime juice
¼ cup chopped pistachios
¼ cup green onions, sliced
1 cup red bell pepper, diced
2 cups medium sized fennel bulb, thinly sliced
1 bunch watercress, trimmed
3 cups Asian pears, cut into matchstick size
Directions:
In a large salad bowl, mix pistachios, green onions, bell pepper, fennel, watercress and pears.
In a small bowl, mix vegetable oil and lime juice. Season with pepper and salt to taste.
Pour dressing to salad and gently mix before.
Nutrition:
Calories 199, Total Fat 7g, Saturated Fat 1g, Total Carbs 34g, Net Carbs 28g, Protein 3g, Sugar: 25g, Fiber 6g, Sodium 49mg, Potassium 508mg

607.   Fruity Salmon-Spinach Salad

Preparation Time: 10 Minutes
Cooking Time: 15 Minutes
Servings: 2
Ingredients:
2 tsp avocado oil
6 oz. wild caught salmon fillet with skin
1/3 cup raw pecans
½ cup cherry tomatoes
½ ripe nectarine
½ avocado
2 cups baby spinach leaves
Vinaigrette Ingredients:
Freshly ground black pepper to taste
¼ tsp Paleo Dijon style mustard
3 tsp walnut oil
2 tsp fresh lemon juice
Directions:
Place a cast iron pan on medium high fire and melt avocado oil. Preheat oven to 400oF.
Once oil is hat sear salmon on both sides for 2 minutes per side. Pop in oven and bake for 10 minutes.
In a small bowl whisk all vinaigrette ingredients until emulsified. Season with pepper to taste and set aside.
Chop pecans into small pieces. Chop avocado, tomatoes, and nectarines into bite-sized pieces and place in a large salad bowl.
Add spinach and chopped pecans in bowl. Pour dressing and toss to coat well.
Serve salad with roasted salmon on top.
Nutrition:

Calories 305, Total Fat 24g, Saturated Fat 3g, Total Carbs 23g, Net Carbs 15g, Protein 4g, Sugar: 13g, Fiber 8g, Sodium 29mg, Potassium 639mg

608.   Summer Jicama & Cabbage Slaw

Preparation Time: 20 Minutes
Cooking Time: 0 Minutes
Servings: 2
Ingredients:
1 handful parsley, finely chopped
½ lb. jicama, peeled, and sliced
½ red onion, sliced thinly
Salt to taste
½ head green cabbage, shredded
½ head purple cabbage, shredded
Dressing Ingredients:
¼ tsp salt
½ lemon, juiced
2 tbsp apple cider vinegar
1/3 cup extra virgin olive oil
½ cup warm filtered water
½ cup coconut concentrate warmed in a bowl of hot water
Directions:
In blender, add all dressing ingredients except for warm water. Puree until smooth and creamy. Add warm water by teaspoonful to reach desired consistency.
In a large salad bowl, add shredded cabbages and add salt. Massage for a minute or two to soften some tough fibers.
Add parsley, jicama, and red onion into bowl. Pour dressing and toss well to combine.
Serve and enjoy.
Nutrition:
Calories 143, Total Fat 1g, Saturated Fat 0g, Total Carbs 33g, Net Carbs g, Protein 6g, Sugar: 13g, Fiber 13g, Sodium 98mg, Potassium 1028mg

609.   Ginger-Broccoli Salad

Preparation Time: 20 Minutes
Cooking Time: 0 Minutes
Servings: 3
Ingredients:
¼ tsp sea salt
¼ tsp ground cinnamon
½ tsp ground turmeric
¾ tsp ground ginger
½ tbsp extra virgin olive oil
½ tbsp apple cider vinegar
2 tbsp chopped green onion
1/3 cup coconut cream

½ cup carrots, shredded

1 small head of broccoli, chopped

Directions:

In a large salad bowl, mix well salt, cinnamon, turmeric, ginger, olive oil, and vinegar.

Add remaining ingredients, tossing well to coat.

Pop in the ref for at least 30 to 60 minutes before.

Nutrition:

Calories 113, Total Fat 10g, Saturated Fat 2g, Total Carbs 5g, Net Carbs 3g, Protein 2g, Sugar: 1g, Fiber 2g, Sodium 233mg, Potassium 198mg

610.   Oregano Dressing on Salad Greens

Preparation Time: 15 Minutes

Cooking Time: 0 Minutes

Servings: 4

Ingredients:

1/3 cup chopped red onion

¾ cup crumbled soft fresh goat cheese

1 ½ cups diced celery

1 ½ large red bell peppers, diced

4 cups baby spinach leaves, coarsely chopped

1 tbsp chopped fresh oregano

2 tbsp fresh lemon juice

2 tbsp extra virgin olive oil

Directions:

In a large salad bowl, mix oregano, lemon juice and oil.

Add pepper and salt to taste.

Mix in red onion, goat cheese, celery, bell peppers and spinach.

Toss to coat well, serve and enjoy.

Nutrition:

Calories 91, Total Fat 4g, Saturated Fat 0g, Total Carbs 11g, Net Carbs 5g, Protein 6g, Sugar: 3g, Fiber 6g, Sodium 207mg, Potassium 720mg

611.   Simple Arugula-Craisins Salad

Preparation Time: 10 Minutes

Cooking Time: 0 Minutes

Servings: 1

Ingredients:

1 cup baby arugula

1 cup spinach

1 tbsp craisins

1 tbsp almonds, shaved or chopped

1 tbsp balsamic vinegar

½ tbsp extra virgin olive oil

Directions:

In a plate, mix arugula and spinach.

Top with craisins and almonds.

Drizzle olive oil and balsamic vinegar.

Serve and enjoy.

Nutrition:

Calories 83, Total Fat 4g, Saturated Fat 0g, Total Carbs 11g, Net Carbs 9g, Protein 2g, Sugar: 8g, Fiber 2g, Sodium 93mg, Potassium 273mg

612.   Nutty 'n Warm Brussels Sprouts Salad

Preparation Time: 10 Minutes

Cooking Time: 10 Minutes

Servings: 4

Ingredients:

1 ½ tbsp toasted walnuts, finely chopped

1/8 tsp black pepper

¼ tsp salt

¾ lb. Brussels sprouts

1/3 cup fresh breadcrumbs

1 garlic clove, minced

1 ½ tsp olive oil, divided

Directions:

Slice Brussels sprouts in half then separate the leaves from the cores. Cut the cores in quarters and set aside.

On medium fire, place a large nonstick saucepan and heat 1 tsp oil. Sauté garlic for a minute.

Add breadcrumbs and sauté for another minute or until lightly browned. Transfer to a bowl.

In same pan, add remaining oil and cook Brussels sprouts until crisp tender around 8 minutes.

Transfer to bowl, pour in breadcrumb mixture and toss to mix.

Garnish with nuts before

Nutrition:

Calories 71, Total Fat 4g, Saturated Fat 0g, Total Carbs 8g, Net Carbs 4g, Protein 4g, Sugar: 2g, Fiber 4g, Sodium 167mg, Potassium 351mg

613.   Salad Greens with Roasted Beets

Preparation Time: 10 Minutes

Cooking Time: 60 Minutes

Servings: 4

Ingredients:

½ cup chopped walnuts

4 cups baby spinach

½ teaspoon Dijon mustard

1 tablespoon minced red onions

2 tablespoons sherry vinegar

¼ cup extra-virgin olive oil

3 medium beets, washed and trimmed

1 tablespoon dried cranberries, chopped roughly

Directions:

In foil, wrap beets and bake in a preheated 400oF oven. Bake until beets are tender, around 1 hour. Once done, open foil and allow to cool. When cool to touch, peel beets and dice.

Mix well mustard, red onions, vinegar, and olive oil. Mix in spinach, beets and cranberries. Toss to coat well.

Nutrition:

Calories 130, Total Fat 13g, Saturated Fat 1g, Total Carbs 3g, Net Carbs 2g, Protein 3g, Sugar: 1g, Fiber 1g, Sodium 147mg, Potassium 227mg

614.   Green Pasta Salad

Preparation Time: 15 Minutes
Cooking Time: 30 Minutes
Servings: 4
5 Ingredients:
2 cups tubular pasta
2 cups green beans, chopped
2 cups shredded spinach
½ cup parmesan cheese
3 cloves of garlic
Salt to taste
4 tablespoons olive oil
Directions:
Cook the pasta according to package instructions. Drain then set aside.
Heat a little olive oil in a skillet over medium heat and add the green beans and garlic. Sauté for 3 to 5 minutes.
Toss the pasta together with the sautéed green beans and garlic. Add in the spinach and parmesan cheese.
Season with salt.
Toss to coat.
Nutrition:
Calories: 280; Fat: 18g; Carbs: 25g; Protein: 7g

615.   Tomato, Peach, And Burrata Salad

Preparation Time: 5 Minutes
Cooking Time: 15 Minutes
Servings: 4
5 Ingredients:
1/3 cup balsamic vinegar
2 large tomatoes, cut into piece
2 large peaches, pitted and cut into pieces
6 ounces burrata cheese, cut into cubes
3 tablespoons chopped basil
Salt to taste
Directions:
Make balsamic reduction by boiling the balsamic vinegar over low heat for 15 minutes. Remove from the heat and set aside.

Arrange the tomatoes, peaches, and cheese on a platter.
Drizzle with balsamic reduction and season with salt to taste.
Garnish with basil.
Nutrition:
Calories: 197; Fat: 11g; Carbs: 17g; Protein: 9g

616.   Watermelon and Cucumber Salad

Preparation Time: 10 Minutes
Cooking Time: 0 Minutes
Servings: 10
5 Ingredients:
½ large watermelon, diced
1 cucumber, peeled and diced
1 red onion, chopped
¼ cup feta cheese
½ cup balsamic vinegar
Salt to taste
Directions:
Place all ingredients in a bowl.
Toss everything to coat.
Place in the fridge to cool before.
Nutrition:
Calories: 24; Fat: 0g; Carbs: 3g; Protein: 0.8g

617.   Pasta Salad

Preparation Time: 5 Minutes
Cooking Time: 10 Minutes
Servings: 4
5 Ingredients:
1-pound dry whole wheat pasta
¾ cup red peppers, seeded and chopped
¾ cup commercial basil pesto
1 small mozzarella cheese ball, diced
3 handfuls of arugulas, washed
Water for boiling
Salt and pepper to taste
Directions:
Boil water in a stock pot and cook the pasta according to package instructions. Drain and allow to cool.
Mix all ingredients in a salad bowl and toss to coat.
Season with salt and pepper to taste.
Nutrition:
Calories: 461; Fat: 6g; Carbs: 88g; Protein: 20g

618.   Marinated Kale Salad

Preparation Time: 10 Minutes
Cooking Time: 0 Minutes
Servings: 2
5 Ingredients:
1 bunch curly kale, washed and torn
1 tablespoon almond butter
2 1/2 tablespoons apple cider vinegar
2 tablespoons liquid aminos or soy sauce
1 tablespoon agave nectar or honey
None
Directions:
Place all ingredients in a container.
Allow to marinate in the fridge for at least 10 minutes before.
Nutrition:
Calories: 114; Fat: 5g; Carbs: 16g; Protein: 4g

619.   Israeli Salad Recipe

Preparation Time:10 Minutes
Cooking Time: 0 Minutes
Servings: 4
5 Ingredients:
2 cups diced cherry tomatoes
2 cups cucumber, diced
¼ cup red onion, sliced
¼ cup chopped mint
2 tablespoons olive oil
Salt to taste
1 tablespoon lemon juice
Directions:
Place all ingredients in salad bowl.
Toss to mix everything.
Place inside the fridge to chill.
Nutrition:
Calories: 81; Fat: 6g; Carbs: 8g; Protein: 1g

620.   Strawberry, Cucumber, And Mozzarella Salad

Preparation Time: 10 Minutes
Cooking Time: 0 Minutes
Servings: 3
5 Ingredients:
5 ounces organic salad greens of your choice
2 medium cucumber, spiralized
2 cups strawberries, hulled and chopped
8 ounces mini mozzarella cheese balls
½ cup balsamic vinegar

Salt to taste
Directions:
Toss all ingredients in a salad bowl.
Allow to chill in the fridge for at least 10 minutes before.
Nutrition:
Calories: 287; Fat: 21g; Carbs: 14g; Protein: 11g

621. Citrusy Brussels Sprouts Salad

Preparation Time: 15 Minutes
Cooking Time: 3 Minutes
Servings: 6
5 Ingredients:
2 tablespoons olive oil
1-pound Brussels sprouts
1 cup walnuts
Juice from 1 lemon
½ cup grated parmesan cheese
Salt and pepper to taste
Directions:
Heat oil in a skillet over medium flame and sauté the Brussels sprouts for 3 minutes until slightly wilted. Removed from heat and allow to cool.
In a bowl, toss together the cooled Brussels sprouts and the rest of the ingredients.
Toss to coat.
Nutrition:
Calories: 259; Fat: 23g; Carbs: 12g; Protein: 6g

622. Crunchy and Salty Cucumber Salad

Preparation Time: 10 Minutes
Cooking Time: 0 Minutes
Servings: 4
5 Ingredients:
2 candy-striped (Chioggiabeets, trimmed and peeled
2 Persian cucumbers, sliced thinly
1 medium radish, trimmed and sliced thinly
Juice from 1 lemon
½ cup parmesan cheese, shredded
A dash of flaky sea salt
A dash of ground black pepper
Olive oil for drizzling
Directions:
Place all vegetables in a bowl.
Stir in the lemon juice and parmesan cheese.
Season with salt and pepper to taste
Add olive oil or salad oil.
Toss to mix everything.

Nutrition:
Calories: 71; Fat: 4g; Carbs: 6g; Protein: 4g

623. Celery Salad

Preparation Time: 5 Minutes
Cooking Time: 0 Minutes
Servings: 4
5 Ingredients:
3 cups celery, thinly sliced
½ cup parmigiana cheese, shaved
1/3 cup toasted walnuts
3 tablespoons extra virgin olive oil
1 tablespoon red wine vinegar
Salt and pepper to taste
Directions:
Place the celery, cheese, and walnuts in a bowl.
In a smaller bowl, combine the olive oil and vinegar. Season with salt and pepper to taste. Whisk to combine everything.
Drizzle over the celery, cheese, and walnuts. Toss to coat.
Nutrition:
Calories: 142; Fat: 4g; Carbs: 13g; Protein: 4

624. Grilled Corn Salad with Feta Cheese

Preparation Time: 5 Minutes
Cooking Time: 15 Minutes
Servings: 6
5 Ingredients:
6 large ears of corn, peeled and hulled
¼ cup chopped red onion
½ cup Feta cheese, crumbled
2 tablespoon extra-virgin olive oil
Chopped mint for garnish
Salt and pepper to taste
Directions:
Heat the grill to medium high and grill the corn for 12 minutes.
Cut the kernels off the cob and place on a bowl.
Add the rest of the ingredients and toss to mix everything.
Nutrition:
Calories: 153; Fat: 8g; Carbs: 18g; Protein: 5g

625. Pear and Pomegranate Salsa

Preparation Time: 10 Minutes
Cooking Time: 0 Minutes
Servings: 3

5 Ingredients:
2 fresh pears, cored and diced
Seeds from 1 fresh pomegranate
½ onion, diced
½ cup fresh cilantro leaves, chopped
Juice from ½ lime
Salt and pepper to taste
Directions:
Toss all ingredients in a bowl to combine.
Serve immediately.
Best served with grilled meats.
Nutrition:
Calories: 122; Fat: 1g; Carbs: 29g; Protein:2 g

626.   Lentil Tomato Salad

Preparation Time: 5 Minutes
Cooking Time: 0 Minutes
Servings: 4
5 Ingredients:
15 ounces canned lentils, rinsed and drained
1 ½ cups cherry tomatoes, sliced
¼ cup white wine vinegar
1/8 cup chives
1 tablespoon olive oil
Salt and pepper to taste
Directions:
Put all ingredients in a bowl.
Toss to combine.
Serve immediately.
Nutrition:
Calories: 231; Fat: 12g; Carbs: 23g; Protein: 10g

627.   Asparagus Niçoise Salad

Preparation Time: 20 Minutes
Cooking Time: 20 Minutes
Servings: 4
5 Ingredients:
1-pound small red potatoes, cleaned and halved
1-pound fresh asparagus, trimmed and halved
2 ½ ounces white tuna in water
½ cup pitted Greek olives, halved
½ cup zesty Italian salad dressing
Water for boiling
Salt and pepper to taste
Directions:

Boil water in a stockpot over medium flame.

Put in the potatoes and cook for 20 minutes or the potatoes are tender.

Blanch the asparagus for 3 minutes and set aside.

Place all ingredients in a bowl.

Toss to mix all ingredients.

Serve.

Nutrition:

Calories: 223; Fat: 8g; Carbs: 23g; Protein: 16g

628.   Bacon and Pea Salad

Preparation Time: 10 Minutes

Cooking Time: 5 Minutes

Servings: 6

5 Ingredients:

4 bacon strips

4 cups fresh peas

½ cup shredded cheddar cheese

½ cup ranch salad dressing

1/3 cup chopped red onions

Salt and pepper to taste

Directions:

Heat skillet over medium flame and fry the bacon until crispy or until the fat has rendered. Transfer into a plate lined with paper towel and crumble.

In a bowl, combine the rest of the ingredients and toss to coat.

Add in the bacon bits last.

Nutrition:

Calories: 218; Fat: 14g; Carbs: 14g; Protein: 9g

629.   Insalata Caprese

Preparation Time: 10 Minutes

Cooking Time: 0 Minutes

Servings: 8

5 Ingredients:

2 ½ pounds tomatoes, cut into 1-inch pieces

8 ounces mozzarella cheese pearls

½ cup ripe olives, pitted

¼ cup fresh basil, sliced thinly

Balsamic vinegar (optional

Salt and pepper to taste

3 tablespoons olive oil

Directions:

Place all ingredients in a bowl.

Season with salt and pepper to taste. Drizzle with balsamic vinegar if available.

Toss to coat.

Serve immediately.

Nutrition:
Calories: 160; Fat: 12g; Carbs: 7g; Protein: 6g

630.   Salmon Salad with Walnuts

Preparation Time: 10 Minutes
Cooking Time: 10 Minutes
Servings: 2
5 Ingredients:
2 salmon fillets
6 tablespoons balsamic vinaigrette, divided
1/8 teaspoon pepper
4 cups mixed salad greens
1/4 cup walnuts
2 tablespoons crumbled cheese
Salt and pepper to taste
Directions:
Brush the salmon with half of the balsamic vinaigrette and sprinkle with pepper.
Grill the salmon over medium heat for 5 minutes on each side.
Crumble the salmon and place in a mixing bowl. Add the rest of the ingredients and season with salt and pepper to taste.
Nutrition:
Calories: 374; Fat: 25g; Carbs: 13g; Protein: 24g

631.   Salmon White Bean Spinach Salad

Preparation Time: 10 Minutes
Cooking Time: 10 Minutes
Servings: 4
5 Ingredients:
4 salmon fillets
15 ounces great northern beans, rinsed and drained
½ cup commercial vinaigrette of your choice
11 ounces baby spinach
1 red onion, cut into thin slices
Salt and pepper to taste
Directions:
Season the salmon fillets with salt and pepper.
Place in a baking pan and bake for 4000F for 10 minutes or until the fish becomes flaky. Cool slightly.
In a large bowl, toss the beans and vinaigrette. Toss in the spinach and onions.
Divide the salad among four plates and top with salmon.
Nutrition:
Calories: 577; Fat: 17; Carbs: 26; Protein: 76g

632.   Balsamic Cucumber Salad

Preparation Time: 10 Minutes
Cooking Time: 0 Minutes
Servings: 6
5 Ingredients:
1 large English cucumber, halved and sliced
2 cups grape tomatoes, halved
1 medium red onion, sliced thinly
½ cup balsamic vinaigrette
¾ cup feta cheese
Salt and pepper to taste
Directions:
Place all ingredients in a bowl.
Toss to coat everything with the dressing.
Allow to chill before.
Nutrition:
Calories: 90; Fat: 5g; Carbs: 9g; Protein: 4g

633.   Sour Cream and Cucumbers

Preparation Time: 15 Minutes
Cooking Time: 0 Minutes
Servings: 8
5 Ingredients:
½ cup sour cream
3 tablespoons white vinegar
1 tablespoon sugar
4 medium cucumbers, sliced thinly
1 small sweet onion, sliced thinly
Salt and pepper to taste
Directions:
In a bowl, whisk the sour cream, vinegar, and sugar. Season with salt and pepper to taste. Whisk until well-combined.
Add in the cucumber and the rest of the ingredients.
Toss to coat.
Allow to chill before.
Nutrition:
Calories: 62; Fat: 3g; Carbs: 7g; Protein: 2g

634.   Minty Watermelon Cucumber Salad

Preparation Time: 10 Minutes
Cooking Time: 0 Minutes
Servings: 12
5 Ingredients:
8 cups cubed seedless watermelon
2 English cucumbers, halved and sliced
¼ cup minced fresh mint

¼ cup balsamic vinegar
¼ cup olive oil
Salt and pepper to taste
Directions:
Place everything in a bowl and toss to coat everything.
Allow to chill before.
Nutrition:
Calories: 60; Fat: 3g; Carbs: 9g; Protein: 1g

635.   Easy Kale Salad

Preparation Time: 10 Minutes
Cooking Time: 0 Minutes
Servings: 8
5 Ingredients:
10 cups kale, sliced thinly
1 apple, thinly sliced
3 tablespoons olive oil
2 tablespoons lemon juice
¼ cup crumbled feta cheese
Salt and pepper to taste
Directions:
Place kale in a bowl and massage kale until the leaves become soft and darkened.
Add in the apples.
In another bowl, whisk the oil, lemon juice, salt, and pepper.
Drizzle the sauce over the kale and sprinkle with cheese on top.
Nutrition:
Calories: 113; Fat: 9g; Carbs: 6g; Protein: 4g

636.   Pear Blue Cheese Salad

Preparation Time: 10 Minutes
Cooking Time: 0 Minutes
Servings: 10
5 Ingredients:
12 cups romaine lettuce, torn
2/3 cup balsamic vinegar
2 medium pears, sliced
2/3 cup crumbled blue cheese
2/3 cup glazed pecans
Salt and pepper to taste
Directions:
Toss all ingredients in a bowl to combine.
Allow to chill before.
Nutrition:
Calories: 133; Fat: 8g; Carbs: 12g; Protein: 3g

637. Salad Greens with Garlic Maple Salad

Preparation Time:10 Minutes
Cooking Time: 0 Minutes
Servings: 4
5 Ingredients:
2 pounds mixed salad greens, washed
1/3 cup olive oil
¼ cup maple syrup
3 cloves of garlic, minced
Juice from 1 lemon
Salt and pepper to taste
Directions:
Place the salad greens in a bowl.
In a smaller bowl, combine the olive oil, maple syrup, garlic, and lemon juice. Season with salt and pepper to taste.
Drizzle over the salad greens and toss.
Nutrition:
Calories: 145; Fat:12 g; Carbs: 10g; Protein: 1g

638. Citrus Avocado Spinach Salad

Preparation Time: 10 Minutes
Cooking Time: 0 Minutes
Servings: 8
5 Ingredients:
8 cups baby spinach; washed and drained
3 cups orange segments, seeded and halved
2 medium ripe avocadoes, peeled and sliced
1 cup blue cheese, crumbled
Salad dressing of your choice
Salt and pepper to taste
Directions:
Place the spinach, oranges, and avocado slices in a bowl.
Add in the cheese and drizzle with the salad dressing of your choice.
Toss to coat everything.
Nutrition:
Calories: 168; Fat:10g; Carbs: 16g; Protein: 5g

639. Kale And Brussels Sprouts Salad

Preparation Time: 10 Minutes
Cooking Time: 0 Minutes
Servings: 6
5 Ingredients:
1 small bunch kale, thinly sliced
½ pound fresh Brussels sprouts, thinly sliced

½ cup pistachios, chopped coarsely
½ cup honey mustard salad dressing
¼ cup parmesan cheese, shredded
Salt and pepper to taste
Directions:
Place all ingredients in a salad bowl.
Toss to coat everything.
Serve.
Nutrition:
Calories: 207; Fat: 14g; Carbs: 16g; Protein: 7g

640.   Pesto Tomato Cucumber Salad

Preparation Time: 10 Minutes
Cooking Time: 0 Minutes
Servings: 8
5 Ingredients:
½ cup Italian salad dressing
¼ cup prepared pesto
3 large tomatoes, sliced
2 medium cucumbers, halved and sliced
1 small red onion, sliced
Salt and pepper to taste
Directions:
In a bowl, whisk the salad dressing and pesto. Season with salt and pepper to taste.
Toss gently to incorporate everything.
Refrigerate before.
Nutrition:
Calories: 82; Fat: 5g; Carbs: 7g; Protein: 2g

641.   Easy Asian Style Chicken Slaw

Preparation Time: 10 Minutes
Cooking Time: 0 Minutes
Servings: 8
5 Ingredients:
3 ounces ramen noodles, cooked according to package Directions:
1 leftover rotisserie chicken, skin removed and shredded
16 ounces coleslaw mix
1 cup toasted sesame salad dressing
6 green onions, finely chopped
Salt and pepper to taste
Directions:
Place the noodles in a bowl and top with the chicken and coleslaw mix.
Drizzle with sesame salad dressing and season with salt and pepper to taste.
Mix and garnish with green onions last.
Nutrition:

Calories: 267; Fat: 10g; Carbs: 18g; Protein: 26g

642. Cucumber and Red Onion Salad

Preparation Time: 10 Minutes
Cooking Time: 0 Minutes
Servings: 4
5 Ingredients:
2 small English cucumbers, sliced thinly
1 cup red onion, sliced thinly
2 tablespoons white wine vinegar
½ teaspoon sugar
¼ teaspoon sesame oil
Salt and pepper to taste
Directions:
Put the cucumbers and red onions in a bowl.
In a small bowl, mix the white vinegar, sugar, and sesame oil. Season with salt and pepper to taste.
Pour over the cucumber and onions.
Toss to coat the ingredients.
Nutrition:
Calories: 31; Fat: 1g; Carbs: 7g; Protein: 1g

643. Bacon Tomato Salad

Preparation Time: 15 Minutes
Cooking Time: 0 Minutes
Servings: 6
5 Ingredients:
12 ounces iceberg lettuce blend
2 cups grape tomatoes, halved
¾ cup coleslaw salad dressing
¾ cup cheddar cheese, shredded
12 bacon strips, cooked and crumbled
Salt and pepper to taste
Directions:
Put the lettuce and tomatoes in a salad bowl.
Drizzle with the dressing and sprinkle with cheese. Season with salt and pepper to taste then mix.
Garnish with bacon bits on top.
Nutrition:
Calories: 268; Fat: 20g; Carbs: 11g; Protein: 10g

Soups and stews

644. Ginger and Spice Carrot Soup

Preparation Time: 10 Minutes
Cooking Time: 30 Minutes
Servings: 6
Ingredients:
¼ cup Greek yogurt
2 tsp fresh lime juice
5 cups low-salt chicken broth
1 ½ tsp finely grated lime peel
4 cups of carrots, peeled, thinly sliced into rounds
2 cups chopped onions
1 tbsp minced and peeled fresh ginger
½ tsp curry powder
3 tbsp expeller-pressed sunflower oil
½ tsp yellow mustard seeds
1 tsp coriander seeds
Directions:
In a food processor, grind mustard seeds and coriander into a powder.
On medium high fire, place a large pot and heat oil.
Add curry powder and powdered seeds and sauté for a minute.
Add ginger, cook for a minute.
Add lime peel, carrots and onions. Sauté for 3 minutes or until onions are softened.
Season with pepper and salt.
Add broth and bring to a boil. Reduce fire to a simmer and simmer uncovered for 20 minutes or until carrots are tender.
Cool broth slightly, and puree in batches. Return pureed carrots into pot.
Add lime juice, add more pepper and salt to taste.
Transfer to a bowl, drizzle with yogurt and serve.
Nutrition:
Calories 94, Total Fat 8g, Saturated Fat 1g, Total Carbs 5g, Net Carbs 4g, Protein 2g, Sugar: 3g, Fiber 1g, Sodium 811mg, Potassium 99mg

645. Turmeric Chickpeas Chowder

Preparation Time: 10 Minutes
Cooking Time: 100 Minutes
Servings: 8
Ingredients:
1 14.5-oz can of petite diced tomatoes, undrained
2 15-oz cans garbanzo beans, rinsed and drained
1 cup lentils
6 cups vegetable broth or stock
¼ tsp ground cayenne pepper
½ tsp ground cumin

1 tsp turmeric

1 tsp garam masala

1 tsp minced garlic

2 tsp grated fresh ginger

1 cup diced carrots

1 cup chopped celery

2 onions, chopped

1 tbsp olive oil

Directions:

On medium high fire, set a large soup pot and heat oil.

Add onions and cook until tender around 3-4 minutes.

Add celery and carrots, continue sautéing for 5 minutes.

Add garlic, cayenne pepper, cumin, turmeric and garam masala and cook until heated through.

Add tomatoes, garbanzo beans, lentils and broth. Cook while covered for 90 minutes or until lentils are tender.

If desired, you can puree half of the soup to make a thick broth.

Serve while hot.

Nutrition:

Calories 212, Total Fat 5g, Saturated Fat 0.6g, Total Carbs 34g, Net Carbs 25g, Protein 10g, Sugar: 8g, Fiber 9g, Sodium 847mg, Potassium 406mg

646. Garbanzo and Lentil Soup

Preparation Time: 10 Minutes

Cooking Time: 10 Minutes

Servings: 8

Ingredients:

1 14.5-oz can petite diced tomatoes, undrained

2 15-oz cans Garbanzo beans, rinsed and drained

1 cup lentils

6 cups vegetable broth

¼ tsp ground cayenne pepper

½ tsp ground cumin

1 tsp turmeric

1 tsp garam masala

1 tsp minced garlic

2 tsp grated fresh ginger

1 cup diced carrots

1 cup chopped celery

2 onions, chopped

Directions:

On medium high fire, place a heavy bottomed large pot and grease with cooking spray.

Add onions and sauté until tender, around three to four minutes.

Add celery and carrots. Cook for another five minutes.

Add cayenne pepper, cumin, garam masala and garlic, cook for half a minute.

Add diced tomatoes, garbanzo beans, lentils and vegetable broth. Bring to a boil.

Once boiling, slow fire to a simmer and cook while covered for 90 minutes. Occasionally stir soup.

If you want a thicker and creamier soup, you can puree ½ of the pot's content and mix in.
Once lentils are soft, turn off fire and serve.
Nutrition:
Calories 196, Total Fat 3g, Saturated Fat 0.2g, Total Carbs 36g, Net Carbs 27g, Protein 9g, Sugar: 9g, Fiber 9g, Sodium 723mg, Potassium 387mg

647.   Pumpkin Soup

Preparation Time: 10 Minutes
Cooking Time: 40 Minutes
Servings: 8
Ingredients:
1 tsp chopped fresh parsley
½ cup half and half
½ tsp chopped fresh thyme
1 tsp salt
4 cups pumpkin puree
6 cups vegetable stock, divided
1 clove garlic, minced
1 1-inch piece gingerroot, peeled and minced
1 cup chopped onion
Directions:
On medium high fire, place a heavy bottomed pot and for 5 minutes heat ½ cup vegetable stock, ginger, garlic and onions or until veggies are tender.
Add remaining stock and cook for 30 minutes.
Season with thyme and salt.
With an immersion blender, puree soup until smooth.
Turn off fire and mix in half and half.
Transfer pumpkin soup into 8 bowls, garnish with parsley, serve and enjoy.
Nutrition:
Calories 66, Total Fat 1g, Saturated Fat 0.4g, Total Carbs 14g, Net Carbs 10g, Protein 3g, Sugar: 5g, Fiber 4g, Sodium 906mg, Potassium 325mg

648.   Cold Cucumber Soup

Preparation Time: 15 Minutes
Cooking Time: 0 Minutes
Servings: 4
Ingredients:
Chopped fresh dill
Pepper and salt to taste
1 cup fat free plain yogurt
1 ½ cups fat free half and half
1 ½ cups low-sodium chicken broth
Juice of 1 lemon
½ cup chopped fresh parsley
6 medium cucumbers, peeled, halved lengthwise, seeds scraped out and chopped

Directions:

In a blender, puree lemon juice, parsley and cucumbers.

Pour half of puree in a bowl and put aside.

In blender, add yogurt plus half and half on remaining pureed cucumber. Mix with a spoon before pureeing to mix well.

Pour back into blender the cucumber puree in a bowl, puree again to mix.

Season with pepper and salt.

Puree to mix.

Refrigerate for at least two hours before cold.

Nutrition:

Calories 150, Total Fat 3, Saturated Fat 1.6g, Total Carbs 22g, Net Carbs 19g, Protein 10g, Sugar: 14g, Fiber 3g, Sodium 168mg, Potassium 902mg

649. Creamy Halibut Soup

Preparation Time: 5 Minutes

Cooking Time: 25 Minutes

Servings: 5

Ingredients:

1 tablespoon olive oil

2 cloves of garlic, minced

1 onion, diced

2 med potatoes, peeled and cubed

6 cups chicken broth

1 cup tomatoes, chopped

2 large carrots, chopped

1 ½ cups coconut milk

2 pounds halibut, chunk

A pinch of red pepper flakes

Salt and pepper to taste

Directions:

Place a heavy bottomed pot on high fire and heat pot for 2 minutes. Add oil and heat for a minute.

Sauté the garlic and onions until fragrant, around 3 minutes.

Stir in the rest of the ingredients.

Cover and bring to a boil. Once boiling, lower fire to a simmer and simmer for 20 minutes.

Adjust seasoning to taste if needed.

Serve and enjoy.

Nutrition:

Calories 172, Total Fat 6.5g, Saturated Fat 3.5g, Total Carbs 12.5g, Net Carbs 5.3g, Protein 15.4g, Sugar:0.8 g, Fiber 7.2g, Sodium 364mg, Potassium 186g

650. Cod and Parsnip Chowder

Preparation Time: 10 Minutes

Cooking Time: 20 Minutes

Servings: 6

Ingredients:

1-pound cod fillets, sliced
½ lemon, freshly squeezed
1 sprig fresh thyme
1-pound parsnips, chopped
½ pound potatoes, peeled and sliced
1 onion, chopped
1 cup coconut milk
Salt and pepper to taste
Directions:
Add all ingredients in a heavy bottomed pot and mix well.
Bring to a boil. Once boiling, lower fire to a simmer and cook for 20 minutes.
Adjust seasoning to taste.
Serve and enjoy.
Nutrition:
Calories 174, Total Fat 2g, Saturated Fat 1g, Total Carbs 25g, Net Carbs 20g, Protein 15g, Sugar: 7g, Fiber 5g, Sodium 258mg, Potassium 730mg

651.   Summer Veggies Stew

Preparation Time: 10 Minutes
Cooking Time: 30 Minutes
Servings: 6
Ingredients:
2 cups okra, sliced
1 cup grape tomatoes
1 cup mushroom, sliced
1 ½ cups onion, sliced
2 cups bell pepper, sliced
2 ½ cups zucchini, sliced
2 tablespoons basil, chopped
1 tablespoon thyme, chopped
½ cups balsamic vinegar
1 tsp olive oil
½ tsp salt
Pepper to taste
2 cups water
Directions:
Place a heavy bottomed pot on medium high fire and heat oil for 3 minutes.
Stir in onions and sauté for 2 minutes.
Stir in tomatoes, mushrooms, bell pepper, thyme, and basil. Sauté for 5 minutes.
Add remaining ingredients, cover and bring to a boil.
Lower fire to a simmer and cook for 15 minutes.
Adjust seasoning to taste, serve and enjoy.
Nutrition:
Calories 78, Total Fat 1g, Saturated Fat 0.2g, Total Carbs 16g, Net Carbs 14g, Protein 2g, Sugar: 10g, Fiber 2g, Sodium 306mg, Potassium 217mg

652. Creamy Mushroom-Kale Stew

Preparation Time: 10 Minutes
Cooking Time: 20 Minutes
Servings: 3
Ingredients:
1 tablespoon coconut oil
3 cloves of garlic, minced
1 onion, chopped
1 bunch kale, stems removed and leaves chopped
5 white button mushrooms, chopped
1/2 cup coconut milk
½ cup water
Salt and pepper to taste
Directions:
Heat oil in a pot.
Sauté the garlic and onion until fragrant for 2 minutes.
Stir in mushrooms. Season with pepper and salt. Cook for 8 minutes.
Stir in kale, water and coconut milk. Simmer for 5 minutes.
Adjust seasoning to taste.
Nutrition:
Calories 164, Total Fat 14g, Saturated Fat 2g, Total Carbs 10g, Net Carbs 6g, Protein 2g, Sugar: 4g,
Fiber 2g, Sodium 11mg, Potassium 319mg

653. Italian White Bean Soup

Preparation Time: 10 Minutes
Cooking Time: 50 Minutes
Servings: 4
Ingredients:
1 (14 ouncecan chicken broth
1 bunch fresh spinach, rinsed and thinly sliced
1 clove garlic, minced
1 stalk celery, chopped
1 tablespoon lemon juice
1 tablespoon vegetable oil
1 onion, chopped
1/4 teaspoon ground black pepper
1/8 teaspoon dried thyme
2 (16 ouncecans white kidney beans, rinsed and drained
2 cups water
Directions:
Place a pot on medium high fire and heat pot for a minute. Add oil and heat for another minute.
Stir in celery and onion. Sauté for 7 minutes.
Stir in garlic and cook for another minute.
Add water, thyme, pepper, chicken broth, and beans. Cover and simmer for 15 minutes.
Remove 2 cups of the bean and celery mixture with a slotted spoon and set aside.

With an immersion blender, puree remaining soup in pot until smooth and creamy.
Return the 2 cups of bean mixture. Stir in spinach and lemon juice. Cook for 2 minutes until heated through and spinach is wilted.
Serve and enjoy.
Nutrition:
Calories 194, Total Fat 12g, Saturated Fat 4g, Total Carbs 13g, Net Carbs 10g, Protein 9g, Sugar: 2g, Fiber 3g, Sodium 406mg, Potassium 1606mg

654.   Black Eyed Peas Stew

Preparation Time: 10 Minutes
Cooking Time: 20 Minutes
Servings: 6
Ingredients:
½ cup extra virgin olive oil, divided
1 cup fresh dill, stems removed, chopped
1 cup fresh parsley, stems removed, chopped
1 cup water
2 bay leaves
2 carrots, peeled and sliced
2 cups black eyed beans, drained and rinsed
2 slices orange with peel and flesh
2 Tablespoons tomato paste
4 green onions, thinly sliced
Salt and pepper, to taste
Directions:
Place a pot on medium high fire and heat. Add ¼ cup oil and heat for 3 minutes.
Stir in bay leaves and tomato paste. Sauté for 2 minutes.
Stir in carrots and a up of water. Cover and simmer for 5 minutes.
Stir in dill, parsley, beans, and orange. Cover and cook for 3 minutes or until heated through.
Season with pepper and salt to taste.
Stir in remaining oil and green onions cook for 2 minutes.
Serve and enjoy.
Nutrition:
Calories 194, Total Fat 8g, Saturated Fat 1g, Total Carbs 25g, Net Carbs 17g, Protein 7g, Sugar: 2g, Fiber 8g, Sodium 198mg, Potassium 471mg

655.   Veggie Jamaican Stew

Preparation Time: 10 Minutes
Cooking Time: 30 Minutes
Servings: 8
Ingredients:
1 tbsp cilantro, chopped
1 tsp salt
1 tsp pepper
1 tbsp lime juice

2 cups collard greens, sliced

3 cups carrots, cut into bite-sized chunks

½ yellow plantain, cut into bite-sized pieces

1 cup okra, cut into ½" pieces

2 cups potatoes, cut into bite-sized cubes

2 cups taro, cut into bite sized cubes

2 cups pumpkin, cut into bite sized cubes

2 cups water

2 cups coconut milk

2 bay leaves

3 green onions, white bottom removed

½ tsp dried thyme

½ tsp ground allspice

4 garlic cloves, minced

1 onion, chopped

1 tbsp olive oil

Directions:

On medium fire, place a stockpot and heat oil. Sauté onions for 4 minutes or until translucent and soft. Add thyme, all spice and garlic. Sauté for a minute.

Pour in water and coconut milk and bring to a simmer. Add bay leaves and green onions.

Once simmering, slow fire to keep broth at a simmer and add taro and pumpkin. Cook for 5 minutes.

Add potatoes and cook for three minutes.

Add carrots, plantain and okra. Mix and cook for five minutes.

Then remove and fish for thyme sprigs, bay leaves and green onions and discard.

Add collard greens and cook for four minutes or until bright green and darker in color.

Turn off fire, add pepper, salt and lime juice to taste. Once it tastes good, mix well, transfer to a bowl, serve and enjoy.

Nutrition:

Calories 330, Total Fat 19g, Saturated Fat 4g, Total Carbs 33g, Net Carbs 26g, Protein 13g, Sugar: 9g, Fiber 7g, Sodium 432mg, Potassium 927mg

656. Lemon-Basil 'n Zucchini Soup

Preparation Time: 10 Minutes

Cooking Time: 20 Minutes

Servings: 4

Ingredients:

1 medium onion, chopped

1/2 cup loosely packed basil

3 cups chicken broth

3-4 cloves garlic, chopped

4 medium zucchinis, peeled and chopped into cubes

Additional Seasonings, Optional and to Taste

Basil leaves, chopped

Lemon wedges

4 tbsp Parmesan cheese, grated

¼ tsp salt
½ tsp Pepper to taste
¼ cup low-fat yogurt
Zest of 1 lemon
Directions:
Place a pot on medium fire and melt butter for 2 minutes. Stir in onions and sauté for 4 minutes.
Add garlic and sauté for a minute.
Stir in zucchini and sauté for 4 minutes.
Mix in lemon zest and chicken broth and simmer for 10 minutes.
Stir in basil and puree with an immersion blender.
Season with pepper and salt to taste.
Ladle into 4 bowls and evenly topped with lemon wedges, Parmesan cheese, lemon zest, and yogurt.
Enjoy.
Nutrition:
Calories 63, Total Fat 2g, Saturated Fat 1g, Total Carbs 8g, Net Carbs 7g, Protein 4g, Sugar: 4g,
Fiber 1g, Sodium 974mg, Potassium 210mg

657.   Seafood Chowder

Preparation Time: 10 Minutes
Cooking Time: 10 Minutes
Servings: 4
Ingredients:
1 can coconut milk
1 cup water
1 tablespoon garlic, minced
salt and pepper to taste
3 cans clams, chopped
1 package fresh shrimps, shelled and deveined
1 can corn, drained
2 med potatoes, diced
2 carrots, peeled and chopped
2 celery stalks, chopped
Directions:
Place all ingredients in a pot and give a good stir to mix everything.
Close the lid and turn on the heat to medium.
Bring to a boil and allow to simmer for 10 minutes.
Place in individual containers.
Put a label and store in the fridge.
Allow to warm at room temperature before heating in the microwave oven.
Nutrition:
Calories 393, Total Fat 15g, Saturated Fat 3g, Total Carbs 39g, Net Carbs 34g, Protein 28g, Sugar:
8g, Fiber 5g, Sodium 622mg, Potassium 1139mg

658.   Chicken Soup Filipino Style

Preparation Time: 10 Minutes

Cooking Time: 45 Minutes
Servings: 6
Ingredients:
1 whole chicken, around 2 lbs, cut into 10-pieces
Hot pepper leaves
2 tbsp fish sauce
1 thumb ginger, cut into strips
1 medium sized onion, chopped
1 tbsp garlic, minced
½ small green papaya, peeled and cut into wedges
5 cups chicken broth
1 tbsp corn oil
Pepper and salt to taste
Directions:
In a heavy bottomed medium pot, heat oil on medium high fire.
Once oil is hot, sauté garlic and ginger for a minute or until garlic begins to brown lightly.
Add onions, sauté for 3 to 5 minutes or until soft and translucent.
Add chicken and sauté for ten minutes.
Season with pepper and salt.
Add 2 cups of Chicken broth or water to pot, cover and cook chicken for another ten minutes.
Add papaya wedges and remaining liquid. Cover and cook until papaya is soft.
Once papaya is soft, add fish sauce and hot pepper leaves, and cook while covered for another minute.
Adjust seasoning to taste, serve and enjoy.
Nutrition:
Calories 143, Total Fat 5g, Saturated Fat 1g, Total Carbs 8g, Net Carbs 7g, Protein 17g, Sugar: 5g, Fiber 1g, Sodium 1338mg, Potassium 341mg

659.   Ramen Miso Soup

Preparation Time: 10 Minutes
Cooking Time: 20 Minutes
Servings: 1
Ingredients:
2 tsp thinly sliced green onion
A pinch of salt
½ tsp shoyu
2 tbsp mellow white miso
1 cup zucchini, cut into angel hair spirals
½ cup thinly sliced cremini mushrooms
½ medium carrot, cut into angel hair spirals
1/2 cup baby spinach leaves – optional
2 ¼ cups water
½ box of medium firm tofu, cut into ¼-inch cubes
1 hardboiled egg
Directions:
In a small bowl, mix ¼ cup of water and miso. Set aside.

In a small saucepan on medium high fire, bring to a boil 2 cups water, mushrooms, tofu and carrots. Add salt, shoyu and miso mixture. Allow to boil for 5 minutes. Remove from fire and add green onion, zucchini and baby spinach leaves if using.

Let soup stand for 5 minutes before transferring to individual bowls.

Garnish with ½ of hardboiled egg per bowl, serve and enjoy.

Nutrition:

Calories 177, Total Fat 8g, Saturated Fat 2g, Total Carbs 15g, Net Carbs 11g, Protein 13g, Sugar: 5g, Fiber 4g, Sodium 1681mg, Potassium 503mg

660.   Creamy Corn Soup

Preparation Time: 10 Minutes
Cooking Time: 20 Minutes
Servings: 4
Ingredients:
2 tbsp cornstarch
1/4 cup water
4 cups chicken broth
1 (14.75 ozcan cream-style corn
2 egg whites
1/2 tsp salt
1/2 lb. skinless, boneless chicken breast meat, finely chopped
Directions:
Combine chicken, egg whites, and salt in a bowl. Stir in the cream style corn. Mix well.

Boil the chicken broth in a wok. Then stir in the chicken mixture, while continue boiling. Then simmer for about 3 minutes, stir frequently to avoid burning.

Mix corn starch and water until well combined. Mix to the simmering broth, while constantly stirring until it slightly thickens. Cook for about 2 minutes more.

Serve and enjoy.

Nutrition:

Calories 186, Total Fat 3g, Saturated Fat 0.5g, Total Carbs 26g, Net Carbs 25g, Protein 17g, Sugar: 5g, Fiber 1g, Sodium 619mg, Potassium 189mg

661.   Hot and Sour Soup

Preparation Time: 10 Minutes
Cooking Time: 25 Minutes
Servings: 4
Ingredients:
½ tsp sesame oil
1 cup fresh bean sprouts
1 egg, lightly beaten
1 tsp black pepper
1 tsp ground ginger
3 tbsp white vinegar
3 tbsp soy sauce
¼ lb. sliced mushrooms

½ lb. tofu, cubed

2 tbsp corn starch

3 ½ cups chicken broth

Directions:

Mix corn starch and ¼ cup chicken broth and put aside.

Over high heat place a pot then combine and boil: pepper, ginger, vinegar, soy sauce, mushrooms, tofu and chicken broth.

Once boiling, add the corn starch mixture. Stir constantly and reduce fire. Once concoction is thickened, drop the slightly beaten egg while stirring vigorously.

Add bean sprouts and for one to two minutes allow simmering.

Remove from fire and transfer to bowls and enjoy while hot.

Nutrition:

Calories 156, Total Fat 8g, Saturated Fat 2g, Total Carbs 13g, Net Carbs 11g, Protein 10g, Sugar: 4g, Fiber 2g, Sodium 716mg, Potassium 247mg

662.   Cioppino Seafood Stew

Preparation Time: 10 Minutes

Cooking Time: 40 Minutes

Servings: 12

Ingredients:

¼ cup Italian parsley, chopped

¼ tsp dried basil

¼ tsp dried thyme

½ cup dry white wine like pinot grigio

½ lb. King crab legs, cut at each joint

½ onion, chopped

½ tsp red pepper flakes (adjust to desired spiciness

1 28-oz can crushed tomatoes

1 lb. mahi mahi, cut into ½-inch cubes

1 lb. raw shrimp

1 tbsp olive oil

2 bay leaves

2 cups clam juice

50 live clams, washed

6 cloves garlic, minced

Pepper and salt to taste

Directions:

On medium fire, place a stockpot and heat oil.

Add onion and for 4 minutes sauté until soft.

Add bay leaves, thyme, basil, red pepper flakes and garlic. Cook for a minute while stirring a bit.

Add clam juice and tomatoes. Once simmering, place fire to medium low and cook for 20 minutes uncovered.

Add white wine and clams. Cover and cook for 5 minutes or until clams have slightly opened.

Stir pot then add fish pieces, crab legs and shrimps. Do not stir soup to maintain the fish's shape.

Cook while covered for 4 minutes or until clams are fully opened; fish and shrimps are opaque and cooked.

Season with pepper and salt to taste.
Transfer Cioppino to bowls and garnish with parsley before.
Nutrition:
Calories 200, Total Fat 4g, Saturated Fat 1g, Total Carbs 11g, Net Carbs 9g, Protein 29g, Sugar: 4g, Fiber 2g, Sodium 1129mg, Potassium 450mg

663.   Chicken 'n Rice Soup

Preparation Time: 10 Minutes
Cooking Time: 25 Minutes
Servings: 4
Ingredients:
6 cups chicken broth homemade or canned
1 1/2 cups diced or shredded cooked chicken
2 Tablespoons olive oil
1 small onion diced about 3/4 cup
1 bay leaf
1/3 cup arborio rice
1 large egg
Juice of half of a lemon
1 cup chopped asparagus
1 cup diced carrots
1/2 cup of fresh chopped dill divided
Kosher salt and fresh pepper to taste
Fresh minced chives for garnish
Directions:
Place a large pot on medium high fire and heat for 2 minutes. Add oil and heat for another 2 minutes.
Stir in onions and sauté for 4 minutes.
Mix in bay leaf, chicken broth, and ¼ cup dill. Mix well, cover and bring to a boil.
Once boiling, add rice and mix well. Once boiling again, lower fire to a simmer and cook for another 10 minutes while covered.
Stir in asparagus and carrots. Cover and cook for another 10 minutes.
In the meantime, in a small bowl whisk well 2 tbsp water, lemon juice, and egg. Slowly whisk into soup. Mixing constantly until soup thickens.
Turn off heat and remove bay leaf.
Stir in remaining dill and adjust seasoning if needed.
Serve and enjoy.
Nutrition:
Calories 326, Total Fat 27g, Saturated Fat 4g, Total Carbs 12g, Net Carbs 8g, Protein 12g, Sugar: 4g, Fiber 4g, Sodium 52mg, Potassium 440mg

664.   Red Lentil Soup

Preparation Time: 10 Minutes
Cooking Time: 25 Minutes
Servings: 6

Ingredients:
1 (14 ouncecan diced tomatoes
1 1/2 cups dried red lentils
1 medium onion, diced
1 tablespoon ground cumin
1 tablespoon olive oil
1 teaspoon ground coriander
2 tablespoons lemon juice, or to taste
4 garlic cloves, minced
5 cups vegetable broth
Fresh chopped cilantro or parsley, for
Harissa paste, to taste (optional
Directions:
Place a pot on medium high fire and heat for 2 minutes.
Add oil and heat for 2 minutes. Add onion and sauté for 5 minutes or until soft.
Stir in coriander, cumin, and garlic for a minute.
Add tomatoes, broth, and lentils. Mix well.
Simmer uncovered for 20 minutes until lentils are soft.
Turn off fire and stir in harissa and lemon juice.
Season with pepper and salt.
Serve and enjoy.
Nutrition:
Calories 222, Total Fat 4g, Saturated Fat 0.6g, Total Carbs 36g, Net Carbs 29g, Protein 13g, Sugar: 3g, Fiber 7g, Sodium 92mg, Potassium 568mg

665.   Green Vegan Soup

Preparation Time: 10 Minutes
Cooking Time: 20 Minutes
Servings: 6
Ingredients:
1 medium head cauliflower, cut into bite-sized florets
1 medium white onion, peeled and diced
2 cloves garlic, peeled and diced
1 bay leaf crumbled
5-oz watercress
 2 cups fresh spinach or frozen spinach
1-liter vegetable stock or bone broth
1 cup cream or coconut milk + 6 tbsp for garnish
1/4 cup ghee or coconut oil
1 tsp salt or to taste
freshly ground black pepper
Optional: fresh herbs such as parsley or chives for garnish
Directions:
On medium-high the fire, place a Dutch the oven greased with ghee. Once hot, sauté garlic for a minute. Add onions and sauté until soft and translucent, about 5 minutes.
Add cauliflower florets and crumbled bay leaf. Mix well and cook for 5 minutes.

Stir in watercress and spinach. Sauté for 3 minutes.

Add vegetable stock and bring to a boil.

When cauliflower is crisp-tender, stir in coconut milk.

Season with pepper and salt.

With a hand blender, puree soup until smooth and creamy.

Serve and enjoy.

Nutrition:

Calories 209, Total Fat 19g, Saturated Fat 4g, Total Carbs 9g, Net Carbs 5g, Protein 4g, Sugar: 3g, Fiber 4g, Sodium 456mg, Potassium 532mg

666.   Spicy Chicken Vegetable Soup

Preparation Time: 10 Minutes

Cooking Time: 25 Minutes

Servings: 4

Ingredients:

1-pound skinless chicken breast

3 bay leaves

½ teaspoon red chili pepper flakes

½ teaspoon sea salt

1 teaspoon dried basil

1 garlic clove, minced

1 can diced tomatoes

1 small onion, diced

1 ½ cups sweet potatoes, cubed

2 cups frozen vegetable mix

2 cups chicken broth

1 jar spicy tomato sauce

Directions:

In a Dutch oven, put all ingredients and mix until well combined.

Season with salt and pepper to taste.

Let it simmer for 15 minutes. Cook for 10 minutes more.

Serve warm.

Nutrition:

Calories 279, Total Fat 11g, Saturated Fat 3g, Total Carbs 18g, Net Carbs 13g, Protein 27g, Sugar: 6g, Fiber 5g, Sodium 451mg, Potassium 614mg

667.   Ginger-Egg Drop Soup with Zoodle

Preparation Time: 20 Minutes

Cooking Time: 15 Minutes

Servings: 4

Ingredients:

½ teaspoons red pepper flakes

2 cups thinly sliced scallions, divided

2 cups, plus 1 tablespoon water, divided

2 tablespoons extra virgin olive oil

2 tablespoons minced ginger

3 tablespoons corn starch

4 large eggs, beaten

4 medium to large zucchini, spiralized into noodles

5 cups shiitake mushrooms, sliced

5 tablespoons low-sodium tamari sauce or soy sauce

8 cups vegetable broth, divided

Salt & pepper to taste

Directions:

On medium-high the fire, place a large pot and add oil.

Once oil is hot, stir in ginger and sauté for two minutes.

Stir in a tablespoon of water and shiitake mushrooms. Cook for 5 minutes or until mushrooms start to give off liquid.

Stir in 1 ½ cups scallions, tamari sauce, red pepper flakes, remaining water, and 7 cups of the vegetable broth. Mix well and bring to a boil.

Meanwhile, in a small bowl whisk well cornstarch and remaining cup of vegetable broth and set aside.

Once pot is boiling, slowly pour in eggs while stirring pot continuously. Mix well.

Add the cornstarch slurry in pot and mix well. Continue mixing every now and then until thickened, about 5 minutes.

Taste and adjust seasoning with pepper and salt.

Stir in zoodles and cook until heated through, about 2 minutes.

Serve with a sprinkle of remaining scallions and enjoy.

Nutrition:

Calories 271, Total Fat 17g, Saturated Fat 4g, Total Carbs 17g, Net Carbs 14g, Protein 15g, Sugar: 3g, Fiber 3g, Sodium 431mg, Potassium 774mg

668.   Moroccan Veggie Soup

Preparation Time: 20 Minutes

Cooking Time: 1 hour and 10 Minutes

Servings: 6

Ingredients:

½ tsp pepper

1 tsp salt

2 oz whole wheat orzo

1 large zucchini, peeled and cut into ¼-insh cubes

8 sprigs fresh cilantro, plus more leaves for garnish

12 sprigs flat leaf parsley, plus more for garnish

A pinch of saffron threads

2 stalks celery leaves included, sliced thinly

2 carrots, diced

2 small turnips, peeled and diced

1 14-oz can diced tomatoes

6 cups water

1 lb. lamb stew meat, trimmed and cut into ½-inch cubes

2 tsp ground turmeric

1 medium onion, diced finely
2 tbsp extra virgin olive oil
Directions:
On medium high fire, place a large Dutch oven and heat oil.
Add turmeric and onion, stir fry for two minutes.
Add meat and sauté for 5 minutes.
Add saffron, celery, carrots, turnips, tomatoes and juice, and water.
With a kitchen string, tie cilantro and parsley sprigs together and into pot.
Cover and bring to a boil. Once boiling reduce fire to a simmer and continue to cook for 45 to 50 minutes or until meat is tender.
Once meat is tender, stir in zucchini. Cover and cook for 8 minutes.
Add orzo; cook for 10 minutes or until soft.
Remove and discard cilantro and parsley sprigs.
Season with pepper and salt.
Transfer to a bowl and garnish with cilantro and parsley leaves before.
Nutrition:
Calories 212, Total Fat 9g, Saturated Fat 2g, Total Carbs 16g, Net Carbs 12g, Protein 18g, Sugar: 5g, Fiber 4g, Sodium 554mg, Potassium 596mg

669.   Tomato Soup

Preparation Time: 15 Minutes
Cooking Time: 40 Minutes
Servings: 2
Ingredients:
Pepper and salt to taste
2 tbsp tomato paste
1 ½ cups vegetable broth
1 tbsp chopped parsley
1 tbsp olive oil
5 garlic cloves
½ medium yellow onion
4 large ripe tomatoes
Directions:
Preheat oven to 350oF.
Chop onion and tomatoes into thin wedges. Place on a rimmed baking sheet. Season with parsley, pepper, salt, and olive oil. Toss to combine well. Hide the garlic cloves inside tomatoes to keep it from burning.
Pop in the oven and bake for 30 minutes.
On medium pot, bring vegetable stock to a simmer. Add tomato paste.
Pour baked tomato mixture into pot. Continue simmering for another 10 minutes.
With an immersion blender, puree soup.
Adjust salt and pepper to taste before.
Nutrition:
Calories 179, Total Fat 8g, Saturated Fat 1g, Total Carbs 27g, Net Carbs 21g, Protein 5g, Sugar: 15g, Fiber 6g, Sodium 445mg, Potassium 1182mg

670. Cajun Jambalaya Soup

Preparation Time: 15 Minutes
Cooking Time: 40 Minutes
Servings: 6
Ingredients:
¼ cup Frank's red-hot sauce
3 tbsp Cajun seasoning
2 cups okra
½ head of cauliflower
4 oz chicken, diced
1 lb. large shrimps, raw and deveined
2 bay leaves
2 cloves garlic, diced
1 large can organic diced tomatoes
1 large onion, chopped
4 pepper
5 cups chicken stock
Directions:
Place a heavy bottomed pot on high fire and add all ingredients except for cauliflower.
Mix well and bring to a boil.
Once boiling, lower fire to a simmer and simmer for 30 minutes.
Meanwhile, in a blender rice the cauliflower. Stir into pot and simmer for another 5 minutes. Adjust seasoning if needed.
Serve and enjoy.
Nutrition:
Calories 143, Total Fat 3g, Saturated Fat 1g, Total Carbs 14g, Net Carbs 11g, Protein 16g, Sugar: 5g, Fiber 3g, Sodium 764mg, Potassium 666mg

671. Cardamom and Carrot Soup

Preparation Time: 10 Minutes
Cooking Time: 45 Minutes
Servings: 4
Ingredients:
Freshly ground black pepper
½ cup full-fat coconut milk
4 cups chicken stock or Bone Broth
½ teaspoon ground cardamom
1 teaspoon minced fresh ginger
¼ cup diced Cortland apple, Empire, McIntosh, or Braeburn
1 ½ pounds peeled large carrots, cut into ½ inch coins
Kosher Salt
2 large green onions, green and white ends only, trimmed and cleaned, and thinly sliced
1 tablespoon coconut oil
Directions:
On medium fire, place large saucepan and heat coconut oil.

Sauté salt and leeks for 5 minutes or until translucent.
Add cardamom, ginger, apple, and carrot. Sauté for 3 minutes.
Add broth and boil on high fire.
When boiling, lower heat to a simmer, cover, and cook for 30 minutes or until carrots and apples are soft.
Add coconut milk, turn off fire, and mix.
With an immersion blender, puree soup.
Season to taste with pepper and salt.
Serve while warm.
Nutrition:
Calories 174, Total Fat 11g, Saturated Fat 2g, Total Carbs 19g, Net Carbs 13g, Protein 2g, Sugar: 10g, Fiber 6g, Sodium 162mg, Potassium 645mg

672.   Gobi Masala Soup

Preparation Time: 15 Minutes
Cooking Time: 35 Minutes
Servings: 4
Ingredients:
1 tsp salt
1 tsp ground turmeric
1 tsp ground coriander
2 tsp cumin seeds
3 tsp dark mustard seeds
1 cup water
3 cups beef broth
1 head cauliflower, chopped
3 carrots, chopped
1 large onion, chopped
2 tbsp coconut oil
Chopped cilantro for topping
Crushed red pepper to taste
Black pepper to taste
1 tbsp lemon juice
Directions:
On medium high fire, place a large heavy bottomed pot and heat coconut oil.
Once hot, sauté garlic cloves for a minute. Add carrots and continue sautéing for 4 minutes more.
Add turmeric, coriander, cumin, mustard seeds, and cauliflower. Sauté for 5 minutes.
Add water and beef broth and simmer for 10 to 15 minutes.
Turn off fire and transfer to blender. Puree until smoot and creamy.
Return to pot, continue simmering for another ten minutes.
Season with crushed red pepper, lemon juice, pepper, and salt.
To serve, garnish with cilantro, and enjoy.
Nutrition:
Calories 143, Total Fat 9g, Saturated Fat 6g, Total Carbs 16g, Net Carbs 11g, Protein 3g, Sugar: 7g, Fiber 5g, Sodium 646mg, Potassium 551mg

673.   Slow Cooked Creamy Chicken Soup

Preparation Time: 10 Minutes
Cooking Time: 7 hours
Servings: 7
Ingredients:
1 lb. skinless and boneless chicken breasts
2 cups unsweetened almond milk
1 tsp balsamic vinegar
4 tbsp whole wheat pastry flour
4 cups chicken broth
Chopped fresh parsley
Pepper and salt to taste
1 tbsp onion powder
1 tbsp garlic powder
¾ cup plain Greek yogurt
Directions:
In a slow cooker, add chicken broth.
Whisk in almond milk and vinegar.
Add chicken and cook for 4 to 6 hours on low setting or until chicken is tender.
Once cooked, remove chicken breast and shred.
Whisk in pepper, salt, onion powder, garlic powder and Greek yogurt into soup inside the slow cooker until well combined.
Return chicken to slow cooker and mix well and cook for another hour.
Serve equally into seven bowls and garnish with parsley.
Serve and enjoy.
Nutrition:
Calories 142, Total Fat 2g, Saturated Fat 0.5g, Total Carbs 10g, Net Carbs 9g, Protein 20g, Sugar: 5g, Fiber 1g, Sodium 79mg, Potassium 471mg

674.   Citrus Acorn Squash Soup

Servings: 3-4
Preparation Time: 10 minutes
Cooking Time: 1 hour 5 minutes
Ingredients:
1 large acorn squash, halved and seeded
½ teaspoon essential olive oil
Salt and freshly ground black pepper, to taste
1 teaspoon fresh orange zest, grated finely
¾ teaspoon ground ginger
2 pinches of cayenne pepper
2 cups vegetable broth
¼ cup fresh orange juice
¼ cup coconut milk
1 tablespoon coconut aminos
Fresh pomegranate seeds, for garnishing

Directions:

Preheat the oven to 400 degrees F. Line a baking sheet with foil paper.

Coat the squash halves with oil evenly and sprinkle with salt and black pepper.

Arrange the squash halves, cut side up within the prepared baking sheet.

Roast approximately one hour.

Remove from oven and allow it to go cool slightly.

Scoop the flesh from roasted squash and transfer right into a blender.

Add remaining all ingredients except pomegranate seeds and pulse till smooth.

Transfer the soup in a very pan on medium heat.

Cook approximately 3-5 minutes or till heated completely.

Serve hot while using garnishing of pomegranate seeds.

Nutrition:

Calories: 300, Fat: 0g, Carbohydrates: 21g, Fiber: 11g, Protein: 22g

675. Tangy Mushroom Soup

Servings: 3-4
Preparation Time: 15 minutes
Cooking Time: 15-20 minutes
Ingredients:
For Soup:
4 cups low-sodium vegetable broth
1 cup button mushrooms, sliced
1 cup cherry tomatoes, chopped
½ of white onion, sliced
3 slices lemongrass
3 fresh ginger pieces
5 fresh kaffir lime leaves
5 Thai chile peppers, seeded and mashed
¼ cup fresh lime juice
2 tablespoons tamari

For Garnishing:
1 cu bean sprouts
¼ cup scallion, chopped
½ cup fresh cilantro, chopped
Directions:
In a sizable pan, add broth on medium-high heat.
Bring with a boil reducing the temperature to medium.
Add remaining soup ingredients and again bring to some gentle simmer.
Simmer approximately 15-20 min.
Remove from heat and discard lemongrass, ginger and lime leaves.
Serve hot while using ingredients of garnishing.
Nutrition:
Calories: 295, Fat: 4g, Carbohydrates: 21g, Fiber: 8g, Protein: 23g

676. Butternut Squash & Lentil Soup

Servings: 6-8
Preparation Time: 15 minutes
Cooking Time 1 hour 40 minutes
Ingredients:
1 medium butternut squash, halved and seeded
2/3 cup celery, divided
¼ cup onion, chopped and divided
3 teaspoons garlic, minced and divided
2 teaspoons dried parsley, crushed and divided
2 teaspoons dried basil, crushed and divided
2 fresh thyme pieces, divided
Salt, to taste
2 tablespoons extra-virgin essential olive oil
½ cup carrot, peeled and chopped
1 medium tomato, chopped
1 teaspoon ground turmeric
1 bay leaf
1 teaspoon freshly squeezed lemon juice
1 vegetable bouillon cube
6 cups water, divided
½ cup split red lentil, soaked and drained
Freshly ground black pepper, to taste
Directions:
Preheat the oven to 375 degrees F. Line a baking sheet with foil paper.
Arrange the squash halves within the prepared baking sheet, cut side up.
Place about ¼ cup from the celery, 2 tablespoons of onion, 1 teaspoon garlic, 1 teaspoon of every dried herbs, 1 thyme piece and salt.
Roast for around 50-60 minutes or till squash becomes tender.
Remove from heat whilst aside to cool completely.
Chop the three cups of flesh and aside.
Meanwhile in a soup pan, heat oil on medium-low heat.

Add carrot, remaining celery, onion and garlic and sauté for approximately 5-7 minutes.
Add tomato, turmeric, bay leaf, fresh lemon juice, bouillon cube, remaining herbs and 1 cup of water and simmer, covered for around 15 minutes.
In the center way, add 1 cup of more water.
Stir in lentils, squash and remaining water and provide to some boil.
Reduce heat to low.
Cover partially and simmer approximately 30-40 minutes.
Remove through the heat and by having an immersion blender, puree the soup completely.
Serve hot together with your desired topping.
Nutrition:
Calories: 317, Fat: 3g, Carbohydrates: 17g, Fiber: 9g, Protein: 22g

677. Tomatoes & Quinoa Soup

Servings: 4
Preparation Time: 15 minutes
Cooking Time: 22 minutes
Ingredients:
5 tablespoons extra-virgin coconut oil
1 brown onion, chopped
1 (3-inchpiece fresh ginger, chopped
4 garlic cloves, chopped
2 teaspoons ground cumin
1 teaspoon ground turmeric
1 teaspoon dried sage
1 teaspoon dried thyme
1/8 teaspoon red pepper cayenne
Salt and freshly ground black pepper, to taste
1½ cups quinoa
4 tomatoes, chopped
1 red bell pepper, seeded and chopped
3 celery stalks, chopped
¾ cup fresh cilantro, chopped and divided
6 cups water
2 tablespoons fresh lemon juice
2 tablespoons extra-virgin extra virgin olive oil
1 avocado, peeled, pitted and sliced
1 lemon, cut into 4 wedges
Directions:
In a big soup pan, heat coconut oil on medium heat.
Add onion, ginger and garlic and sauté for around 4 minutes.
Add cumin, turmeric, sage and thyme and sauté for about 1 minute.
Add cayenne pepper, salt and black pepper and sauté approximately 2 minutes.
Add quinoa, tomatoes, bell pepper, celery, ¼ cup of cilantro, and water and produce with a boil on high heat.
Reduce the warmth to medium-low
Simmer, covered for around 15 minutes.

Stir in remaining cilantro and lemon juice and remove from heat.
Transfer the soup into bowls and drizzle with organic olive oil.
Serve hot using the garnishing of avocado lemon wedges.
Nutrition:
Calories: 437, Fat: 10g, Carbohydrates: 79g, Fiber: 5g, Protein: 8g

### 678.	Tomato & Lentil Soup

Servings: 4
Preparation Time: 15 minutes
Cooking Time: 33 minutes
Ingredients:
2 garlic cloves, peeled
2 tablespoons extra-virgin extra virgin olive oil
1 large yellow onion, sliced
1 cup red lentils
2 carrots, peeled and chopped
1 (28-ouncecan tomatoes
2 teaspoons ground coriander
2 teaspoons ground cumin
1 teaspoon ground ginger
Salt and freshly ground black pepper, to taste
6 cups vegetable broth
Directions:
Crush the garlic cloves whilst in a very bowl for about 5-10 min.
In a large soup pan, heat oil on medium heat.
Add onion and sauté for approximately 3 minutes.
Add lentils, carrots, tomatoes, spices and broth and bring to some boil.
Simmer, covered for around 25 minutes.
Stir in garlic and simmer approximately 5 minutes more.
Remove from heat and having an immersion blender, puree the soup completely.
Serve immediately.
Nutrition:
Calories: 343, Fat: 2g, Carbohydrates: 26g, Fiber: 10g, Protein: 28g

### 679.	Sweet Potato, Spinach & Lentil Soup

Servings: 4
Preparation Time: 15 minutes
Cooking Time: 31 minutes
Ingredients:
1 tbsp extra virgin olive oil
1 large onion, minced
6 garlic cloves, minced
1½ teaspoons garam masala
½ teaspoon ground turmeric
2 pinches red pepper flakes, crushed

4 cups vegetable broth

1 cup lentil

2 sweet potatoes, peeled and cubed into ½-inch size

4 cups fresh spinach, chopped

Directions:

In a substantial soup pan, heat oil on medium heat.

Add onion and garlic and sauté for approximately 2-4 minutes.

Stir in garam masala, turmeric and red pepper flakes and sauté approximately 2 minutes.

Add broth and lentil and provide with a boil.

Reduce heat to low and simmer, covered approximately fifteen minutes.

Stir in sweet potatoes and simmer approximately 10 min.

Stir in spinach and simmer for approximately 3-5 minutes.

Stir in salt and serve hot.

Nutrition:

Calories: 361, Fat: 4.9g, Carbohydrates: 23.7g, Fiber: 20.9g, Protein: 16.9g

680.   Carrot & Lentil Soup

A healthiest soup having a rich and lovely texture. This combo of topping ingredients gives this soup a deluxe and tasty touch.

Servings: 2

Preparation Time: 15 minutes

Cooking Time: 30 minutes

Ingredients:

For Soup:

6 carrots, peeled and sliced
3 tablespoons olive oil, divided
1 tablespoon herbs de Provence
Salt and freshly ground black pepper, to taste
¼ cup split red lentils
1 teaspoon mustard seeds
1 teaspoon ground cumin
1 teaspoon ground turmeric
3 garlic cloves, chopped
1/3 cup coconut milk
1½ cups water
For Topping:

1 tbsp organic olive oil
12 chestnut mushrooms, sliced thinly
1 (14-ouncecan cannellini beans, drained
2 minced garlic cloves
1 tablespoon mixed dried herbs
Directions:
Preheat the oven to 355 degrees F.
Arrange the carrot slices inside a baking dish in the single layer.
Drizzle with 1 tablespoon of oil and sprinkle with herbs de Provence, salt and black pepper.
Roast for around 25 minutes.
Meanwhile in a very pan of boiling water, add lentils and cook for approximately 10 min.
Drain well.
In a sizable frying pan, heat remaining oil on medium heat.
Add mustard seeds, cumin and turmeric and sauté for approximately 30 seconds.
In a blender, add carrots, lentils, mustard seeds mixture, coconut milk and water and pulse till smooth.
Transfer the soup mixture inside a pan on medium heat and cook approximately 4-5 minutes or till heated completely.
For mushroom mixture inside same frying pan, of spices, heat oil on medium heat.
Add mushrooms, beans, garlic and herbs and sauté for about 3-4 minutes.
Transfer soup in bowls and top with mushroom mixture and serve.
Nutrition:
Calories: 354, Fat: 3.4g, Carbohydrates: 25.2g, Fiber: 5.3g, Protein: 32g

681.   Barley, Beans & Veggie Soup

A comforting bowl of soup while using health ingredients combo. barley, beans and vegetables complement the other person nicely.
Servings: 6
Preparation Time: 20 minutes
Cooking Time: 48 minutes
Ingredients:
3 tablespoons extra virgin olive oil
¼ cup pearl barley
1 onion, chopped
2 celery stalks, chopped
2 carrots, peeled and chopped
1 garlic clove, minced
½ teaspoon ground turmeric
½ teaspoon curry powder
Salt and freshly ground black pepper, to taste
6 cups chicken broth
1 small sweet potato, peeled and chopped
1 (14-ouncecan diced tomatoes, drained
1 (19-ouncecan mixed beans, rinsed and drained

Directions:

In a substantial soup pan, heat oil on medium heat.

Add barley, onion, celery, carrots, garlic, turmeric and curry powder and sauté for around 6-8 minutes.

Add salt, black pepper and broth and bring to a boil.

Reduce the heat and simmer, covered for approximately 30 minutes.

Stir in the remaining ingredients and again bring to some boil.

Simmer, covered for around 10 minutes.

Serve hot.

Nutrition:

Calories: 337, Fat: 2.6g, Carbohydrates: 29g, Fiber: 9g, Protein: 32g

682.   Carrot Soup with Chickpeas

Servings: 4

Preparation Time: 15 minutes

Cooking Time: 30 minutes

Ingredients:

1 (15-ouncecan chickpeas, drained

½ teaspoon ground allspice

½ teaspoon ground cinnamon

1 teaspoon extra virgin olive oil

2 tablespoons coconut oil

2-3 teaspoons fresh ginger, chopped finely

2 garlic cloves, chopped finely

1 teaspoon ground turmeric

5 cups carrots, peeled and chopped

1½ cups vegetable broth

Freshly ground black pepper and salt, to taste

½ cup coconut milk

Directions:

Preheat the oven to 375 degrees F.

In a bowl, add chickpeas, allspice, cinnamon and olive oil and toss to coat well.

Transfer a combination in to a baking dish and bake approximately 30 minutes.

In a substantial soup pan, melt coconut oil on medium heat.

Add ginger, garlic and turmeric and sauté for approximately 5 minutes.

Add remaining ingredients except coconut milk and produce with a boil.

Reduce the temperature and simmer approximately 20-25 minutes.

Stir in coconut milk and take off from heat.

With an immersion blender, puree the soup completely.

Serve immediately with all the topping of chickpeas.

Nutrition:

Calories: 301, Fat: 4.7g, Carbohydrates: 25g, Fiber: 7g, Protein: 27g

683.   Black Beans Soup

Servings: 4

Preparation Time: 15 minutes
Cooking Time: 30-45 minutes
Ingredients:
2 (15-ouncecans black beans, rinsed and drained
1 (14½-ouncecan diced tomatoes
1 cup vegetable broth
1 (14-ouncecan coconut milk
2 scallions, chopped
2 minced garlic cloves
1 tablespoon ground cumin
1 tablespoon ground ginger
1 tablespoon ground turmeric
Salt, to taste
Directions:
In a large soup pan, mix together all ingredients except salt on medium-high heat.
Bring to your boil and reduce the heat.
Simmer for approximately 30-45 minutes.
Stir in salt and serve hot.
Nutrition:
Calories: 436, Fat: 22.2g, Carbohydrates: 46.3g, Fiber: 17.8g, Protein: 16.6g

684. Veggies & Quinoa Soup

Servings: 4-6
Preparation Time: 15 minutes
Cooking Time: 43 minutes
Ingredients:
2 tablespoons extra-virgin essential olive oil
1 medium shallot, chopped
1 medium onion, chopped
2 medium turnips, peeled and chopped
5 large carrots, peeled and chopped
2 teaspoons fresh ginger, minced
½ cup uncooked quinoa
3 cups water
3 cups vegetable broth
½ teaspoon ground turmeric
¼ tsp cayenne
Salt and freshly ground black pepper, to taste

Directions:

In a large soup pan, heat oil on medium-high heat.

Add shallot, onion, turnips and carrots and sauté for about 5-7 minutes.

Stir in ginger and sauté for approximately 1 minute.

Stir in remaining ingredients and bring to some boil.

Reduce the heat to low and simmer, covered for around 20-a half-hour.

Remove from heat and make aside to chill slightly.

In an increased speed blender, add soup mixture in batches and pulse till smooth.

Return the soup in pan on medium heat.

Simmer approximately 4-5 minutes or till heated completely.

Nutrition:

Calories: 376, Fat: 5.3g, Carbohydrates: 25g, Fiber: 6g, Protein: 30g

685. Chicken & Veggies Soup

Servings: 10-12

Preparation Time: 15 minutes

Cooking Time: 33 minutes

Ingredients:

1½ tablespoons extra virgin olive oil

1 large onion, chopped

2 large potatoes, peeled and chopped

4 parsnips, peeled and chopped

1-2 zucchinis, chopped

1 cup fresh peas, shelled

2 large raw chicken breasts

2 teaspoons ground cumin

1 tablespoon ground turmeric

4 cups chicken broth

6 cups water

Chopped fresh cilantro, for garnishing

Directions:

In a large soup pan, heat oil on medium heat.

Add onion and sauté approximately 3 minutes.

Stir in vegetables and cook for around 5 minutes.

Stir in remaining ingredients and produce with a boil.

Reduce the heat to medium-low.

Simmer for around 10-fifteen minutes

Remove the chicken breasts from soup with forks, shred them

Return the shredded chicken into soup and simmer for approximately 10 min.

Serve hot while using garnishing of cilantro.

Nutrition:

Calories: 359, Fat: 3.2g, Carbohydrates: 25g, Fiber: 9.1g, Protein: 32.4g

686. Halibut, Quinoa & Veggies Soup

Servings: 8-10

Preparation Time: 15 minutes
Cooking Time: 1 hour 10 minutes
Ingredients:
2 cups onions, chopped
1 cup celeriac root, chopped
2 garlic cloves, chopped
2 tablespoons fresh ginger herb, chopped finely
1 cup shiitake mushrooms, sliced
1 cup quinoa
8 cups vegetable broth
14-ounces halibut fillets
6 cups fresh baby spinach
1cup fresh cilantro, chopped
1 cup coconut milk
Salt, to taste
2 scallions, chopped

Directions:

In a sizable soup pan, onions, celeriac root, garlic, ginger root, mushrooms, quinoa and broth and provide to your boil.

Reduce heat to low and simmer, covered approximately 45 minutes.

Arrange the halibut fillets over soup mixture.

Simmer, covered for around 15 minutes.

Stir in remaining ingredients except scallions and simmer for around 5 minutes.

Serve hot using the garnishing of scallions.

Nutrition:

Calories: 300, Fat: 3g, Carbohydrates: 27g, Fiber: 11g, Protein: 30g

687.   Beef, Mushroom & Broccoli Soup

Servings: 8

Preparation Time: 15 minutes

Cooking Time: 13 minutes

Ingredients:

8 cups beef broth

2-3 cups broccoli, chopped

8-ounces mushrooms, sliced

1 bunch scallion, chopped (reserve dark green part for garnishing

1 (1-inchpiece fresh ginger, minced

5 garlic cloves, minced

1-pound cooked beef, sliced thinly

½ teaspoon red pepper flakes, crushed

3 tablespoons coconut aminos

1 lemon, sliced

Directions:

In a soup pan, add broth and provide to a boil.

Add broccoli and cook for approximately 2 minutes.

Stir in mushroom, scallions, ginger and garlic and simmer for around 7-8 minutes.

Stir in beef, red pepper flakes and coconut aminos minimizing heat to low.

Simmer approximately 2-3 minutes.

Serve hot while using garnishing of reserved green part of scallion and lemon slices.

Nutrition:

Calories: 374, Fat: 7.4g, Carbohydrates: 29g, Fiber: 10.2g, Protein: 30.6g

688.   Butternut Squash & Chickpeas Stew

Servings: 6

Preparation Time: 15 minutes

Cooking Time: 36 minutes

Ingredients:

1 tbsp olive oil

1 medium sweet onion, chopped

1½ teaspoons fresh ginger, grated

2 minced garlic cloves

½ tablespoon coconut sugar

¼ teaspoon ground cumin

¾ teaspoon ground cinnamon

1-2 teaspoons red chili flakes, crushed

3½ cups butternut squash, peeled and chopped

Salt and freshly ground black pepper, to taste

1½ cups water, divided

Salt and freshly ground black pepper, to taste

¼ cup creamy natural almond butter

1½ cups cooked chickpeas

3 cups fresh kale, trimmed and chopped

½ cup raw almonds, chopped

Directions:

In a big soup pan, heat oil on medium heat.

Add onion and cook, covered for about 5 minutes, stirring occasionally.

Stir in ginger, garlic, coconut sugar and spices and sauté approximately 1 minute.

Add squash and stir to mix well.

Add 1¼ glasses of water, salt and black pepper and bring with a boil.

Reduce heat to low.

In a bowl, mix together remaining water and peanut butter.

Add peanut butter mixture in pan and stir to mix.

Simmer, covered for approximately twenty minutes.

Stir in chickpeas, kale and almonds and simmer for around 10 min more.

Nutrition:

Calories: 393, Fat: 10.4g, Carbohydrates: 23g, Fiber: 8.3g, Protein: 27g

689.   Mixed Veggies Stew

Servings: 4
Preparation Time: 15 minutes
Cooking Time: 21 minutes
Ingredients:
2 tablespoons coconut oil
1 large onion, chopped
1 teaspoon ground turmeric
1 teaspoon ground cumin
Salt and freshly ground black pepper, to taste
1-2 cups water, divided
1 cup cabbage, shredded
1 bunch broccoli, chopped
2 large carrots, peeled and sliced
2 teaspoons fresh ginger, grated
Directions:
In a large soup pan, melt coconut oil on medium heat.
Add onion and sauté approximately 5 minutes.
Stir in spices and sauté for about 1 minute.
Add 1 cup of water and convey to some boil.
Simmer approximately 10 min.
Add vegetables and enough water that covers the 50 % of vegetables mixture.
Simmer, covered for about 10-fifteen minutes, stirring occasionally.
Serve hot.
Nutrition:
Calories: 274, Fat: 3.2g, Carbohydrates: 23g, Fiber: 14.1g, Protein: 22g

690.   Root Veggies Stew

A flavorful and aromatic stew for supper table. Freshly squeezed lemon juice offers a refreshing touch to spicy vegetables.
Servings: 6-8
Preparation Time: 15 minutes
Cooking Time: 33 minutes
Ingredients:

2 tablespoons coconut oil
1 large sweet onion, chopped
1 medium parsnips, peeled and chopped
3 tablespoons tomato paste
2 large garlic cloves, minced
½ teaspoon ground cinnamon
½ teaspoon ground ginger
1 teaspoon ground cumin
¼ tsp red pepper cayenne
Salt, to taste
2 medium carrots, peeled and chopped
2 medium purple potatoes, peeled and chopped
2 medium sweet potatoes, peeled and chopped
4 cups vegetable broth
2 tablespoons freshly squeezed lemon juice
2 cups fresh kale, kale, trimmed and chopped
¼ cup fresh cilantro leaves, chopped
Slivered almonds, for garnishing
Directions:
In a sizable soup pan, melt coconut oil on medium-high heat.
Add onion and sauté for approximately 5 minutes.
Add parsnip and sauté for approximately 3 minutes.
Stir in tomato paste, garlic and spices and sauté approximately 2 minutes.
Add carrots, potatoes and sweet potatoes and stir to mix well.
Add broth and produce with a boil and reduce the temperature to medium-low.
Simmer for about twenty or so minutes.
Stir in freshly squeezed lemon juice and kale and simmer approximately 2-3 minutes.
Serve using the garnishing of cilantro and almonds.
Nutrition:
Calories: 366, Fat: 2g, Carbohydrates: 21g, Fiber: 7.5g, Protein: 20g

691.   Chicken & Tomato Stew

Servings: 6-8
Preparation Time: 15 minutes
Cooking Time: 31 minutes
Ingredients:

2 tablespoons olive oil
1 onion, chopped
½ tablespoon fresh ginger, grated finely
1 tablespoon fresh garlic, minced
1 teaspoon ground turmeric
1 teaspoon ground cumin
1 teaspoon ground coriander
1 teaspoon paprika
1 teaspoon red pepper cayenne
6 skinless, boneless chicken thighs, trimmed and cut into 1-inch pieces
3 Roma tomatoes, chopped
1 (14-ouncecoconut milk
Salt and freshly ground black pepper, to taste
1/3 cup fresh cilantro, chopped
Directions:
In a substantial pan, heat oil on medium heat.
Add onion and sauté for around 8-10 minutes.
Add ginger, garlic and spices and sauté for approximately 1 minute.
Add chicken and cook for around 4-5 minutes.
Add tomatoes, coconut milk, salt and black pepper and brig to gentle simmer.
Reduce the heat to low and simmer, covered for around 10-15 minutes or till desired doneness.
Stir in cilantro and take away from heat.
Nutrition:
Calories: 347, Fat: 3.7g, Carbohydrates: 23.3g, Fiber: 7.7g, Protein: 20g

692.　　Chicken, Chickpeas & Olives Stew

Servings: 10-12
Preparation Time: 15 minutes
Cooking Time: 1 hour 9 minutes
Ingredients:
6-pound skinless, boneless grass-fed chicken thighs, trimmed
Salt and freshly ground black pepper, to taste
¼ cup extra-virgin essential olive oil
3 large yellow onions, sliced thinly
8 garlic cloves, crushed
3 small red chiles, stemmed
2 fresh bay leaves
1 tablespoon ground turmeric
2 teaspoon ground coriander
2 teaspoons ground cumin
2 (3-inchcinnamon sticks
4 teaspoons fresh lemon zest, grated finely
½ cup fresh lemon juice, divided
4 cups low-sodium chicken broth
2 cups small green olives, pitted
2 cups canned chickpeas, rinsed and drained

3 tablespoons fresh cilantro, chopped

Directions:

Sprinkle the chicken thighs with salt and black pepper evenly.

In a sizable pan, heat oil on medium-high heat.

Add the chicken thighs in 4 batches and cook for around 3 minutes from each party.

Transfer the chicken into a bowl and make aside.

Reduce the warmth to medium and sauté the onion for about 5-6 minutes.

Add garlic, red chiles, bay leaves and spices and sauté for about 1 minute.

Add lemon zest, 1/3 cup with the lemon juice and broth and produce to your boil.

Reduce the warmth to medium-low and simmer, covered approximately a half-hour.

Stir inside the cooked chicken, olives and chickpeas and boost the heat to medium-high.

Cook, stirring occasionally for about 6-8 minutes.

Stir in remaining fresh lemon juice, salt and black pepper and remove from heat.

Serve hot while using garnishing of cilantro.

Nutrition:

Calories: 490, Fat: 25g, Carbohydrates: 18g, Fiber: 4g, Protein: 48g

693.   Beef & Squash Stew

Servings: 4-6

Preparation Time: 15 minutes

Cooking Time: 1 hour 17 minutes

Ingredients:

1½ tablespoons coconut oil, divided

2-3-pound stew meat, trimmed and cubed into 1½-inch size

1 onion, chopped

1 (2-inchpiece fresh ginger, minced

5 garlic cloves, minced

2 cups bone broth

1 butternut squash, peeled and cubed

¼ teaspoon ground cinnamon

2 pears, cored and chopped

1 cup fresh mushrooms, sliced

1 tablespoon fresh thyme, chopped

Directions:

In a big heavy bottomed pan, heat 1 tablespoon of oil on medium-high heat

Add beef and sear for around 8-10 minutes or till browned completely.

With a slotted spoon, transfer the beef in to a bowl.

Now, decrease the heat to medium.

Add onion and sauté for approximately 5 minutes.

Add ginger and garlic and sauté for about 2 minutes.

Add cooked beef and broth and provide with a boil.

Reduce the warmth to low and simmer, covered approximately 15 minutes.

Stir in squash, cinnamon and salt and simmer, covered for around fifteen minutes.

Stir in pears and simmer, covered for approximately half an hour.

Meanwhile in the small skillet, heat the remainder oil on high heat.

Add mushrooms and cook for approximately 5 minutes or till browned.

Serve the stew with the topping f mushrooms and thyme.
Nutrition:
Calories: 298, Fat: 6.66g, Carbohydrates: 27g, Fiber: 3.4g, Protein: 31g

694.   Baked Lamb Stew

Servings: 4
Preparation Time: 15 minutes
Cooking Time: 1 hour 10 minutes
Ingredients:
For Lamb Marinade:
3 large garlic cloves, minced
1 tablespoon fresh ginger, minced
1 lemongrass stalk, minced
2 tablespoons coconut aminos
2 tablespoons tapioca starch
Salt and freshly ground black pepper, to taste
2-3-pound boneless lamb shoulder, trimmed and cubed into 2-inch pieces
For Stew:
2 tablespoons coconut oil
4 shallots, minced
2 Thai chilies, minced
2 tablespoons tomato paste
4 large tomatoes, chopped
4 carrots, peeled and chopped
1 butternut squash, peeled and cubed
2-star anise
1 cinnamon stick
1 teaspoon Chinese 5-spice powder
2½ cups hot beef broth

Directions:

For lamb marinade in a substantial glass bowl, add all ingredients and mix well.

Cover and refrigerate to marinate for around 2-8 hours.

Preheat the oven to 325 degrees F.

In an oven proof casserole dish, heat oil on medium-high heat.

Add lamb and cook for around 4-5 minutes.

Reduce heat to medium.

Add shallots and chilies and cook for around 2-3 minutes.

Stir in tomato paste and tomatoes and cook approximately 1-2 minutes.

Add remaining ingredients and stir to combine well.

Cover the casserole dish and immediately, transfer into oven.

Bake for approximately one hour or till desired doneness.

Nutrition:

Calories: 291, Fat: 5.6g, Carbohydrates: 23g, Fiber: 5.3g, Protein: 26g

695. Haddock & Potato Stew

Servings: 4

Preparation Time: 15 minutes

Cooking Time: 13 minutes

Ingredients:

2 large Yukon Gold potatoes, sliced into ¼-inch size

1 tbsp. olive oil

1 (2-inchpiece fresh ginger, chopped finely

1 (16-ouncecan whole tomatoes, crushed

½ cup water

1 cup clam juice

¼ teaspoon red pepper flakes, crushed

Salt, to taste

1½ pound boneless haddock, cut into 2inch pieces

2 tablespoons fresh parsley, chopped

Direction:

Arrange a steamer basket in a big pan of water and produce to your boil.

Place the potatoes in steamer basket and cook, covered approximately 8 minutes.

Meanwhile in the pan, heat oil on medium heat.

Add ginger and sauté for about 1 minute.

Add tomatoes and cook, stirring continuously approximately 2 minutes.

Add water, clam juice, red pepper flakes and produce to a boil.

Simmer for around 5 minutes, stirring occasionally.

Gently, stir in haddock pieces and simmer, covered for about 5 minutes or till desired doneness.

In bowls, divide potatoes and top with haddock mixture.

Garnish with parsley and serve.

Nutrition:

Calories: 421, Fat: 3g, Carbohydrates: 14g, Fiber: 9g, Protein: 24g

696. Adzuki Beans & Carrot Stew

One from the best comforting and crave-able stew for those. This pot of stew is undoubtedly a welcome dinner on any weeknight.

Servings: 4

Preparation Time: 15 minutes

Cooking Time: 1 hour 18 minutes

Ingredients:

2 tablespoons extra virgin olive oil

1 large yellow onion, chopped

5 (½-inchfresh ginger slices

Salt, to taste

3 cups water

1 cup dried adzuki beans, soaked for overnight, rinsed and drained

4 large carrots, peeled and sliced into ¾-inch pieces

2 tablespoons brown rice vinegar

3 tablespoons tamari

½ cup fresh parsley, minced

Directions:

In a sizable pan, heat oil on medium heat.

Add onion, ginger and salt and sauté for around 2-3 minutes.

Add water and beans and convey to a boil.

Reduce heat to low and simmer, covered for around 45 minutes.

Arrange carrot slices over beans and simmer, covered for around 20-thirty minutes.

Stir in vinegar and tamari and remove from heat.

Discard the ginger slices before.

Serve hot with garnishing of parsley.

Nutrition:

Calories: 309 Fat: 3g, Carbohydrates: 22g, Fiber: 7g, Protein: 27g

697. Black-Eyed Beans Stew

Servings: 4-5

Preparation Time: 15 minutes

Cooking Time: 2 hours 20 minutes

Ingredients:

2 cups dried black eyed beans, soaked for overnight, rinsed and drained

2 medium onions, chopped and divided

1 (4-inchpiece fresh ginger chopped

4 garlic cloves, chopped

¼ cup essential olive oil

2 scotch bonnet peppers

2 (14-ouncecans plum tomatoes

½-¾ cup water

1 vegetable bouillon cube

Salt, to taste

Directions:

In a big pan of boiling water, add beans and cook, covered approximately 60-90 minutes or till bens become soft.

In a blender, add 1 onion, ginger and garlic and pulse till a puree form.

In a big pan, heat oil on medium heat.

Add onion and sauté for around 2-5 minutes.

Stir in 5 tablespoons of onion puree and cook for approximately 5 minutes.

Meanwhile in blender, add bonnet peppers and tomatoes and pulse till smooth.

Add tomato mixture and stir to blend.

Reduce the warmth to low and simmer, covered for about 30 minutes, stirring occasionally.

Stir in beans, cube and salt and simmer for approximately 10 minutes.

Nutrition:

Calories: 300, Fat: 4g, Carbohydrates: 15g, Fiber: 14g, Protein: 26g

698.   Creamy Chickpeas Stew

Servings: 4-6

Preparation Time: 15 minutes

Cooking Time: 56 minutes

Ingredients:

¼ cup coconut oil

1 medium yellow onion, chopped

2 teaspoons fresh ginger, chopped finely

2 minced garlic cloves

1 teaspoon ground cumin

1 teaspoon ground coriander

¾ teaspoon ground turmeric

¼ teaspoon yellow mustard seeds

¼ tsp cayenne

1 (19-ouncecan chickpeas, rinsed and drained

2 large sweet potatoes, peeled and cubed into 1-inch size

1-pound fresh kale, trimmed and chopped

5 cups vegetable broth

Salt, to taste

1 cup coconut milk

¼ cup red bell pepper, seeded and julienned

2 tablespoons fresh cilantro, chopped

Directions:

In a substantial pan, heat oil on medium heat.

Add onion and sauté for around 3 minutes.

Add ginger and garlic and sauté for about 2 minutes.

Add spices and sauté for around 1 minute.

Add chickpeas, sweet potato, kale and broth and bring with a boil on medium-high heat.

Reduce the temperature to medium-low and simmer, covered for about 35 minutes.

Stir in coconut milk and simmer for about fifteen minutes or till desired thickness of stew.

Serve hot with garnishing of bell pepper and cilantro.

Nutrition:

Calories: 323, Fat: 3g, Carbohydrates: 15g, Fiber: 9g, Protein: 25g

699.   Crab Soup

Preparation Time: 15 minutes
Servings: 4
Ingredients:
1 pound of crab meat
6 tablespoons of butter
1 tablespoon of cooking sherry
2 cups of almond milk
2 cups of heavy whipping cream
Directions:
Add all the ingredients inside your Instant Pot. Stir until well combined.
Lock the lid and cook at high pressure for 5 minutes. When the cooking is done, quick release the pressure and remove the lid. Serve and enjoy!
Nutrition:
Calories: 737
Fat: 70g
Net Carbs: 8g
Protein: 19g

700.   Brown Butter Mushroom Soup

Preparation Time: 13 minutes
Servings: 6
Ingredients:
1 pound of mushrooms, sliced
2 tablespoons of fresh sage, chopped
4 cups of homemade low-sodium chicken stock or vegetable stock
6 tablespoons of butter
½ teaspoon of fine sea salt
½ teaspoon of freshly cracked black pepper
½ cup of heavy cream
Directions:
Press the "Sauté "setting on your Instant Pot and add the butter. Once hot, add the mushrooms and sauté for 4 minutes or until brown, stirring occasionally.
Add the chicken stock and lock the lid. Cook at high pressure for 3 minutes. When the cooking is done, naturally release the pressure and carefully remove the lid.
Use an immersion blender to puree the soup until smooth. Stir in the heavy cream, sea salt, black pepper and chopped fresh sage. Serve and enjoy!
Nutrition:
Calories: 200
Fat: 18g
Net Carbs: 4g
Protein: 5g

701. Lobster Chowder

Preparation Time: 15 minutes
Servings: 6
Ingredients:
6 bacon slices, chopped
1 small onion, finely chopped
¼ cup of coconut oil
2 cups of homemade low-sodium lobster stock
2 cups of cauliflower florets
3 cups of almond milk or coconut milk
2 cups of cooked lobster milk, chopped
1 teaspoon of fine sea salt
1 teaspoon of freshly cracked black pepper
2 tablespoons of fresh parsley, finely chopped
2 tablespoons of apple cider vinegar
¼ teaspoon of xanthan gum
Directions:
Press the "Sauté" setting on your Instant Pot and add the coconut oil, chopped bacon and onion. Cook for 4 minutes or until the onions have softened, stirring frequently.
Add the remaining ingredients and stir until well combined. Lock the lid and cook at high pressure for 3 minutes. When the cooking is done, naturally release the pressure and remove the lid.
Serve and enjoy!
Nutrition:
Calories: 212
Fat: 16g
Net Carbs: 4g
Protein: 13g

702. Creamy Chicken and Mushroom Soup

Preparation Time: 30 minutes
Servings: 8
Ingredients:
1 pound of boneless, skinless chicken breast
2 tablespoons of olive oil
1 large onion, finely chopped
1 cup of celery, chopped
6 garlic cloves, minced
2 cups of mushrooms, sliced
1 teaspoon of fresh rosemary, chopped
1 teaspoon of dried thyme
1/3 cup of dry sherry
8 cups of homemade low-sodium chicken stock
2/3 cups of heavy cream
¼ cup of fresh parsley, finely chopped
Sea salt and freshly cracked black pepper (for taste

Directions:

Press the "Sauté" function on your Instant Pot and add the olive oil. Once hot, add the chopped onions, chopped celery and minced garlic. Sauté for 3 minutes or until softened, stirring frequently. Add the mushrooms and sauté for another 2 minutes, stirring frequently.

Add the remaining ingredients except for the heavy cream. Lock the lid and cook at high pressure for 15 minutes.

When the cooking is done, naturally release the pressure and carefully remove the lid.

Transfer the chicken to a cutting board and shred using two forks. Return the shredded chicken to the soup along with the heavy cream. Stir until well combined and adjust the seasoning if necessary. Serve and enjoy!

Nutrition:
Calories: 218
Fat: 13g
Net Carbs: 8g
Protein: 17g

703.   Beef Stroganoff Soup

Preparation Time: 30 minutes
Servings: 4
Ingredients:
2 pounds of beef sirloin steak, cut into strips
1 pound of brown mushrooms, sliced
¼ cup of butter
2 medium garlic cloves
1 medium onion, finely chopped
5 cups of homemade low-sodium beef broth
1 ½ cup of sour cream or heavy cream
Sea salt and freshly cracked black pepper (to taste
Directions:

Press the "Sauté" setting on your Instant Pot and add the butter. Once hot, add the sirloin strips and cook for 4 minutes or until brown.

Add the mushrooms, garlic cloves and onions. Cook for 4 minutes or until slightly softened, stirring frequently.

Return the sirloin strips along with the beef broth. Lock the lid and cook at high pressure for 20 minutes. When the cooking is done, naturally release the pressure and remove the lid.

Stir in the sour cream and season with salt and black pepper. Serve and enjoy!

Nutrition:
Calories: 520
Fat: 39g
Net Carbs: 8g
Protein: 35g

704.   Thai Curried Butternut Squash Soup

Preparation Time: 25 minutes
Servings: 6

Ingredients:
1 small onion, finely chopped
1 tablespoon of coconut oil
2 medium garlic cloves, minced
2 tablespoons of red curry paste
¼ teaspoon of cayenne pepper
3 cups of homemade low-sodium chicken stock
1 (15-ouncecan of coconut milk
1 pound of butternut squash, peeled, seeds removed and cut into chunks
¼ cup of fresh cilantro, finely chopped
Sea salt and freshly cracked black pepper (to taste
Directions:
Press the "Sauté" setting on your Instant Pot and add the coconut oil. Once hot, add the chopped onions and minced garlic. Sauté for 4 minutes or until translucent, stirring frequently.
Add the cayenne pepper and red curry paste. Sauté for another minute or until fragrant, stirring frequently.
Add the remaining ingredients and stir until well combined. Lock the lid and cook at high pressure for 8 minutes. When the cooking is done, naturally release the pressure and remove the lid.
Use an immersion blender to puree the soup until smooth.
Stir in the fresh cilantro and season with salt and pepper. Serve and enjoy!
Nutrition:
Calories: 198
Fat: 16g
Net Carbs: 8g
Protein: 5g

705.   Cauliflower and Leek Soup with Coconut Cream

Preparation Time: 20 minutes
Servings: 2
Ingredients:
1 large leek, chopped
1 small cauliflower, chopped
½ cup of coconut cream
3 cups of homemade low-sodium chicken stock
Sea salt and freshly cracked black pepper
Directions:
Add all the ingredients inside your Instant Pot except for the coconut cream.
Lock the lid and cook at high pressure for 10 minutes. When the cooking is done, naturally release the pressure and remove the lid.
Use an immersion blender and puree the contents until smooth.
Gently stir in the coconut cream and adjust the seasoning if necessary. Serve and enjoy!
Nutrition:
Calories: 198
Fat: 14.6g
Net Carbs: 11g
Protein: 5g

706.   Creamy Cauliflower Soup

Preparation Time: 25 minutes
Servings: 6
Ingredients:
1 large cauliflower head, cut into florets
2 tablespoons of butter
1 tablespoon of olive oil
1 white onion, finely chopped
3 celery stalks, chopped
3 carrots, chopped
4 medium garlic cloves, minced
1 teaspoon of dried thyme
2 tablespoons of arrowroot powder
2 cups of homemade low-sodium chicken stock
2 cups of heavy whipping cream
Directions:
Press the "Sauté" setting on your Instant Pot and add the butter and olive oil. Once hot, add the chopped onions, garlic cloves, carrots and celery. Sauté for 4 minutes or until softened, stirring frequently.
Pour in the chicken stock and dried thyme. Lock the lid and cook at high pressure for 10 minutes. When the cooking is done, naturally release the pressure and remove the lid.
Stir in the heavy cream and arrowroot powder. Continue to cook until thickens, stirring occasionally. Serve and enjoy!
Nutrition:
Calories: 183
Fat: 11g
Net Carbs: 9g
Protein: 4g

707.   Creamy Leek and Salmon Soup

Preparation Time: 15 minutes
Servings: 4
Ingredients:
1 pound of boneless salmon fillets, cut into bite-sized pieces
2 tablespoons of avocado oil or extra-virgin olive oil
4 leeks, trimmed and sliced
3 medium garlic cloves, minced
6 cups of homemade low-sodium seafood stock or chicken stock
2 teaspoons of dried thyme
2 cups of heavy cream
1 teaspoon of fine sea salt
1 teaspoon of freshly cracked black pepper
Directions:
Press the "Sauté" setting on your Instant Pot and add the avocado oil. Once hot, add the leeks and garlic cloves. Sauté until almost softened, stirring frequently.

Add the remaining ingredients except for the heavy cream. Lock the lid and cook at high pressure for 4 minutes. When the cooking is done, naturally release the pressure and remove the lid. Gently stir in the heavy cream and adjust the seasoning if necessary. Serve and enjoy!

Nutrition:

Calories: 471

Fat: 37g

Net Carbs: 13g

Protein: 25g

708. Asparagus Soup with Parmesan Cheese and Lemon

Preparation Time: 30 minutes

Servings: 6

Ingredients:

2 pounds of asparagus, trimmed and cut into bite-sized pieces

3 tablespoons of butter

2 medium white or yellow onions, finely chopped

3 medium garlic cloves, peeled and crushed

6 cups of homemade low-sodium chicken stock

1 teaspoon of fine sea salt

1 teaspoon of freshly cracked black pepper

2 tablespoons of freshly squeezed lemon juice

½ teaspoon of fresh lemon zest

½ cup of shredded Parmigiano-Reggiano or shredded mozzarella cheese

¼ cup of fresh basil, chopped

Directions:

Press the "Sauté" setting on your Instant Pot and add the butter. Once melted, add the chopped onions, crushed garlic and lemon zest. Sauté for 4 minutes or until softened, stirring frequently. Add the asparagus and sauté for a minute or two, stirring frequently. Turn off the "Sauté" setting and add the chicken stock, salt, black pepper, lemon juice and fresh basil.

Lock the lid and cook at high pressure for 15 minutes. When the cooking is done, naturally release the pressure and remove the lid.

Use an immersion blender to puree the asparagus until smooth. Stir in the shredded cheese and allow to melt, stirring occasionally. Adjust the seasoning if necessary. Serve and enjoy!

Nutrition:

Calories: 170

Fat: 10g

Net Carbs: 8g

Protein: 12g

709. Hearty Green Soup

Preparation Time: 20 minutes

Servings: 4

Ingredients:

1 medium broccoli head, cut into florets

1 medium cauliflower head, cut into florets

3 zucchinis, chopped
3 leeks, chopped
1 medium white or yellow onion, finely chopped
½ cup of butter
2 cups of homemade low-sodium chicken stock
1 cup of heavy cream
Sea salt and freshly cracked black pepper (to taste

Directions:

Press the "Sauté" function on your Instant Pot and add the butter. Once hot, add the chopped onions, chopped leeks, chopped zucchini, broccoli and cauliflower. Sauté for 4 minutes, stirring frequently.

Add the chicken stock and lock the lid. Cook at high pressure for 5 minutes. When the cooking is done, naturally release the pressure and carefully remove the lid.

Use an immersion blender to puree the soup until smooth. Season with sea salt and freshly cracked black pepper. Gently stir in the heavy cream. Serve and enjoy!

Nutrition:

Calories: 425
Fat: 34g
Net Carbs: 13g
Protein: 12g

710.   Creamy Pumpkin Soup

Preparation Time: 20 minutes
Servings: 6
Ingredients:
2 (13-ouncecans of pumpkin
2 cups of homemade low-sodium chicken stock
1 cup of coconut cream
1 teaspoon of onion powder
1 teaspoon of smoked paprika
1 teaspoon of fine sea salt
1 teaspoon of freshly cracked black pepper
1 teaspoon of garlic powder
1 teaspoon of ground cinnamon

Directions:

Add all the ingredients except for the coconut cream inside your Instant Pot and give a good stir. Lock the lid and cook at high pressure for 8 minutes.

When the cooking is done, naturally release the pressure and remove the lid.

Use an immersion blender to puree the soup until smooth. Stir in the coconut cream.Serve and enjoy!

Nutrition:

Calories: 136
Fat: 6g
Net Carbs: 3g
Protein: 4g

711.   Italian Wedding Soup

Preparation Time: 25 minutes
Servings: 4
Meatball Ingredients:
1 pound of ground beef
1 teaspoon of fine sea salt
1 teaspoon of freshly cracked black pepper
1 teaspoon of garlic powder
2 tablespoons of fresh parsley, finely chopped
Soup Ingredients:
2 tablespoons of extra-virgin olive oil
2 tablespoons of fresh parsley, finely chopped
1 beaten egg
3 cups of baby spinach
6 cups of homemade low-sodium bone broth
2 medium garlic cloves, minced
2 celery stalks, chopped
½ onion, finely chopped
Directions:
In a large bowl, add all the meatball ingredients and mix with your hands until well combined. Form meatballs and set aside.
Press the "Sauté" function on your Instant Pot and add the olive oil. Once hot, add the chopped onions, garlic cloves and celery. Sauté for 2 minutes, stirring frequently.
Add the meatballs and remaining soup ingredients inside your Instant Pot. Lock the lid and cook at high pressure for 15 minutes. When the cooking is done, naturally release the pressure and remove the lid. Serve and enjoy!
Nutrition:
Calories: 441
Fat: 13g
Net Carbs: 3.2g
Protein: 36g

712.   Slow-Cooked Vegetable and Beef Soup

Preparation Time: 6 hours: 12
Ingredients:
4 bacon slices, roughly chopped
2 pounds of beef stew meat, cut into 1-inch pieces
2 tablespoons of red wine vinegar
4 cups of homemade low-sodium beef broth
1 medium yellow onion, finely chopped
1 small celeriac, finely chopped
¼ cup of carrots, chopped
1 (28-ouncecan of diced tomatoes
1 (6-ouncecan of tomato paste
2 medium garlic cloves, minced

½ teaspoon of dried rosemary
½ teaspoon of dried thyme
1 teaspoon of fine sea salt
½ teaspoon of freshly cracked black pepper
Instructions:"
Press the "Sauté" setting on your Instant Pot and add the chopped bacon. Cook until brown and crispy. Transfer to a plate lined with paper towels.
Add the beef meat and cook until brown, stirring occasionally.
Add the remaining ingredients and stir until well combined. Lock the lid and press the "Slow Cook" button and set the time to 8 hours. Remove the lid and adjust the seasoning if necessary.
Serve and enjoy!
Nutrition:
Calories: 214
Fat: 14g
Net Carbs: 5g
Protein: 18g

713. Turmeric Chicken Soup

Preparation Time: 30 minutes
Servings: 4
Ingredients:
2 teaspoons of turmeric powder
1 teaspoon of cumin powder
3 boneless, skinless chicken thighs
4 tablespoons of extra-virgin olive oil
1 small onion, finely chopped
1 cup of carrots, chopped
1 cup of cauliflower florets
1 cup of broccoli florets
5 cups of homemade low-sodium bone broth or vegetable broth
1 bay leaf
1 teaspoon of fresh ginger, finely grated
2 cups of chard, stems removed and sliced
½ cup of coconut milk
Directions:
Press the "Sauté" setting on your Instant Pot and add 2 tablespoons of olive oil. Once hot, add the chicken thighs and sear for 2 minutes per side or until brown. Remove and set aside.
Add the remaining tablespoons of olive oil. Add the chopped vegetables and sauté for 4 minutes or until slightly softened, stirring frequently.
Add the remaining ingredients except for the coconut milk inside your Instant Pot.
Lock the lid and cook at high pressure for 15 minutes. When the cooking is done, naturally release the pressure and remove the lid.
Transfer the chicken to a cutting board and shred using two forks. Return the shredded chicken to the soup along with the coconut milk. Stir and add more turmeric as needed. Serve and enjoy!
Nutrition:
Calories: 415

Fat: 30g
Net Carbs: 3g
Protein: 33g
Chicken Avocado Lime Soup
Preparation Time: 30 minutes
Servings: 4
Ingredients:
2 pounds of boneless, skinless chicken thighs
2 tablespoons of avocado oil
1 cup of green onions, finely chopped
2 jalapenos, seeds removed and minced
6 cups of homemade low-sodium chicken stock
2 Roma tomatoes, finely chopped
1/3 cup of fresh cilantro, chopped
1 teaspoon of fine sea salt
1 teaspoon of freshly cracked black pepper
3 tablespoons of freshly squeezed lime juice
3 medium avocados, peeled and finely chopped
Directions:
Press the "Sauté" setting on your Instant Pot and add the 1 tablespoon of avocado oil. Once hot, add the chicken thighs and sear for 2 minutes per side or until brown. Remove and set aside.
Add the remaining tablespoon of avocado oil to the pot and add the chopped green onions and jalapenos. Sauté for 2 minutes or until tender, stirring frequently.
Return the chicken stock along with the stock. Lock the lid and cook at high pressure for 15 minutes. When the cooking is done, naturally release the pressure and remove the lid.
Stir in the lime juice, chopped avocados, salt, black pepper, tomatoes and fresh cilantro.
Serve and enjoy!
Nutrition:
Calories: 370
Fat: 22g
Net Carbs: 8g
Protein: 33g

714. Chicken and Cauliflower Rice Soup

Preparation Time: 50 minutes
Servings: 6
Ingredients:
1 pound of boneless, skinless chicken breasts
2 celery stalks, chopped
2 carrots, chopped
1 small onion, finely chopped
2 tablespoons of olive oil
4 cups of homemade low-sodium chicken stock
1 teaspoon of fresh thyme, finely chopped
1 teaspoon of fine sea salt
1 teaspoon of freshly cracked black pepper

2 cups of cauliflower rice

2 cups of coconut cream

Directions:

Press the "Sauté" setting on your Instant Pot and add 1 tablespoon of olive oil. Once hot, add the chicken breasts and sear for 3 minutes or until brown. Remove and set aside.

Add the remaining tablespoon of olive oil along with the vegetables. Sauté for 4 minutes or until tender, stirring frequently.

Return the chicken along with the chicken stock. Lock the lid and cook at high pressure for 15 minutes. When the cooking is done, naturally release the pressure and remove the lid.

Transfer the chicken to a cutting board and shred using two forks.

Return the shredded chicken and remaining ingredients inside your Instant Pot. Allow the soup to get heated through, stirring occasionally. Serve and enjoy!

Nutrition:

Calories: 576

Fat: 44.1g

Net Carbs: 8.3g

Protein: 36.2g

715.   Pumpkin and Beef Stew

Preparation Time: 1 hour: 6

Ingredients:

2 tablespoons of olive oil

1 pound of beef stew meat, cut into bite-sized pieces

1 pound of pumpkin, peeled and cut into bite-sized pieces

4 cups of homemade low-sodium beef broth

1 (14.5-ouncecan of diced tomatoes, undrained

1 (6-ouncecan of tomato paste

2 bay leaves

2 garlic cloves, minced

1 large onion, finely chopped

½ teaspoon of chili powder

1 teaspoon of fine sea salt

1 teaspoon of freshly cracked black pepper

Directions:

Press the "Sauté" function on your Instant Pot and add the olive oil. Once hot, add the beef meat, onions and garlic. Sauté until the beef has browned and onions are tender, stirring frequently.

Add the beef broth and lock the lid. Cook at high pressure for 30 minutes. When the cooking is done, naturally release the pressure and remove the lid.

Stir in the pumpkin and remaining ingredients. Lock the lid and cook at high pressure for 10 minutes. When the cooking is done, naturally release the pressure and carefully remove the lid.Serve and enjoy!

Nutrition:

Calories: 261

Fat: 8g

Net Carbs: 12g

Protein: 30g

716. Smoky Eggplant Soup

Preparation Time: 15 minutes
Servings: 4
Ingredients:
2 pounds of eggplants, peeled and chopped
5 tablespoons of extra-virgin olive oil
1 large white or yellow onion, finely chopped
1 teaspoon of fine sea salt
1 teaspoon of freshly cracked black pepper
6 cups of homemade low-sodium chicken stock
½ teaspoon of cayenne pepper
1 lemon, juice and zest
2 tablespoons of fresh parsley, finely chopped
Directions:
Press the "Sauté" setting on your Instant Pot and add the olive oil. Once hot, add the chopped onions and minced garlic. Sauté until translucent, stirring occasionally.
Add the remaining ingredients and stir until well combined.
Lock the lid and cook at high pressure for 10 minutes. When the cooking is done, naturally release the pressure and remove the lid.
Use an immersion blender to puree the soup until smooth. Stir the contents again and adjust the seasoning as needed. Serve and enjoy!
Nutrition:
Calories: 200
Fat: 14g
Net Carbs: 7g
Protein: 8g

717. Butternut Squash Soup

Preparation Time: 45 minutes
Servings: 4
Ingredients:
1 (3-poundbutternut squash, peeled and cut into cubes
1 large onion, finely chopped
2 medium garlic cloves, minced
4 tablespoons of extra-virgin olive oil
2 tablespoons of tomato paste
4 cups of homemade low-sodium chicken or vegetable stock
1 cup of coconut cream
1 tablespoon of curry powder
1 teaspoon of fine sea salt
1 teaspoon of freshly cracked black pepper
1 teaspoon of pumpkin pie spice
Directions:
Press the "Sauté" setting on your Instant Pot and add the olive oil. Once hot, add the onion, garlic, and curry powder. Sauté for 4 minutes or until fragrant, stirring occasionally

Add the remaining ingredients except for the coconut cream.

Lock the lid and cook at high pressure for 30 minutes. When the cooking is done, naturally release the pressure and carefully remove the lid.

Use an immersion blender to puree the soup until smooth.

Gently stir in the coconut cream and adjust the seasoning if necessary. Serve and enjoy!

Nutrition:

Calories: 178

Fat: 27.3g

Net Carbs: 11g

Protein: 4.3g

718.   Creamy Tomato Soup

Preparation Time: 20 minutes

Servings: 4

Ingredients:

1 medium onion, finely chopped

4 garlic cloves, minced

1 (28-ouncecan of diced tomatoes

2 tablespoons of extra-virgin olive oil

1 tablespoon of dried oregano

1 tablespoon of dried basil

1 cup of homemade low-sodium chicken or vegetable stock

½ cup of coconut cream or heavy cream

1 teaspoon of apple cider vinegar

1 teaspoon of fine sea salt

1 teaspoon of freshly cracked black pepper

Directions:

Press the "Sauté" setting on your Instant Pot and add the olive oil. Once hot, add the chopped onions and minced garlic. Saute for 4 minutes, stirring frequently.

Add the remaining ingredients except for the cram. Lock the lid and cook at high pressure for 15 minutes. When the cooking is done, naturally release the pressure and remove the lid.

Use an immersion blender to puree the soup until smooth. Stir in the cream. Serve and enjoy!

Nutrition:

Calories: 83

Fat: 3g

Net Carbs: 6g

Protein: 3g

719.   Creamy Garlic Chicken Soup

Preparation Time: 20 minutes

Servings: 4

Ingredients:

2 large boneless, skinless chicken breasts

3 cups of chicken broth

4 garlic cloves, minced

4-ounces of cream cheese, softened
2 tablespoons of butter
2 tablespoons of olive oil or coconut oil
1 tablespoon of parsley, freshly chopped
1 tablespoon of garlic powder
2 teaspoons of onion powder
1 teaspoon of salt
1 teaspoon of black pepper
Directions:
Press the "Sauté" setting on your Instant Pot and add the olive oil. Once hot, add the chicken breasts and sear for4 minutes per side or until brown. Remove the chicken and add the minced garlic. Sauté for 1 minute or until fragrant, stirring frequently.
Return the chicken and add all the ingredients and stir until well combined. Lock the lid and cook at high pressure for 15 minutes. When the cooking is done, naturally release the pressure and remove the lid.
Transfer the chicken to a cutting board and shred using two forks. Return to the soup.Serve and enjoy!
Nutrition:
Calories: 371
Fat: 29g
Net Carbs: 3g
Protein: 15.5g

720.   Cauliflower Parmesan Soup

Preparation Time: 15 minutes
Servings: 6
Ingredients:
4 tablespoons of olive oil or coconut oil
4 garlic cloves, minced
4 cups of homemade low-sodium chicken stock
1 onion, finely chopped
1 leek, chopped
2 large cauliflower heads, cut into florets
½ cup of parmesan cheese, grated
1 teaspoon of fine sea salt
1 teaspoon of freshly cracked black pepper
2 tablespoons of fresh thyme, finely chopped
Directions:
Press the "Sauté" function on your Instant Pot and add olive oil. Once hot, add the chopped onions, leeks and garlic cloves. Sauté until softened, stirring occasionally.
Add the cauliflower florets and cook for another minute. Turn off the "Sauté" setting on your Instant Pot.
Add the remaining ingredients except for the parmesan cheese and stir until well combined. Lock the lid and cook at high pressure for 12 minutes. When the cooking is done, naturally release or quick release the pressure. Remove the lid.

Use an immersion blender to puree the soup until smooth. Stir in the parmesan cheese and allow to melt. Adjust the seasoning if necessary. Serve and enjoy!

Nutrition:

Calories: 180

Fat: 17g

Net Carbs: 5g

Protein: 55g

721.   Broccoli and Cheesy Soup

Preparation Time: 25 minutes

Servings: 4

Ingredients:

3 cups of homemade low-sodium chicken stock

4 cups of broccoli, cut into florets

3 cups of heavy cream

3 cups of cheddar cheese, shredded

1 cup of water

Directions:

Add 1 cup of water and a steamer basket inside your Instant Pot. Place the broccoli in the basket and lock the lid. Cook at high pressure for 3 minutes. When the cooking is done, quick release the pressure and remove the lid.

Discard the steamer basket and water. Add the broccoli to the inner pot.

Press the "Sauté" function on your Instant Pot and add the heavy cream. Allow the heavy cream to get heated through.

Lock the lid and cook at high pressure for 1 minute. When the cooking is done, quick release the pressure and remove the lid.

Stir in the shredded cheddar cheese and allow to melt. Serve and enjoy!

Nutrition:

Calories: 291

Fat: 25g

Net Carbs: 4g

Protein: 14g

722.   Italian-Style Broccoli Cheese Soup

Preparation Time: 30 minutes

Servings: 4

Ingredients:

3 broccoli stalks, chopped

1 large white onion, finely chopped

1 cup of matchsticks carrots

3 large garlic cloves, peeled and minced

3 cups of homemade low-sodium chicken stock

1 tablespoon of Italian parsley, minced

1 teaspoon of dried oregano

1 teaspoon of crushed red pepper flakes

¼ cup of heavy whipping cream
1 cup of shredded Mozzarella cheese
1 cup of shredded Italian cheese mix
¼ cup of parmesan cheese, finely grated
¼ cup of almond flour
Directions:
Add the chopped broccoli, onion, carrots, garlic, salt, black pepper and chicken stock inside your Instant Pot. Lock the lid and cook at high pressure for 3 minutes. When the cooking is done, naturally release the pressure and remove the lid.
Press the "Sauté" function on your Instant Pot and set to the lowest setting. Add the cheeses, parsley, dried oregano, crushed red pepper flakes and almond flour. Cook until the cheese has melted and the liquid thickens, stirring frequently. Serve and enjoy!
Nutrition:
Calories: 421
Fat: 30g
Net Carbs: 11g
Protein: 24g

723.   Winter Kale Vegetable Soup

Preparation Time: 20 minutes
Servings: 6
Ingredients:
1 pound of baby carrots, roughly chopped
5 celery stalks, chopped
5 cups of kale, stemmed and roughly chopped
 2 tablespoons of ghee
2 tablespoons of olive oil
1 onion, finely chopped
9 cups of homemade low-sodium chicken stock or vegetable stock
1 tablespoon of fresh thyme, chopped
3 bay leaves
1 teaspoon of fine sea salt
1 teaspoon of freshly cracked black pepper
Directions:
Press the "Sauté" function on your Instant Pot and add the olive oil. Once hot, add the chopped onions and minced garlic cloves. Cook until fragrant, stirring frequently.
Add the other vegetables and sauté for another minute.
Add the remaining ingredients and lock the lid.
Cook at high pressure for 15 minutes. When the cooking is done, quick release the pressure and remove the lid. Serve and enjoy!
Nutrition:
Calories: 90
Fat: 7g
Net Carbs: 9g
Protein: 7g

724. Sausage and Kale Soup

Preparation Time: 25 minutes
Servings: 6
Ingredients:
2 tablespoons of extra-virgin olive oil
1 pound of Andouille sausage, chopped
1 onion, finely chopped
3 garlic cloves, peeled and minced
1 cup of mushrooms, chopped
5 cups of homemade low-sodium chicken stock
1 cup of dry white wine
1 tablespoon of dried basil
4 cups of kale, stemmed and roughly chopped
2 tablespoons of apple cider vinegar
2 tablespoons of fresh thyme, finely chopped
1 teaspoon of fine sea salt
1 teaspoon of freshly cracked black pepper
Directions:
Press the "Sauté" function on your Instant Pot and add the olive oil. Add the chopped onions and minced garlic. Sauté until softened, stirring frequently.
Add the Andouille sausage and cook for 4 minutes, stirring frequently.
Add the remaining ingredients and lock the lid. Cook at high pressure for 8 minutes. When the cooking is done, quick release the pressure and remove the lid. Adjust the seasoning if necessary. Serve and enjoy!
Nutrition:
Calories: 333
Fat: 7g
Net Carbs: 4g
Protein: 17g

725. Mushroom and Chicken Coconut Soup

Preparation Time: 1 hour and 10 minutes
Servings: 4
Ingredients:
4 boneless, skinless chicken breasts
4 tablespoons of extra-virgin olive oil.
1 large onion, finely chopped
6 cups of homemade low-sodium chicken stock
2 cups of shiitake mushrooms, chopped
4 medium garlic cloves, peeled and minced
1 (14-ouncecan of coconut milk
1 (14.5-ouncecan of diced tomatoes
½ cup of fresh basil, chopped
1 tablespoon of red curry paste
2 tablespoons of fish sauce

1 teaspoon of fine sea salt
1 teaspoon of freshly cracked black pepper
Directions:
Press the "Sauté" setting on your Instant Pot add the olive oil. Once the oil is hot, add the chicken breast and sear until brown on both sides. Remove and set aside.

Add the onions, mushrooms and garlic cloves. Sauté until the vegetables have softened, stirring frequently.

Add the remaining ingredients except for the coconut milk inside your Instant Pot and stir until well combined. Lock the lid and cook at high pressure for 15 minutes. When the cooking is done, naturally release the pressure and remove the lid.

Transfer the chicken to a cutting board and shred using two forks. Return the shredded chicken to the soup along with the coconut milk. Adjust the seasoning if necessary. Serve and enjoy!

Nutrition:
Calories: 318
Fat: 9g
Net Carbs: 6.32g
Protein: 51g

Snacks

726.　　Cabbage and Avocado Salsa

Preparation Time: 15 minutes
Cooking Time: 12 minutes
Serving: 2
Ingredients:
¼ cup veggie stock
2 tablespoons olive oil
2 spring onions, chopped
1 red cabbage head, shredded
1 avocado, peeled, pitted and cubed
Directions:
Add tomatoes and all other ingredients to a suitable cooking pot.
Cover the pot's lid and cook for 12 minutes on medium heat.
Serve fresh and enjoy.
Nutrition:
Calories 132
Total Fat 7.1 g
Saturated Fat 1 g
Cholesterol 101 mg
Sodium 94 mg
Total Carbs 8.2 g
Sugar 1.9 g
Fiber 0.6 g
Protein 13.5 g

727.　　Spinach Cabbage Slaw

Preparation Time: 15 minutes
Cooking Time: 2 minutes
Serving: 2
Ingredients:
2 cups red cabbage, shredded
1 tablespoon mayonnaise
1 spring onion, chopped
1-lb. baby spinach
½ cup chicken stock
Directions:
Start by adding onion to a suitable pan, to sauté for 2 minutes.
Add spinach, stock and mayonnaise then mix well.
Serve fresh and enjoy.
Nutrition:
Calories 194
Total Fat 21.7 g
Saturated Fat 9.4 g

Cholesterol 105 mg
Sodium 384 mg
Total Carbs 8.3 g
Sugar 1.6 g
Fiber 1.3 g
Protein 3.2 g

728. Chicken Pesto Salad

Preparation Time: 15 minutes
Cooking Time: 4 minutes
Serving: 2
Ingredients:
1-lb. chicken breast, skinless, boneless and cubed
2 tablespoons basil pesto
2 tablespoons olive oil
2 tablespoons garlic, chopped
1 cup tomatoes, crushed
Directions:
Start by adding oil, chicken, and garlic to a cooking pan.
Then sauté for 5 minutes.
Stir in pesto and tomatoes.
Cover the pot's lid and cook for 15 minutes on medium heat.
Serve fresh and enjoy.
Nutrition:
Calories 136
Total Fat 18.3 g
Saturated Fat 2.6 g
Cholesterol 75 mg
Sodium 104 mg
Total Carbs 0.6 g
Sugar 6.2 g
Fiber 2.9 g
Protein 5.9 g

729. Peppers Avocado Salsa

Preparation Time: 15 minutes
Cooking Time: 12 minutes
Serving: 2
Ingredients:
1 and ½ lbs. mixed bell peppers, cut into strips
1 tablespoon avocado oil
½ cup tomato passata
1 avocado, peeled, pitted and cubed
Salt and black pepper, to taste
Directions:

Add bell peppers and all other ingredients to a suitable cooking pot.
Cover the pot's lid and cook for 12 minutes on medium heat.
Serve fresh and enjoy.
Nutrition:
Calories 304
Total Fat 20 g
Saturated Fat 3 g
Cholesterol 12 mg
Sodium 645 mg
Total Carbs 9 g
Sugar 2 g
Fiber 5 g
Protein 22 g

730.   Chard Spread

Preparation Time: 10 minutes
Cooking Time: 15 minutes
Servings: 4
Ingredients:
1-lb. salmon fillets, boneless, skinless and cubed
Salt and black pepper, to taste
¼ lb. Swiss chard, torn
1 spring onion, chopped
¼ cup chicken stock
Directions:
Add chard with all other ingredients to a cooking pot.
Cover the pot's lid and cook for 15 minutes on medium heat.
Use an immersion blender to blend the spread until smooth.
Serve fresh and enjoy.
Nutrition:
Calories 294
Total Fat 16.4 g
Saturated Fat 57 g
Cholesterol 120 mg
Sodium 343 mg
Total Carbs 1.1 g
Sugar 0.1 g
Fiber 0.3 g
Protein 35 g

731.   Olives Coconut Dip

Preparation Time: 5 minutes
Cooking Time: 10 minutes
Servings: 4
Ingredients:

4 cups baby spinach
½ cup coconut cream
Salt and black pepper, to taste
4 garlic cloves, roasted and minced
1 cup kalamata olives, pitted and halved
Directions:
Add olives and all other ingredients to a cooking pot.
Cover the pot's lid and cook for 10 minutes on medium heat.
Use an immersion blender to blend the olives mixture until smooth.
Serve fresh and enjoy.
Nutrition:
Calories 135
Total Fat 9.9 g
Saturated Fat 3.2 g
Cholesterol 34 mg
Sodium 10 mg
Total Carbs 3.1 g
Sugar 3.4 g
Fiber 1.5 g
Protein 8.6 g

732. Basil Peppers Dip

Preparation Time: 15 minutes
Cooking Time: 15 minutes
Serving: 2
Ingredients:
3 shallots, minced
1 and ½ lbs. mixed peppers, roughly chopped
¼ cup chicken stock
1 tablespoon olive oil
2 tablespoons basil, chopped
Directions:
Start by sautéing shallots with oil in a pan, then sauté for 2 minutes.
Stir in remaining ingredients and mix well
Cover the pot's lid and cook for 13 minutes on medium heat.
Use an immersion blender to blend the pepper mixture until smooth
Serve fresh and enjoy.
Nutrition:
Calories 199
Total Fat 17.4 g
Saturated Fat 11.3 g
Cholesterol 47 mg
Sodium 192 mg
Total Carbs 9.9 g
Sugar 1.5 g
Fiber 4.3 g

Protein 6.4 g

733.   Watercress Salsa

Preparation Time: 5 minutes
Cooking Time: 12 minutes
Servings: 4
Ingredients:
1 bunch watercress, trimmed
¼ cup chicken stock
1 cup tomato, cubed
1 avocado, peeled, pitted and cubed
2 zucchinis, cubed
Directions:
Start by adding watercress and all other ingredients to a cooking pot.
Cover the pot's lid and cook for 10 minutes on medium heat.
Serve fresh and enjoy.
Nutrition:
Calories 279
Total Fat 4.8 g
Saturated Fat 1 g
Cholesterol 45 mg
Sodium 24 mg
Total Carbs 5.8 g
Sugar 2.3 g
Fiber 4.5 g
Protein 5 g

734.   Beef Bites

Preparation Time: 10 minutes
Cooking Time: 15 minutes
Servings: 4
Ingredients:
1 tablespoon lime juice
2 tablespoons avocado oil
1-lb. beef stew meat, cubed
2 garlic cloves, minced
1 cup beef stock
Directions:
Start by adding oil, and meat to a cooking pan, then sauté for 5 minutes.
Stir in remaining ingredients and mix well
Cover the pot's lid and cook for 30 minutes on medium heat.
Serve fresh and enjoy.
Nutrition:
Calories 142
Total Fat 8.4 g

Saturated Fat 67 g
Cholesterol 743 mg
Sodium 346 mg
Total Carbs 3.4 g
Sugar 1 g
Fiber 0.8 g
Protein 4.1 g

735.   Cheese Stuffed Bell Peppers

Preparation Time: 10 minutes
Cooking Time: 15 minutes
Servings: 4
Ingredients:
4 red bell peppers, tops cut off and deseeded
¼ cup mozzarella, shredded
1 tablespoon garlic, minced
2 teaspoons lemon juice
1 cup baby spinach, torn
Directions:
To prepare the filling, toss all the ingredients in a bowl except the peppers and water.
Stuff the peppers with the prepared filling.
Place the peppers in a baking sheet and bake for 15 minutes at 375 degrees F.
Serve the peppers and enjoy.
Nutrition:
Calories 191
Total Fat 8.4 g
Saturated Fat 0.7 g
Cholesterol 743 mg
Sodium 226 mg
Total Carbs 7.1 g
Sugar 0.1 g
Fiber 1.4 g
Protein 6.3 g

736.   Olives Parsley Spread

Preparation Time: 10 minutes
Cooking Time: 10 minutes
Servings: 4
Ingredients:
2 cups black olives, pitted and halved
2 garlic cloves, minced
1 tablespoon lemon juice
1 tablespoon olive oil
¼ cup chicken stock
Salt and black pepper, to taste

Directions:

Add black olive, stock and all other ingredients to a suitable cooking pot.

Cover the pot's lid and cook for 10 minutes on medium heat.

Blend this mixture using a handheld blender.

Serve fresh and enjoy.

Nutrition:

Calories 124

Total Fat 13.4 g

Saturated Fat 7 g

Cholesterol 20 mg

Sodium 136 mg

Total Carbs 6.4 g

Sugar 2.1 g

Fiber 4.8 g

Protein 4.2 g

737. Basic Mushroom Salsa

Preparation Time: 10 minutes

Cooking Time: 10 minutes

Servings: 4

Ingredients:

1-lb. white mushrooms halved

¼ cup chicken stock

1 tablespoon basil, chopped

2 tomatoes, cubed

1 avocado, peeled, pitted and cubed

Salt and black pepper, to taste

Directions:

Add mushrooms and all other ingredients to a suitable cooking pot.

Cover the pot's lid and cook for 10 minutes on medium heat.

Serve fresh and enjoy.

Nutrition:

Calories 104

Total Fat 3.7 g

Saturated Fat 0.7 g

Cholesterol 33 mg

Sodium 141 mg

Total Carbs 6.5 g

Sugar 1.4 g

Fiber 0.7 g

Protein 5.4 g

738. Shrimp with Okra Bowls

Preparation Time: 10 minutes

Cooking Time: 12 minutes

Servings: 4
Ingredients:
1-lb. okra, trimmed
½ lb. shrimp, peeled and deveined
2 tablespoons olive oil
1 cup tomato passata, chopped
1 tablespoon cilantro, chopped
Salt and black pepper, to taste
Directions:
Add shrimp, okra and all other ingredients to a suitable cooking pot.
Cover the pot's lid and cook for 12 minutes on medium heat.
Serve fresh and enjoy.
Nutrition:
Calories 134
Total Fat 21.4 g
Saturated Fat 1.2 g
Cholesterol 244 mg
Sodium 10 mg
Total Carbs 10.1 g
Sugar 2.7 g
Fiber 5.2 g
Protein 2.3 g

739. Thyme Celery Spread

Preparation Time: 10 minutes
Cooking Time: 12 minutes
Servings: 4
Ingredients:
2 lbs. eggplant, roughly chopped
2 celery stalks, chopped
2 tablespoons olive oil
4 garlic cloves, minced
½ cup veggie stock
Salt and black pepper, to taste
Directions:
Stat by adding oil, celery stalks and garlic to a pan, then sauté for 2 minutes.
Stir in remaining ingredients and mix well
Cover the pot's lid and cook for 10 minutes on medium heat.
Blend the spread using an immersion blender until smooth
Serve fresh and enjoy.
Nutrition:
Calories 204
Total Fat 15.7 g
Saturated Fat 9.7 g
Cholesterol 49 mg
Sodium 141 mg

Total Carbs 12.6 g
Sugar 3.4 g
Fiber 1.5 g
Protein 6.3 g

740. Nutmeg Spiced Endives

Preparation Time: 10 minutes
Cooking Time: 10 minutes
Servings: 4
Ingredients:
4 endives, trimmed and halved
Salt and black pepper to the taste
2 tablespoons olive oil
1 teaspoon nutmeg, ground
1 tablespoon chives, chopped
Directions:
Toss endives with all other ingredients in a baking sheet.
Bake the endives for 5 minutes in a preheated oven at 350 degrees F.
Serve fresh and enjoy.
Nutrition:
Calories 131
Total Fat 10.4 g
Saturated Fat 9.5 g
Cholesterol 10 mg
Sodium 106 mg
Total Carbs 9.1 g
Sugar 0.5 g
Fiber 3.4 g
Protein 2.3 g

741. Fennel with Leeks

Preparation Time: 5 minutes
Cooking Time: 8 minutes
Servings: 4
Ingredients:
4 leeks, roughly sliced
2 fennel bulbs, halved
1 tablespoon smoked paprika
1 teaspoon chili sauce
1 tablespoon ghee, melted
Salt and black pepper, to taste
Directions:
Toss the leeks and fennel bulbs with all other ingredients in a baking tray.
Bake the fennels for 10 minutes in a preheated oven at 350 degrees F.
Toss well then serve.

Nutrition:
Calories 158
Total Fat 14.2 g
Saturated Fat 6.2 g
Cholesterol 35 mg
Sodium 69 mg
Total Carbs 9.1 g
Sugar 0.5 g
Fiber 2.7 g
Protein 3.8 g

742. Sesame Garlic Broccolini

Preparation Time: 10 minutes
Servings: 4
Ingredients:
2 bunches of broccolini
2 tablespoons of toasted sesame oil
1 teaspoon of garlic sea salt
1 lemon, juiced
Directions:
Add 1 cup of water and a steamer basket inside your Instant Pot. Place the broccolini on top.
Lock the lid and cook at high pressure for 2 minutes. When the cooking is done, quick release the pressure and remove the lid.
Drizzle with sesame oil, garlic sea salt and lemon juice.Serve and enjoy!
Nutrition:
Calories: 75
Fat: 6.8g
Net Carbs: 3g
Protein: 1g

743. Southern Collard Greens

Preparation Time: 30 minutes
Servings: 8
Ingredients:
16-ounces of collard greens
1 small onion, finely chopped
2 tablespoons of olive oil
2 bacon slices, uncooked and chopped
4-ounces of ham, sliced and chopped
1/3 cup of apple cider vinegar
¾ cups of homemade low-sodium chicken stock
Fine sea salt and freshly cracked black pepper (to taste
Directions:
Press the "Sauté" Setting on your Instant Pot and add the olive oil. Once hot, add the chopped bacon and ham. Cook for 4 to 5 minutes, stirring occasionally.

Add the onions and continue to cook until golden, stirring occasionally.

Add the remaining ingredients inside your Instant Pot and stir until well combined. Lock the lid and cook at high pressure for 5 minutes. When the cooking is done, naturally release the pressure for 5 minutes, then quick release the remaining pressure. Carefully remove the lid. Serve and enjoy!

Nutrition:

Calories: 92

Fat: 5g

Net Carbs: 3g

Protein: 7g

Sauerkraut

Preparation Time: 25 minutes

Servings: 8

Ingredients:

½ cup of homemade low-sodium chicken stock

2 (14.5-ouncescans of shredded sauerkraut

¾ teaspoons of caraway seeds

1 small onion, finely chopped

3 medium slices of bacon, chopped

½ teaspoon of fine sea salt

½ teaspoon of freshly cracked black pepper

Directions:

Press the "Sauté" setting on your Instant Pot and add the chopped bacon. Continue to cook for 4 minutes or until almost brown, stirring frequently.

Add the chopped onions and continue to cook for 5 to 6 minutes or until golden brown, stirring occasionally.

Add the remaining ingredients. Lock the lid and cook at high pressure for 10 minutes.

When the cooking is done, naturally release the pressure for 10 minutes, then quick release the remaining pressure. Carefully remove the lid. Serve and enjoy!

Nutrition:

Calories: 67

Fat: 4g

Net Carbs: 3g

Protein: 4g

744.   Okra Gumbo

Preparation Time: 30 minutes

Servings: 4

Ingredients:

2 celery stalks, chopped

1 medium onion, finely chopped

2 cups of okra, chopped

1 green bell pepper, chopped

5 medium garlic cloves, peeled and minced

2 bay leaves

1 teaspoon of smoked paprika

1 teaspoon of dried thyme

1 to 2 teaspoons of Cajun seasoning
1 tablespoon of Worcestershire sauce
4 cups of homemade low-sodium vegetable stock
Fine sea salt and freshly cracked black pepper (to taste
Roux Ingredients:
½ cup of olive oil
½ cup of almond or coconut flour
Directions:
Press the "Sauté" setting on your Instant Pot and add the olive oil and flour. Cook for 30 seconds, whisking frequently.
Add the chopped onions, chopped celery and chopped bell peppers. Cook for another 5 minutes, stirring occasionally.
Stir in the remaining ingredients until well combined. Lock the lid and cook at high pressure for 10 minutes. When done, quick release the pressure and remove the lid. Serve and enjoy!
Nutrition:
Calories: 275
Fat: 28g
Net Carbs: 4g
Protein: 2g

745. Glazed Bok Choy

Preparation Time: 10 minutes
Servings: 6
Ingredients:
1 pound of bok choy
½ cup of water
1-inch piece of fresh ginger, peeled and minced
1 medium garlic clove, peeled and minced
3 tablespoons of coconut aminos
1 tablespoon of dry white wine
1 tablespoon of olive oil
Directions:
Press the "Sauté" setting on your Instant Pot and add the olive oil. Once hot, add the ginger and garlic. Sauté for 1 minute, stirring frequently.
Add the bok choy and water inside your Instant Pot. Lock the lid and cook at high pressure for 5 minutes. In another bowl, add the coconut aminos and white wine. Mix well.
Quick release the Instant Pot and remove the lid. Stir in the mixture. Serve and enjoy!
Nutrition:
Calories: 30
Fat: 2.5g
Net Carbs: 1g
Protein: 1.1g

746. Bacon Wrapped Asparagus

Preparation Time: 15 minutes
Servings: 3
Ingredients:
12 asparagus spears
6 slices of bacon
½ cup of heavy cream
1 cup of water
Fine sea salt and freshly cracked black pepper (to taste
Directions:
Add 1 cup of water and a trivet inside your Instant Pot.
Spread the heavy cream over the asparagus and season with sea salt and black pepper.
Divide your asparagus spears into 3 separate portions.
Wrap 2 slices of bacon onto each asparagus group. Place the asparagus onto the trivet.
Lock the lid and cook at high pressure for 3 minutes. When the cooking is done, naturally release the pressure and remove the lid. Serve and enjoy!
Nutrition:
Calories: 294
Fat: 23.4g
Net Carbs: 2.4g
Protein: 16.6g

747.   Simple Cauliflower Rice

Preparation Time: 5 minutes
Servings: 4
Ingredients:
1 large head of cauliflower, cut into florets
2 tablespoons of extra-virgin olive oil
1 teaspoon of fine sea salt
1 tablespoon of fresh parsley, finely chopped
¼ teaspoon of cumin
¼ teaspoon of turmeric
¼ teaspoon of smoked paprika
Directions:
Add 1 cup of water and a steamer basket inside your Instant Pot. Place the cauliflower on the steamer basket. Lock the lid.
Cook at high pressure for 1 minute. When the cooking is done, quick release the pressure and remove the lid. Transfer the cauliflower to a food processor. Pulse until rice-like consistency. Add the olive oil, salt, cumin, turmeric, and smoked paprika. Give another pulse. Serve and enjoy!
Nutrition:
Calories: 98
Fat: 7g
Net Carbs: 4g
Protein: 3g

748.   Creamy Mashed Cauliflower with Kale

Preparation Time: 15 minutes
Servings: 4
Ingredients:
2 pounds of cauliflower florets
1 cup of homemade low-sodium chicken stock
¼ cup of unsalted butter, melted
3 cups of fresh kale, stemmed and roughly chopped
4 medium garlic cloves, crushed
2 scallions, chopped
1 cup of heavy whipping cream (more if needed
1 teaspoon of fine sea salt
1 teaspoon of freshly cracked black pepper
Directions:
Add 1 cup of water and a steamer basket inside your Instant Pot. Place the cauliflower in the steamer basket.
Lock the lid and cook at high pressure for 4 minutes. When the cooking is done, quick release the pressure and remove the lid.
Remove the steamer basket and discard the water. Add the cauliflower florets inside your inner pot. Add the remaining ingredients except for the immersion blender. Use a potato masher to blend the cauliflower until smooth.
Stir in the kale. Lock the lid and cook at high pressure for 1 minutes. When the cooking is done, quick release the pressure and remove the lid. Serve and enjoy!
Nutrition:
Calories: 294
Fat: 23g
Net Carbs: 12g
Protein: 7g

749.   Coconut Cream and Herbed Mashed Potatoes

Preparation Time: 15 minutes
Servings: 6
Ingredients:
2 pounds of cauliflower florets
1 small onion, finely chopped
4 whole garlic cloves, peeled and crushed
1 ½ pounds of fresh rosemary
2 tablespoons of fresh parsley, finely chopped
2 tablespoons of coconut oil, melted
1 ½ cup of coconut milk or coconut cream
1 teaspoon of fine sea salt
1 teaspoon of freshly cracked black pepper
Directions:
Add 1 cup of water and a steamer basket inside your Instant Pot. Place the cauliflower florets and the rosemary onto the steamer basket.
Lock the lid and cook at high pressure for 4 minutes. When the cooking is done, quick release the pressure and remove the lid.

Discard the water and remove the steamer basket. Place the cauliflower florets inside the inner pot along with the remaining ingredients. Use a potato masher to mash the cauliflower until smooth. Serve and enjoy!
Nutrition:
Calories: 321Fat: 23.4gNet Carbs: 8g   Protein: 7.2g

750.   Creamy Mozzarella Mashed Cauliflower

Preparation Time: 20 minutes
Servings: 4
Ingredients:
1 large head of cauliflower, chopped
1 cup of homemade low-sodium chicken stock
4 whole garlic cloves, peeled
6 fresh sprigs of thyme
½ cup of shredded mozzarella cheese
½ cup of plain Greek yogurt
½ teaspoon of fine sea salt
½ teaspoon of freshly cracked black pepper
Directions:
Add the chicken stock, garlic cloves and fresh sprigs of thyme.
Add a trivet inside the Instant Pot and place a cauliflower on top. Lock the lid and cook at high pressure for 12 minutes. When the cooking is done, quick release the pressure and remove the lid. Discard the liquid and remove the trivet. Return the cauliflower inside your Instant Pot along with the mozzarella cheese, Greek yogurt, salt and freshly cracked black pepper.
Use an immersion blender to blend the cauliflower until smooth. Serve and enjoy!
Nutrition:
Calories: 110 Fat: 4gNet Carbs: 7g   Protein: 11g

751.   Creamed Spinach

Preparation Time: 10 minutes
Servings: 4
Ingredients:
1 pound of fresh spinach
¼ cup of unsalted butter
½ cup of heavy whipping cream
½ teaspoon of onion powder
½ teaspoon of garlic powder
1 teaspoon of fine sea salt
1 teaspoon of freshly cracked black pepper
4 tablespoons of parmesan cheese, finely grated
Directions:
Press the "Sauté" function on your Instant Pot and add the butter and spinach. Sauté until the spinach has wilted, stirring frequently.
Add the heavy whipping cream. Lock the lid and cook at high pressure for 3 minutes. When the cooking is done, quick release the pressure and carefully remove the lid.

Stir in the grated parmesan cheese and allow to melt. Season with the onion powder, garlic powder, sea salt and freshly cracked black pepper. Serve and enjoy!
Nutrition:
Calories: 197 Fat: 18gNet Carbs: 2.3g   Protein: 8g

752.   Spinach Saag

Preparation Time: 25 minutes
Servings: 4
Ingredients:
1 pound of spinach
1 pound of mustard leaves
4 tablespoons of ghee
2-inch fresh piece of ginger, peeled and finely minced
4 medium garlic cloves, minced
2 teaspoons of fine sea salt
1 teaspoon of coriander
1 teaspoon of ground cumin
1 teaspoon of garam masala
½ teaspoon of turmeric
½ teaspoon of cayenne pepper
½ teaspoon of freshly cracked black pepper
Instructions;
Press the "Sauté" setting on your Instant Pot and add the ghee. Once hot, add the onion, garlic, ginger and seasonings. Sauté until translucent, stirring frequently.
Add the spinach and mustard greens. Lock the lid and cook at high pressure for 15 minutes. When the cooking is done, quick release the pressure and remove the lid.
Use an immersion blender to blend the contents to your desired consistency. Serve and enjoy!
Nutrition:
Calories: 192
Fat: 19.6g
Net Carbs: 6.32g
Protein: 5.8g

753.   Stuffed Mushrooms

Preparation Time: 30 minutes
Servings: 20
Ingredients:
Around 40 mushrooms, stemmed
1 pound of ground sausage
1 medium onion, finely chopped
2 garlic cloves, peeled and minced
1 (8-ouncepackage of cream cheese, softened
2 large eggs, beaten
1 cup of shredded mozzarella cheese
1/3 cup of homemade low-sodium vegetable broth

Fine sea salt and freshly cracked black pepper (to taste

Directions:

Press the "Sauté" function on your Instant Pot and add the ground sausage. Cook until the sausage has browned, breaking up the meat with a wooden spoon.

Add the chopped onions and minced garlic. Cook for another 3 minutes or until softened, stirring occasionally.

Add the sausage mixture to a large bowl. Stir in the cream cheese, egg yolks and shredded mozzarella cheese, reserve some of the mozzarella cheese.

Spoon the sausage mixture into the mushrooms.

Add the vegetable broth in your inner pot. Place the mushrooms to the inner pot and sprinkle with the shredded mozzarella cheese.

Lock the lid and cook at high pressure for 5 minutes. When the cooking is done, quick release the pressure and carefully remove the lid. Serve and enjoy!

Nutrition:

Calories: 152

Fat: 13g

Net Carbs: 4g

Protein: 8g

754. Balsamic Mushrooms

Preparation Time: 15 minutes

Servings: 4

Ingredients:

1/3 cup of extra-virgin olive oil

3 medium garlic cloves, minced

1 pound of fresh mushrooms, sliced

3 tablespoons of balsamic vinegar

3 tablespoons of red wine

Fine sea salt and freshly cracked black pepper (to taste

Directions:

Press the "Sauté" setting on your Instant Pot and add the olive oil. Once hot, add the minced garlic cloves and mushrooms. Sauté for 3 minutes or until softened, stirring frequently.

Turn off the "Sauté' setting on your Instant Pot. Stir in the balsamic vinegar, red wine, sea salt and freshly cracked black pepper. Stir until well coated, stirring occasionally. Serve and enjoy!

Nutrition:

Calories: 180

Fat: 17.1g

Net Carbs: 3.1g

Protein: 3.6g

755. Garlic Mushrooms with Butter Sauce

Preparation Time: 20 minutes

Servings: 2

Ingredients:

1 pound of small button mushrooms

2 tablespoons of extra-virgin olive oil

2 tablespoons of unsalted butter

1 teaspoon of fresh thyme

2 medium garlic cloves, minced

2 tablespoons of fresh parsley, finely chopped

Fine sea salt and freshly cracked black pepper (to taste

Directions:

Press the "Sauté" setting on your Instant Pot and add the olive oil. Once hot, add the mushrooms, caps down and sauté for 5 minutes.

Add the remaining ingredients and lock the lid. Cook at high pressure for 12 minutes. When the cooking is done, naturally release the pressure for 5 minutes, then quick release the remaining pressure. Carefully remove the lid.

Transfer the mushrooms to a platter and spoon with the butter sauce. Serve and enjoy!

Nutrition:

Calories: 270

Fat: 26.2g

Net Carbs: 5g

Protein: 7.3g

756.   Sri Lankan Coconut Cabbage

Preparation Time: 25 minutes

Servings: 4

Ingredients:

1 medium cabbage, chopped

1 tablespoon of turmeric powder

1 tablespoon of curry powder

1 teaspoon of mustard powder

1 medium onion, finely chopped

2 medium garlic cloves, peeled and crushed

1 medium carrot, sliced

2 tablespoons of freshly squeezed lemon juice

½ cup of desiccated unsweetened coconut

2 tablespoons of olive oil

1/3 cups of water

Directions:

Press the "Sauté" setting on your Instant Pot and add the oil. Once hot, add the chopped onions and sauté until tender, stirring occasionally.

Add the crushed garlic and all seasonings. Sauté for another 30 seconds.

Add the remaining ingredients. Lock the lid and cook at high pressure for 5 minutes. When the cooking is done, quick release the pressure and carefully remove the lid. Serve and enjoy!

Nutrition:

Calories: 549

Fat: 54.6g

Net Carbs: 8.4g

Protein: 4.7g

757. Unstuffed Cabbage Bowls

Preparation Time: 30 minutes
Servings: 4
Ingredients:
1 pound of ground beef
1 tablespoon of olive oil
1 medium onion, finely chopped
4 medium garlic cloves, minced
1 red bell pepper, finely chopped
1 medium cabbage head, chopped
1 cup of cauliflower rice
1 cup of homemade low-sodium beef broth
1 (8-ouncecan of tomato paste
Directions:
Press the "Sauté" setting on your Instant Pot and add the olive oil. Once hot, add the ground beef, onions, garlic and bell peppers. Sauté until the beef is no longer pink.
Add the beef broth and tomato paste. Lock the lid and cook at high pressure for 15 minutes. Quick release the pressure and remove the lid.
Stir in the cauliflower rice and cabbage. Lock the lid and cook for 3 minutes at high pressure. Quick release. Serve and enjoy!
Nutrition:
Calories: 312
Fat: 9g
Net Carbs: 3g
Protein: 30g

758. Sausage Cabbage Bowls

Preparation Time: 35 minutes
Servings: 6
Ingredients:
12 cups of thinly sliced cabbage
¼ cup of fresh parsley, finely chopped
1 pound of Italian chicken sausage
1 tablespoon of olive oil
1 yellow onion, finely chopped
3 medium garlic cloves, minced
1 teaspoon of smoked paprika
1 teaspoon of dried oregano
1 ¼ cup of homemade low-sodium chicken broth
1 cup of diced tomatoes
½ cup of cauliflower rice
½ teaspoon of fine sea salt
½ teaspoon of freshly cracked black pepper
Directions:

Press the "Sauté" setting on your Instant Pot and add the olive oil. Once hot, add the chicken sausage and onions. Cook until the sausage is brow and the onions are tender, stirring occasionally. Stir in the minced garlic, smoked paprika, dried oregano, sea salt and freshly cracked black pepper. Cook for another 30 seconds, stirring frequently.

Add the chicken broth and diced tomatoes. Stir until well combined.

Lock the lid and cook at high pressure for 12 minutes. When the cooking is done, naturally release the pressure and carefully remove the lid.

Stir in the cauliflower rice and cabbage. Lock the lid and cook at high pressure for 3 minutes. When the cooking is done, manually release the pressure and carefully remove the lid.

Stir in the fresh parsley. Serve and enjoy!

Nutrition:

Calories: 80

Fat: 244

Net Carbs: 6g

Protein: 17g

759.   Steamed Artichokes

Preparation Time: 30 minutes

Servings: 4

Ingredients:

4 large artichokes, trimmed

1 cup of water

1 bay leaf

2 whole garlic cloves

1 fresh medium lemon, juice

Directions:

Prepare your artichokes: Cut the tops of the artichokes and remove the stems and outer leaves.

Add the water, bay leaves, garlic cloves inside your Instant Pot. Place a steamer basket inside.

Squeeze the lemon juice over the artichokes and place on top of the steamer basket.

Lock the lid and cook at high pressure for 10 minutes. When the cooking is done, quick release the pressure and carefully remove the lid.

Remove the artichokes from your Instant Pot. Serve and enjoy!

Nutrition:

Calories: 76

Fat: 0.2g

Net Carbs: 8.5g

Protein: 5.3g

760.   Artichokes with Jalapeno Dip

Preparation Time: 20 minutes

Servings: 4

Ingredients:

4 medium artichokes

1 cup of water

1 tablespoon of extra-virgin olive oil

1 tablespoon of freshly squeezed lemon juice
1 tablespoon of dried rosemary
A small pinch of fine sea salt and freshly cracked black pepper (to taste
Jalapeno Dip Ingredients:
½ cup of jalapenos, chopped
½ cup of cream cheese
½ cup of Greek yogurt
2 tablespoons of fresh parsley, finely chopped
Directions:
Prepare your artichokes: Cut the tops of the artichokes and remove the stems and outer leaves.
Add 1 cup of water and a steamer rack inside your Instant Pot. Place the artichokes on top of the steamer rack.
Drizzle with the olive oil and lemon juice. Season with dried rosemary, sea salt and black pepper.
Lock the lid and cook at high pressure for 10 minutes. When the cooking is done, quick release the pressure and remove the lid.
 In a food processor, add all the jalapeno dip ingredients. Pulse until well combined. Transfer to a bowl.
Serve the artichokes with the jalapeno dip. Serve and enjoy!
Nutrition:
Calories: 128
Fat: 6g
Net Carbs: 4g
Protein: 6g

761.   Italian Stuffed Artichokes

Preparation Time: 20 minutes
Servings: 3
Ingredients:
3 artichokes
1 cup of pork rinds, finely crushed
¼ cup of sour cream
3 tablespoons of parmesan cheese, finely grated
1 tablespoon of fresh parsley, finely chopped
1 tablespoon of garlic, minced
1 cup of shredded mozzarella cheese
A small pinch of fine sea salt and freshly cracked black pepper
Directions:
Prepare your artichokes: Cut the tops of the artichokes and remove the stems and outer leaves.
In a bowl, add the crushed pork rinds, sour cream, parmesan cheese, parsley, minced garlic, shredded cheese, sea salt and freshly cracked black pepper. Mix well and spoon the stuffing inside the artichokes.
Add 1 cup of water and a steamer rack inside your Instant Pot. Place the artichokes on top.
Lock the lid and cook at high pressure for 15 minutes. When the cooking is done, quick release the pressure and carefully remove the lid. Serve and enjoy!
Nutrition:
Calories: 391

Fat: 21.7g
Net Carbs: 10g
Protein: 36g

762.   Artichokes with Creamy Herb Dip

Preparation Time: 20 minutes
Servings: 2
Artichoke Ingredients:
2 large artichokes
2 tablespoons of extra-virgin olive oil
2 tablespoons of freshly squeezed lemon juice
Creamy Herb Dip Ingredients:
½ cup of plain Greek yogurt
1-ounce of cream cheese, softened
1 tablespoon of mayonnaise
1 tablespoon of fresh parsley, finely chopped
1 tablespoon of fresh chives
A small pinch of fine sea salt and freshly cracked black pepper
Directions:
Prepare your artichokes: Cut the tops of the artichokes and remove the stems and outer leaves.
In a bowl, add all the creamy herb dip ingredients and stir until well combined. Refrigerate and set aside.
Add 1 cup of water and a steamer basket inside your Instant Pot. Place the artichokes on top. Lock the lid and cook at high pressure for 10 minutes.
When the cooking is done, naturally release the pressure and serve the artichokes along with the dip. Serve and enjoy!
Nutrition:
Calories: 580
Fat: 30g
Net Carbs: 12g
Protein: 46g

763.   Tuscan-Style Baby Artichokes

Preparation Time: 10 minutes
Servings: 4
Ingredients:
Around 9 baby artichokes, washed and trimmed
½ cup of dry white wine
2 tablespoons of freshly squeezed lemon juice
1 medium garlic clove, minced
1 teaspoon of garlic powder
1 teaspoon of fine sea salt
1 cup of water
¼ cup of extra-virgin olive oil
½ cup of Parmesan cheese, finely grated

Directions:

Prepare your artichokes: Cut the tops of the artichokes and remove the stems and outer leaves. Cut the artichokes lengthwise into 4 slices for each artichoke.

Press the "Sauté" Setting on your Instant Pot and add the olive oil. Once hot, add the artichokes and garlic. Sauté for a couple of minutes, stirring frequently.

Add the remaining ingredients except for the parmesan cheese inside your Instant Pot. Lock the lid and cook at high pressure for 5 minutes. When the cooking is done, quick release the pressure and carefully remove the lid

Remove the artichokes from your Instant Pot and place into a large bowl. Add the grated cheese and toss until well combined. Serve and enjoy!

Nutrition:

Calories: 289

Fat: 19g

Net Carbs: 6g

Protein: 10g

764.   Artichokes with Lemon Chive Butter

Preparation Time: 20 minutes

Servings: 3

Ingredients:

3 large artichokes

1 lemon, wedged

3 tablespoons of freshly squeezed lemon juice

¼ teaspoon of fresh lemon zest

4 tablespoons of unsalted butter, melted

2 tablespoons of olive oil or coconut oil

2 tablespoons of fresh chives, minced

A small pinch of fine sea salt

Directions:

Prepare your artichokes: Cut the tops of the artichokes and remove the stems and outer leaves.

Pour 1 cup of water and a steamer basket inside your Instant Pot. Place the artichokes on top of the steamer basket.

Lock the lid and cook at high pressure for 13 minutes. When the cooking is done, naturally release the pressure for 10 minutes, then quick release the remaining pressure. Carefully remove the lid.

In a small bowl, add the olive oil, unsalted butter, lemon juice, lemon zest, fresh chives, and fine sea salt. Mix well. Serve the artichokes with the lemon-chive butter. Enjoy!

Nutrition:

Calories: 298

Fat: 25.6g

Net Carbs: 9g

Protein: 6g

765.   Parmesan Garlic Artichokes

Preparation Time: 15 minutes

Servings: 4

Ingredients:

4 artichokes, washed and prepared

4 medium garlic cloves, peeled and minced

2 tablespoons of olive oil

¼ cup of parmesan cheese, finely grated or shredded

½ cup of homemade low-sodium vegetable stock or chicken stock

Directions:

Prepare your artichokes: Cut the tops of the artichokes and remove the stems and outer leaves. Top each artichoke with 1 minced garlic and drizzle with olive oil.

Sprinkle with parmesan cheese

Pour ½ cup of vegetable stock and a steamer basket inside your Instant Pot. Place the artichokes on the steamer basket.

Place the artichokes on top. Lock the lid and press the "Steam" setting and set the time for 10 minutes.

When the cooking is done, quick release the pressure and remove the lid. Serve and enjoy!

Nutrition:

Calories: 128

Fat: 8g

Net Carbs: 8g

Protein: 6g

766.　　Sautéed Radishes

Preparation Time: 15 minutes

Servings: 4

Ingredients:

1 pound of radishes, quartered

2 tablespoons of unsalted butter

Directions:

Press the "Sauté" setting on your Instant Pot and set to medium setting.

Add the butter. Once melted, add the radishes and sauté for 10 to 15 minutes or until tender.

Serve and enjoy!

Nutrition:

Calories: 69

Fat: 5.9g

Net Carbs: 2g

Protein: 0.8g

767.　　Bok Choy Crisps

Preparation Time: 10 minutes

Servings: 2

INGREDIENTS

2 tbsp olive oil

4 cups packed bok choy

1 tsp vegan seasoning

1 tbsp yeast flakes

Sea salt, to taste
DIRECTIONS
In a bowl, mix oil, bok choy, yeast and vegan seasoning. Dump the coated kale in the Air fryer's basket.
Set the temperature to 360 F and cook for to 5 minutes. Shake after 3 minutes.
Serve sprinkled with sea salt.

768. Ham Rolls with Vegetables and Walnuts

Preparation Time: 15 minutes
Servings: 4
INGREDIENTS
8 rice leaves
4 carrots
4 slices ham
2 oz walnuts, finely chopped
1 zucchini
1 clove garlic
1 tbsp olive oil
1 tbsp ginger powder
¼ cup basil leaves, finely chopped
Salt and black pepper to taste
DIRECTIONS
In a cooking pan, pour olive oil and add the zucchini, carrots, garlic, ginger and salt; cook on low heat for 10 minutes.
Add the basil and walnuts, and keep stirring. Soak the rice leaves in warm water. Then fold one side above the filling and roll in.
Cook the rolls in the preheated Air fryer for 5 minutes at 300 F.

769. Garlic Potato Chips

Preparation Time: 50 minutes
Servings: 3
Ingredients
3 whole potatoes, cut into thin slices
¼ cup olive oil
1 tbsp garlic
½ cup cream
2 tbsp rosemary
Directions
Preheat your Air Fryer to 390 F. In a bowl, add oil, garlic and salt to form a marinade. In a separate bowl, add potato slices and top with cold water. Allow sitting for 30 minutes. Drain the slices and transfer them to marinade.
Allow sitting for 30 minutes. Lay the potato slices onto your Air Fryer's cooking basket and cook for 20 minutes. After 10 minutes, give the chips a turn, sprinkle with rosemary and serve.

770. Simple Parmesan Sandwich

Preparation Time: 20 minutes
Servings: 1
Ingredients
2 tbsp Parmesan cheese, shredded
2 scallions
2 tbsp butter
2 slices bread
¾ cup cheddar cheese
Directions
Preheat your Air Fryer to 360 F. Lay the bread slices on a flat surface. On one slice, spread the exposed side with butter, followed by cheddar and scallions. On the other slice, spread butter and then sprinkle cheese.
Bring the buttered sides together to form sand. Place the sandwich in your Air Fryer's cooking basket and cook for 10 minutes. Serve with berry sauce.

771.   Homemade Cheddar Biscuits

Preparation Time: 35 minutes
Servings: 8
Ingredients
½ cup + 1 tbsp butter
2 tbsp sugar
3 cups flour
1 ⅓ cups buttermilk
½ cup Cheddar cheese, grated
Directions
Preheat your Air Fryer to 380 F. Lay a parchment paper on a baking plate. In a bowl, mix sugar, flour, ½ cup butter, cheese and buttermilk to form a batter. Make 8 balls from the batter and roll in flour.
Place the balls in your air fryer's cooking basket and flatten into biscuit shapes. Sprinkle cheese and the remaining butter on top. Cook for 30 minutes, tossing every 10 minutes. Serve warm.

772.   Molasses Cashew Delight

Preparation Time: 20 minutes
Servings: 12
Ingredients
3 cups cashews
3 tbsp liquid smoke
2 tsp salt
2 tbsp molasses
Directions
Preheat your Air Fryer to 360 F. In a bowl, add salt, liquid, molasses, and cashews; toss to coat well. Place the coated cashews in your Air Fryer's cooking basket and cook for 10 minutes, shaking the basket every 5 minutes.

773.   Ham and Cheese Grilled Sandwich

Preparation Time: 15 minutes
Servings: 2
Ingredients
4 slices bread
¼ cup butter
2 slices ham
2 slices cheese
Directions
Preheat your Air Fryer to 360 degrees F. Place 2 bread slices on a flat surface. Spread butter on the exposed surfaces. Lay cheese and ham on two of the slices. Cover with the other 2 slices to form sandwiches. Place the sandwiches in the cooking basket and cook for 5 minutes.

774.   Simply Parsnip Fries

Preparation Time: 15 minutes
Servings: 3
INGREDIENTS
4 large parsnips
¼ cup flour
¼ cup olive oil
¼ cup water
A pinch of salt
DIRECTIONS
Preheat the Air Fryer to 390 F and cut the parsnip to a half inch by 3 inches. In a bowl, mix the flour, olive oil, water, and parsnip. Mix well and coat. Line the fries in the Air fryer and cook for 15 minutes.
Serve with yogurt and garlic paste.

775.   Crispy Eggplant Fries

Preparation Time: 20 minutes
Servings: 2
Ingredients
1 eggplant, sliced
1 tsp olive oil
1 tsp soy sauce
Salt to taste
Directions
Preheat your Air Fryer to 400 F. Make a marinade of 1 tsp oil, soy sauce and salt. Mix well. Add in the eggplant slices and let stand for 5 minutes. Place the prepared eggplant slices in your Air Fryer's cooking basket and cook for 5 minutes. Serve with a drizzle of maple syrup.

776.   Amul Cabbage Canapes

Preparation Time: 15 minutes
Servings: 2
Ingredients

1 whole cabbage, washed and cut in rounds
1 cube Amul cheese
½ carrot, cubed
¼ onion, cubed
¼ capsicum, cubed
Fresh basil to garnish
Directions
Preheat your Air Fryer to 360 F. Using a bowl, mix onion, carrot, capsicum and cheese. Toss to coat everything evenly. Add cabbage rounds to the Air Fryer's cooking basket.
Top with the veggie mixture and cook for 5 minutes. Serve with a garnish of fresh basil.

777.   Feta Butterbeans with Crispy Bacon

Preparation Time: 10 minutes
Servings: 2
Ingredients
1 (14 oz can butter beans
1 tbsp chives
3 ½ oz feta
Black pepper to taste
1 tsp olive oil
3 ½ oz bacon, sliced
Directions
Preheat your Air Fryer to 340 F. Blend beans, oil and pepper using a blender. Arrange bacon slices on your Air Fryer's cooking basket. Sprinkle chives on top and cook for 10 minutes. Add feta cheese to the butter bean blend and stir. Serve bacon with the dip.

778.   French Beans with Toasted Almonds

Preparation Time: 25 minutes
Servings: 5
Ingredients
1 ½ pounds French beans, washed and drained
1 tbsp salt
1 tbsp pepper
½ pound shallots, chopped
3 tbsp olive oil
½ cup almonds, toasted
Directions
Preheat your Air Fryer to 400 F. Put a pan over medium heat, mix beans in hot water and oil until tender, about 5-6 minutes. Mix the boiled beans with oil, shallots, salt, and pepper. Add the mixture to your Air Fryer's cooking basket and cook for 20 minutes. Serve with almonds and enjoy!

779.   Shrimp with Spices

Preparation Time: 15 minutes
Servings: 3

Ingredients

½ pound shrimp, sauce and deveined

½ tsp Cajun seasoning

Salt as needed

1 tbsp olive oil

¼ tsp black pepper

¼ tsp paprika

Directions

Preheat your Air Fryer to 390 F. Using a bowl, make the marinade by mixing paprika, salt, pepper, oil and seasoning. Cut shrimp and cover with marinade. Place the prepared shrimp in your Air Fryer's cooking basket and cook for 10 minutes, flipping halfway through.

780.   Brussels Sprouts with Garlic

Preparation Time: 25 minutes

Servings: 4

Ingredients

1 block brussels sprouts

½ tsp garlic, chopped

2 tbsp olive oil

½ tsp black pepper

Salt to taste

Directions

Wash the Brussels thoroughly under cold water and trim off the outer leaves, keeping only the head of the sprouts. In a bowl, mix oil and garlic. Season with salt and pepper. Add prepared sprouts to this mixture and let rest for 5 minutes. Place the coated sprouts in your air fryer's cooking basket and cook for 15 minutes.

781.   Yogurt Masala Cashew

Preparation Time: 25 minutes

Servings: 2

Ingredients

8 oz Greek yogurt

2 tbsp mango powder

8¾ oz cashew nuts

Salt and black pepper to taste

1 tsp coriander powder

½ tsp masala powder

½ tsp black pepper powder

Directions

Preheat your Fryer to 240 F. In a bowl, mix all powders. Season with salt and pepper. Add cashews and toss to coat well. Place the cashews in your air fryer's basket and cook for 15 minutes. Serve with a garnish of basil.

782.   Savory Curly Potatoes

Preparation Time: 20 minutes
Servings: 2
Ingredients
2 whole potatoes
1 tbsp extra-virgin olive oil
Salt and black pepper to taste
1 tsp paprika
Directions
Preheat your Fryer to 350 F. Wash the potatoes thoroughly under cold water and pass them through a spiralizer to get curly shaped potatoes. Place the potatoes in a bowl and coat with oil. Transfer them to your air fryer's cooking basket and cook for 15 minutes. Sprinkle a bit of salt and paprika, to serve.

783.   French-Style Fries

Preparation Time: 35 minutes
Servings: 6
Ingredients
6 medium russet potatoes, sauce
2 tbsp olive oil
Salt to taste
Directions
Cut potatoes into ¼ by 3-inch pieces and place in a bowl with cold water; let soak for 30 minutes. Strain and allow to dry. Preheat your Air Fryer to 360 F. Drizzle oil on the dried potatoes and toss to coat. Place the potatoes in your air fryer's cooking basket and cook for 30 minutes. Season with salt and pepper, to serve.

784.   Bacon Wrapped Asparagus

Serves: 4 | Preparation Time: 25 minutes
Servings: 4
Ingredients
20 spears asparagus
4 bacon slices
1 tbsp olive oil
1 tbsp sesame oil
1 tbsp brown sugar
1 garlic clove, crushed
Directions
Preheat your Air Fryer to 380 F. In a bowl, mix the oils, sugar and crushed garlic. Separate the asparagus into 4 bunches (5 spears in 1 bunchand wrap each bunch with a bacon slice. Coat the bunches with the sugar and oil mix. Place the bunches in your air fryer's cooking basket and cook for 8 minutes. Serve immediately.

785.   Cheese and Chives Scones

Preparation Time: 25 minutes
Servings: 10
Ingredients
6 ¼ oz flour
Salt and black pepper to taste
¾ oz butter
1 tsp chives
1 whole egg
1 tbsp milk
2 ¾ cheddar cheese, shredded
Directions
Preheat your Air Fryer to 340 F. In a bowl, mix butter, flour, cheddar cheese, chives, milk and egg to get a sticky dough. Dust a flat surface with flour. Roll the dough into small balls. Place the balls in your Air Fryer's cooking basket and cook for 20 minutes. Serve and enjoy!

786. Pineapple and Mozzarella Pizza

Preparation Time: 15 minutes
Servings: 2
INGREDIENTS
2 tortillas
8 ham slices
8 mozzarella slices
8 thin pineapple slices
2 tbsp tomato sauce
1 tsp dried parsley
DIRECTIONS
Preheat the Air fryer to 330 F and spread the tomato sauce onto the tortillas. Arrange 4 ham slices on each tortilla. Top the ham with the pineapple, top the pizza with mozzarella and sprinkle with parsley. Cook for 10 minutes and enjoy.

787. Marinara Chicken Breasts

Preparation Time: 25 minutes
Servings: 2
Ingredients
2 chicken breasts, skinless, beaten, ½ inch thick
1 egg, beaten
½ cup breadcrumbs
A pinch of salt and black pepper
2 tbsp marinara sauce
2 tbsp Grana Padano cheese, grated
2 slices mozzarella cheese
Directions
Dip the breasts into the egg, then into the crumbs and arrange in the Air fryer. Cook for 5 minutes on 400 F. When ready, turn over and drizzle with marinara sauce, Grana Padano and mozzarella cheese. Cook for 5 more minutes at 400 F. Serve with rice.

788.   Homemade Prosciutto Cheese Croquettes

Preparation Time: 50 minutes
Servings: 6
INGREDIENTS
1 lb. cheddar cheese
12 slices of prosciutto
1 cup flour
2 eggs, beaten
4 tbsp olive oil
1 cup breadcrumbs
DIRECTIONS
Cut the cheese into 6 equal pieces. Wrap each piece of cheese with 2 prosciutto slices. Place them in the freezer just enough to set. I left mine for about 5 minutes; note that they mustn't be frozen. Meanwhile, preheat the Air fryer to 390 F, and dip the croquettes into the flour first, then in the egg, and coat with the breadcrumbs. Place the olive oil in the basket and cook the croquettes for 8 minutes, or until golden.

Desserts

789.   Café-Style Fudge

Preparation Time: 10 minutes + chilling time
Servings: 6
Nutrition: 144 Calories; 15.5g Fat; 2.1g Carbs; 0.8g Protein; 1.1g Fiber
Ingredients
1 tablespoon instant coffee granules
4 tablespoons confectioners' Swerve
4 tablespoons cocoa powder
1 stick butter
1/2 teaspoon vanilla extract
Directions
Beat the butter and Swerve at low speed.
Add in the cocoa powder, instant coffee granules, and vanilla and continue to mix until well combined.
Spoon the batter into a foil-lined baking sheet. Refrigerate for 2 to 3 hours. Enjoy!

790.   Coconut and Seed Porridge

Preparation Time: 15 minutes
Servings: 2
Nutrition: 300 Calories; 25.1g Fat; 8g Carbs; 4.9g Protein; 6g Fiber
Ingredients
6 tablespoons coconut flour
1/2 cup canned coconut milk
4 tablespoons double cream
2 tablespoons flaxseed meal
1 tablespoon pumpkin seeds, ground
Directions
In a saucepan, simmer all of the above the ingredients over medium-low heat. Add in a keto sweetener of choice.
Divide the porridge between bowls and enjoy!

791.   Pecan and Lime Cheesecake

Preparation Time: 30 minutes + chilling time
Servings: 10
Nutrition: 296 Calories; 20g Fat; 6g Carbs; 21g Protein; 3.7g Fiber
Ingredients
1 cup coconut flakes
20 ounces mascarpone cheese, room temperature
1 ½ cups pecan meal

1/2 cup xylitol
3 tablespoons key lime juice
Directions
Combine the pecan meal, 1/4 cup of xylitol, and coconut flakes in a mixing bowl. Press the crust into a parchment-lined springform pan. Freeze for 30 minutes.
Now, beat the mascarpone cheese with 1/4 cup of xylitol with an electric mixer.
Beat in the key lime juice; you can add vanilla extract, if desired.
Spoon the filling onto the prepared crust. Allow it to cool in your refrigerator for about 3 hours.
Bon appétit!

792. Rum Butter Cookies

Preparation Time: 10 minutes + chilling time
Servings: 12
Nutrition: 400 Calories; 40g Fat; 4.9g Carbs; 5.4g Protein; 2.9g Fiber
Ingredients
1/2 cup coconut butter
1 teaspoon rum extract
4 cups almond meal
1 stick butter
1/2 cup confectioners' Swerve
Directions
Melt the coconut butter and butter. Stir in the Swerve and rum extract.
Afterwards, add in the almond meal and mix to combine.
Roll the balls and place them on a parchment-lined cookie sheet. Place in your refrigerator until ready to serve.

793. Fluffy Chocolate Chip Cookies

Preparation Time: 10 minutes + chilling time
Servings: 10
Nutrition: 104 Calories; 9.5g Fat; 4.1g Carbs; 2.1g Protein; 2.6g Fiber
Ingredients
1/2 cup almond meal
4 tablespoons double cream
1/2 cup sugar-free chocolate chips
2 cups coconut, unsweetened and shredded
1/2 cup monk fruit syrup
Directions
In a mixing bowl, combine all of the above ingredients until well combined. Shape the batter into bite-sized balls.
Flatten the balls using a fork or your hand.
Place in your refrigerator until ready to serve.

794. Chewy Almond Blondies

Preparation Time: 55 minutes
Servings: 10
Nutrition: 234 Calories; 25.1g Fat; 3.6g Carbs; 1.7g Protein; 1.4g Fiber
Ingredients
1/2 cup sugar-free bakers' chocolate, chopped into small chunks
1/4 cup erythritol
2 tablespoons coconut oil
1 cup almond meal
1 cup almond butter
Directions
In a mixing bowl, combine almond meal, almond butter, and erythritol until creamy and uniform.
Press the mixture into a foil-lined baking sheet. Freeze for 30 to 35 minutes.
Melt the coconut oil and bakers' chocolate to make the glaze. Spread the glaze over your cake; freeze
until the chocolate is set.
Slice into bars and devour!

795. Light Greek Cheesecake

Preparation Time: 1 hour 35 minutes
Servings: 6
Nutrition: 471 Calories; 45g Fat; 6.9g Carbs; 11.5g Protein; 4g Fiber
Ingredients
10 ounces whipped Greek yogurt cream cheese
6 tablespoons butter, melted
2 cups confectioner's Swerve
2 eggs
2 cups almond meal
Directions
Start by preheating your oven to 325 degrees F.
Combine the almond meal and butter and press the crust into a lightly buttered springform pan.
Beat the Greek-style yogurt with confectioner's Swerve until everything is well mixed. Fold in the
eggs, one at the time, and mix well to make sure that everything is being combined together.
Pour the filling over the crust. Bake in the preheated oven for about 35 minutes until the middle is
still jiggly. Your cheesecake will continue to set as it cools. Bon appétit!

796. Fluffy Chocolate Crepes

Preparation Time: 40 minutes
Servings: 2
Nutrition: 330 Calories; 31.9g Fat; 7.1g Carbs; 7.3g Protein; 3.5g Fiber
Ingredients
1/4 cup coconut milk, unsweetened
2 egg, beaten

1/2 cup coconut flour

1 tablespoon unsweetened cocoa powder

2 tablespoons coconut oil, melted

Directions

In a mixing bowl, thoroughly combine the coconut flour and cocoa powder along with 1/2 teaspoon of baking soda.

In another bowl, whisk the eggs and coconut milk. Add the flour mixture to the egg mixture; mix to combine well.

In a frying pan, preheat 1 tablespoon of the coconut oil until sizzling. Ladle 1/2 of the batter into the frying pan and cook for 2 to 3 minutes on each side.

Melt the remaining tablespoon of coconut oil and fry another crepe for about 5 minutes. Serve with your favorite keto filling. Bon appétit!

797. Crispy Peanut Fudge Squares

Preparation Time: 1 hour

Servings: 10

Nutrition: 218 Calories; 21.2g Fat; 5.1g Carbs; 3.8g Protein; 0.7g Fiber

Ingredients

1/2 cup peanuts, toasted and coarsely chopped

1 vanilla paste

2 tablespoons Monk fruit powder

1 stick butter

1/3 cup coconut oil

Directions

Melt the butter, coconut oil, and vanilla. Add in Monk fruit powder and mix to combine well.

Place the chopped peanuts in an ice cube tray. Pour the batter over the peanuts.

Place in your freezer for about 1 hour. Bon appétit!

798. Almond Butter Cookies

Preparation Time: 15 minutes + chilling time

Servings: 8

Nutrition: 322 Calories; 28.9g Fat; 3.4g Carbs; 13.9g Protein; 0.6g Fiber

Ingredients

1 ½ cups almond butter

1/2 cup sugar-free chocolate, cut into chunks

1/2 cup double cream

1/2 cup Monk fruit powder

3 cups pork rinds, crushed

Directions

Melt almond butter and Monk fruit powder; add in crushed pork rinds along with vanilla, if desired. Spread the mixture onto a cookie sheet and place in your refrigerator.

Microwave the chocolate with double cream; spread the chocolate layer over the first layer. Place in your refrigerator until ready to serve. Enjoy!

799.   Basic Almond Cupcakes

Preparation Time: 35 minutes
Servings: 9
Nutrition: 134 Calories; 11.6g Fat; 2.9g Carbs; 5.4g Protein; 1.3g Fiber
Ingredients
1 cup almond milk, unsweetened
2 tablespoons coconut oil
1/2 cup almond meal
1/4 cup Swerve
3 eggs
Directions
Mix all of the above ingredients until well combined. Line a muffin pan with cupcake liners.
Spoon the batter into the muffin pan.
Bake in the preheated oven at 350 degrees F for 18 to 20 minutes or until a toothpick comes out dry
and clean. Enjoy!

800.   Blueberry Cheesecake Bowl

Preparation Time: 10 minutes + chilling time
Servings: 8
Nutrition: 244 Calories; 24.2g Fat; 4.7g Carbs; 3.7g Protein; 1g Fiber
Ingredients
2 cups cream cheese
1/2 cup blueberries
1/2 teaspoon coconut extract
6 tablespoons pecans, chopped
1/4 cup coconut cream
Directions
Beat the cream cheese and coconut cream until well mixed.
Fold in the coconut extract, pecans, and 1/4 cup of blueberries and mix again. Refrigerate for 2 to 3
hours.
Serve garnished with the remaining 1/4 cup of blueberries. Enjoy!

801.   Energy Chocolate Chip Candy

Preparation Time: 10 minutes + chilling time
Servings: 10
Nutrition: 102 Calories; 7.8g Fat; 5.8g Carbs; 2.6g Protein; 1.8g Fiber
Ingredients
2 tablespoons milk
1/2 cup peanut butter, melted
1 cup coconut flour

1/4 cup erythritol
1/4 cup chocolate chips, sugar-free
Directions
Mix all of the above ingredients until everything is well combined.
Spoon the mixture into an ice-cube tray.
Place in your refrigerator for about 2 hours. Bon appétit!

802.   Fudgy Mug Brownie

Preparation Time: 10 minutes
Servings: 2
Nutrition: 336 Calories; 31.5g Fat; 6g Carbs; 9.1g Protein; 3.1g Fiber
Ingredients
2 eggs
1/2 teaspoon Monk fruit powder
2 dollops heavy whipping cream
1/2 cup coconut milk
2 tablespoons coconut flour
Directions
Whip the eggs and coconut milk until well combined.
In another bowl, mix the coconut flour and Monk fruit powder; add vanilla and cinnamon to taste.
Add the egg mixture to the dry mixture and stir to combine well. Scrape the batter into microwave-safe mugs.
Microwave for about 1 minute 30 seconds. Garnish with a dollop of whipping cream and serve!

803.   Basic Keto Brownies

Preparation Time: 1 hour 25 minutes
Servings: 10
Nutrition: 123 Calories; 12.9g Fat; 3.1g Carbs; 0.9g Protein; 1.7g Fiber
Ingredients
1/2 cup butter, melted
1 ¼ cups coconut flour
1 teaspoon baking powder
1/3 cup cocoa powder, unsweetened
1 cup Xylitol
Directions
Start by preheating your oven to 355 degrees F.
Mix all ingredients until everything is well combined. Spread the batter onto the bottom of a parchment-lined baking pan.
Bake in the preheated oven for 15 to 20 minutes or until a toothpick comes out dry and clean.
Transfer to wire racks until firm enough to slice. Bon appétit!

804.   Dad's Rum Brownies

Preparation Time: 30 minutes
Servings: 8
Nutrition: 245 Calories; 23.2g Fat; 3.1g Carbs; 3.1g Protein; 1.8g Fiber
Ingredients
6 ounces butter, melted
3 ounces baking chocolate, unsweetened and melted
1 cup almond flour
2 eggs
2 tablespoons rum
Directions
Start by preheating your oven to 365 degrees F.
Thoroughly combine almond flour and baking powder. In another bowl, combine the eggs, butter, chocolate and rum. Add the flour mixture to the wet mixture.
Spoon the batter into the bottom of a foil-lined baking pan.
Bake in the preheated oven approximately 20 minutes. Enjoy!

805. Chia Smoothie Bowl

Preparation Time: 5 minutes
Servings: 2
Nutrition: 280 Calories; 16g Fat; 7g Carbs; 25g Protein; 4g Fiber
Ingredients
1/2 cup coconut milk
2 tablespoons chia seeds
4 tablespoons powdered erythritol
A pinch of freshly grated nutmeg
4 tablespoons peanut butter
Directions
Blend all ingredients in your food processor.
Serve in individual bowls and devour!

806. Chocolate Cheesecake Fudge

Preparation Time: 35 minutes + chilling time
Servings: 6
Nutrition: 411 Calories; 38g Fat; 7.5g Carbs; 5.8g Protein; 1.1g Fiber
Ingredients
16 ounces cream cheese, at room temperature
2 tablespoons unsweetened cocoa powder
3/4 cup coconut flour
1/3 cup butter, at room temperature
6 ounces sour cream
Directions
Combine the coconut flour and butter; press the crust into the bottom of a lightly buttered baking pan; freeze for 30 minutes.

Make the filling by mixing the cream cheese, sour cream, and cocoa powder, add in Erythritol to taste. Spoon the filling over the crust.

Bake in the preheated oven at 420 degrees F for 8 to 10 minutes; decrease temperature to 365 degrees F and continue to bake for 15 to 20 minutes more.

Enjoy!

807.   Favorite Keto Frisuelos

Preparation Time: 20 minutes
Servings: 6
Nutrition: 137 Calories; 12.3g Fat; 3.2g Carbs; 4.1g Protein; 0g Fiber
Ingredients
1 tablespoon butter, melted
3 eggs
2 ounces double cream
4 ounces mascarpone cheese
6 tablespoons confectioners' Swerve
Directions
Whisk the eggs until pale and frothy. Fold in double cream and mascarpone cheese. Mix until everything is well combined. Add maple extract and salt to taste.

Melt the batter in a frying pan over medium-high heat.

Spoon 1/6 of the batter into the hot frying pan. Cook for 2 to 3 minutes per side. Repeat until you run out of the ingredients. Serve with confectioners' Swerve. Enjoy!

808.   Candy Bar Cheesecake Balls

Preparation Time: 10 minutes + chilling time
Servings: 10
Nutrition: 293 Calories; 26g Fat; 5.6g Carbs; 5.3g Protein; 1g Fiber
Ingredients
9 ounces sugar-free chocolate chips
2 ounces butter, at room temperature
9 ounces mascarpone cheese, at room temperature
1 teaspoon butterscotch extract
2 cups powdered erythritol
Directions
In a mixing bowl, combine the butter, mascarpone cheese, erythritol, chocolate chips, and butterscotch extract.

Refrigerate for 2 hours and then, shape the mixture into bite-sized balls. Bon appétit!

809.   Old-Fashion Coffee Mousse

Preparation Time: 15 minutes + chilling time
Servings: 4

Nutrition: 289 Calories; 27.6g Fat; 5g Carbs; 5.9g Protein; 0g Fiber
Ingredients
1/2 teaspoon instant coffee
1 teaspoon pure coconut extract
2 cups double cream
4 egg yolks
6 tablespoons Xylitol
Directions
Warm double cream in a saucepan over low heat. Let it cool at room temperature.
Then, combine the egg yolks, instant coffee, coconut extract, and Xylitol; whisk to combine well.
Spoon the egg mixture into the lukewarm cream. Cook the mixture over the lowest setting until the liquid has thickened slightly.
Serve well-chilled and enjoy!

810.   Blueberry Pot de Crème

Preparation Time: 10 minutes
Servings: 1
Nutrition: 235 Calories; 17.7g Fat; 8.9g Carbs; 8.1g Protein; 7g Fiber
Ingredients
2 tablespoons Greek-style yogurt
1 tablespoon peanut butter
1 tablespoon chia seeds
1/2 avocado, pitted and peeled
2 tablespoons blueberries
Directions
Blend the avocado, blueberries, and Greek-style yogurt in your food processor. Add in Swerve to taste.
Garnish with peanut butter and chia seeds. Bon appétit!

811.   Chocolate Blechkuchen

Preparation Time: 30 minutes + chilling time
Servings: 8
Nutrition: 182 Calories; 17.1g Fat; 5.8g Carbs; 5.5g Protein; 3.1g Fiber
Ingredients
1 cup almond meal
3 eggs
1/3 cup coconut oil
1/4 cup powdered erythritol
1/4 cup cocoa powder, unsweetened
Directions
Start by preheating your oven to 330 degrees F.
Combine the almond meal and cocoa powder; add in 1/2 teaspoon of baking powder and mix until well combined.

Fold in the eggs, one at a time, whisking after each addition. Add in coconut oil and powdered erythritol.

Press the batter into a buttered springform pan. Bake in the preheated oven for about 20 minutes. Frost the cake with whipped cream, if desired.

10 Tips for Maintaining an Anti-Inflammatory Diet

Need help getting started? We have compiled a few of the very helpful hints:

1) Meal prep. Over the weekend, decide your foods for the week. It will be easier to eat healthy for the whole week if you've got a plan in place.
2) Write a shopping list. Prepare a grocery list before you step foot in the store. You will be less tempted to buy convenience foods and snacks.
3) Choose an assortment of fruits, veggies and wholesome fats. Having options will save you from getting bored. Additionally, diversifying your meals will provide you a complete range of nutrients.
4) Keep healthful snacks on hand. You'll be less inclined to reach for chips and biscuits if a better choice is nearby.
5) Drink more water. Proper hydration boosts your energy level, brain function and general health.
6) You should always speak to your doctor before integrating dietary changes. Together, you and your Physician, you can discuss how to start building the best meal plan to boost your health.

1000-DAYS MEAL PLAN

DAYS	BREAKFAST	LUNCH/DINNER	DESSERT
1.	Chili Tomato Salad	Poached Halibut and Mushrooms	Café-Style Fudge
2.	Cumin Mushroom Bowls	Halibut Stir Fry	Coconut and Seed Porridge
3.	Bell Peppers and Tomato Salad	Steamed Garlic-Dill Halibut	Pecan and Lime Cheesecake
4.	Avocado and Spinach Salad	Italian Halibut Chowder	Fluffy Chocolate Chip Cookies
5.	Zucchini Bowls	Pomegranate-Molasses Glazed Salmon	Chewy Almond Blondies
6.	Lime Berries Salad	Salmon with Sun-Dried Tomatoes and Capers	Rum Butter Cookies
7.	Zucchini Spread	Quick Thai Cod Curry	Light Greek Cheesecake
8.	Greek Tomato and Olives Salad	Island Style Sardines	Fluffy Chocolate Crepes
9.	Garlicky Green Beans and Olives Pan	Greek Chicken Stew	Crispy Peanut Fudge Squares
10.	Paprika Olives Spread	Herbed Chicken Salad	Almond Butter Cookies
11.	Chives Avocado Mix	Easy Stir-Fried Chicken	Basic Almond Cupcakes
12.	Zucchini Pan	Poached Cod Asian Style	Blueberry Cheesecake Bowl
13.	Chili Spinach and Zucchini Pan	Chicken in Pita Bread	Energy Chocolate Chip Candy
14.	Basil Tomato and Cabbage Bowls	Multi-Spice Cod Curry	Fudgy Mug Brownie
15.	Spinach and Zucchini Hash	Slow Cooked Spanish Cod	Basic Keto Brownies
16.	Tomato and Zucchini Fritters	Roasted Chicken	Chocolate Cheesecake Fudge
17.	Cottage Cheese Fluff	Chicken and Avocado Lettuce Wraps	Candy Bar Cheesecake Balls
18.	Microwaved Egg and Cheese Breakfast Burrito	Spicy & Creamy Ground Beef Curry	Chocolate Blechkuchen

19.	Microwaved Ham and Mushroom Coffee Cup Scramble	Curried Beef Meatballs	Dad's Rum Brownies
20.	Mini Breakfast Pizza	Ground Beef & Veggies Curry	Chia Smoothie Bowl
21.	Apple Yogurt Parfait	Ground Beef with Greens & Tomatoes	Favorite Keto Frisuelos
22.	Basic Poached Eggs	Beef & Veggies Chili	Blueberry Pot de Crème
23.	Easy Sweet Potatoes and Eggs	Ground Beef with Cashews & Veggies	Old-Fashion Coffee Mousse
24.	Sweet Onion and Egg Pie	Ground Beef with Veggies	Café-Style Fudge
25.	Eggs Baked in Avocado	Beef with Asparagus & Bell Pepper	Coconut and Seed Porridge
26.	Baked Egg Stuffed Cups	African Chicken Stew Turkey Meatballs	Pecan and Lime Cheesecake
27.	Strawberries and Cream Trifle	Brussels Sprouts and Paprika Chicken Thighs	Fluffy Chocolate Chip Cookies
28.	Maple Toast and Eggs	Chicken Breasts with Stuffing	Chewy Almond Blondies
29.	Crème Brulee	Chicken-Bell Pepper Sauté	Rum Butter Cookies
30.	Peppers Casserole	Avocado-Orange Grilled Chicken	Light Greek Cheesecake
31.	Chili Tomato Salad	Poached Halibut and Mushrooms	Fluffy Chocolate Crepes
32.	Cumin Mushroom Bowls	Halibut Stir Fry	Crispy Peanut Fudge Squares
33.	Bell Peppers and Tomato Salad	Steamed Garlic-Dill Halibut	Almond Butter Cookies
34.	Avocado and Spinach Salad	Italian Halibut Chowder	Basic Almond Cupcakes
35.	Zucchini Bowls	Pomegranate-Molasses Glazed Salmon	Blueberry Cheesecake Bowl
36.	Lime Berries Salad	Salmon with Sun-Dried Tomatoes and Capers	Energy Chocolate Chip Candy
37.	Zucchini Spread	Quick Thai Cod Curry	Fudgy Mug Brownie

38.	Greek Tomato and Olives Salad	Island Style Sardines	Basic Keto Brownies
39.	Garlicky Green Beans and Olives Pan	Greek Chicken Stew	Chocolate Cheesecake Fudge
40.	Paprika Olives Spread	Herbed Chicken Salad	Candy Bar Cheesecake Balls
41.	Chives Avocado Mix	Easy Stir-Fried Chicken	Chocolate Blechkuchen
42.	Zucchini Pan	Poached Cod Asian Style	Dad's Rum Brownies
43.	Chili Spinach and Zucchini Pan	Chicken in Pita Bread	Chia Smoothie Bowl
44.	Basil Tomato and Cabbage Bowls	Multi-Spice Cod Curry	Favorite Keto Frisuelos
45.	Spinach and Zucchini Hash	Slow Cooked Spanish Cod	Blueberry Pot de Crème
46.	Tomato and Zucchini Fritters	Roasted Chicken	Old-Fashion Coffee Mousse
47.	Cottage Cheese Fluff	Chicken and Avocado Lettuce Wraps	Café-Style Fudge
48.	Microwaved Egg and Cheese Breakfast Burrito	Spicy & Creamy Ground Beef Curry	Coconut and Seed Porridge
49.	Microwaved Ham and Mushroom Coffee Cup Scramble	Curried Beef Meatballs	Pecan and Lime Cheesecake
50.	Mini Breakfast Pizza	Ground Beef & Veggies Curry	Fluffy Chocolate Chip Cookies
51.	Apple Yogurt Parfait	Ground Beef with Greens & Tomatoes	Chewy Almond Blondies
52.	Basic Poached Eggs	Beef & Veggies Chili	Rum Butter Cookies
53.	Easy Sweet Potatoes and Eggs	Ground Beef with Cashews & Veggies	Light Greek Cheesecake
54.	Sweet Onion and Egg Pie	Ground Beef with Veggies	Fluffy Chocolate Crepes
55.	Eggs Baked in Avocado	Beef with Asparagus & Bell Pepper	Crispy Peanut Fudge Squares
56.	Baked Egg Stuffed Cups	African Chicken Stew Turkey Meatballs	Almond Butter Cookies
57.	Strawberries and Cream Trifle	Brussels Sprouts and Paprika Chicken	Basic Almond Cupcakes

		Thighs	
58.	Maple Toast and Eggs	Chicken Breasts with Stuffing	Blueberry Cheesecake Bowl
59.	Crème Brulee	Chicken-Bell Pepper Sauté	Energy Chocolate Chip Candy
60.	Peppers Casserole	Avocado-Orange Grilled Chicken	Fudgy Mug Brownie
61.	Chili Tomato Salad	Poached Halibut and Mushrooms	Basic Keto Brownies
62.	Cumin Mushroom Bowls	Halibut Stir Fry	Chocolate Cheesecake Fudge
63.	Bell Peppers and Tomato Salad	Steamed Garlic-Dill Halibut	Candy Bar Cheesecake Balls
64.	Avocado and Spinach Salad	Italian Halibut Chowder	Chocolate Blechkuchen
65.	Zucchini Bowls	Pomegranate-Molasses Glazed Salmon	Dad's Rum Brownies
66.	Lime Berries Salad	Salmon with Sun-Dried Tomatoes and Capers	Chia Smoothie Bowl
67.	Zucchini Spread	Quick Thai Cod Curry	Favorite Keto Frisuelos
68.	Greek Tomato and Olives Salad	Island Style Sardines	Blueberry Pot de Crème
69.	Garlicky Green Beans and Olives Pan	Greek Chicken Stew	Old-Fashion Coffee Mousse
70.	Paprika Olives Spread	Herbed Chicken Salad	Café-Style Fudge
71.	Chives Avocado Mix	Easy Stir-Fried Chicken	Coconut and Seed Porridge
72.	Zucchini Pan	Poached Cod Asian Style	Pecan and Lime Cheesecake
73.	Chili Spinach and Zucchini Pan	Chicken in Pita Bread	Fluffy Chocolate Chip Cookies
74.	Basil Tomato and Cabbage Bowls	Multi-Spice Cod Curry	Chewy Almond Blondies
75.	Spinach and Zucchini Hash	Slow Cooked Spanish Cod	Rum Butter Cookies
76.	Tomato and Zucchini Fritters	Roasted Chicken	Light Greek Cheesecake
77.	Cottage Cheese Fluff	Chicken and Avocado Lettuce Wraps	Fluffy Chocolate Crepes

78.	Microwaved Egg and Cheese Breakfast Burrito	Spicy & Creamy Ground Beef Curry	Crispy Peanut Fudge Squares
79.	Microwaved Ham and Mushroom Coffee Cup Scramble	Curried Beef Meatballs	Almond Butter Cookies
80.	Mini Breakfast Pizza	Ground Beef & Veggies Curry	Basic Almond Cupcakes
81.	Apple Yogurt Parfait	Ground Beef with Greens & Tomatoes	Blueberry Cheesecake Bowl
82.	Basic Poached Eggs	Beef & Veggies Chili	Energy Chocolate Chip Candy
83.	Easy Sweet Potatoes and Eggs	Ground Beef with Cashews & Veggies	Fudgy Mug Brownie
84.	Sweet Onion and Egg Pie	Ground Beef with Veggies	Basic Keto Brownies
85.	Eggs Baked in Avocado	Beef with Asparagus & Bell Pepper	Chocolate Cheesecake Fudge
86.	Baked Egg Stuffed Cups	African Chicken Stew Turkey Meatballs	Candy Bar Cheesecake Balls
87.	Strawberries and Cream Trifle	Brussels Sprouts and Paprika Chicken Thighs	Chocolate Blechkuchen
88.	Maple Toast and Eggs	Chicken Breasts with Stuffing	Dad's Rum Brownies
89.	Crème Brulee	Chicken-Bell Pepper Sauté	Chia Smoothie Bowl
90.	Peppers Casserole	Avocado-Orange Grilled Chicken	Favorite Keto Frisuelos
91.	Chili Tomato Salad	Poached Halibut and Mushrooms	Blueberry Pot de Crème
92.	Cumin Mushroom Bowls	Halibut Stir Fry	Old-Fashion Coffee Mousse
93.	Bell Peppers and Tomato Salad	Steamed Garlic-Dill Halibut	Café-Style Fudge
94.	Avocado and Spinach Salad	Italian Halibut Chowder	Coconut and Seed Porridge
95.	Zucchini Bowls	Pomegranate-Molasses Glazed Salmon	Pecan and Lime Cheesecake
96.	Lime Berries Salad	Salmon with Sun-Dried Tomatoes and Capers	Fluffy Chocolate Chip Cookies

97.	Zucchini Spread	Quick Thai Cod Curry	Chewy Almond Blondies
98.	Greek Tomato and Olives Salad	Island Style Sardines	Rum Butter Cookies
99.	Garlicky Green Beans and Olives Pan	Greek Chicken Stew	Light Greek Cheesecake
100.	Paprika Olives Spread	Herbed Chicken Salad	Fluffy Chocolate Crepes
101.	Chives Avocado Mix	Easy Stir-Fried Chicken	Crispy Peanut Fudge Squares
102.	Zucchini Pan	Poached Cod Asian Style	Almond Butter Cookies
103.	Chili Spinach and Zucchini Pan	Chicken in Pita Bread	Basic Almond Cupcakes
104.	Basil Tomato and Cabbage Bowls	Multi-Spice Cod Curry	Blueberry Cheesecake Bowl
105.	Spinach and Zucchini Hash	Slow Cooked Spanish Cod	Energy Chocolate Chip Candy
106.	Tomato and Zucchini Fritters	Roasted Chicken	Fudgy Mug Brownie
107.	Cottage Cheese Fluff	Chicken and Avocado Lettuce Wraps	Basic Keto Brownies
108.	Microwaved Egg and Cheese Breakfast Burrito	Spicy & Creamy Ground Beef Curry	Chocolate Cheesecake Fudge
109.	Microwaved Ham and Mushroom Coffee Cup Scramble	Curried Beef Meatballs	Candy Bar Cheesecake Balls
110.	Mini Breakfast Pizza	Ground Beef & Veggies Curry	Chocolate Blechkuchen
111.	Apple Yogurt Parfait	Ground Beef with Greens & Tomatoes	Dad's Rum Brownies
112.	Basic Poached Eggs	Beef & Veggies Chili	Chia Smoothie Bowl
113.	Easy Sweet Potatoes and Eggs	Ground Beef with Cashews & Veggies	Favorite Keto Frisuelos
114.	Sweet Onion and Egg Pie	Ground Beef with Veggies	Blueberry Pot de Crème
115.	Eggs Baked in Avocado	Beef with Asparagus & Bell Pepper	Old-Fashion Coffee Mousse
116.	Baked Egg Stuffed Cups	African Chicken Stew Turkey Meatballs	Café-Style Fudge

117.	Strawberries and Cream Trifle	Brussels Sprouts and Paprika Chicken Thighs	Coconut and Seed Porridge
118.	Maple Toast and Eggs	Chicken Breasts with Stuffing	Pecan and Lime Cheesecake
119.	Crème Brulee	Chicken-Bell Pepper Sauté	Fluffy Chocolate Chip Cookies
120.	Peppers Casserole	Avocado-Orange Grilled Chicken	Chewy Almond Blondies
121.	Chili Tomato Salad	Poached Halibut and Mushrooms	Rum Butter Cookies
122.	Cumin Mushroom Bowls	Halibut Stir Fry	Light Greek Cheesecake
123.	Bell Peppers and Tomato Salad	Steamed Garlic-Dill Halibut	Fluffy Chocolate Crepes
124.	Avocado and Spinach Salad	Italian Halibut Chowder	Crispy Peanut Fudge Squares
125.	Zucchini Bowls	Pomegranate-Molasses Glazed Salmon	Almond Butter Cookies
126.	Lime Berries Salad	Salmon with Sun-Dried Tomatoes and Capers	Basic Almond Cupcakes
127.	Zucchini Spread	Quick Thai Cod Curry	Blueberry Cheesecake Bowl
128.	Greek Tomato and Olives Salad	Island Style Sardines	Energy Chocolate Chip Candy
129.	Garlicky Green Beans and Olives Pan	Greek Chicken Stew	Fudgy Mug Brownie
130.	Paprika Olives Spread	Herbed Chicken Salad	Basic Keto Brownies
131.	Chives Avocado Mix	Easy Stir-Fried Chicken	Chocolate Cheesecake Fudge
132.	Zucchini Pan	Poached Cod Asian Style	Candy Bar Cheesecake Balls
133.	Chili Spinach and Zucchini Pan	Chicken in Pita Bread	Chocolate Blechkuchen
134.	Basil Tomato and Cabbage Bowls	Multi-Spice Cod Curry	Dad's Rum Brownies
135.	Spinach and Zucchini Hash	Slow Cooked Spanish Cod	Chia Smoothie Bowl
136.	Tomato and Zucchini Fritters	Roasted Chicken	Favorite Keto Frisuelos

137.	Cottage Cheese Fluff	Chicken and Avocado Lettuce Wraps	Blueberry Pot de Crème
138.	Microwaved Egg and Cheese Breakfast Burrito	Spicy & Creamy Ground Beef Curry	Old-Fashion Coffee Mousse
139.	Microwaved Ham and Mushroom Coffee Cup Scramble	Curried Beef Meatballs	Café-Style Fudge
140.	Mini Breakfast Pizza	Ground Beef & Veggies Curry	Coconut and Seed Porridge
141.	Apple Yogurt Parfait	Ground Beef with Greens & Tomatoes	Pecan and Lime Cheesecake
142.	Basic Poached Eggs	Beef & Veggies Chili	Fluffy Chocolate Chip Cookies
143.	Easy Sweet Potatoes and Eggs	Ground Beef with Cashews & Veggies	Chewy Almond Blondies
144.	Sweet Onion and Egg Pie	Ground Beef with Veggies	Rum Butter Cookies
145.	Eggs Baked in Avocado	Beef with Asparagus & Bell Pepper	Light Greek Cheesecake
146.	Baked Egg Stuffed Cups	African Chicken Stew Turkey Meatballs	Fluffy Chocolate Crepes
147.	Strawberries and Cream Trifle	Brussels Sprouts and Paprika Chicken Thighs	Crispy Peanut Fudge Squares
148.	Maple Toast and Eggs	Chicken Breasts with Stuffing	Almond Butter Cookies
149.	Crème Brulee	Chicken-Bell Pepper Sauté	Basic Almond Cupcakes
150.	Peppers Casserole	Avocado-Orange Grilled Chicken	Blueberry Cheesecake Bowl
151.	Chili Tomato Salad	Poached Halibut and Mushrooms	Energy Chocolate Chip Candy
152.	Cumin Mushroom Bowls	Halibut Stir Fry	Fudgy Mug Brownie
153.	Bell Peppers and Tomato Salad	Steamed Garlic-Dill Halibut	Basic Keto Brownies
154.	Avocado and Spinach Salad	Italian Halibut Chowder	Chocolate Cheesecake Fudge
155.	Zucchini Bowls	Pomegranate-Molasses Glazed Salmon	Candy Bar Cheesecake Balls

156.	Lime Berries Salad	Salmon with Sun-Dried Tomatoes and Capers	Chocolate Blechkuchen
157.	Zucchini Spread	Quick Thai Cod Curry	Dad's Rum Brownies
158.	Greek Tomato and Olives Salad	Island Style Sardines	Chia Smoothie Bowl
159.	Garlicky Green Beans and Olives Pan	Greek Chicken Stew	Favorite Keto Frisuelos
160.	Paprika Olives Spread	Herbed Chicken Salad	Blueberry Pot de Crème
161.	Chives Avocado Mix	Easy Stir-Fried Chicken	Old-Fashion Coffee Mousse
162.	Zucchini Pan	Poached Cod Asian Style	Café-Style Fudge
163.	Chili Spinach and Zucchini Pan	Chicken in Pita Bread	Coconut and Seed Porridge
164.	Basil Tomato and Cabbage Bowls	Multi-Spice Cod Curry	Pecan and Lime Cheesecake
165.	Spinach and Zucchini Hash	Slow Cooked Spanish Cod	Fluffy Chocolate Chip Cookies
166.	Tomato and Zucchini Fritters	Roasted Chicken	Chewy Almond Blondies
167.	Cottage Cheese Fluff	Chicken and Avocado Lettuce Wraps	Rum Butter Cookies
168.	Microwaved Egg and Cheese Breakfast Burrito	Spicy & Creamy Ground Beef Curry	Light Greek Cheesecake
169.	Microwaved Ham and Mushroom Coffee Cup Scramble	Curried Beef Meatballs	Fluffy Chocolate Crepes
170.	Mini Breakfast Pizza	Ground Beef & Veggies Curry	Crispy Peanut Fudge Squares
171.	Apple Yogurt Parfait	Ground Beef with Greens & Tomatoes	Almond Butter Cookies
172.	Basic Poached Eggs	Beef & Veggies Chili	Basic Almond Cupcakes
173.	Easy Sweet Potatoes and Eggs	Ground Beef with Cashews & Veggies	Blueberry Cheesecake Bowl
174.	Sweet Onion and Egg Pie	Ground Beef with Veggies	Energy Chocolate Chip Candy

175.	Eggs Baked in Avocado	Beef with Asparagus & Bell Pepper	Fudgy Mug Brownie
176.	Baked Egg Stuffed Cups	African Chicken Stew Turkey Meatballs	Basic Keto Brownies
177.	Strawberries and Cream Trifle	Brussels Sprouts and Paprika Chicken Thighs	Chocolate Cheesecake Fudge
178.	Maple Toast and Eggs	Chicken Breasts with Stuffing	Candy Bar Cheesecake Balls
179.	Crème Brulee	Chicken-Bell Pepper Sauté	Chocolate Blechkuchen
180.	Peppers Casserole	Avocado-Orange Grilled Chicken	Dad's Rum Brownies
181.	Chili Tomato Salad	Poached Halibut and Mushrooms	Chia Smoothie Bowl
182.	Cumin Mushroom Bowls	Halibut Stir Fry	Favorite Keto Frisuelos
183.	Bell Peppers and Tomato Salad	Steamed Garlic-Dill Halibut	Blueberry Pot de Crème
184.	Avocado and Spinach Salad	Italian Halibut Chowder	Old-Fashion Coffee Mousse
185.	Zucchini Bowls	Pomegranate-Molasses Glazed Salmon	Café-Style Fudge
186.	Lime Berries Salad	Salmon with Sun-Dried Tomatoes and Capers	Coconut and Seed Porridge
187.	Zucchini Spread	Quick Thai Cod Curry	Pecan and Lime Cheesecake
188.	Greek Tomato and Olives Salad	Island Style Sardines	Fluffy Chocolate Chip Cookies
189.	Garlicky Green Beans and Olives Pan	Greek Chicken Stew	Chewy Almond Blondies
190.	Paprika Olives Spread	Herbed Chicken Salad	Rum Butter Cookies
191.	Chives Avocado Mix	Easy Stir-Fried Chicken	Light Greek Cheesecake
192.	Zucchini Pan	Poached Cod Asian Style	Fluffy Chocolate Crepes
193.	Chili Spinach and Zucchini Pan	Chicken in Pita Bread	Crispy Peanut Fudge Squares
194.	Basil Tomato and Cabbage Bowls	Multi-Spice Cod Curry	Almond Butter Cookies

195.	Spinach and Zucchini Hash	Slow Cooked Spanish Cod	Basic Almond Cupcakes
196.	Tomato and Zucchini Fritters	Roasted Chicken	Blueberry Cheesecake Bowl
197.	Cottage Cheese Fluff	Chicken and Avocado Lettuce Wraps	Energy Chocolate Chip Candy
198.	Microwaved Egg and Cheese Breakfast Burrito	Spicy & Creamy Ground Beef Curry	Fudgy Mug Brownie
199.	Microwaved Ham and Mushroom Coffee Cup Scramble	Curried Beef Meatballs	Basic Keto Brownies
200.	Mini Breakfast Pizza	Ground Beef & Veggies Curry	Chocolate Cheesecake Fudge
201.	Apple Yogurt Parfait	Ground Beef with Greens & Tomatoes	Candy Bar Cheesecake Balls
202.	Basic Poached Eggs	Beef & Veggies Chili	Chocolate Blechkuchen
203.	Easy Sweet Potatoes and Eggs	Ground Beef with Cashews & Veggies	Dad's Rum Brownies
204.	Sweet Onion and Egg Pie	Ground Beef with Veggies	Chia Smoothie Bowl
205.	Eggs Baked in Avocado	Beef with Asparagus & Bell Pepper	Favorite Keto Frisuelos
206.	Baked Egg Stuffed Cups	African Chicken Stew Turkey Meatballs	Blueberry Pot de Crème
207.	Strawberries and Cream Trifle	Brussels Sprouts and Paprika Chicken Thighs	Old-Fashion Coffee Mousse
208.	Maple Toast and Eggs	Chicken Breasts with Stuffing	Café-Style Fudge
209.	Crème Brulee	Chicken-Bell Pepper Sauté	Coconut and Seed Porridge
210.	Peppers Casserole	Avocado-Orange Grilled Chicken	Pecan and Lime Cheesecake
211.	Chili Tomato Salad	Poached Halibut and Mushrooms	Fluffy Chocolate Chip Cookies
212.	Cumin Mushroom Bowls	Halibut Stir Fry	Chewy Almond Blondies
213.	Bell Peppers and Tomato Salad	Steamed Garlic-Dill Halibut	Rum Butter Cookies

214.	Avocado and Spinach Salad	Italian Halibut Chowder	Light Greek Cheesecake
215.	Zucchini Bowls	Pomegranate-Molasses Glazed Salmon	Fluffy Chocolate Crepes
216.	Lime Berries Salad	Salmon with Sun-Dried Tomatoes and Capers	Crispy Peanut Fudge Squares
217.	Zucchini Spread	Quick Thai Cod Curry	Almond Butter Cookies
218.	Greek Tomato and Olives Salad	Island Style Sardines	Basic Almond Cupcakes
219.	Garlicky Green Beans and Olives Pan	Greek Chicken Stew	Blueberry Cheesecake Bowl
220.	Paprika Olives Spread	Herbed Chicken Salad	Energy Chocolate Chip Candy
221.	Chives Avocado Mix	Easy Stir-Fried Chicken	Fudgy Mug Brownie
222.	Zucchini Pan	Poached Cod Asian Style	Basic Keto Brownies
223.	Chili Spinach and Zucchini Pan	Chicken in Pita Bread	Chocolate Cheesecake Fudge
224.	Basil Tomato and Cabbage Bowls	Multi-Spice Cod Curry	Candy Bar Cheesecake Balls
225.	Spinach and Zucchini Hash	Slow Cooked Spanish Cod	Chocolate Blechkuchen
226.	Tomato and Zucchini Fritters	Roasted Chicken	Dad's Rum Brownies
227.	Cottage Cheese Fluff	Chicken and Avocado Lettuce Wraps	Chia Smoothie Bowl
228.	Microwaved Egg and Cheese Breakfast Burrito	Spicy & Creamy Ground Beef Curry	Favorite Keto Frisuelos
229.	Microwaved Ham and Mushroom Coffee Cup Scramble	Curried Beef Meatballs	Blueberry Pot de Crème
230.	Mini Breakfast Pizza	Ground Beef & Veggies Curry	Old-Fashion Coffee Mousse
231.	Apple Yogurt Parfait	Ground Beef with Greens & Tomatoes	Café-Style Fudge
232.	Basic Poached Eggs	Beef & Veggies Chili	Coconut and Seed Porridge

233.	Easy Sweet Potatoes and Eggs	Ground Beef with Cashews & Veggies	Pecan and Lime Cheesecake
234.	Sweet Onion and Egg Pie	Ground Beef with Veggies	Fluffy Chocolate Chip Cookies
235.	Eggs Baked in Avocado	Beef with Asparagus & Bell Pepper	Chewy Almond Blondies
236.	Baked Egg Stuffed Cups	African Chicken Stew Turkey Meatballs	Rum Butter Cookies
237.	Strawberries and Cream Trifle	Brussels Sprouts and Paprika Chicken Thighs	Light Greek Cheesecake
238.	Maple Toast and Eggs	Chicken Breasts with Stuffing	Fluffy Chocolate Crepes
239.	Crème Brulee	Chicken-Bell Pepper Sauté	Crispy Peanut Fudge Squares
240.	Peppers Casserole	Avocado-Orange Grilled Chicken	Almond Butter Cookies
241.	Chili Tomato Salad	Poached Halibut and Mushrooms	Basic Almond Cupcakes
242.	Cumin Mushroom Bowls	Halibut Stir Fry	Blueberry Cheesecake Bowl
243.	Bell Peppers and Tomato Salad	Steamed Garlic-Dill Halibut	Energy Chocolate Chip Candy
244.	Avocado and Spinach Salad	Italian Halibut Chowder	Fudgy Mug Brownie
245.	Zucchini Bowls	Pomegranate-Molasses Glazed Salmon	Basic Keto Brownies
246.	Lime Berries Salad	Salmon with Sun-Dried Tomatoes and Capers	Chocolate Cheesecake Fudge
247.	Zucchini Spread	Quick Thai Cod Curry	Candy Bar Cheesecake Balls
248.	Greek Tomato and Olives Salad	Island Style Sardines	Chocolate Blechkuchen
249.	Garlicky Green Beans and Olives Pan	Greek Chicken Stew	Dad's Rum Brownies
250.	Paprika Olives Spread	Herbed Chicken Salad	Chia Smoothie Bowl
251.	Chives Avocado Mix	Easy Stir-Fried Chicken	Favorite Keto Frisuelos
252.	Zucchini Pan	Poached Cod Asian Style	Blueberry Pot de Crème

253.	Chili Spinach and Zucchini Pan	Chicken in Pita Bread	Old-Fashion Coffee Mousse
254.	Basil Tomato and Cabbage Bowls	Multi-Spice Cod Curry	Café-Style Fudge
255.	Spinach and Zucchini Hash	Slow Cooked Spanish Cod	Coconut and Seed Porridge
256.	Tomato and Zucchini Fritters	Roasted Chicken	Pecan and Lime Cheesecake
257.	Cottage Cheese Fluff	Chicken and Avocado Lettuce Wraps	Fluffy Chocolate Chip Cookies
258.	Microwaved Egg and Cheese Breakfast Burrito	Spicy & Creamy Ground Beef Curry	Chewy Almond Blondies
259.	Microwaved Ham and Mushroom Coffee Cup Scramble	Curried Beef Meatballs	Rum Butter Cookies
260.	Mini Breakfast Pizza	Ground Beef & Veggies Curry	Light Greek Cheesecake
261.	Apple Yogurt Parfait	Ground Beef with Greens & Tomatoes	Fluffy Chocolate Crepes
262.	Basic Poached Eggs	Beef & Veggies Chili	Crispy Peanut Fudge Squares
263.	Easy Sweet Potatoes and Eggs	Ground Beef with Cashews & Veggies	Almond Butter Cookies
264.	Sweet Onion and Egg Pie	Ground Beef with Veggies	Basic Almond Cupcakes
265.	Eggs Baked in Avocado	Beef with Asparagus & Bell Pepper	Blueberry Cheesecake Bowl
266.	Baked Egg Stuffed Cups	African Chicken Stew Turkey Meatballs	Energy Chocolate Chip Candy
267.	Strawberries and Cream Trifle	Brussels Sprouts and Paprika Chicken Thighs	Fudgy Mug Brownie
268.	Maple Toast and Eggs	Chicken Breasts with Stuffing	Basic Keto Brownies
269.	Crème Brulee	Chicken-Bell Pepper Sauté	Chocolate Cheesecake Fudge
270.	Peppers Casserole	Avocado-Orange Grilled Chicken	Candy Bar Cheesecake Balls
271.	Chili Tomato Salad	Poached Halibut and Mushrooms	Chocolate Blechkuchen

272.	Cumin Mushroom Bowls	Halibut Stir Fry	Dad's Rum Brownies
273.	Bell Peppers and Tomato Salad	Steamed Garlic-Dill Halibut	Chia Smoothie Bowl
274.	Avocado and Spinach Salad	Italian Halibut Chowder	Favorite Keto Frisuelos
275.	Zucchini Bowls	Pomegranate-Molasses Glazed Salmon	Blueberry Pot de Crème
276.	Lime Berries Salad	Salmon with Sun-Dried Tomatoes and Capers	Old-Fashion Coffee Mousse
277.	Zucchini Spread	Quick Thai Cod Curry	Café-Style Fudge
278.	Greek Tomato and Olives Salad	Island Style Sardines	Coconut and Seed Porridge
279.	Garlicky Green Beans and Olives Pan	Greek Chicken Stew	Pecan and Lime Cheesecake
280.	Paprika Olives Spread	Herbed Chicken Salad	Fluffy Chocolate Chip Cookies
281.	Chives Avocado Mix	Easy Stir-Fried Chicken	Chewy Almond Blondies
282.	Zucchini Pan	Poached Cod Asian Style	Rum Butter Cookies
283.	Chili Spinach and Zucchini Pan	Chicken in Pita Bread	Light Greek Cheesecake
284.	Basil Tomato and Cabbage Bowls	Multi-Spice Cod Curry	Fluffy Chocolate Crepes
285.	Spinach and Zucchini Hash	Slow Cooked Spanish Cod	Crispy Peanut Fudge Squares
286.	Tomato and Zucchini Fritters	Roasted Chicken	Almond Butter Cookies
287.	Cottage Cheese Fluff	Chicken and Avocado Lettuce Wraps	Basic Almond Cupcakes
288.	Microwaved Egg and Cheese Breakfast Burrito	Spicy & Creamy Ground Beef Curry	Blueberry Cheesecake Bowl
289.	Microwaved Ham and Mushroom Coffee Cup Scramble	Curried Beef Meatballs	Energy Chocolate Chip Candy
290.	Mini Breakfast Pizza	Ground Beef & Veggies Curry	Fudgy Mug Brownie

291.	Apple Yogurt Parfait	Ground Beef with Greens & Tomatoes	Basic Keto Brownies
292.	Basic Poached Eggs	Beef & Veggies Chili	Chocolate Cheesecake Fudge
293.	Easy Sweet Potatoes and Eggs	Ground Beef with Cashews & Veggies	Candy Bar Cheesecake Balls
294.	Sweet Onion and Egg Pie	Ground Beef with Veggies	Chocolate Blechkuchen
295.	Eggs Baked in Avocado	Beef with Asparagus & Bell Pepper	Dad's Rum Brownies
296.	Baked Egg Stuffed Cups	African Chicken Stew Turkey Meatballs	Chia Smoothie Bowl
297.	Strawberries and Cream Trifle	Brussels Sprouts and Paprika Chicken Thighs	Favorite Keto Frisuelos
298.	Maple Toast and Eggs	Chicken Breasts with Stuffing	Blueberry Pot de Crème
299.	Crème Brulee	Chicken-Bell Pepper Sauté	Old-Fashion Coffee Mousse
300.	Peppers Casserole	Avocado-Orange Grilled Chicken	Café-Style Fudge
301.	Chili Tomato Salad	Poached Halibut and Mushrooms	Coconut and Seed Porridge
302.	Cumin Mushroom Bowls	Halibut Stir Fry	Pecan and Lime Cheesecake
303.	Bell Peppers and Tomato Salad	Steamed Garlic-Dill Halibut	Fluffy Chocolate Chip Cookies
304.	Avocado and Spinach Salad	Italian Halibut Chowder	Chewy Almond Blondies
305.	Zucchini Bowls	Pomegranate-Molasses Glazed Salmon	Rum Butter Cookies
306.	Lime Berries Salad	Salmon with Sun-Dried Tomatoes and Capers	Light Greek Cheesecake
307.	Zucchini Spread	Quick Thai Cod Curry	Fluffy Chocolate Crepes
308.	Greek Tomato and Olives Salad	Island Style Sardines	Crispy Peanut Fudge Squares
309.	Garlicky Green Beans and Olives Pan	Greek Chicken Stew	Almond Butter Cookies
310.	Paprika Olives Spread	Herbed Chicken Salad	Basic Almond Cupcakes

311.	Chives Avocado Mix	Easy Stir-Fried Chicken	Blueberry Cheesecake Bowl
312.	Zucchini Pan	Poached Cod Asian Style	Energy Chocolate Chip Candy
313.	Chili Spinach and Zucchini Pan	Chicken in Pita Bread	Fudgy Mug Brownie
314.	Basil Tomato and Cabbage Bowls	Multi-Spice Cod Curry	Basic Keto Brownies
315.	Spinach and Zucchini Hash	Slow Cooked Spanish Cod	Chocolate Cheesecake Fudge
316.	Tomato and Zucchini Fritters	Roasted Chicken	Candy Bar Cheesecake Balls
317.	Cottage Cheese Fluff	Chicken and Avocado Lettuce Wraps	Chocolate Blechkuchen
318.	Microwaved Egg and Cheese Breakfast Burrito	Spicy & Creamy Ground Beef Curry	Dad's Rum Brownies
319.	Microwaved Ham and Mushroom Coffee Cup Scramble	Curried Beef Meatballs	Chia Smoothie Bowl
320.	Mini Breakfast Pizza	Ground Beef & Veggies Curry	Favorite Keto Frisuelos
321.	Apple Yogurt Parfait	Ground Beef with Greens & Tomatoes	Blueberry Pot de Crème
322.	Basic Poached Eggs	Beef & Veggies Chili	Old-Fashion Coffee Mousse
323.	Easy Sweet Potatoes and Eggs	Ground Beef with Cashews & Veggies	Café-Style Fudge
324.	Sweet Onion and Egg Pie	Ground Beef with Veggies	Coconut and Seed Porridge
325.	Eggs Baked in Avocado	Beef with Asparagus & Bell Pepper	Pecan and Lime Cheesecake
326.	Baked Egg Stuffed Cups	African Chicken Stew Turkey Meatballs	Fluffy Chocolate Chip Cookies
327.	Strawberries and Cream Trifle	Brussels Sprouts and Paprika Chicken Thighs	Chewy Almond Blondies
328.	Maple Toast and Eggs	Chicken Breasts with Stuffing	Rum Butter Cookies
329.	Crème Brulee	Chicken-Bell Pepper Sauté	Light Greek Cheesecake

330.	Peppers Casserole	Avocado-Orange Grilled Chicken	Fluffy Chocolate Crepes
331.	Chili Tomato Salad	Poached Halibut and Mushrooms	Crispy Peanut Fudge Squares
332.	Cumin Mushroom Bowls	Halibut Stir Fry	Almond Butter Cookies
333.	Bell Peppers and Tomato Salad	Steamed Garlic-Dill Halibut	Basic Almond Cupcakes
334.	Avocado and Spinach Salad	Italian Halibut Chowder	Blueberry Cheesecake Bowl
335.	Zucchini Bowls	Pomegranate-Molasses Glazed Salmon	Energy Chocolate Chip Candy
336.	Lime Berries Salad	Salmon with Sun-Dried Tomatoes and Capers	Fudgy Mug Brownie
337.	Zucchini Spread	Quick Thai Cod Curry	Basic Keto Brownies
338.	Greek Tomato and Olives Salad	Island Style Sardines	Chocolate Cheesecake Fudge
339.	Garlicky Green Beans and Olives Pan	Greek Chicken Stew	Candy Bar Cheesecake Balls
340.	Paprika Olives Spread	Herbed Chicken Salad	Chocolate Blechkuchen
341.	Chives Avocado Mix	Easy Stir-Fried Chicken	Dad's Rum Brownies
342.	Zucchini Pan	Poached Cod Asian Style	Chia Smoothie Bowl
343.	Chili Spinach and Zucchini Pan	Chicken in Pita Bread	Favorite Keto Frisuelos
344.	Basil Tomato and Cabbage Bowls	Multi-Spice Cod Curry	Blueberry Pot de Crème
345.	Spinach and Zucchini Hash	Slow Cooked Spanish Cod	Old-Fashion Coffee Mousse
346.	Tomato and Zucchini Fritters	Roasted Chicken	Café-Style Fudge
347.	Cottage Cheese Fluff	Chicken and Avocado Lettuce Wraps	Coconut and Seed Porridge
348.	Microwaved Egg and Cheese Breakfast Burrito	Spicy & Creamy Ground Beef Curry	Pecan and Lime Cheesecake

349.	Microwaved Ham and Mushroom Coffee Cup Scramble	Curried Beef Meatballs	Fluffy Chocolate Chip Cookies
350.	Mini Breakfast Pizza	Ground Beef & Veggies Curry	Chewy Almond Blondies
351.	Apple Yogurt Parfait	Ground Beef with Greens & Tomatoes	Rum Butter Cookies
352.	Basic Poached Eggs	Beef & Veggies Chili	Light Greek Cheesecake
353.	Easy Sweet Potatoes and Eggs	Ground Beef with Cashews & Veggies	Fluffy Chocolate Crepes
354.	Sweet Onion and Egg Pie	Ground Beef with Veggies	Crispy Peanut Fudge Squares
355.	Eggs Baked in Avocado	Beef with Asparagus & Bell Pepper	Almond Butter Cookies
356.	Baked Egg Stuffed Cups	African Chicken Stew Turkey Meatballs	Basic Almond Cupcakes
357.	Strawberries and Cream Trifle	Brussels Sprouts and Paprika Chicken Thighs	Blueberry Cheesecake Bowl
358.	Maple Toast and Eggs	Chicken Breasts with Stuffing	Energy Chocolate Chip Candy
359.	Crème Brulee	Chicken-Bell Pepper Sauté	Fudgy Mug Brownie
360.	Peppers Casserole	Avocado-Orange Grilled Chicken	Basic Keto Brownies
361.	Chili Tomato Salad	Poached Halibut and Mushrooms	Chocolate Cheesecake Fudge
362.	Cumin Mushroom Bowls	Halibut Stir Fry	Candy Bar Cheesecake Balls
363.	Bell Peppers and Tomato Salad	Steamed Garlic-Dill Halibut	Chocolate Blechkuchen
364.	Avocado and Spinach Salad	Italian Halibut Chowder	Dad's Rum Brownies
365.	Zucchini Bowls	Pomegranate-Molasses Glazed Salmon	Chia Smoothie Bowl
366.	Lime Berries Salad	Salmon with Sun-Dried Tomatoes and Capers	Favorite Keto Frisuelos
367.	Zucchini Spread	Quick Thai Cod Curry	Blueberry Pot de Crème
368.	Greek Tomato and Olives Salad	Island Style Sardines	Old-Fashion Coffee Mousse

369.	Garlicky Green Beans and Olives Pan	Greek Chicken Stew	Café-Style Fudge
370.	Paprika Olives Spread	Herbed Chicken Salad	Coconut and Seed Porridge
371.	Chives Avocado Mix	Easy Stir-Fried Chicken	Pecan and Lime Cheesecake
372.	Zucchini Pan	Poached Cod Asian Style	Fluffy Chocolate Chip Cookies
373.	Chili Spinach and Zucchini Pan	Chicken in Pita Bread	Chewy Almond Blondies
374.	Basil Tomato and Cabbage Bowls	Multi-Spice Cod Curry	Rum Butter Cookies
375.	Spinach and Zucchini Hash	Slow Cooked Spanish Cod	Light Greek Cheesecake
376.	Tomato and Zucchini Fritters	Roasted Chicken	Fluffy Chocolate Crepes
377.	Cottage Cheese Fluff	Chicken and Avocado Lettuce Wraps	Crispy Peanut Fudge Squares
378.	Microwaved Egg and Cheese Breakfast Burrito	Spicy & Creamy Ground Beef Curry	Almond Butter Cookies
379.	Microwaved Ham and Mushroom Coffee Cup Scramble	Curried Beef Meatballs	Basic Almond Cupcakes
380.	Mini Breakfast Pizza	Ground Beef & Veggies Curry	Blueberry Cheesecake Bowl
381.	Apple Yogurt Parfait	Ground Beef with Greens & Tomatoes	Energy Chocolate Chip Candy
382.	Basic Poached Eggs	Beef & Veggies Chili	Fudgy Mug Brownie
383.	Easy Sweet Potatoes and Eggs	Ground Beef with Cashews & Veggies	Basic Keto Brownies
384.	Sweet Onion and Egg Pie	Ground Beef with Veggies	Chocolate Cheesecake Fudge
385.	Eggs Baked in Avocado	Beef with Asparagus & Bell Pepper	Candy Bar Cheesecake Balls
386.	Baked Egg Stuffed Cups	African Chicken Stew Turkey Meatballs	Chocolate Blechkuchen
387.	Strawberries and Cream Trifle	Brussels Sprouts and Paprika Chicken Thighs	Dad's Rum Brownies
388.	Maple Toast and Eggs	Chicken Breasts with Stuffing	Chia Smoothie Bowl

389.	Crème Brulee	Chicken-Bell Pepper Sauté	Favorite Keto Frisuelos
390.	Peppers Casserole	Avocado-Orange Grilled Chicken	Blueberry Pot de Crème
391.	Chili Tomato Salad	Poached Halibut and Mushrooms	Old-Fashion Coffee Mousse
392.	Cumin Mushroom Bowls	Halibut Stir Fry	Café-Style Fudge
393.	Bell Peppers and Tomato Salad	Steamed Garlic-Dill Halibut	Coconut and Seed Porridge
394.	Avocado and Spinach Salad	Italian Halibut Chowder	Pecan and Lime Cheesecake
395.	Zucchini Bowls	Pomegranate-Molasses Glazed Salmon	Fluffy Chocolate Chip Cookies
396.	Lime Berries Salad	Salmon with Sun-Dried Tomatoes and Capers	Chewy Almond Blondies
397.	Zucchini Spread	Quick Thai Cod Curry	Rum Butter Cookies
398.	Greek Tomato and Olives Salad	Island Style Sardines	Light Greek Cheesecake
399.	Garlicky Green Beans and Olives Pan	Greek Chicken Stew	Fluffy Chocolate Crepes
400.	Paprika Olives Spread	Herbed Chicken Salad	Crispy Peanut Fudge Squares
401.	Chives Avocado Mix	Easy Stir-Fried Chicken	Almond Butter Cookies
402.	Zucchini Pan	Poached Cod Asian Style	Basic Almond Cupcakes
403.	Chili Spinach and Zucchini Pan	Chicken in Pita Bread	Blueberry Cheesecake Bowl
404.	Basil Tomato and Cabbage Bowls	Multi-Spice Cod Curry	Energy Chocolate Chip Candy
405.	Spinach and Zucchini Hash	Slow Cooked Spanish Cod	Fudgy Mug Brownie
406.	Tomato and Zucchini Fritters	Roasted Chicken	Basic Keto Brownies
407.	Cottage Cheese Fluff	Chicken and Avocado Lettuce Wraps	Chocolate Cheesecake Fudge
408.	Microwaved Egg and Cheese Breakfast	Spicy & Creamy Ground Beef Curry	Candy Bar Cheesecake Balls

	Burrito		
409.	Microwaved Ham and Mushroom Coffee Cup Scramble	Curried Beef Meatballs	Chocolate Blechkuchen
410.	Mini Breakfast Pizza	Ground Beef & Veggies Curry	Dad's Rum Brownies
411.	Apple Yogurt Parfait	Ground Beef with Greens & Tomatoes	Chia Smoothie Bowl
412.	Basic Poached Eggs	Beef & Veggies Chili	Favorite Keto Frisuelos
413.	Easy Sweet Potatoes and Eggs	Ground Beef with Cashews & Veggies	Blueberry Pot de Crème
414.	Sweet Onion and Egg Pie	Ground Beef with Veggies	Old-Fashion Coffee Mousse
415.	Eggs Baked in Avocado	Beef with Asparagus & Bell Pepper	Café-Style Fudge
416.	Baked Egg Stuffed Cups	African Chicken Stew Turkey Meatballs	Coconut and Seed Porridge
417.	Strawberries and Cream Trifle	Brussels Sprouts and Paprika Chicken Thighs	Pecan and Lime Cheesecake
418.	Maple Toast and Eggs	Chicken Breasts with Stuffing	Fluffy Chocolate Chip Cookies
419.	Crème Brulee	Chicken-Bell Pepper Sauté	Chewy Almond Blondies
420.	Peppers Casserole	Avocado-Orange Grilled Chicken	Rum Butter Cookies
421.	Chili Tomato Salad	Poached Halibut and Mushrooms	Light Greek Cheesecake
422.	Cumin Mushroom Bowls	Halibut Stir Fry	Fluffy Chocolate Crepes
423.	Bell Peppers and Tomato Salad	Steamed Garlic-Dill Halibut	Crispy Peanut Fudge Squares
424.	Avocado and Spinach Salad	Italian Halibut Chowder	Almond Butter Cookies
425.	Zucchini Bowls	Pomegranate-Molasses Glazed Salmon	Basic Almond Cupcakes
426.	Lime Berries Salad	Salmon with Sun-Dried Tomatoes and Capers	Blueberry Cheesecake Bowl
427.	Zucchini Spread	Quick Thai Cod Curry	Energy Chocolate Chip Candy

428.	Greek Tomato and Olives Salad	Island Style Sardines	Fudgy Mug Brownie
429.	Garlicky Green Beans and Olives Pan	Greek Chicken Stew	Basic Keto Brownies
430.	Paprika Olives Spread	Herbed Chicken Salad	Chocolate Cheesecake Fudge
431.	Chives Avocado Mix	Easy Stir-Fried Chicken	Candy Bar Cheesecake Balls
432.	Zucchini Pan	Poached Cod Asian Style	Chocolate Blechkuchen
433.	Chili Spinach and Zucchini Pan	Chicken in Pita Bread	Dad's Rum Brownies
434.	Basil Tomato and Cabbage Bowls	Multi-Spice Cod Curry	Chia Smoothie Bowl
435.	Spinach and Zucchini Hash	Slow Cooked Spanish Cod	Favorite Keto Frisuelos
436.	Tomato and Zucchini Fritters	Roasted Chicken	Blueberry Pot de Crème
437.	Cottage Cheese Fluff	Chicken and Avocado Lettuce Wraps	Old-Fashion Coffee Mousse
438.	Microwaved Egg and Cheese Breakfast Burrito	Spicy & Creamy Ground Beef Curry	Café-Style Fudge
439.	Microwaved Ham and Mushroom Coffee Cup Scramble	Curried Beef Meatballs	Coconut and Seed Porridge
440.	Mini Breakfast Pizza	Ground Beef & Veggies Curry	Pecan and Lime Cheesecake
441.	Apple Yogurt Parfait	Ground Beef with Greens & Tomatoes	Fluffy Chocolate Chip Cookies
442.	Basic Poached Eggs	Beef & Veggies Chili	Chewy Almond Blondies
443.	Easy Sweet Potatoes and Eggs	Ground Beef with Cashews & Veggies	Rum Butter Cookies
444.	Sweet Onion and Egg Pie	Ground Beef with Veggies	Light Greek Cheesecake
445.	Eggs Baked in Avocado	Beef with Asparagus & Bell Pepper	Fluffy Chocolate Crepes
446.	Baked Egg Stuffed Cups	African Chicken Stew Turkey Meatballs	Crispy Peanut Fudge Squares
447.	Strawberries and Cream Trifle	Brussels Sprouts and Paprika Chicken	Almond Butter Cookies

		Thighs	
448.	Maple Toast and Eggs	Chicken Breasts with Stuffing	Basic Almond Cupcakes
449.	Crème Brulee	Chicken-Bell Pepper Sauté	Blueberry Cheesecake Bowl
450.	Peppers Casserole	Avocado-Orange Grilled Chicken	Energy Chocolate Chip Candy
451.	Chili Tomato Salad	Poached Halibut and Mushrooms	Fudgy Mug Brownie
452.	Cumin Mushroom Bowls	Halibut Stir Fry	Basic Keto Brownies
453.	Bell Peppers and Tomato Salad	Steamed Garlic-Dill Halibut	Chocolate Cheesecake Fudge
454.	Avocado and Spinach Salad	Italian Halibut Chowder	Candy Bar Cheesecake Balls
455.	Zucchini Bowls	Pomegranate-Molasses Glazed Salmon	Chocolate Blechkuchen
456.	Lime Berries Salad	Salmon with Sun-Dried Tomatoes and Capers	Dad's Rum Brownies
457.	Zucchini Spread	Quick Thai Cod Curry	Chia Smoothie Bowl
458.	Greek Tomato and Olives Salad	Island Style Sardines	Favorite Keto Frisuelos
459.	Garlicky Green Beans and Olives Pan	Greek Chicken Stew	Blueberry Pot de Crème
460.	Paprika Olives Spread	Herbed Chicken Salad	Old-Fashion Coffee Mousse
461.	Chives Avocado Mix	Easy Stir-Fried Chicken	Café-Style Fudge
462.	Zucchini Pan	Poached Cod Asian Style	Coconut and Seed Porridge
463.	Chili Spinach and Zucchini Pan	Chicken in Pita Bread	Pecan and Lime Cheesecake
464.	Basil Tomato and Cabbage Bowls	Multi-Spice Cod Curry	Fluffy Chocolate Chip Cookies
465.	Spinach and Zucchini Hash	Slow Cooked Spanish Cod	Chewy Almond Blondies
466.	Tomato and Zucchini Fritters	Roasted Chicken	Rum Butter Cookies
467.	Cottage Cheese Fluff	Chicken and Avocado Lettuce Wraps	Light Greek Cheesecake

468.	Microwaved Egg and Cheese Breakfast Burrito	Spicy & Creamy Ground Beef Curry	Fluffy Chocolate Crepes
469.	Microwaved Ham and Mushroom Coffee Cup Scramble	Curried Beef Meatballs	Crispy Peanut Fudge Squares
470.	Mini Breakfast Pizza	Ground Beef & Veggies Curry	Almond Butter Cookies
471.	Apple Yogurt Parfait	Ground Beef with Greens & Tomatoes	Basic Almond Cupcakes
472.	Basic Poached Eggs	Beef & Veggies Chili	Blueberry Cheesecake Bowl
473.	Easy Sweet Potatoes and Eggs	Ground Beef with Cashews & Veggies	Energy Chocolate Chip Candy
474.	Sweet Onion and Egg Pie	Ground Beef with Veggies	Fudgy Mug Brownie
475.	Eggs Baked in Avocado	Beef with Asparagus & Bell Pepper	Basic Keto Brownies
476.	Baked Egg Stuffed Cups	African Chicken Stew Turkey Meatballs	Chocolate Cheesecake Fudge
477.	Strawberries and Cream Trifle	Brussels Sprouts and Paprika Chicken Thighs	Candy Bar Cheesecake Balls
478.	Maple Toast and Eggs	Chicken Breasts with Stuffing	Chocolate Blechkuchen
479.	Crème Brulee	Chicken-Bell Pepper Sauté	Dad's Rum Brownies
480.	Peppers Casserole	Avocado-Orange Grilled Chicken	Chia Smoothie Bowl
481.	Chili Tomato Salad	Poached Halibut and Mushrooms	Favorite Keto Frisuelos
482.	Cumin Mushroom Bowls	Halibut Stir Fry	Blueberry Pot de Crème
483.	Bell Peppers and Tomato Salad	Steamed Garlic-Dill Halibut	Old-Fashion Coffee Mousse
484.	Avocado and Spinach Salad	Italian Halibut Chowder	Café-Style Fudge
485.	Zucchini Bowls	Pomegranate-Molasses Glazed Salmon	Coconut and Seed Porridge
486.	Lime Berries Salad	Salmon with Sun-Dried Tomatoes and Capers	Pecan and Lime Cheesecake

487.	Zucchini Spread	Quick Thai Cod Curry	Fluffy Chocolate Chip Cookies
488.	Greek Tomato and Olives Salad	Island Style Sardines	Chewy Almond Blondies
489.	Garlicky Green Beans and Olives Pan	Greek Chicken Stew	Rum Butter Cookies
490.	Paprika Olives Spread	Herbed Chicken Salad	Light Greek Cheesecake
491.	Chives Avocado Mix	Easy Stir-Fried Chicken	Fluffy Chocolate Crepes
492.	Zucchini Pan	Poached Cod Asian Style	Crispy Peanut Fudge Squares
493.	Chili Spinach and Zucchini Pan	Chicken in Pita Bread	Almond Butter Cookies
494.	Basil Tomato and Cabbage Bowls	Multi-Spice Cod Curry	Basic Almond Cupcakes
495.	Spinach and Zucchini Hash	Slow Cooked Spanish Cod	Blueberry Cheesecake Bowl
496.	Tomato and Zucchini Fritters	Roasted Chicken	Energy Chocolate Chip Candy
497.	Cottage Cheese Fluff	Chicken and Avocado Lettuce Wraps	Fudgy Mug Brownie
498.	Microwaved Egg and Cheese Breakfast Burrito	Spicy & Creamy Ground Beef Curry	Basic Keto Brownies
499.	Microwaved Ham and Mushroom Coffee Cup Scramble	Curried Beef Meatballs	Chocolate Cheesecake Fudge
500.	Mini Breakfast Pizza	Ground Beef & Veggies Curry	Candy Bar Cheesecake Balls
501.	Apple Yogurt Parfait	Ground Beef with Greens & Tomatoes	Chocolate Blechkuchen
502.	Basic Poached Eggs	Beef & Veggies Chili	Dad's Rum Brownies
503.	Easy Sweet Potatoes and Eggs	Ground Beef with Cashews & Veggies	Chia Smoothie Bowl
504.	Sweet Onion and Egg Pie	Ground Beef with Veggies	Favorite Keto Frisuelos
505.	Eggs Baked in Avocado	Beef with Asparagus & Bell Pepper	Blueberry Pot de Crème
506.	Baked Egg Stuffed Cups	African Chicken Stew Turkey Meatballs	Old-Fashion Coffee Mousse

507.	Strawberries and Cream Trifle	Brussels Sprouts and Paprika Chicken Thighs	Café-Style Fudge
508.	Maple Toast and Eggs	Chicken Breasts with Stuffing	Coconut and Seed Porridge
509.	Crème Brulee	Chicken-Bell Pepper Sauté	Pecan and Lime Cheesecake
510.	Peppers Casserole	Avocado-Orange Grilled Chicken	Fluffy Chocolate Chip Cookies
511.	Chili Tomato Salad	Poached Halibut and Mushrooms	Chewy Almond Blondies
512.	Cumin Mushroom Bowls	Halibut Stir Fry	Rum Butter Cookies
513.	Bell Peppers and Tomato Salad	Steamed Garlic-Dill Halibut	Light Greek Cheesecake
514.	Avocado and Spinach Salad	Italian Halibut Chowder	Fluffy Chocolate Crepes
515.	Zucchini Bowls	Pomegranate-Molasses Glazed Salmon	Crispy Peanut Fudge Squares
516.	Lime Berries Salad	Salmon with Sun-Dried Tomatoes and Capers	Almond Butter Cookies
517.	Zucchini Spread	Quick Thai Cod Curry	Basic Almond Cupcakes
518.	Greek Tomato and Olives Salad	Island Style Sardines	Blueberry Cheesecake Bowl
519.	Garlicky Green Beans and Olives Pan	Greek Chicken Stew	Energy Chocolate Chip Candy
520.	Paprika Olives Spread	Herbed Chicken Salad	Fudgy Mug Brownie
521.	Chives Avocado Mix	Easy Stir-Fried Chicken	Basic Keto Brownies
522.	Zucchini Pan	Poached Cod Asian Style	Chocolate Cheesecake Fudge
523.	Chili Spinach and Zucchini Pan	Chicken in Pita Bread	Candy Bar Cheesecake Balls
524.	Basil Tomato and Cabbage Bowls	Multi-Spice Cod Curry	Chocolate Blechkuchen
525.	Spinach and Zucchini Hash	Slow Cooked Spanish Cod	Dad's Rum Brownies
526.	Tomato and Zucchini Fritters	Roasted Chicken	Chia Smoothie Bowl

527.	Cottage Cheese Fluff	Chicken and Avocado Lettuce Wraps	Favorite Keto Frisuelos
528.	Microwaved Egg and Cheese Breakfast Burrito	Spicy & Creamy Ground Beef Curry	Blueberry Pot de Crème
529.	Microwaved Ham and Mushroom Coffee Cup Scramble	Curried Beef Meatballs	Old-Fashion Coffee Mousse
530.	Mini Breakfast Pizza	Ground Beef & Veggies Curry	Café-Style Fudge
531.	Apple Yogurt Parfait	Ground Beef with Greens & Tomatoes	Coconut and Seed Porridge
532.	Basic Poached Eggs	Beef & Veggies Chili	Pecan and Lime Cheesecake
533.	Easy Sweet Potatoes and Eggs	Ground Beef with Cashews & Veggies	Fluffy Chocolate Chip Cookies
534.	Sweet Onion and Egg Pie	Ground Beef with Veggies	Chewy Almond Blondies
535.	Eggs Baked in Avocado	Beef with Asparagus & Bell Pepper	Rum Butter Cookies
536.	Baked Egg Stuffed Cups	African Chicken Stew Turkey Meatballs	Light Greek Cheesecake
537.	Strawberries and Cream Trifle	Brussels Sprouts and Paprika Chicken Thighs	Fluffy Chocolate Crepes
538.	Maple Toast and Eggs	Chicken Breasts with Stuffing	Crispy Peanut Fudge Squares
539.	Crème Brulee	Chicken-Bell Pepper Sauté	Almond Butter Cookies
540.	Peppers Casserole	Avocado-Orange Grilled Chicken	Basic Almond Cupcakes
541.	Chili Tomato Salad	Poached Halibut and Mushrooms	Blueberry Cheesecake Bowl
542.	Cumin Mushroom Bowls	Halibut Stir Fry	Energy Chocolate Chip Candy
543.	Bell Peppers and Tomato Salad	Steamed Garlic-Dill Halibut	Fudgy Mug Brownie
544.	Avocado and Spinach Salad	Italian Halibut Chowder	Basic Keto Brownies
545.	Zucchini Bowls	Pomegranate-Molasses Glazed Salmon	Chocolate Cheesecake Fudge

546.	Lime Berries Salad	Salmon with Sun-Dried Tomatoes and Capers	Candy Bar Cheesecake Balls
547.	Zucchini Spread	Quick Thai Cod Curry	Chocolate Blechkuchen
548.	Greek Tomato and Olives Salad	Island Style Sardines	Dad's Rum Brownies
549.	Garlicky Green Beans and Olives Pan	Greek Chicken Stew	Chia Smoothie Bowl
550.	Paprika Olives Spread	Herbed Chicken Salad	Favorite Keto Frisuelos
551.	Chives Avocado Mix	Easy Stir-Fried Chicken	Blueberry Pot de Crème
552.	Zucchini Pan	Poached Cod Asian Style	Old-Fashion Coffee Mousse
553.	Chili Spinach and Zucchini Pan	Chicken in Pita Bread	Café-Style Fudge
554.	Basil Tomato and Cabbage Bowls	Multi-Spice Cod Curry	Coconut and Seed Porridge
555.	Spinach and Zucchini Hash	Slow Cooked Spanish Cod	Pecan and Lime Cheesecake
556.	Tomato and Zucchini Fritters	Roasted Chicken	Fluffy Chocolate Chip Cookies
557.	Cottage Cheese Fluff	Chicken and Avocado Lettuce Wraps	Chewy Almond Blondies
558.	Microwaved Egg and Cheese Breakfast Burrito	Spicy & Creamy Ground Beef Curry	Rum Butter Cookies
559.	Microwaved Ham and Mushroom Coffee Cup Scramble	Curried Beef Meatballs	Light Greek Cheesecake
560.	Mini Breakfast Pizza	Ground Beef & Veggies Curry	Fluffy Chocolate Crepes
561.	Apple Yogurt Parfait	Ground Beef with Greens & Tomatoes	Crispy Peanut Fudge Squares
562.	Basic Poached Eggs	Beef & Veggies Chili	Almond Butter Cookies
563.	Easy Sweet Potatoes and Eggs	Ground Beef with Cashews & Veggies	Basic Almond Cupcakes
564.	Sweet Onion and Egg Pie	Ground Beef with Veggies	Blueberry Cheesecake Bowl

565.	Eggs Baked in Avocado	Beef with Asparagus & Bell Pepper	Energy Chocolate Chip Candy
566.	Baked Egg Stuffed Cups	African Chicken Stew Turkey Meatballs	Fudgy Mug Brownie
567.	Strawberries and Cream Trifle	Brussels Sprouts and Paprika Chicken Thighs	Basic Keto Brownies
568.	Maple Toast and Eggs	Chicken Breasts with Stuffing	Chocolate Cheesecake Fudge
569.	Crème Brulee	Chicken-Bell Pepper Sauté	Candy Bar Cheesecake Balls
570.	Peppers Casserole	Avocado-Orange Grilled Chicken	Chocolate Blechkuchen
571.	Chili Tomato Salad	Poached Halibut and Mushrooms	Dad's Rum Brownies
572.	Cumin Mushroom Bowls	Halibut Stir Fry	Chia Smoothie Bowl
573.	Bell Peppers and Tomato Salad	Steamed Garlic-Dill Halibut	Favorite Keto Frisuelos
574.	Avocado and Spinach Salad	Italian Halibut Chowder	Blueberry Pot de Crème
575.	Zucchini Bowls	Pomegranate-Molasses Glazed Salmon	Old-Fashion Coffee Mousse
576.	Lime Berries Salad	Salmon with Sun-Dried Tomatoes and Capers	Café-Style Fudge
577.	Zucchini Spread	Quick Thai Cod Curry	Coconut and Seed Porridge
578.	Greek Tomato and Olives Salad	Island Style Sardines	Pecan and Lime Cheesecake
579.	Garlicky Green Beans and Olives Pan	Greek Chicken Stew	Fluffy Chocolate Chip Cookies
580.	Paprika Olives Spread	Herbed Chicken Salad	Chewy Almond Blondies
581.	Chives Avocado Mix	Easy Stir-Fried Chicken	Rum Butter Cookies
582.	Zucchini Pan	Poached Cod Asian Style	Light Greek Cheesecake
583.	Chili Spinach and Zucchini Pan	Chicken in Pita Bread	Fluffy Chocolate Crepes
584.	Basil Tomato and Cabbage Bowls	Multi-Spice Cod Curry	Crispy Peanut Fudge Squares

585.	Spinach and Zucchini Hash	Slow Cooked Spanish Cod	Almond Butter Cookies
586.	Tomato and Zucchini Fritters	Roasted Chicken	Basic Almond Cupcakes
587.	Cottage Cheese Fluff	Chicken and Avocado Lettuce Wraps	Blueberry Cheesecake Bowl
588.	Microwaved Egg and Cheese Breakfast Burrito	Spicy & Creamy Ground Beef Curry	Energy Chocolate Chip Candy
589.	Microwaved Ham and Mushroom Coffee Cup Scramble	Curried Beef Meatballs	Fudgy Mug Brownie
590.	Mini Breakfast Pizza	Ground Beef & Veggies Curry	Basic Keto Brownies
591.	Apple Yogurt Parfait	Ground Beef with Greens & Tomatoes	Chocolate Cheesecake Fudge
592.	Basic Poached Eggs	Beef & Veggies Chili	Candy Bar Cheesecake Balls
593.	Easy Sweet Potatoes and Eggs	Ground Beef with Cashews & Veggies	Chocolate Blechkuchen
594.	Sweet Onion and Egg Pie	Ground Beef with Veggies	Dad's Rum Brownies
595.	Eggs Baked in Avocado	Beef with Asparagus & Bell Pepper	Chia Smoothie Bowl
596.	Baked Egg Stuffed Cups	African Chicken Stew Turkey Meatballs	Favorite Keto Frisuelos
597.	Strawberries and Cream Trifle	Brussels Sprouts and Paprika Chicken Thighs	Blueberry Pot de Crème
598.	Maple Toast and Eggs	Chicken Breasts with Stuffing	Old-Fashion Coffee Mousse
599.	Crème Brulee	Chicken-Bell Pepper Sauté	Café-Style Fudge
600.	Peppers Casserole	Avocado-Orange Grilled Chicken	Coconut and Seed Porridge
601.	Chili Tomato Salad	Poached Halibut and Mushrooms	Pecan and Lime Cheesecake
602.	Cumin Mushroom Bowls	Halibut Stir Fry	Fluffy Chocolate Chip Cookies
603.	Bell Peppers and Tomato Salad	Steamed Garlic-Dill Halibut	Chewy Almond Blondies

604.	Avocado and Spinach Salad	Italian Halibut Chowder	Rum Butter Cookies
605.	Zucchini Bowls	Pomegranate-Molasses Glazed Salmon	Light Greek Cheesecake
606.	Lime Berries Salad	Salmon with Sun-Dried Tomatoes and Capers	Fluffy Chocolate Crepes
607.	Zucchini Spread	Quick Thai Cod Curry	Crispy Peanut Fudge Squares
608.	Greek Tomato and Olives Salad	Island Style Sardines	Almond Butter Cookies
609.	Garlicky Green Beans and Olives Pan	Greek Chicken Stew	Basic Almond Cupcakes
610.	Paprika Olives Spread	Herbed Chicken Salad	Blueberry Cheesecake Bowl
611.	Chives Avocado Mix	Easy Stir-Fried Chicken	Energy Chocolate Chip Candy
612.	Zucchini Pan	Poached Cod Asian Style	Fudgy Mug Brownie
613.	Chili Spinach and Zucchini Pan	Chicken in Pita Bread	Basic Keto Brownies
614.	Basil Tomato and Cabbage Bowls	Multi-Spice Cod Curry	Chocolate Cheesecake Fudge
615.	Spinach and Zucchini Hash	Slow Cooked Spanish Cod	Candy Bar Cheesecake Balls
616.	Tomato and Zucchini Fritters	Roasted Chicken	Chocolate Blechkuchen
617.	Cottage Cheese Fluff	Chicken and Avocado Lettuce Wraps	Dad's Rum Brownies
618.	Microwaved Egg and Cheese Breakfast Burrito	Spicy & Creamy Ground Beef Curry	Chia Smoothie Bowl
619.	Microwaved Ham and Mushroom Coffee Cup Scramble	Curried Beef Meatballs	Favorite Keto Frisuelos
620.	Mini Breakfast Pizza	Ground Beef & Veggies Curry	Blueberry Pot de Crème
621.	Apple Yogurt Parfait	Ground Beef with Greens & Tomatoes	Old-Fashion Coffee Mousse
622.	Basic Poached Eggs	Beef & Veggies Chili	Café-Style Fudge

623.	Easy Sweet Potatoes and Eggs	Ground Beef with Cashews & Veggies	Coconut and Seed Porridge
624.	Sweet Onion and Egg Pie	Ground Beef with Veggies	Pecan and Lime Cheesecake
625.	Eggs Baked in Avocado	Beef with Asparagus & Bell Pepper	Fluffy Chocolate Chip Cookies
626.	Baked Egg Stuffed Cups	African Chicken Stew Turkey Meatballs	Chewy Almond Blondies
627.	Strawberries and Cream Trifle	Brussels Sprouts and Paprika Chicken Thighs	Rum Butter Cookies
628.	Maple Toast and Eggs	Chicken Breasts with Stuffing	Light Greek Cheesecake
629.	Crème Brulee	Chicken-Bell Pepper Sauté	Fluffy Chocolate Crepes
630.	Peppers Casserole	Avocado-Orange Grilled Chicken	Crispy Peanut Fudge Squares
631.	Chili Tomato Salad	Poached Halibut and Mushrooms	Almond Butter Cookies
632.	Cumin Mushroom Bowls	Halibut Stir Fry	Basic Almond Cupcakes
633.	Bell Peppers and Tomato Salad	Steamed Garlic-Dill Halibut	Blueberry Cheesecake Bowl
634.	Avocado and Spinach Salad	Italian Halibut Chowder	Energy Chocolate Chip Candy
635.	Zucchini Bowls	Pomegranate-Molasses Glazed Salmon	Fudgy Mug Brownie
636.	Lime Berries Salad	Salmon with Sun-Dried Tomatoes and Capers	Basic Keto Brownies
637.	Zucchini Spread	Quick Thai Cod Curry	Chocolate Cheesecake Fudge
638.	Greek Tomato and Olives Salad	Island Style Sardines	Candy Bar Cheesecake Balls
639.	Garlicky Green Beans and Olives Pan	Greek Chicken Stew	Chocolate Blechkuchen
640.	Paprika Olives Spread	Herbed Chicken Salad	Dad's Rum Brownies
641.	Chives Avocado Mix	Easy Stir-Fried Chicken	Chia Smoothie Bowl
642.	Zucchini Pan	Poached Cod Asian Style	Favorite Keto Frisuelos

643.	Chili Spinach and Zucchini Pan	Chicken in Pita Bread	Blueberry Pot de Crème
644.	Basil Tomato and Cabbage Bowls	Multi-Spice Cod Curry	Old-Fashion Coffee Mousse
645.	Spinach and Zucchini Hash	Slow Cooked Spanish Cod	Café-Style Fudge
646.	Tomato and Zucchini Fritters	Roasted Chicken	Coconut and Seed Porridge
647.	Cottage Cheese Fluff	Chicken and Avocado Lettuce Wraps	Pecan and Lime Cheesecake
648.	Microwaved Egg and Cheese Breakfast Burrito	Spicy & Creamy Ground Beef Curry	Fluffy Chocolate Chip Cookies
649.	Microwaved Ham and Mushroom Coffee Cup Scramble	Curried Beef Meatballs	Chewy Almond Blondies
650.	Mini Breakfast Pizza	Ground Beef & Veggies Curry	Rum Butter Cookies
651.	Apple Yogurt Parfait	Ground Beef with Greens & Tomatoes	Light Greek Cheesecake
652.	Basic Poached Eggs	Beef & Veggies Chili	Fluffy Chocolate Crepes
653.	Easy Sweet Potatoes and Eggs	Ground Beef with Cashews & Veggies	Crispy Peanut Fudge Squares
654.	Sweet Onion and Egg Pie	Ground Beef with Veggies	Almond Butter Cookies
655.	Eggs Baked in Avocado	Beef with Asparagus & Bell Pepper	Basic Almond Cupcakes
656.	Baked Egg Stuffed Cups	African Chicken Stew Turkey Meatballs	Blueberry Cheesecake Bowl
657.	Strawberries and Cream Trifle	Brussels Sprouts and Paprika Chicken Thighs	Energy Chocolate Chip Candy
658.	Maple Toast and Eggs	Chicken Breasts with Stuffing	Fudgy Mug Brownie
659.	Crème Brulee	Chicken-Bell Pepper Sauté	Basic Keto Brownies
660.	Peppers Casserole	Avocado-Orange Grilled Chicken	Chocolate Cheesecake Fudge
661.	Chili Tomato Salad	Poached Halibut and Mushrooms	Candy Bar Cheesecake Balls

662.	Cumin Mushroom Bowls	Halibut Stir Fry	Chocolate Blechkuchen
663.	Bell Peppers and Tomato Salad	Steamed Garlic-Dill Halibut	Dad's Rum Brownies
664.	Avocado and Spinach Salad	Italian Halibut Chowder	Chia Smoothie Bowl
665.	Zucchini Bowls	Pomegranate-Molasses Glazed Salmon	Favorite Keto Frisuelos
666.	Lime Berries Salad	Salmon with Sun-Dried Tomatoes and Capers	Blueberry Pot de Crème
667.	Zucchini Spread	Quick Thai Cod Curry	Old-Fashion Coffee Mousse
668.	Greek Tomato and Olives Salad	Island Style Sardines	Café-Style Fudge
669.	Garlicky Green Beans and Olives Pan	Greek Chicken Stew	Coconut and Seed Porridge
670.	Paprika Olives Spread	Herbed Chicken Salad	Pecan and Lime Cheesecake
671.	Chives Avocado Mix	Easy Stir-Fried Chicken	Fluffy Chocolate Chip Cookies
672.	Zucchini Pan	Poached Cod Asian Style	Chewy Almond Blondies
673.	Chili Spinach and Zucchini Pan	Chicken in Pita Bread	Rum Butter Cookies
674.	Basil Tomato and Cabbage Bowls	Multi-Spice Cod Curry	Light Greek Cheesecake
675.	Spinach and Zucchini Hash	Slow Cooked Spanish Cod	Fluffy Chocolate Crepes
676.	Tomato and Zucchini Fritters	Roasted Chicken	Crispy Peanut Fudge Squares
677.	Cottage Cheese Fluff	Chicken and Avocado Lettuce Wraps	Almond Butter Cookies
678.	Microwaved Egg and Cheese Breakfast Burrito	Spicy & Creamy Ground Beef Curry	Basic Almond Cupcakes
679.	Microwaved Ham and Mushroom Coffee Cup Scramble	Curried Beef Meatballs	Blueberry Cheesecake Bowl
680.	Mini Breakfast Pizza	Ground Beef & Veggies Curry	Energy Chocolate Chip Candy
681.	Apple Yogurt Parfait	Ground Beef with Greens & Tomatoes	Fudgy Mug Brownie

682.	Basic Poached Eggs	Beef & Veggies Chili	Basic Keto Brownies
683.	Easy Sweet Potatoes and Eggs	Ground Beef with Cashews & Veggies	Chocolate Cheesecake Fudge
684.	Sweet Onion and Egg Pie	Ground Beef with Veggies	Candy Bar Cheesecake Balls
685.	Eggs Baked in Avocado	Beef with Asparagus & Bell Pepper	Chocolate Blechkuchen
686.	Baked Egg Stuffed Cups	African Chicken Stew Turkey Meatballs	Dad's Rum Brownies
687.	Strawberries and Cream Trifle	Brussels Sprouts and Paprika Chicken Thighs	Chia Smoothie Bowl
688.	Maple Toast and Eggs	Chicken Breasts with Stuffing	Favorite Keto Frisuelos
689.	Crème Brulee	Chicken-Bell Pepper Sauté	Blueberry Pot de Crème
690.	Peppers Casserole	Avocado-Orange Grilled Chicken	Old-Fashion Coffee Mousse
691.	Chili Tomato Salad	Poached Halibut and Mushrooms	Café-Style Fudge
692.	Cumin Mushroom Bowls	Halibut Stir Fry	Coconut and Seed Porridge
693.	Bell Peppers and Tomato Salad	Steamed Garlic-Dill Halibut	Pecan and Lime Cheesecake
694.	Avocado and Spinach Salad	Italian Halibut Chowder	Fluffy Chocolate Chip Cookies
695.	Zucchini Bowls	Pomegranate-Molasses Glazed Salmon	Chewy Almond Blondies
696.	Lime Berries Salad	Salmon with Sun-Dried Tomatoes and Capers	Rum Butter Cookies
697.	Zucchini Spread	Quick Thai Cod Curry	Light Greek Cheesecake
698.	Greek Tomato and Olives Salad	Island Style Sardines	Fluffy Chocolate Crepes
699.	Garlicky Green Beans and Olives Pan	Greek Chicken Stew	Crispy Peanut Fudge Squares
700.	Paprika Olives Spread	Herbed Chicken Salad	Almond Butter Cookies
701.	Chives Avocado Mix	Easy Stir-Fried Chicken	Basic Almond Cupcakes

702.	Zucchini Pan	Poached Cod Asian Style	Blueberry Cheesecake Bowl
703.	Chili Spinach and Zucchini Pan	Chicken in Pita Bread	Energy Chocolate Chip Candy
704.	Basil Tomato and Cabbage Bowls	Multi-Spice Cod Curry	Fudgy Mug Brownie
705.	Spinach and Zucchini Hash	Slow Cooked Spanish Cod	Basic Keto Brownies
706.	Tomato and Zucchini Fritters	Roasted Chicken	Chocolate Cheesecake Fudge
707.	Cottage Cheese Fluff	Chicken and Avocado Lettuce Wraps	Candy Bar Cheesecake Balls
708.	Microwaved Egg and Cheese Breakfast Burrito	Spicy & Creamy Ground Beef Curry	Chocolate Blechkuchen
709.	Microwaved Ham and Mushroom Coffee Cup Scramble	Curried Beef Meatballs	Dad's Rum Brownies
710.	Mini Breakfast Pizza	Ground Beef & Veggies Curry	Chia Smoothie Bowl
711.	Apple Yogurt Parfait	Ground Beef with Greens & Tomatoes	Favorite Keto Frisuelos
712.	Basic Poached Eggs	Beef & Veggies Chili	Blueberry Pot de Crème
713.	Easy Sweet Potatoes and Eggs	Ground Beef with Cashews & Veggies	Old-Fashion Coffee Mousse
714.	Sweet Onion and Egg Pie	Ground Beef with Veggies	Café-Style Fudge
715.	Eggs Baked in Avocado	Beef with Asparagus & Bell Pepper	Coconut and Seed Porridge
716.	Baked Egg Stuffed Cups	African Chicken Stew Turkey Meatballs	Pecan and Lime Cheesecake
717.	Strawberries and Cream Trifle	Brussels Sprouts and Paprika Chicken Thighs	Fluffy Chocolate Chip Cookies
718.	Maple Toast and Eggs	Chicken Breasts with Stuffing	Chewy Almond Blondies
719.	Crème Brulee	Chicken-Bell Pepper Sauté	Rum Butter Cookies
720.	Peppers Casserole	Avocado-Orange Grilled Chicken	Light Greek Cheesecake

721.	Chili Tomato Salad	Poached Halibut and Mushrooms	Fluffy Chocolate Crepes
722.	Cumin Mushroom Bowls	Halibut Stir Fry	Crispy Peanut Fudge Squares
723.	Bell Peppers and Tomato Salad	Steamed Garlic-Dill Halibut	Almond Butter Cookies
724.	Avocado and Spinach Salad	Italian Halibut Chowder	Basic Almond Cupcakes
725.	Zucchini Bowls	Pomegranate-Molasses Glazed Salmon	Blueberry Cheesecake Bowl
726.	Lime Berries Salad	Salmon with Sun-Dried Tomatoes and Capers	Energy Chocolate Chip Candy
727.	Zucchini Spread	Quick Thai Cod Curry	Fudgy Mug Brownie
728.	Greek Tomato and Olives Salad	Island Style Sardines	Basic Keto Brownies
729.	Garlicky Green Beans and Olives Pan	Greek Chicken Stew	Chocolate Cheesecake Fudge
730.	Paprika Olives Spread	Herbed Chicken Salad	Candy Bar Cheesecake Balls
731.	Chives Avocado Mix	Easy Stir-Fried Chicken	Chocolate Blechkuchen
732.	Zucchini Pan	Poached Cod Asian Style	Dad's Rum Brownies
733.	Chili Spinach and Zucchini Pan	Chicken in Pita Bread	Chia Smoothie Bowl
734.	Basil Tomato and Cabbage Bowls	Multi-Spice Cod Curry	Favorite Keto Frisuelos
735.	Spinach and Zucchini Hash	Slow Cooked Spanish Cod	Blueberry Pot de Crème
736.	Tomato and Zucchini Fritters	Roasted Chicken	Old-Fashion Coffee Mousse
737.	Cottage Cheese Fluff	Chicken and Avocado Lettuce Wraps	Café-Style Fudge
738.	Microwaved Egg and Cheese Breakfast Burrito	Spicy & Creamy Ground Beef Curry	Coconut and Seed Porridge
739.	Microwaved Ham and Mushroom Coffee Cup Scramble	Curried Beef Meatballs	Pecan and Lime Cheesecake

740.	Mini Breakfast Pizza	Ground Beef & Veggies Curry	Fluffy Chocolate Chip Cookies
741.	Apple Yogurt Parfait	Ground Beef with Greens & Tomatoes	Chewy Almond Blondies
742.	Basic Poached Eggs	Beef & Veggies Chili	Rum Butter Cookies
743.	Easy Sweet Potatoes and Eggs	Ground Beef with Cashews & Veggies	Light Greek Cheesecake
744.	Sweet Onion and Egg Pie	Ground Beef with Veggies	Fluffy Chocolate Crepes
745.	Eggs Baked in Avocado	Beef with Asparagus & Bell Pepper	Crispy Peanut Fudge Squares
746.	Baked Egg Stuffed Cups	African Chicken Stew Turkey Meatballs	Almond Butter Cookies
747.	Strawberries and Cream Trifle	Brussels Sprouts and Paprika Chicken Thighs	Basic Almond Cupcakes
748.	Maple Toast and Eggs	Chicken Breasts with Stuffing	Blueberry Cheesecake Bowl
749.	Crème Brulee	Chicken-Bell Pepper Sauté	Energy Chocolate Chip Candy
750.	Peppers Casserole	Avocado-Orange Grilled Chicken	Fudgy Mug Brownie
751.	Chili Tomato Salad	Poached Halibut and Mushrooms	Basic Keto Brownies
752.	Cumin Mushroom Bowls	Halibut Stir Fry	Chocolate Cheesecake Fudge
753.	Bell Peppers and Tomato Salad	Steamed Garlic-Dill Halibut	Candy Bar Cheesecake Balls
754.	Avocado and Spinach Salad	Italian Halibut Chowder	Chocolate Blechkuchen
755.	Zucchini Bowls	Pomegranate-Molasses Glazed Salmon	Dad's Rum Brownies
756.	Lime Berries Salad	Salmon with Sun-Dried Tomatoes and Capers	Chia Smoothie Bowl
757.	Zucchini Spread	Quick Thai Cod Curry	Favorite Keto Frisuelos
758.	Greek Tomato and Olives Salad	Island Style Sardines	Blueberry Pot de Crème
759.	Garlicky Green Beans and Olives Pan	Greek Chicken Stew	Old-Fashion Coffee Mousse

760.	Paprika Olives Spread	Herbed Chicken Salad	Café-Style Fudge
761.	Chives Avocado Mix	Easy Stir-Fried Chicken	Coconut and Seed Porridge
762.	Zucchini Pan	Poached Cod Asian Style	Pecan and Lime Cheesecake
763.	Chili Spinach and Zucchini Pan	Chicken in Pita Bread	Fluffy Chocolate Chip Cookies
764.	Basil Tomato and Cabbage Bowls	Multi-Spice Cod Curry	Chewy Almond Blondies
765.	Spinach and Zucchini Hash	Slow Cooked Spanish Cod	Rum Butter Cookies
766.	Tomato and Zucchini Fritters	Roasted Chicken	Light Greek Cheesecake
767.	Cottage Cheese Fluff	Chicken and Avocado Lettuce Wraps	Fluffy Chocolate Crepes
768.	Microwaved Egg and Cheese Breakfast Burrito	Spicy & Creamy Ground Beef Curry	Crispy Peanut Fudge Squares
769.	Microwaved Ham and Mushroom Coffee Cup Scramble	Curried Beef Meatballs	Almond Butter Cookies
770.	Mini Breakfast Pizza	Ground Beef & Veggies Curry	Basic Almond Cupcakes
771.	Apple Yogurt Parfait	Ground Beef with Greens & Tomatoes	Blueberry Cheesecake Bowl
772.	Basic Poached Eggs	Beef & Veggies Chili	Energy Chocolate Chip Candy
773.	Easy Sweet Potatoes and Eggs	Ground Beef with Cashews & Veggies	Fudgy Mug Brownie
774.	Sweet Onion and Egg Pie	Ground Beef with Veggies	Basic Keto Brownies
775.	Eggs Baked in Avocado	Beef with Asparagus & Bell Pepper	Chocolate Cheesecake Fudge
776.	Baked Egg Stuffed Cups	African Chicken Stew Turkey Meatballs	Candy Bar Cheesecake Balls
777.	Strawberries and Cream Trifle	Brussels Sprouts and Paprika Chicken Thighs	Chocolate Blechkuchen
778.	Maple Toast and Eggs	Chicken Breasts with Stuffing	Dad's Rum Brownies
779.	Crème Brulee	Chicken-Bell Pepper Sauté	Chia Smoothie Bowl

780.	Peppers Casserole	Avocado-Orange Grilled Chicken	Favorite Keto Frisuelos
781.	Chili Tomato Salad	Poached Halibut and Mushrooms	Blueberry Pot de Crème
782.	Cumin Mushroom Bowls	Halibut Stir Fry	Old-Fashion Coffee Mousse
783.	Bell Peppers and Tomato Salad	Steamed Garlic-Dill Halibut	Café-Style Fudge
784.	Avocado and Spinach Salad	Italian Halibut Chowder	Coconut and Seed Porridge
785.	Zucchini Bowls	Pomegranate-Molasses Glazed Salmon	Pecan and Lime Cheesecake
786.	Lime Berries Salad	Salmon with Sun-Dried Tomatoes and Capers	Fluffy Chocolate Chip Cookies
787.	Zucchini Spread	Quick Thai Cod Curry	Chewy Almond Blondies
788.	Greek Tomato and Olives Salad	Island Style Sardines	Rum Butter Cookies
789.	Garlicky Green Beans and Olives Pan	Greek Chicken Stew	Light Greek Cheesecake
790.	Paprika Olives Spread	Herbed Chicken Salad	Fluffy Chocolate Crepes
791.	Chives Avocado Mix	Easy Stir-Fried Chicken	Crispy Peanut Fudge Squares
792.	Zucchini Pan	Poached Cod Asian Style	Almond Butter Cookies
793.	Chili Spinach and Zucchini Pan	Chicken in Pita Bread	Basic Almond Cupcakes
794.	Basil Tomato and Cabbage Bowls	Multi-Spice Cod Curry	Blueberry Cheesecake Bowl
795.	Spinach and Zucchini Hash	Slow Cooked Spanish Cod	Energy Chocolate Chip Candy
796.	Tomato and Zucchini Fritters	Roasted Chicken	Fudgy Mug Brownie
797.	Cottage Cheese Fluff	Chicken and Avocado Lettuce Wraps	Basic Keto Brownies
798.	Microwaved Egg and Cheese Breakfast Burrito	Spicy & Creamy Ground Beef Curry	Chocolate Cheesecake Fudge

799.	Microwaved Ham and Mushroom Coffee Cup Scramble	Curried Beef Meatballs	Candy Bar Cheesecake Balls
800.	Mini Breakfast Pizza	Ground Beef & Veggies Curry	Chocolate Blechkuchen
801.	Apple Yogurt Parfait	Ground Beef with Greens & Tomatoes	Dad's Rum Brownies
802.	Basic Poached Eggs	Beef & Veggies Chili	Chia Smoothie Bowl
803.	Easy Sweet Potatoes and Eggs	Ground Beef with Cashews & Veggies	Favorite Keto Frisuelos
804.	Sweet Onion and Egg Pie	Ground Beef with Veggies	Blueberry Pot de Crème
805.	Eggs Baked in Avocado	Beef with Asparagus & Bell Pepper	Old-Fashion Coffee Mousse
806.	Baked Egg Stuffed Cups	African Chicken Stew Turkey Meatballs	Café-Style Fudge
807.	Strawberries and Cream Trifle	Brussels Sprouts and Paprika Chicken Thighs	Coconut and Seed Porridge
808.	Maple Toast and Eggs	Chicken Breasts with Stuffing	Pecan and Lime Cheesecake
809.	Crème Brulee	Chicken-Bell Pepper Sauté	Fluffy Chocolate Chip Cookies
810.	Peppers Casserole	Avocado-Orange Grilled Chicken	Chewy Almond Blondies
811.	Chili Tomato Salad	Poached Halibut and Mushrooms	Rum Butter Cookies
812.	Cumin Mushroom Bowls	Halibut Stir Fry	Light Greek Cheesecake
813.	Bell Peppers and Tomato Salad	Steamed Garlic-Dill Halibut	Fluffy Chocolate Crepes
814.	Avocado and Spinach Salad	Italian Halibut Chowder	Crispy Peanut Fudge Squares
815.	Zucchini Bowls	Pomegranate-Molasses Glazed Salmon	Almond Butter Cookies
816.	Lime Berries Salad	Salmon with Sun-Dried Tomatoes and Capers	Basic Almond Cupcakes
817.	Zucchini Spread	Quick Thai Cod Curry	Blueberry Cheesecake Bowl
818.	Greek Tomato and Olives Salad	Island Style Sardines	Energy Chocolate Chip Candy

819.	Garlicky Green Beans and Olives Pan	Greek Chicken Stew	Fudgy Mug Brownie
820.	Paprika Olives Spread	Herbed Chicken Salad	Basic Keto Brownies
821.	Chives Avocado Mix	Easy Stir-Fried Chicken	Chocolate Cheesecake Fudge
822.	Zucchini Pan	Poached Cod Asian Style	Candy Bar Cheesecake Balls
823.	Chili Spinach and Zucchini Pan	Chicken in Pita Bread	Chocolate Blechkuchen
824.	Basil Tomato and Cabbage Bowls	Multi-Spice Cod Curry	Dad's Rum Brownies
825.	Spinach and Zucchini Hash	Slow Cooked Spanish Cod	Chia Smoothie Bowl
826.	Tomato and Zucchini Fritters	Roasted Chicken	Favorite Keto Frisuelos
827.	Cottage Cheese Fluff	Chicken and Avocado Lettuce Wraps	Blueberry Pot de Crème
828.	Microwaved Egg and Cheese Breakfast Burrito	Spicy & Creamy Ground Beef Curry	Old-Fashion Coffee Mousse
829.	Microwaved Ham and Mushroom Coffee Cup Scramble	Curried Beef Meatballs	Café-Style Fudge
830.	Mini Breakfast Pizza	Ground Beef & Veggies Curry	Coconut and Seed Porridge
831.	Apple Yogurt Parfait	Ground Beef with Greens & Tomatoes	Pecan and Lime Cheesecake
832.	Basic Poached Eggs	Beef & Veggies Chili	Fluffy Chocolate Chip Cookies
833.	Easy Sweet Potatoes and Eggs	Ground Beef with Cashews & Veggies	Chewy Almond Blondies
834.	Sweet Onion and Egg Pie	Ground Beef with Veggies	Rum Butter Cookies
835.	Eggs Baked in Avocado	Beef with Asparagus & Bell Pepper	Light Greek Cheesecake
836.	Baked Egg Stuffed Cups	African Chicken Stew Turkey Meatballs	Fluffy Chocolate Crepes
837.	Strawberries and Cream Trifle	Brussels Sprouts and Paprika Chicken Thighs	Crispy Peanut Fudge Squares
838.	Maple Toast and Eggs	Chicken Breasts with Stuffing	Almond Butter Cookies

839.	Crème Brulee	Chicken-Bell Pepper Sauté	Basic Almond Cupcakes
840.	Peppers Casserole	Avocado-Orange Grilled Chicken	Blueberry Cheesecake Bowl
841.	Chili Tomato Salad	Poached Halibut and Mushrooms	Energy Chocolate Chip Candy
842.	Cumin Mushroom Bowls	Halibut Stir Fry	Fudgy Mug Brownie
843.	Bell Peppers and Tomato Salad	Steamed Garlic-Dill Halibut	Basic Keto Brownies
844.	Avocado and Spinach Salad	Italian Halibut Chowder	Chocolate Cheesecake Fudge
845.	Zucchini Bowls	Pomegranate-Molasses Glazed Salmon	Candy Bar Cheesecake Balls
846.	Lime Berries Salad	Salmon with Sun-Dried Tomatoes and Capers	Chocolate Blechkuchen
847.	Zucchini Spread	Quick Thai Cod Curry	Dad's Rum Brownies
848.	Greek Tomato and Olives Salad	Island Style Sardines	Chia Smoothie Bowl
849.	Garlicky Green Beans and Olives Pan	Greek Chicken Stew	Favorite Keto Frisuelos
850.	Paprika Olives Spread	Herbed Chicken Salad	Blueberry Pot de Crème
851.	Chives Avocado Mix	Easy Stir-Fried Chicken	Old-Fashion Coffee Mousse
852.	Zucchini Pan	Poached Cod Asian Style	Café-Style Fudge
853.	Chili Spinach and Zucchini Pan	Chicken in Pita Bread	Coconut and Seed Porridge
854.	Basil Tomato and Cabbage Bowls	Multi-Spice Cod Curry	Pecan and Lime Cheesecake
855.	Spinach and Zucchini Hash	Slow Cooked Spanish Cod	Fluffy Chocolate Chip Cookies
856.	Tomato and Zucchini Fritters	Roasted Chicken	Chewy Almond Blondies
857.	Cottage Cheese Fluff	Chicken and Avocado Lettuce Wraps	Rum Butter Cookies
858.	Microwaved Egg and Cheese Breakfast	Spicy & Creamy Ground Beef Curry	Light Greek Cheesecake

	Burrito		
859.	Microwaved Ham and Mushroom Coffee Cup Scramble	Curried Beef Meatballs	Fluffy Chocolate Crepes
860.	Mini Breakfast Pizza	Ground Beef & Veggies Curry	Crispy Peanut Fudge Squares
861.	Apple Yogurt Parfait	Ground Beef with Greens & Tomatoes	Almond Butter Cookies
862.	Basic Poached Eggs	Beef & Veggies Chili	Basic Almond Cupcakes
863.	Easy Sweet Potatoes and Eggs	Ground Beef with Cashews & Veggies	Blueberry Cheesecake Bowl
864.	Sweet Onion and Egg Pie	Ground Beef with Veggies	Energy Chocolate Chip Candy
865.	Eggs Baked in Avocado	Beef with Asparagus & Bell Pepper	Fudgy Mug Brownie
866.	Baked Egg Stuffed Cups	African Chicken Stew Turkey Meatballs	Basic Keto Brownies
867.	Strawberries and Cream Trifle	Brussels Sprouts and Paprika Chicken Thighs	Chocolate Cheesecake Fudge
868.	Maple Toast and Eggs	Chicken Breasts with Stuffing	Candy Bar Cheesecake Balls
869.	Crème Brulee	Chicken-Bell Pepper Sauté	Chocolate Blechkuchen
870.	Peppers Casserole	Avocado-Orange Grilled Chicken	Dad's Rum Brownies
871.	Chili Tomato Salad	Poached Halibut and Mushrooms	Chia Smoothie Bowl
872.	Cumin Mushroom Bowls	Halibut Stir Fry	Favorite Keto Frisuelos
873.	Bell Peppers and Tomato Salad	Steamed Garlic-Dill Halibut	Blueberry Pot de Crème
874.	Avocado and Spinach Salad	Italian Halibut Chowder	Old-Fashion Coffee Mousse
875.	Zucchini Bowls	Pomegranate-Molasses Glazed Salmon	Café-Style Fudge
876.	Lime Berries Salad	Salmon with Sun-Dried Tomatoes and Capers	Coconut and Seed Porridge
877.	Zucchini Spread	Quick Thai Cod Curry	Pecan and Lime Cheesecake

878.	Greek Tomato and Olives Salad	Island Style Sardines	Fluffy Chocolate Chip Cookies
879.	Garlicky Green Beans and Olives Pan	Greek Chicken Stew	Chewy Almond Blondies
880.	Paprika Olives Spread	Herbed Chicken Salad	Rum Butter Cookies
881.	Chives Avocado Mix	Easy Stir-Fried Chicken	Light Greek Cheesecake
882.	Zucchini Pan	Poached Cod Asian Style	Fluffy Chocolate Crepes
883.	Chili Spinach and Zucchini Pan	Chicken in Pita Bread	Crispy Peanut Fudge Squares
884.	Basil Tomato and Cabbage Bowls	Multi-Spice Cod Curry	Almond Butter Cookies
885.	Spinach and Zucchini Hash	Slow Cooked Spanish Cod	Basic Almond Cupcakes
886.	Tomato and Zucchini Fritters	Roasted Chicken	Blueberry Cheesecake Bowl
887.	Cottage Cheese Fluff	Chicken and Avocado Lettuce Wraps	Energy Chocolate Chip Candy
888.	Microwaved Egg and Cheese Breakfast Burrito	Spicy & Creamy Ground Beef Curry	Fudgy Mug Brownie
889.	Microwaved Ham and Mushroom Coffee Cup Scramble	Curried Beef Meatballs	Basic Keto Brownies
890.	Mini Breakfast Pizza	Ground Beef & Veggies Curry	Chocolate Cheesecake Fudge
891.	Apple Yogurt Parfait	Ground Beef with Greens & Tomatoes	Candy Bar Cheesecake Balls
892.	Basic Poached Eggs	Beef & Veggies Chili	Chocolate Blechkuchen
893.	Easy Sweet Potatoes and Eggs	Ground Beef with Cashews & Veggies	Dad's Rum Brownies
894.	Sweet Onion and Egg Pie	Ground Beef with Veggies	Chia Smoothie Bowl
895.	Eggs Baked in Avocado	Beef with Asparagus & Bell Pepper	Favorite Keto Frisuelos
896.	Baked Egg Stuffed Cups	African Chicken Stew Turkey Meatballs	Blueberry Pot de Crème

897.	Strawberries and Cream Trifle	Brussels Sprouts and Paprika Chicken Thighs	Old-Fashion Coffee Mousse
898.	Maple Toast and Eggs	Chicken Breasts with Stuffing	Café-Style Fudge
899.	Crème Brulee	Chicken-Bell Pepper Sauté	Coconut and Seed Porridge
900.	Peppers Casserole	Avocado-Orange Grilled Chicken	Pecan and Lime Cheesecake
901.	Chili Tomato Salad	Poached Halibut and Mushrooms	Fluffy Chocolate Chip Cookies
902.	Cumin Mushroom Bowls	Halibut Stir Fry	Chewy Almond Blondies
903.	Bell Peppers and Tomato Salad	Steamed Garlic-Dill Halibut	Rum Butter Cookies
904.	Avocado and Spinach Salad	Italian Halibut Chowder	Light Greek Cheesecake
905.	Zucchini Bowls	Pomegranate-Molasses Glazed Salmon	Fluffy Chocolate Crepes
906.	Lime Berries Salad	Salmon with Sun-Dried Tomatoes and Capers	Crispy Peanut Fudge Squares
907.	Zucchini Spread	Quick Thai Cod Curry	Almond Butter Cookies
908.	Greek Tomato and Olives Salad	Island Style Sardines	Basic Almond Cupcakes
909.	Garlicky Green Beans and Olives Pan	Greek Chicken Stew	Blueberry Cheesecake Bowl
910.	Paprika Olives Spread	Herbed Chicken Salad	Energy Chocolate Chip Candy
911.	Chives Avocado Mix	Easy Stir-Fried Chicken	Fudgy Mug Brownie
912.	Zucchini Pan	Poached Cod Asian Style	Basic Keto Brownies
913.	Chili Spinach and Zucchini Pan	Chicken in Pita Bread	Chocolate Cheesecake Fudge
914.	Basil Tomato and Cabbage Bowls	Multi-Spice Cod Curry	Candy Bar Cheesecake Balls
915.	Spinach and Zucchini Hash	Slow Cooked Spanish Cod	Chocolate Blechkuchen
916.	Tomato and Zucchini Fritters	Roasted Chicken	Dad's Rum Brownies

917.	Cottage Cheese Fluff	Chicken and Avocado Lettuce Wraps	Chia Smoothie Bowl
918.	Microwaved Egg and Cheese Breakfast Burrito	Spicy & Creamy Ground Beef Curry	Favorite Keto Frisuelos
919.	Microwaved Ham and Mushroom Coffee Cup Scramble	Curried Beef Meatballs	Blueberry Pot de Crème
920.	Mini Breakfast Pizza	Ground Beef & Veggies Curry	Old-Fashion Coffee Mousse
921.	Apple Yogurt Parfait	Ground Beef with Greens & Tomatoes	Café-Style Fudge
922.	Basic Poached Eggs	Beef & Veggies Chili	Coconut and Seed Porridge
923.	Easy Sweet Potatoes and Eggs	Ground Beef with Cashews & Veggies	Pecan and Lime Cheesecake
924.	Sweet Onion and Egg Pie	Ground Beef with Veggies	Fluffy Chocolate Chip Cookies
925.	Eggs Baked in Avocado	Beef with Asparagus & Bell Pepper	Chewy Almond Blondies
926.	Baked Egg Stuffed Cups	African Chicken Stew Turkey Meatballs	Rum Butter Cookies
927.	Strawberries and Cream Trifle	Brussels Sprouts and Paprika Chicken Thighs	Light Greek Cheesecake
928.	Maple Toast and Eggs	Chicken Breasts with Stuffing	Fluffy Chocolate Crepes
929.	Crème Brulee	Chicken-Bell Pepper Sauté	Crispy Peanut Fudge Squares
930.	Peppers Casserole	Avocado-Orange Grilled Chicken	Almond Butter Cookies
931.	Chili Tomato Salad	Poached Halibut and Mushrooms	Basic Almond Cupcakes
932.	Cumin Mushroom Bowls	Halibut Stir Fry	Blueberry Cheesecake Bowl
933.	Bell Peppers and Tomato Salad	Steamed Garlic-Dill Halibut	Energy Chocolate Chip Candy
934.	Avocado and Spinach Salad	Italian Halibut Chowder	Fudgy Mug Brownie
935.	Zucchini Bowls	Pomegranate-Molasses Glazed Salmon	Basic Keto Brownies

936.	Lime Berries Salad	Salmon with Sun-Dried Tomatoes and Capers	Chocolate Cheesecake Fudge
937.	Zucchini Spread	Quick Thai Cod Curry	Candy Bar Cheesecake Balls
938.	Greek Tomato and Olives Salad	Island Style Sardines	Chocolate Blechkuchen
939.	Garlicky Green Beans and Olives Pan	Greek Chicken Stew	Dad's Rum Brownies
940.	Paprika Olives Spread	Herbed Chicken Salad	Chia Smoothie Bowl
941.	Chives Avocado Mix	Easy Stir-Fried Chicken	Favorite Keto Frisuelos
942.	Zucchini Pan	Poached Cod Asian Style	Blueberry Pot de Crème
943.	Chili Spinach and Zucchini Pan	Chicken in Pita Bread	Old-Fashion Coffee Mousse
944.	Basil Tomato and Cabbage Bowls	Multi-Spice Cod Curry	Café-Style Fudge
945.	Spinach and Zucchini Hash	Slow Cooked Spanish Cod	Coconut and Seed Porridge
946.	Tomato and Zucchini Fritters	Roasted Chicken	Pecan and Lime Cheesecake
947.	Cottage Cheese Fluff	Chicken and Avocado Lettuce Wraps	Fluffy Chocolate Chip Cookies
948.	Microwaved Egg and Cheese Breakfast Burrito	Spicy & Creamy Ground Beef Curry	Chewy Almond Blondies
949.	Microwaved Ham and Mushroom Coffee Cup Scramble	Curried Beef Meatballs	Rum Butter Cookies
950.	Mini Breakfast Pizza	Ground Beef & Veggies Curry	Light Greek Cheesecake
951.	Apple Yogurt Parfait	Ground Beef with Greens & Tomatoes	Fluffy Chocolate Crepes
952.	Basic Poached Eggs	Beef & Veggies Chili	Crispy Peanut Fudge Squares
953.	Easy Sweet Potatoes and Eggs	Ground Beef with Cashews & Veggies	Almond Butter Cookies
954.	Sweet Onion and Egg Pie	Ground Beef with Veggies	Basic Almond Cupcakes

955.	Eggs Baked in Avocado	Beef with Asparagus & Bell Pepper	Blueberry Cheesecake Bowl
956.	Baked Egg Stuffed Cups	African Chicken Stew Turkey Meatballs	Energy Chocolate Chip Candy
957.	Strawberries and Cream Trifle	Brussels Sprouts and Paprika Chicken Thighs	Fudgy Mug Brownie
958.	Maple Toast and Eggs	Chicken Breasts with Stuffing	Basic Keto Brownies
959.	Crème Brulee	Chicken-Bell Pepper Sauté	Chocolate Cheesecake Fudge
960.	Peppers Casserole	Avocado-Orange Grilled Chicken	Candy Bar Cheesecake Balls
961.	Chili Tomato Salad	Poached Halibut and Mushrooms	Chocolate Blechkuchen
962.	Cumin Mushroom Bowls	Halibut Stir Fry	Dad's Rum Brownies
963.	Bell Peppers and Tomato Salad	Steamed Garlic-Dill Halibut	Chia Smoothie Bowl
964.	Avocado and Spinach Salad	Italian Halibut Chowder	Favorite Keto Frisuelos
965.	Zucchini Bowls	Pomegranate-Molasses Glazed Salmon	Blueberry Pot de Crème
966.	Lime Berries Salad	Salmon with Sun-Dried Tomatoes and Capers	Old-Fashion Coffee Mousse
967.	Zucchini Spread	Quick Thai Cod Curry	Café-Style Fudge
968.	Greek Tomato and Olives Salad	Island Style Sardines	Coconut and Seed Porridge
969.	Garlicky Green Beans and Olives Pan	Greek Chicken Stew	Pecan and Lime Cheesecake
970.	Paprika Olives Spread	Herbed Chicken Salad	Fluffy Chocolate Chip Cookies
971.	Chives Avocado Mix	Easy Stir-Fried Chicken	Chewy Almond Blondies
972.	Zucchini Pan	Poached Cod Asian Style	Rum Butter Cookies
973.	Chili Spinach and Zucchini Pan	Chicken in Pita Bread	Light Greek Cheesecake
974.	Basil Tomato and Cabbage Bowls	Multi-Spice Cod Curry	Fluffy Chocolate Crepes

975.	Spinach and Zucchini Hash	Slow Cooked Spanish Cod	Crispy Peanut Fudge Squares
976.	Tomato and Zucchini Fritters	Roasted Chicken	Almond Butter Cookies
977.	Cottage Cheese Fluff	Chicken and Avocado Lettuce Wraps	Basic Almond Cupcakes
978.	Microwaved Egg and Cheese Breakfast Burrito	Spicy & Creamy Ground Beef Curry	Blueberry Cheesecake Bowl
979.	Microwaved Ham and Mushroom Coffee Cup Scramble	Curried Beef Meatballs	Energy Chocolate Chip Candy
980.	Mini Breakfast Pizza	Ground Beef & Veggies Curry	Fudgy Mug Brownie
981.	Apple Yogurt Parfait	Ground Beef with Greens & Tomatoes	Basic Keto Brownies
982.	Basic Poached Eggs	Beef & Veggies Chili	Chocolate Cheesecake Fudge
983.	Easy Sweet Potatoes and Eggs	Ground Beef with Cashews & Veggies	Candy Bar Cheesecake Balls
984.	Sweet Onion and Egg Pie	Ground Beef with Veggies	Chocolate Blechkuchen
985.	Eggs Baked in Avocado	Beef with Asparagus & Bell Pepper	Dad's Rum Brownies
986.	Baked Egg Stuffed Cups	African Chicken Stew Turkey Meatballs	Chia Smoothie Bowl
987.	Strawberries and Cream Trifle	Brussels Sprouts and Paprika Chicken Thighs	Favorite Keto Frisuelos
988.	Maple Toast and Eggs	Chicken Breasts with Stuffing	Blueberry Pot de Crème
989.	Crème Brulee	Chicken-Bell Pepper Sauté	Old-Fashion Coffee Mousse
990.	Peppers Casserole	Avocado-Orange Grilled Chicken	Café-Style Fudge
991.	Chili Tomato Salad	Poached Halibut and Mushrooms	Coconut and Seed Porridge
992.	Cumin Mushroom Bowls	Halibut Stir Fry	Pecan and Lime Cheesecake
993.	Bell Peppers and Tomato Salad	Steamed Garlic-Dill Halibut	Fluffy Chocolate Chip Cookies
994.	Avocado and Spinach Salad	Italian Halibut Chowder	Chewy Almond Blondies

995.	Zucchini Bowls	Pomegranate-Molasses Glazed Salmon	Rum Butter Cookies
996.	Lime Berries Salad	Salmon with Sun-Dried Tomatoes and Capers	Light Greek Cheesecake
997.	Zucchini Spread	Quick Thai Cod Curry	Fluffy Chocolate Crepes
998.	Greek Tomato and Olives Salad	Island Style Sardines	Crispy Peanut Fudge Squares
999.	Garlicky Green Beans and Olives Pan	Greek Chicken Stew	Almond Butter Cookies
1000.	Paprika Olives Spread	Herbed Chicken Salad	Basic Almond Cupcakes
1001.	Chives Avocado Mix	Easy Stir-Fried Chicken	Blueberry Cheesecake Bowl

Conclusion

Although the anti-inflammatory diet is generally good for health, it is especially suitable for some health problems. For example; the anti-inflammatory diet reduces the risk of heart disease, keeps existing heart problems under control, reduces blood pressure and triglycerides in the blood (natural fats formed by the combination of fatty acids and glyceroland soothes hard rheumatic joints. This diet aims to increase physical and mental health by recommending healthy, fat, fiber-rich fruits and vegetables, abundant water, and a limited amount of animal protein (excluding fish, providing a constant source of energy and reducing the risk of age-related diseases.

Made in the USA
Middletown, DE
04 March 2020